DATE DUE

A LIBRARY, MEDIA, AND ARCHIVAL PRESERVATION HANDBOOK

A LIBRARY, MEDIA, AND ARCHIVAL PRESERVATION HANDBOOK

John N. DePew

ABC-CLIO

Santa Barbara, California
Denver, Colorado
Oxford, England

Copyright © 1991 by John N. DePew

Library of Congress Cataloging-in-Publication Data

DePew, John N.
   A library, media, and archival preservation handbook / John N. DePew
     p.   cm.
   Includes bibliographical references and index.
    1. Library materials—Conservation and restoration—Handbooks, manuals, etc. 2. Audio-visual materials—Conservation and restoration—Handbooks, manuals, etc. 3. Archival materials—Conservation and restoration—Handbooks, manuals, etc. I. Title.
   Z701.D45   1991   025.8′4—dc20   91-16501

ISBN 0-87436-543-0 (alk. paper)

98 97 96 95 94 93   10 9 8 7 6 5 4 3 2

ABC-CLIO, Inc.
130 Cremona Drive, P.O. Box 1911
Santa Barbara, California 93116-1911

The paper used in this publication meets the minimum requirements of the American National Standard for Information Services—Permanence of Paper for Printed Library Materials, ANSI Z39.48—1984.

This book is Smyth-sewn and printed on acid-free paper ∞ .
Manufactured in the United States of America

CONTENTS

FIGURES

TABLES

CHARTS

PREFACE

In this age of environmental awareness, fragile collections in the nation's libraries are gaining attention from an increasingly aware and anxious public. Books, paper records, and audio-visual materials are deteriorating at a spiralling rate in libraries, media centers, and archives throughout the United States and Canada. Over the last 20 to 30 years, numerous library leaders have warned their colleagues and the general public about the "slow fires" that are consuming collections across North America.

It has been estimated that approximately 30 to 40 percent of the holdings of our research libraries are too brittle to use without causing them serious physical damage. Library users discover insects in volumes just taken off the shelf. Mildew appears on entire shelves of books overnight. Bound periodicals are cracked and torn at the spine as patrons press them tightly against the glass platens of copying machines. Collections are damaged by fire and destroyed by the water used to quench the flames. These problems are occurring everywhere, motivating archivists, librarians, and media specialists to become educated, conduct research, and implement programs to reduce short and long term damage to their collections and help avoid such problems in the future.

A tremendous amount of information on the conservation and preservation of library material has been published in books, periodical articles, and technical reports during the last two decades. The 1980s, in particular, was a rich period in the production of information about the preservation of library materials. This information should be easily available to those who need the tools to successfully fight preservation problems in their own libraries or to study preservation in library schools. Unfortunately, much of it is scattered across the literature and difficult to find, especially for those who do not have access to major libraries. This work is an attempt to bring a portion of that literature together.

A Library, Media, and Archival Preservation Handbook is designed to introduce those who have little knowledge of the preservation of library materials to the basic environmental controls, materials, processes, and techniques that are required to house and preserve library materials in all types and sizes of collections. It also introduces the reader to procedures, such as aqueous deacidification, that are widely used by archivists, but not normally performed in libraries or media centers.

Topics are grouped into nine chapters according to subject areas commonly used to organize preservation literature. Chapter 1 is on the physical nature and manufacture of paper; Chapter 2, on the environment in which archives, books, paper, and audio-visual media are housed and used; Chapter 3, on the care and handling of library materials; Chapter 4, on binding and in-house repair of books and paper; Chapter 5, on solutions to the problems created by acid paper and brittle books; Chapter 6, on photographic, audio, and magnetic media; Chapter 7, on surveying the building and collection; Chapter 8, on disaster preparedness; and Chapter 9, on advisory and preservation treatment services and sources of equipment and supplies.

Each chapter is divided into discrete sections dealing with specific aspects of the chapter's primary subject. In most cases the information is keyed to a bibliographic reference through the use of a citation reference number and the cited pages, both set within brackets. For example, a reference to an item on page 132 in Morrow's book, which is number four in the list of references at the end of this preface, would appear as [4:132]. A second reference in the same sentence to page 8 in Roper's work (number five in the reference list) would follow a semicolon: [4:132; 5:8].

Many companies and organizations are included in the directories in Chapter 9. Although they have appeared in many reputable lists published over the years, their inclusion in this volume does not in any way imply endorsement of their products or services. If readers are aware of sources (providing a product or service nationally) that should be included in future lists, the author would be most grateful if names, addresses, telephone numbers, and the products or services rendered be sent to him in care of the School of Library and Information Studies (R-106), Florida State University, Tallahassee, Florida 32306-2048.

Many conservation and preservation terms require definition to avoid confusion or misunderstanding in meaning. A short glossary is provided at the end of the book, but since the language of preservation literature is often complex and technical, a more complete glossary of preservation nomenclature is planned as a companion volume.

The field of preservation is steadily changing and expanding; there are often conflicting points of view concerning a strategy, technique, or solution to a problem. The author has attempted to include the better-known points of view but realizes that some approaches may have been omitted. Because of space limitations, one area of preservation is deliberately not addressed, i.e., the administration and organization of preservation activities. The Association of Research Libraries' *Preservation Organization and Staffing*, SPEC Kit #160 [1], various issues of the *Conservation Administration News (CAN)* [2], The Harris, Mandel, and Wolven article on a cost model for preservation [3], Carolyn Morrow's *The Preservation Challenge: A Guide to Conserving Library Materials* [4], and Michael Roper's *Planning, Equipping, and Staffing an Archival Preservation and Conservation Service: A RAMP Study with Guidelines* [5], among others, should be consulted for specific information on establishing preservation departments.

Many people deserve thanks for helping—either directly or indirectly—to publish this book: Mary Platt, Jannette Hill, and Beth Harden, my graduate assistants in the School of Library and Information Studies at Florida State University, who ran errands, did research, typed and retyped reams of material, always in good humor; my students in LIS 5766, Conservation and Preservation of Library Materials, who were often the guinea pigs, sometimes unknowingly, in checking the clearness and comprehensibility of the text; Michael Trinkley of the Chicora Foundation, who kindly reviewed portions of Chapter 2; and Heather Cameron of ABC-CLIO, who steadily and patiently encouraged me and kept me on the track. Finally, my wife, Joan, who spent many hours proofing, correcting my English, and offering suggestions that invariably improved the manuscript, and who, with incredible fortitude and patience, encouraged and sustained me in the effort to bring this work to fruition; and my daughter, Cathy, for her support.

Even though help was received from numerous sources, the author takes full responsibility for any errors of omission or commission that may occur in this work. It would be appreciated if such errors were brought to the author's attention. With these caveats in mind, it is hoped that this compendium will be of use to librarians, archivists, media specialists, and students.

REFERENCES

1. Association of Research Libraries, Systems and Procedures Exchange Center. *Preservation Organization and Staffing*. SPEC Kit 160. Washington, DC: Association of Research Libraries, Office of Management Studies, 1990.

2. *Conservation Administration News (CAN)*. Tulsa, OK: University of Tulsa, McFarlin Library, 1979– .

3. Harris, Carolyn, Carol Mandel, and Robert Wolven. "A Cost Model for Preservation: The Columbia University Libraries' Approach." *Library Resources & Technical Services* 35 (January 1991): 33–54.

4. Morrow, Carolyn Clark. *The Preservation Challenge: A Guide to Conserving Library Materials*. White Plains, NY: Knowledge Industry Publications, 1983.

5. Roper, Michael. *Planning, Equipping, and Staffing an Archival Preservation and Conservation Service: A RAMP Study with Guidelines*. Paris: General Information Programme and UNISIST, United Nations Educational, Scientific, and Cultural Organization, 1989.

A LIBRARY, MEDIA, AND ARCHIVAL PRESERVATION HANDBOOK

1.
PAPER AND PAPERMAKING

1.A. Introduction

Most students of the subject believe that paper was first made in China about 105 A.D. Tsai Lun, an advisor to the Chinese emperor, Ho Ti, probably developed the first true paper, although some think he may have stolen the process and appropriated the patents for making paper. In any event, he was the first to record that it existed. Other authorities claim that paper for writing was first made in India. Papermaking spread rapidly through the Orient, and by the year 750 A.D. it had reached Persia and the Middle East. The Crusaders discovered paper in the Holy Land and brought the secrets of papermaking back to Europe. The Spanish took the craft to Mexico and South America in the sixteenth century. William Rittenhouse began making paper near Philadelphia in 1690, and by the end of the eighteenth century American papermakers were able to produce enough to supply most of the newly formed United States. [11:371]

Paper is defined by the *Random House Dictionary* as "a substance made from rags, straw, bark, wood, or other fibrous material, usually in thin sheets, used to bear writing or printing. . . ." [28:1044] Dard Hunter elaborates: "To be classed as true paper the thin sheets must be made from fiber that has been macerated until each individual filament is a separate unit; the fibers are intermixed with water, and by the use of a sieve-like screen, lifted from the water in the form of a thin stratum, the water draining through the small openings of the screen, leaving a sheet of matted fiber upon the screen's surface. This thin layer of intertwined fiber is paper." [15:5]

1.B. Paper Fibers

In order to appreciate the problems of preserving paper, one must first understand its composition and manufacture. The trunk fibers of both softwood and hardwood trees have provided the principal source of fibers for the commercial paper industry for the past 100 years.

Depending upon the wood species, trunk fibers vary greatly in length, from about one-half millimeter to five or six millimeters. Wood provides a renewable resource of raw material; without it the paper industry could not exist.

Minerals, resins, and gums, generally called extractives, are usually removed before forming the fibers into paper. After they are gone, three major constituents remain—cellulose, hemicellulose, and lignin.

Cellulose is the basis of all natural fibers and is the fundamental building block from which they are formed. It is a product of photosynthesis and is the most abundant organic material on earth; with an annual growth rate estimated at 100 billion tons per year, it far exceeds the growth or production of any other material. Cellulose occurs principally in nature as the hollow, elongated biological cell called fiber, found in all plant life. [36:37]

Chemically, cellulose is a long chain polymer of glucose, which is a common sugar. Cellulose and glucose are both carbohydrates, which means that they are composed of carbon, hydrogen, and oxygen, with the hydrogen and oxygen atoms always present in the same ratio as in water (H_2O). A chemical polymer is a large molecule made up of many smaller molecules through the process of bonding together. The mechanism of building up a polymer can proceed in a variety of ways. For example, the bonding may take place randomly in all directions to form a three-dimensional structure. The bonding is different in cellulose, however, forming a straight-chain polymer. That is, each new glucose unit adds on to form a chain, which can be represented much like a long string of beads. Cellulose, from which "paper is fabricated, is built from glucose molecules bonded covalently together into these chains. Each alternating glucose ring of the cellulose molecule is flipped over and the water molecule (H_2O) is split out, leaving an oxygen molecule between each ring. This chain or ribbon (the cellulose molecule) will continue for several thousand glucose units as illustrated" in Figure 1.1. [10:4]

"It is dangerous to generalize, but often the longer the chain, the more resistant is the cellulose to degradation and deterioration. Cotton, for example, is a very stable and resistant fiber, and it has a very long chain length." [36:37] Thus, pulp made from cotton makes very good paper.

Hemicelluloses are similar to cellulose in composition. They are straight-chain polymers of sugars other than glucose, but the chain length is usually shorter than cellulose—a few hundred repeating units rather than a few thousand. They are generally much less resistant to degradation and to attack by chemicals or atmospheric conditions.

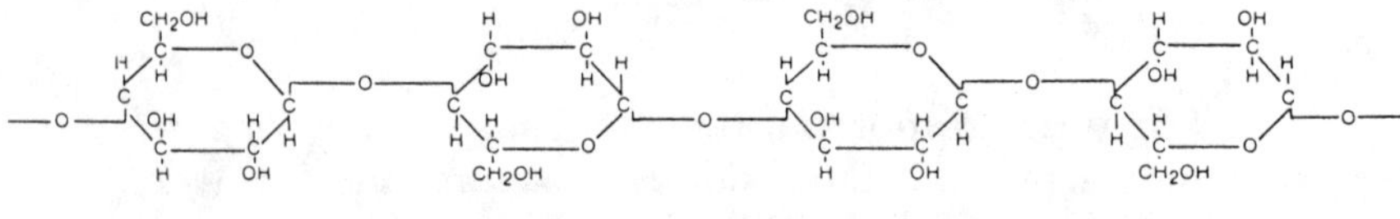

FIGURE 1.1. Alpha cellulose molecule or chain. Reprinted, with permission, from the Conservation Resources International *Catalogue*. Springfield, VA: Conservation Resources International, June 1988, p. 4.

Hemicelluloses bond even more readily than cellulose, in fact, so readily that they sometimes form sheets that are much too dense and translucent. Depending on the kind of paper being made, however, hemicelluloses are sometimes retained in the fibers.

Lignin is often called the cement that glues fibers together in a shrub or tree. It gives the plant the structural strength to stand straight and grow tall. Lignin is a three-dimensional polymer; it is amorphous and it has no ordered structure. It is not fibrous and, in contrast with cellulose, hates water, just as does a petroleum product. Thus it is defined as being hydrophobic.

Unlike cellulose, lignins do not have a specific chemical composition or structure. Their composition and structures vary considerably among plants. Lignins are undesirable material in making paper for books and archival materials, and they should be extracted from the pulp to the greatest extent possible.

The proportion of these three major components varies greatly among various trees and shrubs, as indicated in Table 1.1. Percentages are only approximate and average.

The figures indicate one reason why cotton is such a good papermaking material. It is the purest form of cellulose occurring in nature, hence not much pulping or purification is necessary before the fibers can be used. Flax and other bast fibers are not quite as good; nevertheless, they are attractive. Excellent papermaking fibers can be derived from wood, but extensive pulping and purification are necessary, which is expensive. The great virtue of wood is its continuing availability in tremendous quantities.

Figure 1.2 is a scanning electron micrograph of a section of jack pine, showing both the radial and the transverse planes. The radial plane, near the top of the picture, is cut horizontally across the tree trunk and shows a cross section of the vertical fibers. The transverse plane, near the bottom, is cut lengthwise along the trunk and fibers. [36:38]

These are springwood or earlywood fibers, formed in the spring of the year when the growth rate is high; such fibers are always characterized by thin walls. In the transverse section, the pits in the fiber walls are evident. Pits are characteristic of softwood fibers, and they form connecting horizontal passages between fibers to permit fluids to be

TABLE 1.1. Cellulose, hemicellulose, and lignin content of four common components of paper.

| | APPROXIMATE COMPOSITION (EXTRACTIVE-FREE BASIS) | | | |
	COTTON LINTERS (%)	RAW FLAX (%)	TYPICAL SOFTWOOD (%)	TYPICAL HARDWOOD (%)
Cellulose	96	85	50	50
Hemicelluloses	3	10	20	30
Lignins	1	5	30	20

Source: Roy P. Whitney "Chemistry of Paper." In *Paper—Art & Technology*, edited by Paulette Long. San Francisco: World Print Council, 1979, p. 38.

transported up the tree through the lumens. In different trees and plants, the lumens in the fibers may be large or small, and the cell walls may be thin or thick. The relative size of the lumen and the thickness of the cell wall is very important in papermaking. [36:38]

If these fibers are isolated and subjected to beating and violent treatment, as they are in Oriental hand beating or in a Hollander beater [see 1.C.2.b], they will collapse and look much more like ribbons than filled-out fibers. This is what happens when typical springwood fibers, particularly softwoods, are used in papermaking.

Figure 1.3 is a radial section showing fiber cross sections in aspen, a hardwood. Again, these are typical springwood fibers with very thin walls and large lumens. Essentially, all of the cellulose and the hemicelluloses are in the cell walls. The boundaries between the walls of adjacent fibers are rather ragged and contain lignin, the cement, in an area called the middle lamella. However, not all of the lignin is

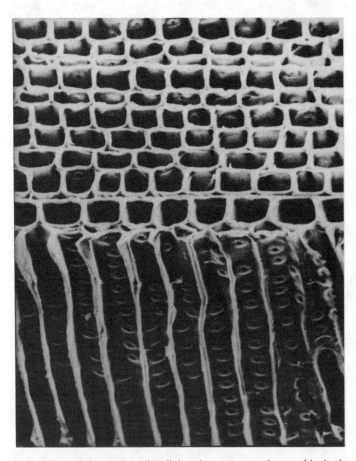

FIGURE 1.2. Intersection of radial and transverse planes of jack pine. Scanning Electron Micrograph (SEM) magnified 200 times. Reprinted, with permission, from *Papermaking Materials: An Atlas of Electron Micrographs*, by Russell A. Parham and Hilkka M. Kaustinen. Appleton, WI: The Institute of Paper Chemistry, 1974, p. 9.

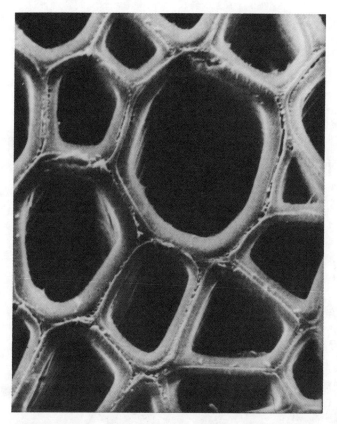

FIGURE 1.3. Fiber cross sections in aspen, a hardwood. SEM magnified 2200 times. Reprinted, with permission, from *Papermaking Materials: An Atlas of Electron Micrographs,* by Russell A. Parham and Hilkka M. Kaustinen. Appleton, WI: The Institute of Paper Chemistry, 1974, p. 11.

located here; about half of it is in the middle lamella, and the other half is interspersed throughout the cell wall. The middle lamella lignin is relatively easy to remove in pulping, but the cell-wall lignin is very difficult to remove and cannot be taken out without some degradation of the cellulose. [36:39-40]

1.C. Papermaking

Modern papermaking consists of converting raw wood into separate fibers by removing the bark, pulping the stripped logs, then cleaning, bleaching, beating, and refining the pulp. The pulp, which is about 99 percent water and 1 percent fiber, is then sent to the papermaking machine where it flows onto a fast moving, vibrating screen that

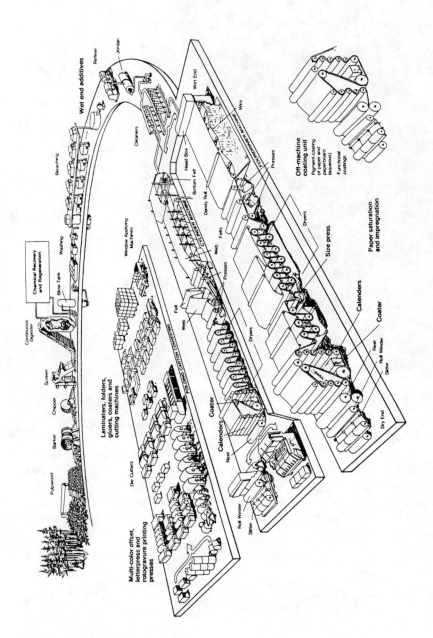

FIGURE 1.4. Pictorial view of papermaking. Originally printed as a poster. TAPPI, 1983. Reprinted with permission.

makes the fibers interlock and mat together. Water is removed from the pulp with the help of suction pumps, pressing rolls, and dryers. Coatings are applied to make the paper slick and shiny, and it is pressed by calenders to give it a smooth, hard surface. Then it is wound onto large reels, taken off the machine, trimmed to take off the rough edges, and cut to the desired width.

1.C.1. PULPING

Paper mills cover many acres and employ hundreds of workers. The process begins with the arrival of logs or chips at the wood yard from the tree farms. Water, circulating at the rate of thousands of gallons per minute, floats the logs along a flume to a jack ladder that carries them into the wood room for processing. Debarkers the size of railroad cars tumble the logs, stripping the bark from the wood by friction.

The wood fibers are then separated and liberated by pulping, either mechanically, chemically, or both. If the pulping is solely mechanical, as in making groundwood, all of the lignin remains in the pulp, and the resulting papers are of very poor quality: they have poor strength and yellow rapidly on aging. They are used in products where quality and long life are not important, such as in newsprint and the groundwood printing paper used in most mass market paperback books.

There are three chemical methods for pulping wood. In 1850 chemists in England developed the soda process, which involves cooking the wood with caustic soda (sodium hydroxide). By the late 1850s European papermakers had learned how to increase their output by cooking chips with calcium bisulfite, which became known as the sulfite process. These two processes were in general use in the United States in the late nineteenth century. Unfortunately, the "lignin residues in sulfite pulps are an important source of the paper-destroying sulfonic acids which, combined with alum/rosin sizing, result in early self-destruction of sulfite paper, on which so many books have been printed." [5]

The sulfate process was perfected in 1889 by German chemists. The wood is cooked with sodium sulfate, which is a more economical method for recovering the cellulose fiber than those developed earlier. The process produces kraft paper, which is known for its strength (*kraft* is a German word meaning "strong"). Its natural unbleached color is brown (e.g., wrapping paper), but when bleached with chlorine, it is excellent for printing. Kraft paper was first manufactured in the United States in 1909.

Chemical pulping begins with either softwood or hardwood chips. In the chipper, steel blades, rotating like a giant pencil sharpener, chew the logs into chips the size of quarters. At the pulp mill the wood chips are fed into a high-rise continuous digester, where they are cooked in chemicals under pressure in a dissolving agent to soften their lignin and reduce them to fiber form. This process releases the individual fibers without reducing their length. The kraft process used today removes most of the lignin and other non-cellulose materials, resulting in pulp that is virtually all fiber.

In mechanical pulping, fibers are separated by physical abrasion. One of the oldest methods, that of making stone groundwood, employs a circular grindstone against which whole logs are forced. Because the fibers are tightly bound by lignin, this action generally forces them to fragment and tear, sometimes in chunks, rather than to separate cleanly. The result is a pulp with a high percentage of short, broken fibers, fiber debris, and fiber chunks or bundles. Although this pulp is then washed and screened, very little of the lignin or other impurities are removed, which means the pulp contains a high percentage of materials that may seriously detract from paper quality.

There are other mechanical methods of pulping, e.g., chemi-mechanical, chemical thermo-mechanical, semi-mechanical, and thermo-mechanical, but most are not suitable for the production of quality printing papers.

1.C.2. CLEANING AND PROCESSING

After pulping, the fibers are thoroughly washed to remove dissolved lignin and screened to remove fiber chunks or bundles. But washing does not affect the lignin that has stained the fibers a dark brown. Because of this staining, the end-product of pulping is usually referred to as brown stock. Before it can be used in the manufacture of printing papers, it passes through a multistage chemical process that bleaches it into a white pulp.

1.C.2.a. Bleaching

Bleaching can be considered a continuation of pulping, to whiten and further purify the fibers. Particularly with wood pulp, bleaching is effective in removing much of the lignin in the cell wall.

Early papers, made from colored rags or vegetable fibers, retained the color of the original material and were considered poor in quality. Good quality, clean white rags were always in short supply, so papermakers bleached their materials to make them usable for writing and printing. Originally cloth was bleached by sunlight and air as the craftsmen sprinkled it frequently with cold water—a process that was very slow and often took months to accomplish. In 1774 the Swedish chemist Karl Wilhelm Scheele isolated and identified chlorine (Cl_2), which led to the development of chlorine bleach.

"Papermakers soon learned that they could increase the supply and reduce the cost of fiber by bleaching filthy rags, normally unsuitable for papermaking, with that chemical." [11:372] While its early uses in papermaking were disastrous (books often crumbled even before they were sold because it was not known how much bleach to use), it rapidly came into use throughout the papermaking industry. But while chemical bleaching enabled papermakers to expand the range of pulp materials to include fibers such as wood, straw, and esparto grass, the chlorine bleach created other problems. Most bleaching today is conducted with chlorined compounds, and it must be done very carefully to avoid cellulose degradation. Residual chlorine, sometimes left in the paper after bleaching, becomes hydrochloric acid (HCl), which will result in the decomposition of the paper if not washed completely out of the pulp after being used. The acid residue becomes a leading factor in paper deterioration. Like pulping, bleaching is a necessary operation, but it must be conducted with care and a thorough understanding of what is going on. [26:48–49]

1.C.2.b. Beating

"The next major step in preparing the pulp is beating and refining. Beating is always necessary to make good paper. The dimensions and the surface of the cellulose fiber must be controlled to obtain the desired properties." [36:41] Originally, the Chinese beat the wet pulp by hand in a stone mortar to separate the fibers. Two other methods used by early papermakers included shredding the materials by using stone rollers or manpowered trip-hammers, and cutting rags into bits and soaking them in limewater until they began to disintegrate. The waterpowered stamping mill was invented in 1151 in Valencia and served for five centuries as the papermaker's principal mechanical aid. Dutch papermakers invented the beating engine or Hollander in the last half of the seventeenth century. The early Hollander consisted of a roller with 30 or more blades set into an oblong tub. The revolving motion of the roller kept the pulp circulating around the tub and against a bedplate positioned under the cylinder. In five or six hours the machine could make the same amount of pulp that the earlier stampers required 24 hours to prepare. The Hollander, however, chopped the fibers into short pieces rather than spreading the long rag fibers as the stampers did. Thus, paper strength and durability began to be compromised. [26:44–47]

"Two major effects of beating are cutting and fibrillation. Cutting results in shortening of the average fiber length and is necessary, particularly with long fibers, to obtain good sheet formation . . . Fibrillation involves altering the surface of the fibers by macerating, fraying, brooming, and generally causing the intricate fibrillar structure to be disrupted. This creates much more surface, which is then available for bonding in the papermaking step. Beaten fibers are much less well defined than unbeaten ones, but they bond together much better and produce stronger, smoother, and generally better paper." [36:41]

The development of surface, the freeing of the surface fibrils, and the interfiber bonding that results from beating are illustrated in Figure 1.5. The picture clearly shows how the process strengthens the paper by binding the fibers tightly together.

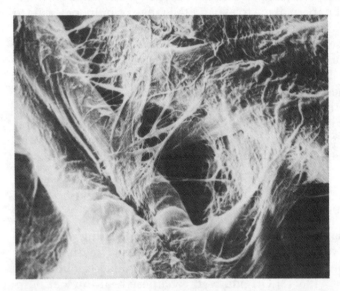

FIGURE 1.5. Interfiber bonding in natural fiber filter paper. SEM magnified 1,650 times. Reprinted, with permission, from *Papermaking Materials: An Atlas of Electron Micrographs*, by Russell A. Parham and Hilkka M. Kaustinen. Appleton, WI: The Institute of Paper Chemistry, 1974, p. 53.

1.C.2.c. Sizing

After bleaching and beating, the pulp may be blended with other papermaking materials such as sizing, fillers, and dyes. "In the Orient, starch, brushed on the handmade sheets, has always been the principle additive to make the otherwise too-soft material suitable for receiving ink. In the West, hot animal gelatine, in which the newly formed sheets were dipped, replaced starch as the 'sizing' material for handmade paper." [11:372] Until the nineteenth century the principal sizing agents were animal gelatin or glue obtained from cartilaginous material. Over 300 years ago, however, papermakers learned that dipping paper sheets in solutions of alum water, after they had been previously dip-sized with gelatin, would harden their surfaces, making them even more suitable for printing than gelatin sizing alone. That is why some papers made before 1800 are highly acidic and have become brown stained. "But they are often not brittle, because alpha cellulose fibers, which are common in handmade paper, are acid resistant." [11:372] Alpha cellulose is long chain cellulose with no additives or impurities of any kind. [See Figure 1.1 for an illustration of an alpha cellulose molecule.]

"Papermakers, in their constant efforts to increase production and reduce costs, also learned how to avoid the centuries-old but costly practice of sizing the newly formed sheets by dipping them in hot solutions of gelatin. They did this by 'tub-sizing' the paper, that is, by adding a mixture of alum and rosin to the wet fiber slurry before the sheet was formed on the machine, thereby coating the paper fibers with rosin to prevent the feathering of writing or printing ink when applied to the paper." [11:372] This procedure is also called internal sizing.

Until recently, rosin was a basic material used in sizing paper. Today it is being replaced in alkaline papermaking mills by synthetic sizes. As a sizing agent, rosin makes paper resistant to water; however, in order for the rosin to do this it must be rendered insoluble, which is one of the functions of alum. Alum enables the rosin to come out of solution and precipitate while it is in close contact with the fibers of the papermaking slurry. The fibers are coated and impregnated with a solid and water-resistant mixture of rosin and what is probably a compound of rosin and aluminum oxide. [31:9]

Alum, or aluminum sulfate, $Al_2(SO_4)_3$, must be added to the pulp to ensure uniform distribution of the rosin throughout the paper. Aluminum sulfate reacts with the water in paper to form aluminum hydroxide, $Al_2(OH)_2$, and sulfuric acid, H_2SO_4, and it is one of the major causes of acid in paper: [11:372]

$$Al_2(SO_4)_3 + 2H_2O \rightarrow Al_2(OH)_2(SO_4)_2 + H_2SO_4$$
$$Al_2(OH)_2(SO_4)_2 + H_2O \rightarrow Al_2(OH)_4(SO_4) + H_2SO_4$$
$$\text{etc. to } Al(OH)_3$$

The rosin is precipitated on the paper fibers as aluminum resinate. It works best at pH 4.5 to 5.0, but leaves free sulfuric acid as a by-product of the reaction between the alum and the rosin soap. William J. Barrow concluded that it contributed more to the destruction of paper than any other development in papermaking of the nineteenth century. [9:16]

In contrast to engine or internal sizing, "surface sizing is applied after the sheet is formed and dried, and it is therefore mostly on or near the surface. It is used to impart surface finish and to control surface properties." Glue, gelatin, casein, and starch, which are not acidic, are used. "Most bonds and writing papers and many art papers are surface sized." [36:43]

1.C.2.d. Filling and loading

Filling and loading are also practiced extensively with many papers. Fillers improve the opacity and also provide further control of surface properties. Most fillers are minerals that have been very finely ground. Kaolin clay is the most common filler, and calcium carbonate (ground limestone, precipitated chalk) is used extensively in alkaline papers. Some synthetic materials are also used. Titanium dioxide is a preferred filler, but it is also about the most expensive. Fillers always weaken the sheet. Retention of fillers is also poor, since they have no affinity for cellulose and wash out readily during the sheet forming process.

Coloring or dyeing is an essential part of papermaking. Practically all papers are dyed, even all white papers. Other chemical additives

include beater adhesives, such as starch, natural gums, modified cellu-
loses, and wet-strength resins. [36:43]

1.C.2.e. Forming the paper

In the actual forming of paper the cellulose fibers are drawn together into a thin, somewhat irregular mesh. Unlike cloth, in which fibers
are bound by the mechanical processes of twisting and weaving, paper
forms primarily from chemical bonds occurring between the fibers either
directly or indirectly with the aid of other materials.

Two characteristics of cellulose fiber make such bonds possible.
First, it is hydrophilic (which means that cellulose has a great affinity for
water) and swells, becoming flexible and even gelatinous in water without dissolving or losing its shape. Second, the fiber's structure resembles
that of a rope, having walls composed of several layers of threads, called
fibrils or microfibrils, that wrap round and round in spirals. When two
wet cellulose chains are brought into close proximity to each other, they
bond very tenaciously. [36:37] The cellulose chains (molecules) are held
together side to side by hydrogen bonding between the chains to form
sheets. [See Figure 1.6.]

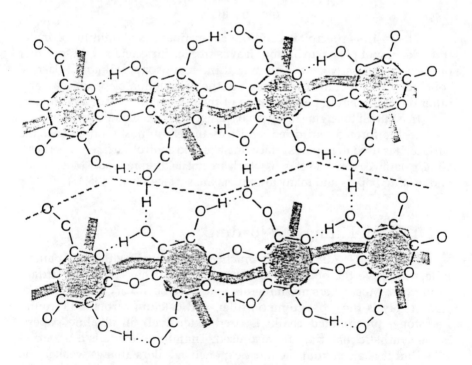

FIGURE 1.6. Cellulose molecules forming into sheets.The long ribbonlike molecules
are held together side to side to form sheets, by hydrogen bonds (O . . . H).
Reprinted, with permission, from the Conservation Resources International
Catalogue. Springfield, VA: Conservation Resources International, June 1988, p. 5.

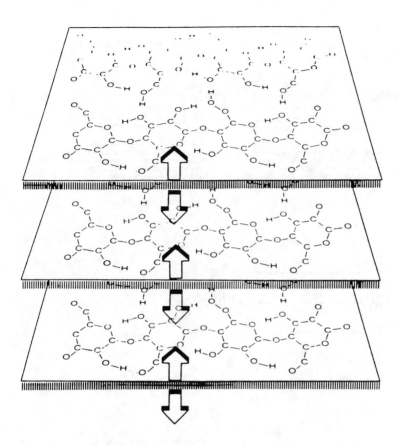

FIGURE 1.7. The sheets of cellulose are held in layers by Van der Waals forces. Reprinted, with permission, from the Conservation Resources International *Catalogue.* Springfield, VA: Conservation Resources International, June 1988, p. 5.

"The sheets of cellulose are held in staggered layers, one on top of another, by Van der Waals forces. The geometry of the short carbon-hydrogen bonds minimizes the distance between layers and, therefore, Van der Waals forces . . . are maximized. [See Figure 1.7.]

"Since cellulose is hydrophilic, cellulose molecules have a great affinity for each other when they are wet. When these cellulose chains are brought into close proximity, they bond together very tenaciously to form sub-units called fibrils or microfibrils, and these bond together to form fibers. [33:37] These microfibrils will crystallize . . . into bundles, and the bundles will crystallize into fibers, by the same side-by-side hydrogen bonding and layer-to-layer Van der Waals interaction that formed the microfibrils. The microfibrils have nearly perfect bonding, both side-by-side and layer-to-layer; however, each successive stage of formation has a progressively less perfect degree of bonding, because any imperfection in the first stages of crystallization will be progressively magnified during the progression to the final fiber formation. These fibers are mixed with water and often other chemicals, beaten into a slurry and spread

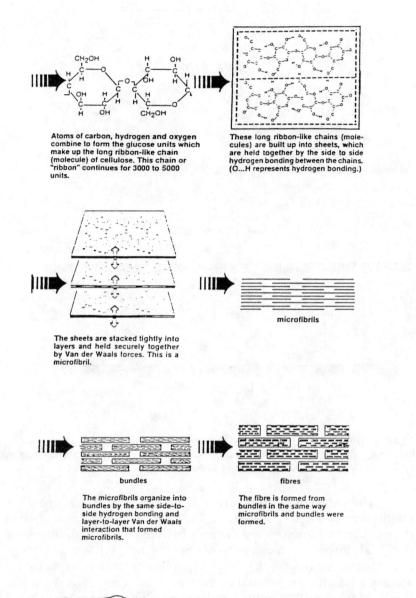

Atoms of carbon, hydrogen and oxygen combine to form the glucose units which make up the long ribbon-like chain (molecule) of cellulose. This chain or "ribbon" continues for 3000 to 5000 units.

These long ribbon-like chains (molecules) are built up into sheets, which are held together by the side to side hydrogen bonding between the chains. (O...H represents hydrogen bonding.)

The sheets are stacked tightly into layers and held securely together by Van der Waals forces. This is a microfibril.

microfibrils

bundles

The microfibrils organize into bundles by the same side-to-side hydrogen bonding and layer-to-layer Van der Waals interaction that formed microfibrils.

fibres

The fibre is formed from bundles in the same way microfibrils and bundles were formed.

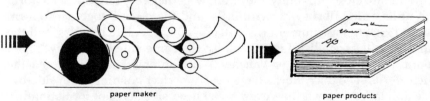

paper maker

paper products

FIGURE 1.8. Steps in the formation of paper. Reprinted, with permission, from the Conservation Resources International *Catalogue*. Springfield, VA: Conservation Resources International, June 1988, p 6.

onto a forming screen. They are then pressed together and dried to produce a finished sheet of paper. The overall sequence of steps in the formation of paper, from subatomic particles to paper products, is shown in [Figure 1.8]." [10:4–5]

Fiber bonding occurs between molecules with extremely short-range attraction. For two fibers to bond, therefore, they must conform to one another and come into very close contact. The strength of their bond is determined not only by the amount of the area over which contact is made, but also by how deeply the contact is made.

Preparing fibers for bonding actually started with pulping and bleaching. Both processes occur in large quantities of water, where the fibers begin to soften. The softer and more flexible they become, the more bonding area they develop and the stronger the bonds will be.

Refining continues the process. In a slurry containing about 95 percent water, pulp is pumped between serrated metal disks that collapse the fibers and rupture their outer walls. Thus, flexibility is increased, and many of the fibrils unravel, swelling with water to create additional bonding sites.

At this point, there are important differences between chemical pulp and groundwood pulp and their relative suitability for papermaking. In refined chemical pulp, the majority of fibers are whole, collapsed, highly fibrillated, and very flexible. These are characteristics that produce a strong paper. Also in chemical pulp, lignin and other impurities have been washed away, and the pure cellulose fibers have been bleached to a bright white. It takes only a few additives (e.g., internal sizing for water resistance, dye for shade, and/or some mineral pigment for opacity and greater brightness, depending on the type of paper being made) to complete the combination of papermaking materials, known as furnish.

1.C.3. PAPERMAKING MACHINES

The furnish now moves on to the paper machine. This mixture of 0.5 percent fiber and 99.5 percent water flows into the headbox and onto a fast-moving, fine-mesh wire screen that weaves the fibers together as the water drains. "Since about 1800, two types of continuous paper machines have been in commercial use." [36:42] These are the fourdrinier machine and the cylinder machine, which are the papermaking machines normally used in the manufacture of all grades of paper and board. The fourdrinier comprises an endless wire screen, with the pulp slurry flowing onto it at one end and the wet sheet couched off, pressed, and dried at the other. The cylinder machine is a wire-covered cylinder that rotates in a vat containing the fiber slurry. The sheet is formed on the cylinder surface and couched off. The pressing and drying operations are about the same as with the fourdrinier. Paper machines can be hundreds of feet long, yet are composed essentially of just four main parts: the headbox and the wire, which comprise the "wet end," and the press section and dryers, which make up the "dry end." [31:189]

1.C.3.a. Fourdrinier papermaking machine

Most of the paper produced in the United States is made on a machine that was patented by a Frenchman, Nicholas-Louis Robert, in 1798 and developed in England by Brian Donkin for the Fourdrinier brothers, who were the leading British wholesale stationers at that time. [See Figure 1.9 for a drawing of a typical modern papermaking machine.]

1.C.3.a.1. Wet end

The machine has a tank called a headbox. Furnish is uniformly delivered to the headbox, where it is fed from the slice onto a continuous fine-mesh wire screen called the fourdrinier wire. Paper is formed during the first few feet of travel on the wire. As the newly formed paper mat moves along on the wire, water drains out of the pulp and down through the screen. The wire runs over a breast roll, which is next to the headbox, and then over a series of foils that keep the wire level and aid in water removal. The wet mat passes under a metal roller, called a dandy roll, that presses it down into a smoother sheet. The dandy roll may contain a design called the watermark that will be pressed into the sheet of fibers. Near the end of the wet end, the wire passes over a series of suction boxes, over the bottom suction couch roll (which drives the wire), and then down and back over various guide rolls and a stretch roll to the breast roll. Meanwhile, the screen vibrates to make the fibers interlock and mat together. The paper consists of about 75 percent water as it leaves the wet end and enters the press section.

Twin wire wet ends were introduced in the late 1960s. "By the early 1980s, twin wire designs had come to outnumber conventional fourdrinier arrangements in new, high speed installations." [12:3425] In most operations, "twin [paper web] formers drain the forming web from both sides, in contrast to forming on a standard [single wire] fourdrinier. This action reduces the length of the drainage zone and delivers a product that is more symmetrical from top to bottom." [12:3425]

1.C.3.a.2. Dry end

The wet web of paper is transferred from the fourdrinier wire to the felt at the couch roll and is carried through the press section on the felts, the texture and character of which vary according to the grade of paper being made. The press section, the first component of the dry end, usually consists of two or more presses that remove more water from the web mechanically and equalize the surface characteristics of the felt and wire sides. The dryers consist of two or more tiers of steam-heated cylinders. As the web passes from one dryer to another, first the felt side and then the wire side are pressed against the heated surface of the dryer. The web, having a water content of approximately 65 percent, enters the dryer train where the bulk of the water is evaporated. Hot air blowing onto the sheets and in between the dryers helps to remove water vapor. About half

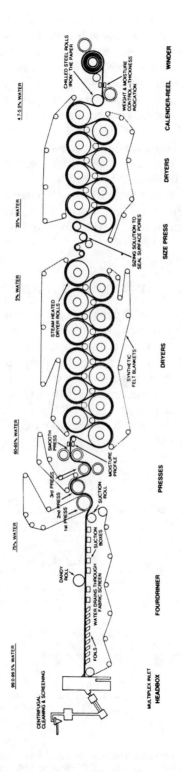

FIGURE 1.9. Fourdrinier papermaking machine. This diagram was provided by Hammermill Papers, Memphis, Tennessee, and is reprinted with their permission.

way along the drying curve there may be a size press that seals the surface pores of the paper with a sizing solution. The moisture content of the paper at the end of the dryer section is approximately 5 percent.

The calender section consists of one to three calender stacks with a device for winding the paper onto a reel as it leaves the machine. The calender finishes the paper, i.e., smooths it and imparts the desired finish, thickness, or gloss. Water, starch, wax emulsions, and so on may also be used to obtain additional finishes. The reel winds the finished paper, which may or may not undergo further processing.

The wire, press section, dryer section or sections, the calender stacks, and the reel are controlled so that proper tension is maintained in the web of paper throughout its passage through the machine, which may run at speeds of several thousand feet per minute. The overall speed of fourdrinier machines is determined by the grade and weight of the paper being manufactured. [31:108–109]

1.C.3.b. Cylinder papermaking machine

The cylinder machine is "a papermaking machine which utilizes a wire curved around one or more cylinders or molds that are partially immersed and rotated in vats containing a dilute stock suspension." [31:72] A vacuum inside the cylinder hugs the pulp to the screen while sucking out the water, which drains out of the ends of the cylinder; on the down turn of the cylinder, it transfers the mat of fibers to a continuous felt. The press section and the dry end of the cylinder machine are essentially the same as those of the fourdrinier machine. The cylinder machine was patented in 1805 by the Englishman Joseph Bramah, and

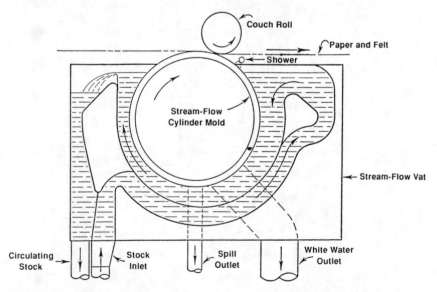

FIGURE 1.10. The cylinder papermaking machine. Source: Edwin Sutermeister. *The Story of Paper Making*. Boston: S. D. Warren Company, 1954, p. 165.

was improved considerably in 1808 by John Dickinson. In England it is called a board machine or vat machine. [31:72]

The cylinder machine is generally used for making paperboard and heavy building paper. It is also used for the production of fine mold-made paper. The fourdrinier is much faster and more versatile, and it dominates the commercial scene. Both machines are showing signs of obsolescence, and other forming devices are coming into use. The newer machines still, however, use the original concept of draining water through a porous screen. [36:42]

1.D. Paper Acidity

Conservation International describes the problem of acidity in paper very clearly:

> The paper described and depicted in [Figure 1.8] is a completely pristine sheet made entirely from long chain, alpha cellulose fibers with no additives or impurities of any kind. Unfortunately, most paper available today contains a variety of additives, impurities and other less stable plant products that cause acid deterioration of paper. Other culprits which also have a deleterious effect on paper are environmental and atmospheric acids and pollutants. The destruction of the paper fiber follows essentially the same route as in its construction, but in the reverse direction. Acids attack the bonds which hold together the glucose rings, the cellulose chains, the microfibrils, the bundles and the fibers. [10:5]

Specifically, an acid is any substance that can donate a proton.

> The hydrogen atom is the only element which has only one proton in the nucleus and one electron in "orbit." When hydrogen loses that negatively charged electron, it becomes positively charged (an "ion"), consisting of only one proton. This proton is strongly attracted to negatively charged electrons which overlap and share outer energy levels or "orbits" with other atoms to form the chemical (in this case, covalent) bonds which hold the long chain, cellulose molecule together. [10:5]

When an acid (a positively charged hydrogen ion) is introduced to the cellulose chain, it combines with one of the electrons being shared in the outer energy orbits of one of the carbon or oxygen atoms and breaks the bond between two of the glucose rings of the chain. The single long chain then becomes two shorter, weaker chains. One side of the glucose ring is stable because it is still intact, but the other side is not stable. If a water molecule is introduced into the situation, the unstable side of the ring will seek to achieve stability by taking an electron from the water molecule. Now both sides of the glucose ring are again stable; but in becoming so, a hydrogen nucleus (which is a proton or acid) is freed, and it will break another covalent bond connecting the rings of the chain, which will release yet another hydrogen ion, etc. As the chain is broken into successively shorter lengths, it becomes progressively weaker. When 0.5 to 1 percent of the bonds are broken, the paper will be virtually useless.

When the cellulose chain is broken, it also weakens and often breaks the hydrogen bonds that bind the ribbons, or chains, into sheets. The layers held by Van der Waals forces suffer the same fate, and the bonding between layers of bundles of microfibrils is weakened and broken, which in turn breaks the bonds between the fibers.

Impurities such as lignin, hemicellulose and hydrolyzed cellulose oxidize and produce substantial quantities of acidic degradation products to be present in paper. Alum-rosin sizing [$Al_2(SO_4)3 \cdot 18H_2O$] added during the paper making process is a prime acid producer. There are also acidic gases and pollutants from the atmosphere such as sulfur dioxide which forms sulfuric acid (H_2SO_4), nitrogen dioxide which forms nitric acid, and glucuronic acid. Other culprits are ozone, various peroxides, peroxyacyl nitrates and cupric and ferric ions which promote carbohydrate acid through the oxidation of carbonyl and hydroxyl groups. [10:8]

These acids in paper do their damage by weakening the molecular bonds of the cellulose fibers, resulting in the yellowing of paper and its embrittlement.

When testing the acidity of paper, acidity is most often expressed by specifying the concentration of positive hydrogen ions, or pH, in the paper on a scale of zero to 14.0. A pH of 7.0 is considered neutral; paper with a pH of less than 7.0 would be acidic, while paper with a pH of more than 7.0 would be alkaline. As the pH moves progressively below 7.0, the paper becomes more and more acidic. Conversely, as the pH moves above 7.0, it becomes more alkaline. Since the scale is logarithmic, paper with a pH of 5.0 has ten times the acidity of one at pH 6.0. At pH 4.0, the solution is 100 times more acid than at pH 6.0. Paper with a pH in either extreme can be expected to have a relatively short life expectancy because the excess acidity or alkalinity will degrade the cellulose fibers. This process can be further aggravated by humidity, pollution, heat, light, and abuse.

Most rosin-sized papers are made in the pH range of 4.5 to 5.5. This is much too acid for the papers to show any great degree of permanence, and they will deteriorate significantly in a few years. Papers of archival quality must be made at essentially neutral pH. In fact, they often contain alkaline materials that neutralize any acids that may form over years of storage. The addition of those materials is called buffering. Other internal sizing agents that can be used under neutral or slightly alkaline conditions, such as Aquapel and Hercon, are now available. [21:125]

Acid books are those whose pages have a pH of less than 7.0. The pages are not yet brittle, but because of their acidity they will become brittle in time. An acid free book is one made with paper produced by alkaline manufacturing processes. Although the paper may not be totally free of acid, its pH is nearly neutral. [35:107]

Acid migration, i.e., the ability of acid to transfer from an acidic material to adjacent less acidic or nonacidic material, will cause staining, weakening, and embrittlement of the nonacidic material. The migration takes place either through direct physical contact or through vapor action if acidic and less- or nonacidic items are stored in the same container. [30:87] Therefore, lining an acidic box with acid-free paper will not protect the non-acidic items.

1.D.1. TESTING THE pH OF PAPER

All of the following methods for testing the pH of paper should be performed only in accordance with the instructions supplied with the equipment or chemicals used for each test. Prior to using any tests, it should be determined whether any of the chemicals to be used are potentially hazardous. If the chemicals pose a health threat, the safety procedures specified by the manufacturer and state and federal authorities should be followed.

1.D.1.a. Cold extraction method

The pH of paper may be determined by the TAPPI T 509 hydrogen ion concentration (pH) of paper extracts (cold extraction method). This is a testing procedure published by the Technical Association of the Pulp and Paper Industry (TAPPI), located in Technology Park, Atlanta, Georgia. [34] To test for pH, weigh one gram of paper (cut into 10mm squares) to the nearest 0.01 grams into a 100 ml beaker. Fill a graduated cylinder to the 70 ml mark with distilled water. Add 5 ml of water to the beaker. Macerate the paper with a glass stirring rod (flattened on one end) until it is thoroughly wet. Add the remainder of water from the graduated cylinder, stir, and allow to stand one hour or longer. Stir again and measure the pH of the extract, using a pH meter with a glass electrode and a reference electrode, following the directions supplied by the manufacturer for the specific pH meter. None of the pieces of paper should be allowed to touch either electrode during the measurement. Consult TAPPI T 509 for more detailed information. [34]

1.D.1.b. Hot extraction method

The TAPPI T 435 hydrogen ion concentration (pH) of paper extractions (hot extraction method) is another testing procedure published by

TAPPI. The hot extraction method is a relatively accurate and widely accepted procedure for testing pH in paper. It requires boiling one gram of paper in distilled water for one hour before testing the solution with a pH meter. [13:49; 34] Since most archivists and librarians are not equipped to conduct the TAPPI hot and cold extraction tests, however, there are alternatives that will give an adequate indication as to the acid content (or not) of paper.

1.D.1.c. pH indicator strips

The following pH testing procedures are reprinted, with permission, from the Society of American Archivists, *Archives & Manuscripts: Conservation: A Manual on Physical Care and Management*. Chicago: SAA, 1983. (Not to be reprinted without permission.) [30:99–100]

A number of methods available for testing the pH of paper do not require laboratory facilities or sophisticated technical training. These methods provide indications of the surface pH of the paper. The pH indicators respond chemically with a color range when brought into contact with specific levels of acidity or alkalinity. They are easy to use and are accurate enough to indicate whether a paper is neutral or decidedly or mildly acidic or alkaline. Test results with coated papers are not entirely satisfactory using the methods to be described, since the coatings tend to obscure the true character of the interior of the paper. Coatings may also dissolve with the application of water and other solvents.

Within an archival context, these techniques are most useful for checking the quality of archival supplies, such as boxes, folders, interleaving sheets, and mat board, to determine whether or not the product meets specifications and the manufacturer's claims regarding pH level. The surface layer of such supplies may be scraped away with a microspatula or scalpel to allow testing of the interior pH level of the products. Archival documents may be tested as well to help determine paper quality, condition, and need for treatment. These tests also provide a quick and easy means of checking a collection *after* deacidification to determine whether or not the neutralization and buffering processes successfully brought the paper to the required pH level.

Several of the testing methods leave a permanent mark or stain on the paper and thus are not desirable for direct use on archival materials. EM Laboratory colorpHast™ Indicator [Strips] are non-bleeding and leave no stain on the paper, so they are recommended for use on archival papers and other materials of value. ColorpHast™ Indicator [Strips] are strips of plastic impregnated with indicating agents that respond with a color change to indicate the pH of the paper being tested.

Care must be taken to avoid touching the sensitive portion of the [strip]. ColorpHast™ Indicator [Strips] are available in the following pH ranges: 0–14, 0–6, 7.5–14, 6.5–10, 4.0–7.0, and 2.5–4.5; the smaller the range, the more accurate the reading. The test procedure is as follows:

1. Slip a small piece of polyester under the area to be tested.
2. Place a drop of distilled water on the area to be tested [see Figure 1.11]. Do not test areas close to ink or a coloring agent. If the spot being tested contains ink, the results cannot be assumed to be accurate for the paper, as the pH of the ink may alter the results. Paper does not necessarily have a uniform pH over its entire surface. Areas near the margin are likely to be more acidic due to handling. Thus, for greater accuracy, it may be advisable to check the paper in several spots and compare results.
3. Lay the active end of the pH indicator paper in the droplet and move it back and forth slightly to ensure that the entire sensitive portion is wetted [see Figure 1.12].

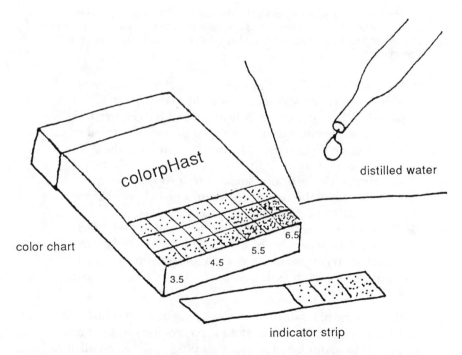

FIGURE 1.11. pH testing with colorpHast™. Reprinted, with permission, from the Society of American Archivists, *Archives & Manuscripts: Conservation; A Manual on Physical Care and Management.* Chicago: SAA, 1983, p. 99. Not to be reprinted without permission.

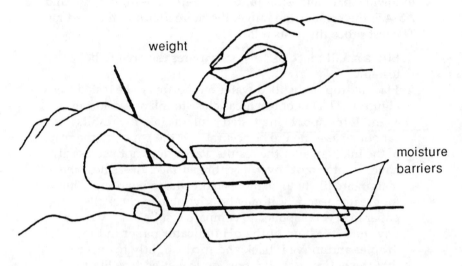

weight

moisture
barriers

pH indicator strip placed on
water droplet

FIGURE 1.12. pH testing with colorpHast™. Reprinted, with permission, from the
Society of American Archivists, *Archives & Manuscripts: Conservation; A Manual on
Physical Care and Management.* Chicago: SAA, 1983, p. 99. Not to be reprinted
without permission.

4. Place a second piece of polyester over the pH indicator
   [strip] and cover with a light weight to ensure that the test
   [strip] and the paper are in firm contact [see Figure 1.13].
5. After three to five minutes, remove the polyester and test
   stick and determine the pH value by matching the colors
   of the wet indicators to the color chart on the EM box. To
   ensure that the indicator squares are properly oriented
   with the chart, the test [strip] should be held so that the
   non-sensitive portion is at the top of the box.
6. Blot up any water remaining on the paper tested; place
   the paper between dry blotters under a light weight to
   complete drying. Small water marks sometimes remain
   on the paper, even with the application of a tiny drop of
   water.

Paper with pH values below 7.0 are acidic; deacidification
should definitely be considered for papers having a pH below
6.0. A pH of about 8.5 indicates that the paper has an alkaline
reserve.

Because several color indicators appear on each test strip,
depending on the test range selected, colorpHast™ Indicator

[Strips] are quite precise. The multiple indicator response increases the degree of accuracy. The test sticks may be used to determine the pH of solutions such as paste as well as papers. They are especially useful for testing colored or toned papers, for which it is difficult to differentiate color changes with spot tests. ColorpHast™ Indicator [Strips], however, have a limited shelf life; they should be kept in an airtight container and replaced every two years. It must also be understood that although this process is theoretically accurate and simple to use, in actual practice the pH of the water can alter the test results: for example, dissolved carbon dioxide in distilled water may lower the pH below the neutral 7.0 level. Nevertheless, colorpHast™ Indicator [Strips] are the preferred method for testing most non-archival library materials.

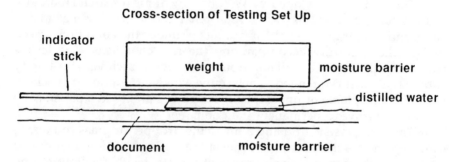

Cross-section of Testing Set Up

indicator
stick

weight   moisture barrier

distilled water

document   moisture barrier

FIGURE 1.13. pH testing with colorpHast™. Reprinted, with permission, from the Society of American Archivists, *Archives & Manuscripts: Conservation; A Manual on Physical Care and Management*. Chicago: SAA, 1983, p. 99. Not to be reprinted without permission.

1.D.1.d. pH pens

Chlorophenol red felt-tipped pens are widely available from a variety of suppliers for testing the surface pH of paper. This method, while not accurate for determining the pH value, will indicate if the paper is acidic. Since the pens leave permanent stains, they should not be used on materials in the collection; they are more appropriate for testing archival supplies.

A small mark should be made in an unobtrusive part of the object to be tested. Since the natural color of the indicator is red, it has to be applied in a thin enough layer for it to be affected by the paper's pH, and must be read as soon as it is dry. If it sits for an hour or longer, it will absorb CO_2 and SO_2 from the air and show the paper to be more acidic than it is. If the mark turns purple, the paper is neutral or alkaline; yellow or green means that it is acidic. Since coated paper may have a different pH on its surface than in the base sheet, it must be torn on a slant to get a diagonal cross section. The pen should then be run along the torn exposed surface. [1]

The indicator does not lose efficacy with time, but the cotton wadding in the fillers of some pens may not be of very high quality and may eventually deteriorate. Shelf life is not known, but pens probably should be replaced within 18 months after purchase. [22:30] Newer pens have polyester fiber reservoirs, which are guaranteed not to deteriorate or affect the indicator fluid's accuracy. [23:19]

Another type of fiber-tipped pen contains Bromcresol Green, a bright green chemical ink that changes color from blue (acid-free) to green (some acid content) to yellow (high acid content) when applied to paper. A small dot is made in an unobtrusive place on the paper or in the book. The same cautions apply to its use as to the chlorophenol red testing pen, since the dot is permanent.

1.D.1.e. Barrow spot test

The spot test developed by W. J. Barrow at his research laboratory in Richmond, Virginia, is based upon reliable research findings and is sufficiently accurate to accept if conducted under the conditions specified in the literature accompanying the test chemicals. The test is reasonably priced and available from a number of archival and library supply houses. It is intended to determine whether the amount of acidity present is acceptable or unacceptable for good stability in a paper. Note that the test leaves a permanent stain on paper.

The test consists of using a medicine dropper or glass rod applicator to spread a thin, inch-long line of the testing solution on uninked portions of the paper. If the line or spot turns a decided yellow, strong acid (pH 6.0 and below) is present. If the spot turns a definite purple, either a near neutral or an alkaline condition (pH 6.6 and above) exists in the paper. The spot should be allowed to dry before the results are determined. If the color changes from yellow through yellow-green, green, or grayish, it may be in the 6.0 to 6.7 pH range. Certain impurities in the paper may gradually change these colors. This is of little practical importance, however, since in almost every case observed, the color of the spot test was either definitely yellow (acidic and undesirable) or definitely purple (more alkaline and desirable). Where the spot tests give conflicting or equivocal results, they should not be relied upon. [5:12–13] The test kit contains a color chart for aid in matching the color changes.

1.D.2. GROUNDWOOD, ALUM, AND ROSIN TESTS

Two other test chemicals are packaged with the Barrow acidity test described above: one to detect the presence of groundwood and the other to detect alum. It is recommended that the indicator solutions be refrigerated to prolong their useful life. [30:100]

"The groundwood papermaking process mechanically reduces wood to fiber with little or no chemical processing to remove deteriorative components such as lignin. It is generally accepted that papers containing groundwood are unstable; they quickly discolor and become brittle on exposure to light and air. If the groundwood content is high, as in modern newsprint, the life expectancy of the paper is only 10 to 20 years, and somewhat longer if an alkaline filler has been used, such as in magazine papers." [5:11–12]

The groundwood test should be run first, before the test for acidity. Then if groundwood is found present, the paper may be classified as unstable and will require no further testing. To conduct the test, a thin line of the solution is spread on uninked portions of the paper with a medicine dropper or glass rod applicator. If the line remains colorless, there is no groundwood. It will turn a deep purplish red if groundwood is present. [5:11–12]

The alum test is run by spreading a thin line of the testing solution on uninked portions of the paper in the same fashion as with the first two tests. When no alum is present in the paper, the spot will turn colorless or remain a very faint pink, which is the color of the test solution. It will turn bright to deep pink if alum is present. The test indicates the presence of alum (aluminum sulfate) resulting from the use of alum-rosin size or from alum in other manufacturing processes. [5:13]

There is a test for rosin, but since it is relatively dangerous to a person conducting it without the benefit of a laboratory, a protective coat, and training in the use of sulfuric acid, it is not packaged with the other test solutions.

1.D.3. TESTING PAPER STRENGTH

TAPPI has developed a definitive body of standards for testing the permanence and durability of paper. Permanence is a measure of the chemical stability of paper; durability is a measure of the stability of its physical and mechanical properties. Paper that is roughly treated for a short time and then discarded (e.g., a newspaper) should be durable, but not necessarily permanent. A paper that is meant to last for a century, on the other hand, must be compounded for chemical stability. That chemical stability can be reinforced by storing paper at a low temperature, at a constant, low relative humidity, in the dark, and in an atmosphere free of pollutants.

Four of the TAPPI test methods evaluate the strength properties of paper: (1) T 403 for bursting strength, (2) T 404 and T 494 for tensile strength, (3) T 414 for tearing resistance, and (4) T 511 for folding endurance. Each of these properties is widely accepted as a measure of the permanence of paper. [8:31] Although there is some question about its usefulness, a description of the accelerated aging test (T 453 and T 544) is included in this discussion because it is so often mentioned in the literature. There are tests in addition to those named, but they are referred to in the Library Binding Institute *Standard for Library Binding* (with the exceptions of T 453, T 494, and T 544) for its specifications for the mechanical characteristics of endpapers. [18:10] Most of the laboratories and large paper mills in the United States recognize the TAPPI standards, and most paper testing equipment is calibrated and used according to those references. [8:31]

1.D.3.a. Bursting strength (T 403)

The Mullen paper tester, invented by John W. Mullen in 1887, is used to test the bursting strength of paper. "The bursting strength is the combined tensile strength and stretch of a material as measured by the ability of the material to resist rupture when pressure is applied under specified conditions to one of its sides by an instrument used for testing the property. Testing for the bursting strength of paper is a very common procedure, although its value in determining the potential permanence or durability of paper is suspect." [31:43] According to Caulfield, the test apparently originated from the older practice of papermakers who, in a hands-on quality control evaluation of paper strength, would attempt to push their thumbs through the sheet. [8:33]

In Mullen's apparatus, the paper specimen is clamped over a circular diaphragm of thin rubber. A piston presses against the paper with increasing force until the fibers are pulled apart [see Figure 1.14].

The pressure at bursting point is recorded on a dial by a pointer. A Mullen test generally indicates how long a pulp has been beaten and how high or low its quality. The higher the number recorded on the dial, the more the resistance to bursting is indicated. The burst failure usually results in a roughly H-shaped tearing pattern in the specimen [see Figure 1.15]. The orientation of the H with the two directions of the machine-made paper indicates that failure initiates in tension along the line at right angles to the machine direction. [8:33]

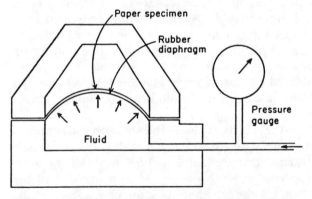

FIGURE 1.14. Schematic of bursting test apparatus. Source: D. F. Caulfield and D. E. Gunderson. *Paper Testing and Strength Characteristics.* Madison, WI: USDA Forest Service, Forest Products Laboratory, 1988. In *TAPPI Proceedings: 1988 Paper Preservation Symposium.* Atlanta, GA: TAPPI Press, 1988, p. 39.

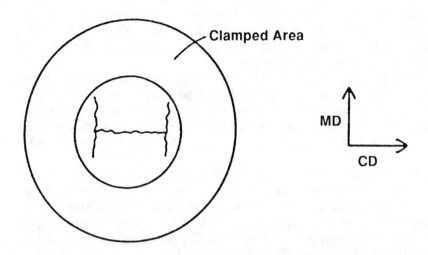

FIGURE 1.15. Appearance of a typical bursting test specimen after failure; failure initiates along the rip at right angles to the machine direction. MD: Machine direction. CD: Cross-machine direction. Source: D. F. Caulfield and D. E. Gunderson. *Paper Testing and Strength Characteristics.* Madison, WI: USDA Forest Service, Forest Products Laboratory, 1988. In *TAPPI Proceedings: 1988 Paper Preservation Symposium.* Atlanta, GA: TAPPI Press, 1988, p. 39.

The Library Binding Institute specifications for library binding stipulate that endpapers (80 pound basis weight, 25 x 38 - 500) have a bursting strength (Mullen) of 40 pounds per square inch. [18:10]

1.D.3.b. Tensile strength (T 404 and T 494)

Measuring the tensile strength of a paper is a way of measuring the relative bonding between the fibers. Tensile test results reflect the intimate structure of paper and the properties of its individual fibers. The dimensions and strength of the individual fibers, their arrangement, and the extent to which they are bonded to each other are all important factors contributing to test results. Papers made with long fibers generally have higher tensile strength properties than papers made of short fibers. However, the extent of interfiber bonding is considered the most important factor contributing to tensile strength properties. [6]

"TAPPI method T 404 measures tensile breaking strength and elongation of paper and paperboard using a pendulum-type tester, and T 494 measures tensile breaking properties of paper and paperboard using constant rate of elongation apparatus." [8:31] This measurement is done by an instrument devised to ascertain what strain, expressed in pounds, is required to break a strip of paper a given length and width. In separate tests for each direction, standard-sized strips cut from the paper in both machine direction and cross direction are attached top and bottom to clamps or grips in the device. The lower clamp is pulled down at a slow, even speed by an electric motor. The strip of paper pulls down the clamp to which the upper end is attached, transmitting the movement along an arm to a weighted lever that is pulled along a scale. When the test strip breaks, the lever remains fixed and indicates on the scale the force in pounds required to break the paper.

"The tensile strength of a paper is described by one number indicating the pressure required to pull the fibers apart in the machine direction and another number for the cross direction. Since tensile strength is tested by a pulling action (instead of a tearing action or a bursting action), the results should be higher in the machine direction than in the cross direction." [13:48]

Papers that measure a high tensile strength are commonly formed from well-beaten pulp because beating maximizes interfiber bonding. The Library Binding Institute specifications for endpapers call for a paper having a tensile strength with the grain of not less than 40 pounds per inch and across the grain of not less than 25 pounds per inch strip for 80 pound basis weight paper (25 x 38 - 500). [18:10]

1.D.3.c. Resistance to tear (T 414)

The T 414, or Elmendorf test, "named after its inventor, Armin Elmendorf, determines the average force in grams required to tear a single sheet of paper after the tear has been started." [31:87] The test measures the internal tearing resistance of paper rather than its edge-tear strength, which is described in T 470. [34] Internal tearing resistance is a measure of the force perpendicular to the plane of the paper necessary to tear a single sheet through a specified distance after the tear has already been started. Edge-tearing strength (T 470) is a measure of the force needed to start a tear, which may be several times the force needed to continue it once it is started. An example of this difference is the difficulty of opening a cellophane bag, which, once nicked, tears open easily. [8:33]

The "tester consists essentially of a stationary clamp, a moveable clamp carried on a pendulum formed by a sector of a circle free to swing on a ball bearing, a knife mounted on a stationary post for starting the tear, means for leveling the instrument, means for holding the pendulum in a raised position and for releasing it instantaneously, and means for registering the maximum arc through which the pendulum swings when released." [31:87]

In the test, several thin pieces of paper are fixed between the two clamps. The pieces to be torn are slit so that a known distance must still be torn to completely separate them. When the pendulum is released, the paper is torn between the fixed and the moveable clamp. The greater resistance the paper has to tearing, the more the swing of the pendulum is impeded and brought to a standstill, as indicated by a friction pointer. The pointer indicates a number on a scale, which is the measure of the "tearing resistance." The higher the number, the greater the paper's resistance to tearing. [13:47]

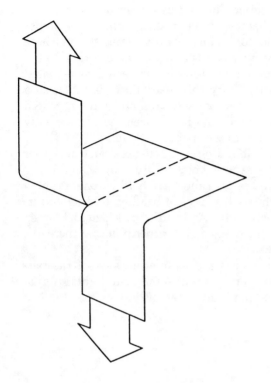

FIGURE 1.16. Out-of-plane
tearing mode used in the
Elmendorf tearing resistance
test. Source: D. F. Caulfield
and D. E. Gunderson. *Paper
Testing and Strength
Characteristics.* Madison, WI:
USDA Forest Service, Forest
Products Laboratory, 1988. In
*TAPPI Proceedings: 1988
Paper Preservation
Symposium.* Atlanta, GA:
TAPPI Press, 1988, p. 39.

The Elmendorf method measures the tearing resistance of paper perpendicular to the plane of the sheet or when paper is torn in the out-of-plane mode, "for example when deliberately tearing strips of newspaper [Figure 1.16]. . . . An example of in-plane tearing is the separation of computer printout sheets along a perforation while both sheets are held on the surface of a desk. In-plane tearing is representative of the tearing failure that can occur during the transport of a paper web through a printing press. The out-of-plane tearing mode, used in the Elmendorf test, resembles the type of tearing that occurs when a nicked sheet in a book is accidentally torn by a reader while turning pages." [8:33]

The Library Binding Institute specifications stipulate that the paper for endpapers (80 pound basis weight, 25 x 38 - 500) have a tearing resistance per 1-inch strip of 114 grams with the grain and 140 grams across the grain. [18:10]

1.D.3.d. Folding endurance (T 511)

A paper's durability and resistance to handling and abuse can be evaluated from a standardized test known as the M.I.T. folding endurance test. Folding provides a means of measuring the built-in ruggednes and permanence of paper. The folding endurance is the number of folds a paper will withstand under testing conditions before breaking. A paper will tend to fold more readily along the machine direction without rupturing the fiber bonds than across the grain. In the M.I.T. test, the paper is held under tension and subjected to repeated folding; the number of folds necessary to cause failure is taken as a measure of folding endurance. The test closely "resembles the repeated action of opening and closing a book, and it has been found especially valuable in measuring the deterioration of paper with aging." [8:34]

Short fiber length, poor fiber bonding, or brittleness can cause poor folding endurance. Rag pulp papers are usually "high in folding endurance, whereas groundwood papers and heavily filled papers show poorer folding endurance. In the early stages of beating, folding endurance increases as does tensile strength. As beating proceeds, however, folding endurance eventually decreases as interfiber bonding increases the brittleness of the paper." [8:34]

Folding endurance is considered a sensitive measure of the permanence of paper: the ability of paper to withstand heat, light, internal and external chemical attack, aging, and other influences that tend to

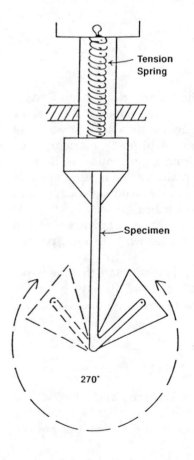

FIGURE 1.17. Schematic of the M.I.T. folding endurance apparatus. Source: D. F. Caulfield and D. E. Gunderson. *Paper Testing and Strength Characteristics.* Madison, WI: USDA Forest Service, Forest Products Laboratory, 1988. In *TAPPI Proceedings: 1988 Paper Preservation Symposium.* Atlanta, GA: TAPPI Press, 1988, p. 39.

deteriorate the fiber. One of the ways such correlations are confirmed is by subjecting test samples to heat and dryness for a specified number of days and then measuring any loss of strength by comparing the paper's folding endurance before and after this artificial heat aging. "A decline in folding endurance is the most sensitive indicator of aging and deterioration of paper." [31:105]

The Library Binding Institute specifications stipulate that paper for endpapers (80 pound basis weight, 25 x 38 - 500) have a folding endurance with the grain of 275 double folds and across the grain of 200 double folds. [18:10]

1.D.3.e. Accelerated aging (T 453 and T 544)

"Accelerated aging is exposing paper to high temperatures and varying humidity to simulate natural aging." [35:107] Accelerated aging consists of heating a specimen of the paper to be tested in an environmentally controlled oven. Ideally, the environment inside the oven will simulate a condition whereby the *rate* of the paper's deterioration will increase but its *nature* will not. A commonly accepted measure of aging in this process is "that heating paper for three days in an oven at 100 °C is equivalent in its effect to approximately 25 years under normal library storage conditions." [31:3]

Although sound in theory, accelerated aging tests are, at this time, of limited usefulness. The reason is that conditions of storage, which vary widely, have a considerable influence on the degree of permanence; also, it is difficult to verify empirically the accuracy of such tests except by experiments conducted over a number of years. [31:4]

1.E. Standards

There are several organizations writing standard specifications for permanence of paper.

American Society for Testing and Materials (ASTM)
1916 Race Street
Philadelphia, PA 19103

Founded in 1898, ASTM is a scientific and technical association formed for the development of standards on characteristics and performance of materials, products, systems, and service, and for the promotion of related knowledge. Committee D6 on Paper and Paper Products has the responsibility for developing the standards for those products.

The American National Standards Institute (ANSI)
1430 Broadway
New York, NY 10018

ANSI is the United States coordinator of voluntary standards development and the clearinghouse for information on national and international standards. Its federated membership includes a wide range of voluntary organizations representing every technical discipline, every facet of trade and commerce, organized labor, and consumer interest. It does not develop standards, per se, as they are developed by the member organizations referred to as secretariats. All of the actions of a secretariat must meet the voluntary consensus procedures established by ANSI. [4:41]

National Information Standards Organization (NISO)
P.O. Box 1056
Bethesda, MD 20817

NISO is a nonprofit association that develops voluntary technical standards used in a wide range of information services and products. NISO is accredited to develop standards by the American National Standards Institute.

An important ANSI/NISO standard for librarians and archivists is that for the permanence of paper for printed library materials (ANSI Z39.48-1984) published in 1985. The standard establishes the criteria for permanence of *uncoated* paper with the intention of having that paper last several hundred years under normal library circulation and storage conditions. It applies to uncoated paper used in the production of library materials in the following categories:

1. Important works of fiction and nonfiction.
2. Scholarly periodicals, monographs, and reprints.
3. Collected editions.
4. Encyclopedias, dictionaries, bibliographies, directories, indexes, abstracts, and other reference works that require permanent retention.
5. Publications intended primarily for the library market.
6. Titles not appropriate for transfer to other formats. [2:7]

In 1990 the National Information Standards Organization (NISO) voted on and submitted to ANSI a proposal for the revision of the ANSI Z39.48-1984 standard for uncoated paper. The revision establishes criteria for the manufacture of both *"coated* and *uncoated* paper that will last several hundred years under normal conditions of library and archives circulation and storage without significant deterioration."* [25:1] The revised standard, if accepted by ANSI, will bear the designation of ANSI/NISO Z39.48-199X. The "X" will be replaced by the digit indicating the year the standard was accepted.

The proposal adds "original documents and records" to the list of materials likely to be produced and/or acquired by libraries and archives. According to the revision, both uncoated and coated permanent paper should meet all of the minimum requirements in Table 1.2 plus a number of others.

TABLE 1.2. Proposed minimum requirements for the permanence of uncoated and coated paper for publications and documents for libraries and archives.[a]

	UNCOATED PAPER	COATED PAPER
pH	7.5[b]	7.0 in the core, exclusive of coating[c]
Tear resistance	Minimum average machine direction tear index of 5.25 mNm^2/g[d]	Minimum average machine direction tear index of 5.25 mNm^2/g when the value of g is the weight of the core paper, exclusive of coating
Alkaline reserve equivalent of calcium carbonate based on oven-dry weight of paper	2%[e]	2%[f]
Amount of lignin in the paper stock by weight of the fiber component	No more than 1%[g]	No more than 1% in core paper[h]

[a] These and several other requirements are being reviewed by the NISO Standards Committee II.

[b] In accordance with the cold extraction method described in TAPPI T 509 om-88, *Hydrogen Ion Concentration (pH) of Paper Extracts—Cold Extraction Method.*

[c] As described in TAPPI T 529 pm-74, *Surface pH Measurement of Paper.* TAPPI T 509 om-88 is *not* an appropriate pH test for coated paper.

[d] See ISO 1974 Paper, *Determination of Tear Resistance,* 2nd ed., 1985.

[e] See TAPPI UM 531, *Carbonates in Coated Paper (Qualitative).*

[f] The oven-dry weight of the entire paper including the coating. See TAPPI UM 531.

[g] See TAPPI T 401 om-88, *Fiber Analysis of Paper and Paperboard.*

[h] Ibid.

Source: National Information Standards Organization (Z39). *ANSI/NISO Z39.48-199X, Revision of Z39.48-1984; Proposed American National Standard for Permanence of Paper for Publications and Documents in Libraries and Archives.* Gaithersburg, MD: National Institute of Standards and Technology, 1989.

It is interesting to note that the participants in a recent symposium on permanent paper held by the Deutsche Bibliothek (the Library of the Federal Republic of Germany) agreed that the specifications for book paper should be:

1. 100 percent bleached cellulose without pulp fibers.
2. A pH value of 7.5 to 9.
3. A calcium carbonate buffer of at least 3 percent.

These requirements are somewhat more stringent than those in the current and proposed ANSI standards. [14:4]

Publications printed on paper that meets the ANSI/NISO Z39.48-1984 standards can carry a statement to the effect that the paper meets the minimum requirements of the ANSI standard. They can also display the mathematical symbol for infinity, set inside a circle, on the verso of the title page of a book (for example, see the verso of the title page of this book) or on the masthead or copyright area of a periodical publication. [2:7–8] The proposal for the new standard contains a somewhat revised statement of compliance, but the meaning is virtually the same.

For detailed information consult the complete standard, which is available from ANSI. Other ANSI or ASTM standards of interest to librarians and archivists relating to paper, storage containers, and copying are briefly discussed below. More complete information on these standards is available from the ASTM.

ANSI/ASTM D 3290-86, Standard Specification for Bond and Ledger Papers for Permanent Records.

Bond papers are used for writing or printing and [bond] is a grade which historically was used where permanence, strength and durability was required. [Bonds are] used mostly for letterheads and forms today. Documents published or generated on ledger paper are often heavily used and must be very durable. If documents produced on either of these types of papers will be stored or used for long periods of time, papers complying with [the ANSI/ASTM D 3290-86] standard should be used. [4:43]

ANSI/ASTM D 3458-85, Standard Specification for Copies from Office Copying Machines for Permanent Records.

This is a two-part specification with the first covering paper and the second covering imaged copy. The paper is covered by standard D 3290. The Imaged Copy portion allows for copies made on either direct or indirect electrostatic copy processes and other types of copiers. The lack of good test methods to evaluate images and the inability to relate tests that do exist to archival properties of a document limit the means of evaluating that characteristic. [4:43]

ASTM D 3301-85, Standard Specification for File Folders for Storage of Permanent Records.

Folder stock is a paperboard used for manufacture of filing folders. The storage medium is often overlooked when considering specifications for the permanent retention of files. Folders made from board complying with this specification will ensure the long life of archival materials. [4:43]

Technical Association of the Pulp and Paper Industry (TAPPI)
Technology Park/Atlanta
P.O. Box 105113
Atlanta, GA 30348

TAPPI's purpose is to collect and disseminate technical information for executives, engineers, consultants, and students who work in the pulp and paper, packaging and converting, nonwovens, and allied industries. It does not develop product standards.

International Organization for Standardization (ISO)
One Rue de Varenbe
Case Postale 56
CH-1121 Geneva 20
Switzerland

National standards bodies united to promote standardization worldwide. The organization develops and publishes international standards, facilitates exchanging of goods and services, and fosters mutual cooperation in intellectual, scientific, technical, and economic spheres of endeavor. ISO is affiliated with ANSI, and its standards can be purchased from the latter.

1.F. Alkaline Papers and the Future

Until recently, most of the free sheet paper produced in the United States was alum-rosin sized and therefore contained acids that, as described above, dramatically shorten its usable life. This has serious consequences for libraries and archives, especially those charged with the responsibility of maintaining the nation's cultural, economic, and social heritage for the use of citizens and scholars in the future. "Nearly 80 million books in North American research libraries are threatened with destruction because they are printed on acidic paper." [3:I-A-1] Public and school librarians have felt that such statistics have little relevance for them because their collections are much smaller and newer than those in the average research library, and their holdings are often duplicated elsewhere. Public librarians in particular, however, are beginning to change their attitudes; they too are discovering that significant percentages of their own collections are printed on acidic paper, and many of these materials, especially adult nonfiction, are important parts of their collections that cannot be replaced. [29:128–129]

The problem of acid books and paper, as well as some solutions, are covered in more detail in Chapter 5. This chapter will close with a discussion of the developments in the production of alkaline papers and the types of action information professionals can take to encourage publishers to use such papers in their publications.

"There were no significant changes in machine papermaking after the development of the sulfate process until the S. D. Warren Company began using waste carbonates, from their pulp cooking, as fillers for their commercial papers. Intended originally as a means of getting rid of a nuisance (lime mud), it became apparent over the years that the carbonate fillers, by making the paper acid-resistant, were making it longer lasting." [11:373] The *Encyclopedia Britannica*, 11th Edition (© 1911), is an excellent example. Its paper remains white and flexible in contrast to its companion alum-rosin paper editions, which are discolored and brittle. Nevertheless, Dr. Edwin Sutermeister, the scientist who experimented with the lime mud and tested the encyclopedias, concluded that the amount of clay present in the paper was not as much a factor in the deteriorating editions as the alum-rosin sizing. [32:128]

Cunha, in his 1987 report on mass deacidification for libraries says:

In the 1950's, in response to an urgent need for a long-lasting durable paper for bookmaking and record keeping, chemists at the B. W. Wilson Paper Company in Richmond, Virginia, working with the W. J. Barrow Research Laboratory, also in Richmond, perfected a method of making high quality alkaline acid-free paper from fibers derived from wood. Essentially the process consists of selecting wood from trees that produce very long cellulose fibers; careful manufacturing control to eliminate unwanted residual chemicals from the cooking and bleaching processes; substituting chemically stable synthetic resin for the commonly used alum/rosin sizing; and using acid-inhibiting carbonates as fillers. This permanent/durable/acid-free paper, as it is called, can be as good as any fine-quality, handmade, rag paper that has ever been made. [11:373]

In the 1950s and early 1960s there were three significant events that led to the development of long-life paper.

1. The lithographic offset printing process put a greater stress on paper and required the development of papers with greater surface and internal binding strength. High speed web offset presses became widely used for book manufacturing. The stresses produced by these machines required greater tensile strength and tear resistance in the paper to ensure good runability and adequate strength for book conversion.
2. W. J. Barrow's work on paper permanence and durability, sponsored by the Virginia State Library, laid the foundation for the ANSI Z39.48-1984 specifications for permanent paper and eventually brought publicity to and understanding of the processes of paper deterioration.
3. Perhaps the most important event was the development of new technology in the papermaking industry, i.e., synthetic sizing chemicals. (The two main types of alkaline synthetic sizing

materials are alkyl-ketene-dimer (AKD) and alkenyl succinic anhydride (ASA). Calcium carbonate is generally used as the filler and alum is not required as a co-reactant. [35:98]) This development enabled papermakers to change the paper machine wet end chemistry from acid pH levels of 4.5 to 5.0 to the neutral 7.0. "It is this breakthrough that brought about an alternate source of printing papers that are now commonly referred to as 'permanent' or 'acid free.' " [17:15–16] These synthetic sizes have enabled many papermakers to convert their operations to alkaline systems.

Alkaline systems should be very attractive to papermakers because they enable the industry to reduce manufacturing costs as a result of

the ability to use cheaper calcium carbonate pigment, which can replace titanium dioxide and part of the fiber;

reduced energy consumption due to less required refining and easier drying;

better runability due to more stable chemistry and cleaner operation;

reduced equipment corrosion;

the potential for machine speedup due to easier drying;

easier pollution control;

and brightness and opacity specs being easier to achieve. [16:213]

The most important of these are the use of calcium carbonate as a filler instead of more expensive fiber, reduced water consumption in the manufacturing process, and improved waste management.

"With so many advantages to the alkaline process, it might be expected that the paper industry would have completely converted by now." [16:213] Unfortunately, many papermakers still produce acidic products, although this is rapidly changing. Alkaline paper presently makes up about 40 to 45 percent of all sized paper. [24:5] There are several reasons that the industry has not rapidly shifted to alkaline production, but probably the most important is lack of demand (or perceived lack of demand). For many years it was thought that book paper made up only 1 or 2 percent of the total paper market. Figures published in 1988, however, reveal that possibly as much as 13 percent of the paper produced in this country goes into books. [19:7] Since the demand was thought to be small, and since alkaline papers sell for the same cost as acidic papers, there was little market incentive for the conversion. The new statistics and the efforts of librarians, archivists, and others are causing publishers to require that more of their materials be produced on alkaline paper.

The most effective means of convincing papermakers to produce more alkaline products is for publishers to demand permanent/durable paper for their books and other publications. While some publishers, notably Random House, Simon & Schuster, ABC-CLIO, and the university presses, are using acid-free paper, much needs to be done to convince all publishers to convert. A list of "ideas for advocates" was recently published to assist persons interested in lobbying paper manufacturers and publishers. Parts of it are reprinted here. [29:11–12]

> Make bumper stickers, e.g., "Achieve Immortality! Write on permanent paper."
>
> Assemble teaching aids and kits about the manufacture and use of permanent paper for school classes in history or science.
>
> Monitor the use of alkaline paper in selected parts of the market, e.g., books reviewed by various publications, or all books received at the local library. Keep records and follow trends. These activities make good student projects, and might provide material for an interesting article in a professional publication.
>
> Petition large organizations, urging them to switch to alkaline paper for their copy paper, for government records (city, county, and state officials), for office supplies and letterheads (the local university or employer). The possibilities are endless. The first step, of course, would be to determine the kind of paper already in use, since it may already be alkaline.
>
> Increase awareness of the standards for paper permanence among people who ought to know, e.g., publishers and purchasing agents. The ANSI standard is the easiest to understand and apply.
>
> Test the books you buy and any other item made of paper that is intended for use over a long period of time; then feed back results to the sources. This is a form of consciousness-raising.
>
> Whenever there is a choice among papers, request the alkaline brand. When dealing with a printer, insist on alkaline paper.
>
> At convention exhibits where books are displayed, ask the company representative whether the books are on permanent paper. If they don't know, the question opens up the topic and often provides the opportunity for a little education. Informed librarians and archivists need to stamp out the myth that paper is only good if it is 100 percent rag. Information professionals and the public need to learn that they can trust purified wood pulp. Everyone needs to learn that permanent paper costs no more than the other stuff; in fact, it is cheaper to make. [20:11–12]

These ideas were gathered by Ellen McCrady, one of the most forceful and articulate champions for the use of alkaline papers in the country. Her newsletter, the *Alkaline Paper Advocate*, promotes with energy and enthusiasm the cause of permanent paper. Due to her efforts and those of the Association of Research Libraries, the Council on Library Resources, the Commission on Preservation and Access, the Library of Congress, the National Humanities Alliance, the National Library of Medicine, the National Endowment for the Humanities, and other organizations and concerned individuals, the public is becoming aware of the need to use permanent/durable papers for publications of enduring value.

In October 1990, Public Law 101-423, which makes urgent recommendations concerning the use of acid-free permanent papers for the publication of important government documents, was signed by President Bush. Six states (Arizona, Colorado, Connecticut, Indiana, North Carolina, and Virginia) have laws requiring the use of alkaline or permanent paper for books and/or records. More and more paper mills are converting to alkaline paper production, which will make it much easier to convince publishers and government agencies to require such papers for their publications and records. It is expected that most papers manufactured for publishing and record-keeping purposes will be alkaline by the middle of the 1990s. "Paper industry analysts predict that by 1992 approximately 80 percent of the uncoated, free-sheet paper—that is, paper free from partially processed fiber—produced in the United States will be alkaline." [3:I-A-3]

REFERENCES

1. *ABBEY pH Pens (Cholorphenol Red) Instructions for Use.* Provo, UT: Abbey Publications, n.d.

2. American National Standards Institute. *American National Standards for Information Sciences—Permanence of Paper for Printed Library Materials (ANSI) Z39.48-1984.* New York: American National Standards Institute, 1985.

3. Association of Research Libraries. *Preserving Knowledge: The Case for Alkaline Paper.* Revised August 1990. Washington, DC: Association of Research Libraries in Collaboration with American Library Association, Commission on Preservation and Access, National Humanities Alliance, 1990.

4. Aubey, Rolland. "Specifications and Test Methods Associated with Papers for Permanent Books, Records, and Documents." In *TAPPI Proceedings: 1988 Paper Preservation Symposium,* 41–45. Atlanta, GA: TAPPI Press, 1988.

5. Barrow, William J. *Tri-Test: A Spot Testing Kit for Unstable Papers.* Richmond, VA: W. J. Barrow Research Laboratory, 1969.

6. Browning, B. L. "Nature and Sources of Acid in Paper." Paper presented at The Institute of Paper Chemistry, Seminar for Conservators of Paper Objects. Appleton, WI: The Institute for Paper Chemistry, October 1971.

7. Casey, J. P. *Pulp and Paper.* New York: Interscience Publishers, 1966.

8. Caulfield, D. F., and D. E. Gunderson. *Paper Testing and Strength Characteristics.* Madison, WI: USDA Forest Service, Forest Products Laboratory, 1988. In *TAPPI Proceedings: 1988 Paper Preservation Symposium,* 31–40. Atlanta, GA: TAPPI Press, 1988.

9. Clapp, Verner W. "The Story of Permanent/Durable Book-Paper, 1115–1970." *Restaurator* Supplement No. 3 (1972): 1–51.

10. *Conservation Resources Catalogue.* Springfield, VA: Conservation Resources International, Inc., June 1988.

11. Cunha, George Martin. "Mass Deacidification for Libraries." *Library Technology Reports* 23 (May-June 1987): 362–472.

12. *Encyclopedia of Materials Science and Engineering*, edited by Michael B. Bever. 8 vols. Cambridge, MA: MIT Press, 1986.

13. Farnsworth, Donald. "Laboratory Paper Testing." In *Paper—Art & Technology*, edited by Paulette Long, 45–49. San Francisco: World Print Council, 1979.

14. "Federal Republic of Germany Holds Permanent Paper Symposium." *Commission on Preservation and Access Newsletter*. 23 (May 1990): 3–4.

15. Hunter, Dard. *Papermaking: The History and Technique of an Ancient Craft*. New York: Dover Publications, 1978.

16. Kindler, W. A., Jr. "Collection Preservation: The Practical Choices." In *TAPPI Proceedings: 1988 Paper Preservation Symposium*, 211–214. Atlanta, GA: TAPPI Press, 1988.

17. Liberatore, Anthony M. "Production of Paper for Libraries." In *TAPPI Proceedings: 1988 Paper Preservation Symposium*, 15–21. Atlanta, GA: TAPPI Press, 1988.

18. Library Binding Institute. *Standard for Library Binding*, edited by Paul A. Parisi and Jan Merrill-Oldham. 8th ed. Rochester, NY: Library Binding Institute, 1986.

19. McCrady, Ellen. "Fine Paper is a Significant Part of the Market." *Alkaline Paper Advocate* 1 (March 1988): 7.

20. McCrady, Ellen. "Ideas for Advocates." *Alkaline Paper Advocate* 1 (March 1988): 11–12.

21. McCrady, Ellen. "Paper & Book Intensive '88." *The Abbey Newsletter* 12 (November 1988): 124–126.

22. McCrady, Ellen. "pH and pH Pens." *Alkaline Paper Advocate* 1 (October 1988): 29–30.

23. McCrady, Ellen. "Prices Will Rise." *Alkaline Paper Advocate* 2 (July 1989): 19–20.

24. McCrady, Ellen. "TAPPI Paper Preservation Symposium." *Alkaline Paper Advocate* 2 (April 1989): 1–2, 5–7.

25. National Information Standards Organization (Z39). *ANSI/NISO Z39.48-199X, Revision of Z39.48-1984; Proposed American National Standard for Permanence of Paper for Publications and Documents in Libraries and Archives*. Gaithersburg, MD: National Institute of Standards and Technology, 1989.

26. *Papermaking: Art and Craft; An Account Derived from the Exhibition Presented in the Library of Congress, Washington, D.C. and Opened on April 21, 1963*. Washington, DC: Library of Congress, 1963.

27. Parham, Russell A., and Hilkka M. Kaustinen. *Papermaking Materials: An Atlas of Electron Micrographs*. Appleton, WI: The Institute of Paper Chemistry, 1974.

28. *The Random House Dictionary of the English Language*, edited by Jess Stein. New York: Random House, 1981.

29. Reynolds, Anne L., Nancy C. Schrock, and Joanna Walsh. "Preservation: The Public Library Response." *Library Journal* 114 (February 15, 1989): 128–132.

30. Ritzenthaler, Mary Lynn. *Archives & Manuscripts: Conservation. A Manual on Physical Care and Management*. SAA Basic Manual Series. Chicago: Society of American Archivists, 1983.

31. Roberts, Matt T., and Don Etherington. *Bookbinding and the Conservation of Books: A Dictionary of Descriptive Terminology*. Washington, DC: Library of Congress, 1982.

32. Smith, Richard D. "Deacidification Technologies: State of the Art." In *TAPPI Proceedings: 1988 Paper Preservation Symposium*, 125–140. Atlanta, GA: TAPPI Press, 1988.

33. Sutermeister, Edwin. *The Story of Paper Making*. Boston: S. D. Warren Co., 1954.

34. *TAPPI Test Methods, 1989*. Atlanta, GA: TAPPI Press, 1988.

35. U.S. Congress. Office of Technology Assessment. *Book Preservation Technologies*. OTA-O-375. Washington, DC: U.S. Government Printing Office, 1988.

36. Whitney, Roy P. "Chemistry of Paper." In *Paper—Art & Technology*, edited by Paulette Long, 36–44. San Francisco: World Print Council, 1979.

2.
THE ENVIRONMENT

2.A. Introduction

The most critical element affecting the longevity of library materials, other than their own inherent physical composition, is the environment in which they are used and stored. The siting of the building, both in regard to its orientation to the sun and the building's location in areas safe from flooding and other natural disasters; the presence of planted areas and trees near perimeter walls; the design of roofs and basements and the location of windows in relation to stack areas; the orientation and type of shelving; the type and capacity of heating and air-conditioning systems (HVAC)—all these factors, and more, affect the health of library materials. In light of these facts, it is extremely important that conservators and/or librarians knowledgeable about the role the environment plays in the preservation of library materials participate in planning new facilities or in the renovation of older buildings. [20:99] If such individuals had participated in the past (and their advice had been followed), many of the problems endemic in libraries and archives could have been avoided.

But it is not only the buildings and their design that cause problems. As was discussed in Chapter 1, libraries house millions of books published on acidic paper. High temperatures and humidity cause chemical reactions between the cellulose in paper, the acids residing in the fibers, and pollutants in the atmosphere, all of which accelerate deterioration. Fluctuations in temperature and humidity cause the expansion and contraction of cellulose, adhesives in the bindings, and boards and cloth in covers, all at different rates. Over time, this literally pulls books apart. An unstable environment will also weaken and degrade other media such as computer disks, film, magnetic tape, photographs, prints, slides, and video disks.

This chapter will discuss the proper environmental conditions necessary to maintain the collection safely in a stable condition. HVAC systems, relative humidity, temperature, pollutants in the air, monitoring equipment and methods, mold and mildew, insects, vermin and fumigation—all elements of environmental conservation (EC)—will be addressed. EC is a preventative preservation program for the entire collection and, therefore, is more cost effective in the long run than individual treatment of library materials. It pays for itself very quickly by avoiding the conditions that create preservation problems.

2.B. Heating, Ventilation, and Air-Conditioning (HVAC)

Timothy Padfield described the HVAC conditions within library buildings very clearly in the abstract of his paper presented at the conference on the preservation of library materials in Vienna in April 1986:

"The climate maintained within a library is the result of a compromise between the needs of the readers and the staff, the structure of the building, the need to minimize the deterioration rate of the collection, and maintenance demands and running costs of mechanical air-conditioning. Passive climate control by careful design of storage containers and by slowing down the heat and moisture transfer through walls allows simpler air-handling systems that are less troublesome, less costly to run, and less dangerous if they fail. Orthodox air-conditioning systems can produce air at a dew point of about 5 °C (41 °F),* allowing the building to be held at 18 °C (64.4 °F) and about 42 percent relative humidity (RH). A lower temperature can only be obtained by allowing the relative humidity to rise, or vice versa. A lower dew point can be obtained by drying the air with a silica gel desiccant system after the initial dehydration with a cooling coil. Bound books are liable to physical damage below about 35 percent RH, however, and people feel cold below about 18 °C (64.4 °F). Therefore, colder or dryer conditions are only suitable for carefully insulated storage vaults, in which only a minimum amount of air need be circulated. The relative humidity in vaults should be maintained slightly below that in the reading room so the moisture content of the book does not change when it is warmed for the reader. A stable relative humidity is desirable, but the value can be chosen, within the limits of 40 to 62 percent, to take account of peculiarities of the local climate and of the building. Buildings that are humidified in winter may be damaged by condensation and freezing of water in the walls. Sudden changes of relative humidity can be entirely prevented by enclosing books in close-fitting, nearly airtight containers, which are safe if there is no permanent temperature gradient from one side to the other and no sudden temperature drop around them. The small danger of locally generated air pollution can be minimized by sealing interior wooden surfaces and by incorporating alkaline buffered paper into boxes and shelf liners." [16:124]

"The simplest way to control the climate in a building is to distribute air from a central conditioning plant through ducts to the individual rooms. An air-distribution system allows control of dust, pollution, and

---

* The literature often uses Celsius instead of Fahrenheit when discussing recommended temperatures in the field of conservation and preservation. A temperature converter is included for convenience.

Conversion of Celsius to Fahrenheit: (C x 9/5) + 32 = F
Conversion of Fahrenheit to Celsius: (F - 32) x 5/9 = C

humidity as well as temperature regulation, all within the same system."
[16:125] Buildings lose heat only from their perimeters. The relative
humidity is controlled by holding the moisture content of the air in the
duct at a value that gives the correct relative humidity when the air has
warmed to the correct room temperature. The relative humidity is therefore not independently controlled from room to room as is the
temperature. Putting dryer air into the room cannot compensate for
sources of humidity such as fountains, people, and plants.

2.C. Temperature

Scientific experiments have shown that the deterioration
rate of cellulose (the main component of paper) is increased 2.5 times as
the temperature is increased from 68°F to 77°F. [4:1] In addition, it is
commonly believed that the rate of deterioration of library materials
doubles with every 10°C (18°F) increase in temperature. This belief is
based on the fact that the speed of chemical reactions depends in large
part on temperature and, on the average, doubles in speed with each 10°C
rise in temperature (conversely halving with each 10°C drop in temperature). Because the chemical reactions in cellulose may double at each 5°C
change, however, libraries may not have to drop their temperatures so
much. The actual deterioration rate will vary considerably because books
and other paper-based media contain a variety of materials, each having
a different rate of reaction. [20:99; 23:51]

The recommended temperature in which most library materials
should be housed is 65°F ±5 degrees. This causes problems, however,
because it is uncomfortable for most people and, in many areas, is not
energy efficient. Furthermore, in humid climates condensation can be a
problem: water vapor will condense on books, papers, and other objects
brought directly from cold storage to a warmer reading room or circulation area. For example, the dew point in a room at 68°F and 55 percent
relative humidity is 52°F, so water will condense on any object whose
temperature is below 52°F. Therefore, items kept in cold storage have to
be acclimatized, i.e., warmed slowly to the temperature of the area in
which they will be used before being released to the user. [27:45] [See
section 2.D for a discussion of relative humidity and an explanation of
dew point.]

Although condensation can be a problem, libraries with valuable
materials that need to be preserved for future generations should investigate the possibility of cold storage. Cool temperatures can also reduce
bio-deterioration problems. Many authorities agree that if a lower temperature cannot be maintained, a *nonfluctuating* temperature of 70°F or
less is acceptable for storage purposes. [23:51]

Recommended temperature ranges for a variety of library materials
are listed below. If the target temperature cannot be accurately maintained, the library should strive to stay within the recommended limits.

It is probably impractical to maintain a building or stack temperature at one setting throughout the year, especially in areas of the country that experience extreme temperature variations. Since rapid changes do the most damage to collections, internal temperature fluctuations due to seasonal changes should be gradual. The temperatures listed in Table 2.1 are the ideal and should be followed whenever possible, especially in libraries serving research institutions. But what about the average library that does not have significant amounts of material that demand cool temperatures? Academic, public, and school libraries, in general, must maintain an environment that is comfortable for both patrons and staff and safe for the housing of collections, yet is still economically feasible to support during all seasons of the year. In a library that is being used by the public, 72 °F has often been cited as a reasonable level to implement. [2:339] This is at the upper level of the 68 °F to 72 °F range that is most often cited as acceptable. The temperature could be allowed to rise as high as 76 °F as long as the relative humidity remains in the area of 50 percent. In fact, the relative humidity must be kept at 50 percent regardless of the temperature that is finally chosen to be effective in terms of cost, comfort, and environment. Reasons for this will be discussed in the next section.

If the temperature rises above 76 °F and the RH is above 60 percent, there is an excellent chance that mold and mildew will appear in the collection. While heat accelerates the deterioration of paper fibers, creating serious problems over time, mold and mildew are more immediate concerns in many libraries, especially in humid climates. Consequently, regardless of the size, type, or mission of the library, it behooves the staff to maintain a nonfluctuating temperature in the low seventies (or less) in the building year-round. Fungal outbreaks can occur overnight. The most serious and common mistake building administrators and/or maintenance staff make is to turn off air-conditioning systems in the evening after the building is closed, or on weekends and during vacation periods. Experience has shown that such a policy is penny wise and pound foolish. The cost of the energy saved is usually far less than the money necessary to

TABLE 2.1. Recommended temperature ranges.

TYPE OF MATERIALS	TEMPERATURE (FAHRENHEIT)	RANGE ±
Books, paper, and people	68° a	3°
Books and paper alone	60°	3°
Books and photographic materials	60°	3°
Photographic materials	55°	3°

aUpper safe limit is 76°

Source: *Environmental Specifications for the Storage of Library Materials*, 2. SOLINET Preservation Program Leaflet, No. 1. Atlanta, GA: Southeastern Library Network, Inc., April 24, 1985.

recover from an outbreak of mold and mildew and the accelerated degradation of materials that will occur over decades of fluctuating temperature and RH.

2.D. Relative Humidity and Its Control

2.D.1. RELATIVE HUMIDITY

Relative humidity (RH) is the ratio of the amount of water vapor actually present in the air to the greatest amount of vapor the air could hold at that temperature. The term describes the wetness or dryness of air at a given temperature and pressure. It is expressed as a percentage:

$$\frac{\text{Pounds of water present in air at } x°F \times 100}{\text{Absolute humidity at } x°F}$$

where absolute humidity = pounds of water the air could hold at $x°F$.

For example, a pound of air can hold .017 pounds of water vapor at 72°F:

$$RH = .017 \text{ pounds of water at } 72°F \times 100 = 100\% \text{ RH}$$

If the amount of water actually present in the air at that temperature is .017 pounds, the relative humidity is 100 percent and the air is saturated, i.e., it cannot hold any more water. Any additional water will be precipitated as dew, fog, or rain. Likewise, half the amount of water vapor actually in the air at that temperature will result in 50 percent relative humidity:

$$RH = .0085 \text{ pounds of water at } 72°F \times 100 = 50\% \text{ RH}$$

One quarter of the water vapor will produce 25 percent RH and so on:

$$RH = .00425 \text{ pounds of water at } 72°F \times 100 = 25\% \text{ RH}$$

A certain amount of relative humidity is necessary for paper to retain its flexibility. But scientists disagree about the optimum relative humidity desirable, because increased moisture content increases the rate of deteriorative chemical reactions and, if it is too high (i.e., above 65 to 70 percent), mold will grow. [27:87] If the relative humidity is too low, in the neighborhood of 25 percent, then brittle paper will break more easily because it is less flexible. Complicating matters even more, film and other photographic media require a lower level of relative humidity for optimum storage conditions (30 to 50 percent RH is the preferred range).

Low relative humidity also contributes to paper deterioration. Individual leaves of paper may be dried without catastrophic effect, but books react differently because they are made of various materials

TABLE 2.2. Recommended relative humidity ranges.

TYPE OF MATERIALS	RELATIVE HUMIDITY	RANGE ±
General collections	50%	3%
Books, paper and photos	50% [a]	3%
Photographic materials	40%	3%
Film and magnetic tape alone	20%	3%

[a] **May be reduced to 30%–40% in winter to help prevent condensation.**

Source: *Environmental Specifications for the Storage of Library Materials*, 2. SOLINET Preservation Program Leaflet, No. 1. Atlanta, GA: Southeastern Library Network, Inc., April 24, 1985.

laminated together. As the relative humidity is lowered, these materials change their physical properties in different ways. Paper and leather will shrink and stiffen, but in different manners and directions. Cloth, on the other hand, will expand in area as the relative humidity diminishes. Glue becomes extremely hard and brittle as it dries. These materials appear to work against one another, causing book covers to warp, although these effects are not yet documented by reliable published data. Apparently a relative humidity below 35 percent is rather risky for books (in contrast, the optimum relative humidity for film and tape is between 30 to 50 percent).

The upper limit for relative humidity for good preservation is set by the danger of mold growth at about 65 to 70 percent. Within the general limits of 40 to 60 percent RH, the choice should be controlled by the local climate and by the nature of the outer wall of the building, as will be explained later. It is better to have a constant relative humidity within this range than to strive towards an ideal relative humidity that can only be obtained in some seasons of the year. [16:131]

All organic materials are hygroscopic: they take up and give off moisture in response to the percentage of moisture in the air. The moisture content of most natural organic materials ranges from 3 to 20 percent. Paper takes up moisture from the surrounding air quickly but releases it back into the air much more slowly. Therefore, the relative humidity of the air may not be equal to the moisture content of the books stored in that air, especially if the books go out of the building on loan. Because the moisture content of books may be higher than that of the surrounding air, mold can grow on books even though the relative humidity measures within accepted levels. Fluctuations in relative humidity contribute to this problem. Storage under constant conditions of relative humidity will slowly stabilize the equilibrium moisture content of books.

The recommended level of relative humidity is a compromise among several requirements: (1) a level of moisture high enough to maintain flexibility, (2) a level low enough to slow deterioration of

TABLE 2.3. Recommended relative humidity ranges by geographic area.

TYPE OF MATERIALS	RELATIVE HUMIDITY [a]
Mixed collections in humid tropics (Air must circulate to discourage mold growth)	65%
Mixed collections in Europe and North America (May cause frosting and condensation problems in libraries where winter temperatures are low)	55%
Compromise for mixed collections in libraries where winter temperatures are low	45%–50%

[a] **All levels should be maintained to within ±5%. The danger limits of 65% and 40% should not be exceeded.**

Source: Based on a table from Sarah Staniforth, "Environmental Conservation," in *Manual of Curatorship; A Guide to Museum Practice,* ed. John M. A. Thompson, et al., 196 (London: Butterworth, 1984).

materials and control insects and mold, and (3) a level that will do no structural harm to library buildings due to condensation in cold weather. The important controlling factor in establishing an appropriate level of relative humidity is the need to maintain it within a narrow range (3 percent). Again, maintaining humidity at a constant level is more important than attaining any one particular level. [4:2]

Authorities tend to agree that the practical limits for relative humidity in libraries range from 40 to 65 percent, plus or minus 3 percent of whatever optimum is recommended.

The geographic location as well as the nature of the collection should also be taken into consideration when considering safe (and practical) RH ranges [see Table 2.3].

2.D.2. DEW POINT

Dew point is the saturation temperature corresponding to the relative humidity and pressure of a given moist air state. Warm air will hold much more moisture than an equal amount of cool air. As air cools, the relative humidity increases until a temperature is reached in which the air becomes saturated and liquid water begins to condense. That temperature is the dew point. The higher the initial relative humidity of the air, the less the air must cool before condensation can occur. In other words, the dew point is the surface temperature at which moisture begins to condense on that surface. For example, if a book is in cold storage (at sea level) and its surface temperature is 60°F when it is brought into a room heated to 72 °F with a relative humidity of 80 percent, water vapor will condense on the book because its dew point temperature is 65 °F, 5 degrees above the book's surface temperature. The more humid the air, the higher the dew point temperature; conversely, the dryer the air, the lower the dew point temperature. [14:3] If that same book is brought into the same room, but the relative humidity has been lowered to 50 percent, there will be no condensation on the book because its dew point temperature will have dropped to 52.3 °F, 7.7 degrees below the surface temperature of the book. The dew point temperature has implications not only for cold storage, but also for the design of library buildings and the location of shelving within the building.

2.D.3. CONTROL OF RELATIVE HUMIDITY

Modern air-conditioning systems, if they are equipped to add or remove moisture in the air, can enable libraries and archives to completely control relative humidity . Not all systems can do this. What every library should have is a well-designed system that rigidly controls both temperature and relative humidity day and night, seven days a week, all year long. A central air-conditioning unit with a reheat or similar capability can control the atmospheric environment well enough to meet the minimum standards of 50 percent (±5 percent) relative humidity and 68 °F to 72 °F (±3 °F). Problems usually occur because of administrative decisions to reduce the amount of energy required to operate the systems by raising the temperature in the evening, on weekends and during holidays, or turning the systems off altogether during these periods. Another source of difficulty is cutting off the air-conditioning during repair of buildings or repair, expansion, or installation of new systems. This is especially true in hot and humid climates or during the summer season. Any HVAC system, however, will find it difficult to reduce RH much below ambient levels.

In areas of low humidity, maintaining the recommended relative humidity may lead to serious damage to the exterior walls of buildings during the coldest months of the year. This is especially true of buildings constructed of brick or masonry. Water vapor will diffuse through the walls from the region of high humidity inside to the low humidity outside. In colder areas within the walls, water vapor may condense and leach salts out of the walls. These salts will show up on the exterior surface as a white discoloration or efflorescence. Freezing of the water or precipitation of salts within the wall can cause stresses that shatter the brick or masonry and cause it to spall off. In the coldest periods it is possible for water vapor to condense even on the inside of an exterior wall, causing the destruction of plaster or wall board. [13:13] The usual remedy for this problem is the use of a vapor barrier, usually plastic film. The barrier should be incorporated into the building (as close as possible to the warm side) by the architect. If condensation is a problem, an engineer should be consulted; don't tamper with the RH. Vinyl wallpaper or special vapor barrier paints may be used in existing buildings.

Libraries that do not have adequate air-conditioning or whose systems are incapacitated do have some other options to consider. Portable humidifiers or dehumidifiers can be installed either to raise or lower the moisture content of the air. Relative humidity control may be achieved within a room by using free-standing humidifier and dehumidifier units that are automatically controlled by humidistats, although the latter must be monitored constantly. These units provide an inexpensive and satisfactory method of keeping relative humidity within acceptable limits. [24:197]

2.D.3.a. Humidifiers

Humidifiers are designed to add water quickly to the air in a controlled manner. Staniforth describes three types of humidifiers that are in general use.

1. Atomizing (or adiabatic process) humidifiers draw water onto rapidly rotating blades which disperse particles into fine droplets which vaporize near the machine. Unless distilled or deionized water is used, the minerals that are present in tap water and a film of salts will be deposited on all exposed surfaces. A further problem is that if the humidistat fails and the machine does not switch off, water will continue to be added until the air is saturated and water condenses.
2. Steam (or isothermal process) humidifiers heat water (like a kettle) so that it evaporates into the air; these are used in air-conditioning plants, but usually only in emergencies for rooms.
3. The most suitable humidifier for library use is the unheated evaporated humidifier. A drum which carries a sponge belt slowly revolves, dipping the sponge into a reservoir filled with water. A fan blows room air through the wet sponge. Unlike the atomizing humidifier, if the humidistat fails in the 'on' position the relative humidity will not rise to much above 70 percent since damp air can only absorb a certain amount of water from a damp material. The minerals are left behind on the sponge, so tap water may be used in evaporative humidifiers. [24:197]

2.D.3.b. Dehumidifiers

There are two types of room dehumidifiers, desiccant and refrigerant. Which is more suitable depends on the climate. In a desiccant dehumidifier, room air is passed over a salt that absorbs water from the air. A drum containing the desiccant slowly rotates, passing, in turn, through a region where hot air drives moisture from the desiccant, through an exhaust, out of the room, and then into a region where room air is again passed through the desiccant. Refrigerant dehumidifiers work on a principle similar to a domestic refrigerator. They contain refrigerant gases (usually fluorinated hydrocarbons) that liquefy when compressed. Liquefaction occurs in the condensing coils, which are warm because of the heat that is given off when a gas turns into a liquid. In the cooling coils the liquid expands and vaporizes, absorbing heat from its surroundings. Room air is passed over the cooling coils, where it is cooled below its dew point and deposits moisture. It is reheated by passing over the warm condensing coils. Refrigerant dehumidifiers are preferred for warm climates, but they frost up too readily in very cold conditions. In colder environments, therefore, desiccant dehumidifiers are preferred.

Dehumidification can be achieved by heating alone, and this is a possible solution where the damp air is also cold; however, heating consumes more energy than either of the other dehumidifiers. [24:197]

2.D.3.c. Heat pipes

A new type of internal atmospheric control is the heat pipe. Working under a NASA contract in cooperation with the Florida Solar Energy Center (FSEC), the Dinh Company of Alachua, Florida has developed a prototype heat pipe dehumidification system that can double the moisture removal capacity of any air-conditioner and save substantial amounts of energy. The heat pipe, a technology that has been available only in the last 20 years, offers a unique, efficient, and highly reliable approach for providing additional dehumidification with relatively little cost. Added to a typical air-conditioning system [see Figure 2.1], an air-to-air heat pipe exchanger (HPHX) can recover heat from the warm return air to heat the cold supply air. The return air is precooled in this process by the HPHX, and the cooling energy requirement of the air-conditioner is reduced. An HPHX is a passive heat transfer device that has been used successfully in NASA's space program and has been successfully tested in a number of libraries. [9]

Recently, a library in Florida experienced relative humidity levels of 80 percent and more, causing the growth of mold and mildew on the books and concern for the health of the staff. A dehumidifying heat pipe (DHP) was installed in the air-conditioning duct work, causing the humidity level to drop to 58 percent within 24 hours. After the walls and books were dry, the humidity was maintained at 50 to 55 percent. There is no extra annual operating cost because of the passive nature of the HPHX which, in effect, turns it into a sort of perpetual motion machine when the air-conditioning system is operating. Libraries that have continuing problems with high relative humidity might wish to explore the installation of this equipment in their central air-conditioning systems. It should be noted, however, that the heat pipe works only when the air-conditioning system is running. [6]

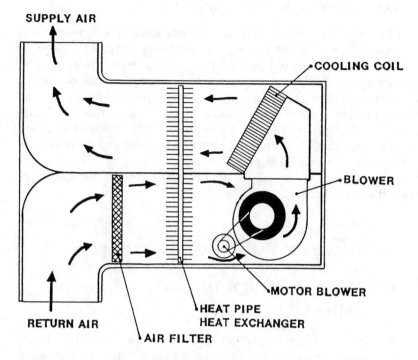

SUPPLY AIR

COOLING COIL

BLOWER

MOTOR BLOWER

RETURN AIR

HEAT PIPE
HEAT EXCHANGER

AIR FILTER

FIGURE 2.1. Heat pipe. Reproduced with the permission of the Dinh Company, Alachua, Florida.

2.D.3.d. Silica gel

Silica gel, a colloidal form of silica, can be used as a dehumidifier. It is available in small cloth bags or metal containers and is placed near objects on display or in storage that are prone to cockling or other damage. If it is used in a very dry condition, it will take moisture out of the atmosphere and will help in the prevention of mold, softening of water-soluble coatings, cockling, and warping. An indicator is usually mixed in with the granules; the indicator is blue when the granules are dry, but as the silica gel's drying capacity becomes exhausted, its color changes to pink. It can be dried by heating it to between 230°F and 482°F, whereupon the indicator will turn back to blue. [26:109]

The relative humidity of small enclosed spaces can be controlled by using silica gel conditioned to maintain the relative humidity at a predetermined level. When the relative humidity drops below that level, the gel will give off water, and when the humidity rises, the gel will absorb water. Before being used in an exhibition case or packing case, however, the gel must be preconditioned to the environment in the chamber for at least two weeks. To test whether a bag of the gel has reached the required RH, place it in a polyethylene bag together with an accurate (calibrated) dial hygrometer that can be read through the bag, and leave it for 30 minutes. [26:109]

2.D.3.e. Monitoring air circulation

When using any type of humidity controller, it is important to ensure that all areas of the room or space being supplied receive its benefit. A hygrometer should be used to check that there are no pockets of stagnant air, particularly in the corners of rooms. Fans can be used to improve air circulation. The size of humidity controllers and the number of units depend on such factors as the size of the room, the speed with which the air changes in the room (determined by the number of doors, vents, and windows), the difference between internal and external considerations, and the number of people who pass through the room. Check with air-conditioning engineers and the manufacturers of the equipment to obtain the correct calculations. [24:197]

2.E. Air Pollution

2.E.1. EXTERNAL SOURCES OF AIR POLLUTION

Both gaseous and particulate air pollutants are harmful to library materials. Gases such as sulphur dioxide, oxides of nitrogen, and ozone are absorbed from the air into paper. These gases increase the rate of paper deterioration. Sulphur dioxide reacts with the moisture in paper to produce sulphurous acid, which, in turn, reacts with oxygen in the presence of metal ionic impurities in paper to produce sulfuric acid. This acid then breaks down the fiber structure of paper and causes embrittlement. Particulate pollution is made up of dust, ash, smoke, dirt, and mold spores. Particulate pollution causes abrasion, disfigures and obscures text, and adds acid, acid catalysts, and mold spores to paper materials. [5:3]

Libraries should strive to remove nearly all the airborne dust in the building. Several filters are needed to do this, including a coarse filter to remove large particles, and a very fine filter capable of removing nearly all dust over one micron in size. Another filtration method is the electrostatic precipitator, which removes dust particles in the air by forcing them through an electric field and then attracting them to oppositely charged plates. Electrostatic precipitators tend to produce large agglomerations of particles, however; these eventually get caught up in the air stream, so a fiber filter is placed farther down the air duct to catch the large particles. Electrostatic filters have been criticized for generating ozone, but the amount produced seems to depend on the design of the device, since ozone can be removed by a pollutant absorber downstream of the precipitator. [16:128] Particulate filters that produce filtering efficiencies of at least 60 percent are a good compromise in air systems that recirculate 90 percent of the air. Very high efficiency filters such as HEPA filters are best suited to small closed areas, but they are generally too costly, energy inefficient, and maintenance intensive to use throughout buildings. [5:3]

Most air-conditioning systems are not designed to remove gaseous pollutants. Active carbon filters or activated microporous alumina pellets impregnated with potassium permanganate are believed to be the best methods of removing this type of pollutant from libraries. The latter filter needs the impregnant to ensure complete removal of sulphur dioxide, which is a very damaging pollutant. One brand name for the activated alumina is Pureafill™. It costs more initially than charcoal, but lasts indefinitely. Established standards for gaseous pollutants specify levels of ten micrograms per cubic centimeter for sulphur dioxide and two micrograms per cubic centimeter for ozone. [5:3]

Air-conditioning equipment itself can generate some pollutants. Chemicals are used in the humid parts of the equipment, such as drain pans for humidifiers, to prevent algae growth; but if they are not checked periodically, mold may still grow. Steam humidifiers are free of this problem, but chemicals such as diethylaminoethanol are customarily added to the steam pipes leading to them in order to inhibit corrosion. The best solution at present seems to be to use high pressure steam to generate steam from purified water brought through plastic tubes to stainless steel heat exchangers. [16:128]

Good air circulation is also important for the preservation of library and archival materials. Pockets of dead air should be eliminated, as these make regulation of the relative humidity and temperature levels more difficult and promote the growth of biological agents, mold, and insects. Rates of air exchange are set by building codes and are based upon the requirements of the people who use the buildings. Repositories usually have one air change per hour. [5:3]

2.E.2. INTERNAL SOURCES OF AIR POLLUTION

Many air pollutants, such as formaldehyde, formic acid, and acetic acid (emitted by plywood and particle board), originate within the building itself. Diethylaminoethanol [see above] is a hygroscopic alkaline vapor that probably reacts with the acid pollutants in air to form nonvolatile salts that precipitate as a slimy film on surfaces. Librarians should be aware of the chemicals that emerge from the outside surface of books, such as the oxides of nitrogen released by the proxylin cloth used to cover cases. [16:136]

Wood should not be used for shelving libraries and archives, but in those facilities that already have wooden bookcases, precautions should be taken. Wooden shelves can outgas volatile acids that can harm collections, so they should be tested. Since gas chromatography and mass spectrometry tests are required to detect the ability of wood to produce harmful agents, the average library should probably just assume that all wooden shelves need treatment. The shelves are treated with a primer and then at least two coats of a high quality solvent-based acrylic paint.

If the natural appearance of the shelves is preferred, a good solvent-based acrylic varnish or polyurethane can be used instead; however, it must be tested by painting it on a piece of wood, placing the wood in a closed glass container with a piece of clean lead metal (available from chemical supply houses) or a lead fishing weight, and leaving it for about two weeks. A chalky white powder will appear on the lead if formaldehyde is present in the polyurethane, indicating the polyurethane should not be used. Continue the test with other brands of polyurethane until an acceptable one is found. Note that each container of polyurethane should be tested before use, since manufacturers frequently change their formulations. [28:1]

All surfaces of the wood should be painted, including the ends, which need several coats. Shelves should be allowed to dry for at least four to six weeks before books are placed on them. [28:1]

"If treatment of the wood is not possible, bookshelves should be lined with 100 percent ragboard or polyester film (Mylar™ Type D and Melinex™ 516 are recommended) held in position with 3M Scotch brand double-coated tape #415. Although lining shelves will not protect books as well as sealing the wood, lining will provide some protection." [28:1]

2.F. Passive Climate Control

Books should be kept in a stable environment. This is best effected by preventing temperature changes around the collection, or at least ensuring that any changes made will be very gradual. In addition to maintaining a stable temperature, books in fragile condition should be placed in close-fitting, nearly airtight enclosures.

Enclosures protect materials from dust and airborne pollutants and have other advantages such as reducing the exchange of moisture between the paper in the books and the air. The dimensions and stiffness of paper depend on its moisture content, which is usually around 6 percent. This water is loosely bound and will be taken up in the surrounding air in low relative humidity. More water will be absorbed in the paper if the surrounding air has a high relative humidity. If the air surrounding the book is isolated from the rest of the atmosphere and its volume kept small compared with the volume of the book, then the exchange of water will be very small. The book also regulates the moisture in the air trapped around it. [16:134]

Slow changes in air temperature around a book will not cause harm. Even sudden upward temperature changes are not too damaging. If a book in a protective enclosure is suddenly cooled, however, water will condense on the container's interior walls when the temperature drops below the dew point of the air within the container. The book will release more water vapor to compensate for that lost, and the water will condense and drip on the book or flood the bottom of the enclosure. From there it will re-evaporate, setting up a cyclic process that will stain the book. [16:135]

The same thing can happen to books housed in glass-fronted cases placed against uninsulated outer walls. Cold winter exterior air can cool the back of the case, while the books remain warm because the glass front readily transmits the heat of the room. The books maintain the relative humidity of the air in the container, creating the cycle described above, and condensed water runs unseen down the back of the bookcase. [16:135]

The solution to these problems is to (1) maintain a stable temperature; (2) avoid changing the temperature rapidly, especially by lowering it; (3) refrain from placing bookcases against outside walls; (4) avoid using glass-fronted enclosed bookcases; (5) keep the air moving; and (6) insulate walls, covering the insulation with an impermeable membrane. [16:135]

The condition of collections in European libraries demonstrates that if the average exterior climate is less than 77°F and between 40 and 65 percent relative humidity, then no great harm will come to collections that are not air-conditioned.

Adjusting the environment near the building can help considerably in reducing problems inside. Plants, trees, and light-colored paint will reduce heat gain in the sun, although there is a trade-off [see sections 2.J.1 and 7.B] because plants near the perimeter of the building can be a source of problems for the roof and can attract insects. Grass and plants around the building will reflect less solar energy onto the facade than will concrete or marble concourses.

Roof ducts and ventilators in attic spaces will reduce heat conduction through the roof and prevent roof condensation in a humidified building. Do not install an ornamental fountain in the lobby, however, as it could humidify or dehumidify the air; control of the water temperature is critical and difficult to maintain. Fountains should never be allowed in libraries. [16:136]

2.G. Light

"All wavelengths of light are damaging to library and archival materials. Ultraviolet light, which is not needed for seeing, is the most damaging. Light causes fading of bindings, inks, and dyes; darkening and yellowing of paper; and weakening of cellulosic fibers through bleaching and oxidation. The damage light can do is dependent upon the intensity and the duration of the radiation. Total exposure is a product of intensity and duration so that a short exposure to a high level of light is as damaging as a long exposure to a low level." [4:3–4]

Figure 2.2 shows a chart of the major divisions of the electromagnetic spectrum. As the wavelength changes, the properties of the radiation change, not sharply as suggested by the schematic representation, but gradually from one major type of radiation to the next.

Wavelength, nanometers (nm)

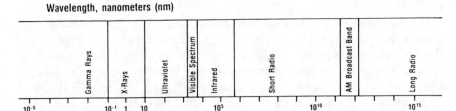

FIGURE 2.2. The electromagnetic spectrum. Source: Washington, DC: Preservation Information and Education Office, Library of Congress, 1985.

Wavelength, nanometers (nm)

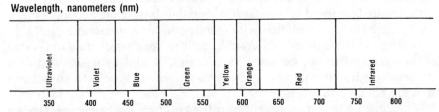

FIGURE 2.3. The visible spectrum. Source: Washington, DC: Preservation Information and Education Office, Library of Congress, 1985.

Figure 2.3 shows the very small portion of the total electromagnetic spectrum that is the visible region, i.e., the wavelengths associated with spectral colors, and portions of the ultraviolet and infrared spectral regions immediately adjacent. The band in Figure 2.3 shows the location of visible light in the 400 to 760 nanometer (nm) range of the spectrum. (A nanometer is a thousand millionth of a meter; 1 nm = 10^{-9} meters.) At either end of the band lies invisible light—ultraviolet radiation (UV) at the short end (300 to 400 nm) and infrared radiation (IR) at the long end (above 700 nm). Ultraviolet radiation is energetic enough to induce photochemical reactions in cellulosic materials; infrared radiation causes temperature to rise and can also cause photochemical reactions. The shorter the wavelength, the greater the damage to materials.

Light consists of photons that bombard molecules when they get excited. Giving off light and heat, they break apart and rearrange their bonds; e.g., the dye molecules in a manuscript will generate hydrogen peroxide and form bubbles on the paper. A few definitions from Macleod's *Museum Lighting* [11] are useful in understanding the effects of light:

"*Radiant flux* is the radiant energy emitted or received by a surface in a unit of time. It is measured in fractions of a watt, usually microwatts." [12:7]

Luminous flux is a quantity expressing the capacity of the radiant flux to produce visual sensation. The unit of luminous flux is the *lumen*.

"The *lumen* is the luminous flux received on an area of one square foot contained on a sphere of radius one foot (or on an area of one square meter contained on a sphere of radius one meter) from a point source having a uniform luminous intensity of one *candela*. "The *candela* (formerly candle) is defined as equal to one-sixtieth of the luminous intensity per square centimeter of a black body radiator operating at the temperature of solidification of platinum, the *luminous intensity* in a given direction being the quotient of the luminous flux in an infinitesimal cone containing the given direction by the solid angle of that cone." [12:7]

The international unit of illumination is the *lux*, defined as one lumen per square meter. It can be visualized as the illumination on the surface of a sphere of radius of one meter when a point source of one candela is at the center of the sphere.

1 lux = 1 lumen per square meter

"Another common unit of illumination is the *foot candle* (fc) which is defined as one lumen per square foot. The foot candle represents a greater illumination than the lux; the exact relationship is:

1 foot candle = 10.76 lux" [12:8]
(1 lux = .0929368 foot candles)
or
1 fc = 1 lumen per square foot

"Light from a full moon is a little under 0.5 lux (.05 fc). Direct sunlight plus skylight may be as high as 10,000 lux (929.4 fc); however, on a dark day the illumination outdoors may be only 1,000 lux (93 fc). A bare 100 watt incandescent bulb provides about 14 lux (1.3 fc) on a surface 10 feet away." [12:8] The Illuminating Engineering Society has recommended illumination levels for various tasks. For example, 1,000 lux (93 fc) is recommended for a library; 1500 lux (139.4 fc) for proof-reading; 500 to 10,000 lux (46.5 to 929.4 fc) for inspecting manufactured parts (the level depending on the inspection difficulty); and 5,000 lux (465 fc) for sewing. These figures only illustrate what a lux is and do not take into account the deteriorating effects on a collection. Table 2.4 illustrates recommended footcandles for various areas and activities in a library.

2.G.1. RECOMMENDED LIGHTING LEVELS

Scientific studies have enabled museum curators to estimate the extent of probable damage per footcandle (D/fc values) that objects can sustain before disintegrating. [Section 2.H.1 explains how to monitor UV and footcandle levels.] Experts are not in total agreement, but a near consensus is that maximum illumination of particularly vulnerable objects (watercolors, tapestries, etc.) should be 50 lux (4.6 fc). For other objects a maximum of 150 lux (14 fc) may be permitted. [12:10]

TABLE 2.4. Recommended levels of illumination.

LIBRARY AREA	FOOTCANDLES ON TASK [a]
Reading Areas	
Reading printed materials	30 [b]
Study and note taking	70 [b]
Conference Area	30 [b]
Seminar Rooms	70 [b]
Book Stacks (30 inches above floor)	
Active stacks	30 [c]
Inactive stacks	5 [c]
Book Repair and Binding	70
Cataloging	70 [b]
Card Files	100 [b]
Carrels, Individual Study Areas	70 [b]
Circulation Desks	70 [b]
Rare Book Rooms—Archives	
Storage areas	30
Reading areas	100 [b]
Map, Picture, and Print Rooms	
Storage areas	30
Use areas	100 [b]
Audiovisual Areas	
Preparation rooms	70
Viewing rooms (variable)	70
Television receiving room (shield viewing screen)	70
Audio Listening Area	
General	30
For note taking	70 [b]
Record inspection table	100 [d]
Microform Areas	
Files	70 [b]
Viewing areas	30

[a] Minimum on the task at any time for young adults with normal or better than 20/30 corrected vision.

[b] Evaluation of Equivalent Sphere Illumination. The extent to which a given lighting installation will satisfy the IES visual performance criterion requires calculation of values of the Equivalent Sphere Illumination, E_s. Calculation of E_s involves describing the visual performance potential of a real environment of known actual illumination in terms of the illumination under the reference conditions of a photometric sphere providing performance potential. The value of E_s is computed from the actual task illumination after allowance for the veiling reflection and disability glare effects, and the transient adaptive effects if desired. This is accomplished in terms of a standard curve relating contrast sensitivity to illumination.

[c] Vertical.

[d] Obtained with a combination of general lighting plus specialized supplementary lighting. Care should be taken to keep within recommended luminance ratios. These seeing tasks generally involve the discrimination of fine detail for long periods of time and under conditions of poor contrast. The design and installation of the combination system must not only provide a sufficient amount of light, but also the proper direction of light, diffusion, color, and eye protection. As far as possible it should eliminate direct and reflected glare as well as objectionable shadows.

Source: *Simpson's Operator's Manual; Model 408-2 Illumination Level Meter,* 8-6–8-7, 8-10, 8-13–8-15, 4th ed. Elgin, IL: Simpson Electric Co., 1987.

Since the effect of light is cumulative, many traditional pigments show significant fading after exposure to 80 million lux hours of illumination by daylight fluorescent lighting. Assuming that a museum is lighted 3,600 hours per year, this would mean a life expectancy of 70 years at 300 lux, 220 years at 100 lux and 440 years at 50 lux. Fading at this rate is a consequence of the reciprocity law that states that the rate of photochemical change is proportional to the product of illuminance and the length of exposure (in other words, if the amount of illumination is cut in half, the damage rate will be cut in half). Particularly sensitive materials such as watercolor pigments may show fading at only one-eighth of this total exposure, so their lifetime would only be 55 years, even at 50 lux (440 years divided by eight). [12:10]

The total permissible exposure time as stated by the reciprocity law can be expressed as follows:

Total exposure = Intensity x time (length of exposure)

For example:

50 fc hours = 5 fc x 10 hours

50 fc hours = 50 fc x 1 hour

200 fc hours = 20 fc x 10 hours

18,000 fc hours = 5 fc x 3600 hours (10 hours a day for every day of the year for 440 years)

While libraries do not have the same problems as museums, many do have valuable books and manuscripts that are occasionally displayed. The total exposure formula enables informed decisions to be made regarding prudent display time.

Incandescent lighting has almost disappeared from libraries, being replaced almost exclusively by fluorescent lamps. Although the quality and general appearance of the light emitted by incandescent lamps varies little from one type of bulb to the other, wide differences exist among fluorescent lamps. "Most fluorescent lamps are made with tubular glass bulbs, varying in diameter from 5/8 inch to 2-1/8 inches and in over-all length from 6 to 96 inches. They are available in various wattages from 4 to 215 watts. The standard designation for fluorescent lamps is explained in [Figure 2.4].

F	15	T	8	CW
Fluorescent Lamp	Wattage (e.g., 15 watts)	Bulb Shape (e.g., tubular)	Bulb Diameter in eights of an inch (e.g., 8/8" or one inch)	Color Appearance (e.g., cool white)

FIGURE 2.4. Standard designation for fluorescent lamps. Source: Raymond H. Lafontaine and Patricia A. Wood. *Fluorescent Lamps.* Rev. ed. Technical Bulletin, No. 7. Ottawa: Canadian Conservation Institute, 1982, p. 3.

The popular 4 foot, 40 watt tubes are normally designated as F40CW, F40WW, F40D, etc., without the shape and diameter of the bulb." [10:3]

The public often mistakenly associates the quantity of light given off by a fluorescent lamp with the lamp's wattage. "The wattage of a lamp is the amount of electrical energy it consumes. This electrical energy is converted into light energy by various means, such as incandescence of a tungsten filament, fluorescence of phosphors, etc. The efficiency of each mechanism varies considerably. The term 'luminous efficacy' is used to describe the total quantity of visible light given off for each watt of electricity consumed. Fluorescent lamps have typical luminous efficacies of from 40 to 75 lumen/watt. On the other hand, incandescent bulbs vary from 6 to about 15 lumen/watt." [10:7]

A four-foot-long fluorescent tube (F40), rated at 40 watts, can emit from 1700 to 3400 lumens of light. A 40-watt household incandescent bulb gives off only 360 lumens. For comparison, an R40, 150-watt spot or floodlight emits 1825 lumens. Thus, many people are misled by lamp wattages, and consequently purchase excessively strong lighting, especially for display cases lit by fluorescent lamps. [10:7]

Ultraviolet radiation in libraries should not exceed 75 microwatts per lumen. It can be controlled by using incandescent lamps or fluorescent lamps that emit little or no UV, shielding fluorescent tubes and windows with UV filters, and using fixed window blinds or other forms of indirect lighting. [5:4]

Lamps that emit less than 75 µw/lm (µw is the abbreviation for microwatt—one millionth of a watt; lm is the abbreviation for lumen) will not require filters, but some are more expensive. The library or archive should determine whether it would be cheaper to use a low UV-emitting lamp or a combination of a high UV-emitting lamp and a UV filter. [10:3] Many UV filter sleeves can be reused and will last for two or three years. [24:193]

"Tungsten-halogen lamps, which are increasingly used because of their high light output, emit a small amount of highly energetic, and therefore dangerous, short-wavelength UV; these lamps should always be used with a piece of glass in front of the bulb since glass absorbs short-wavelength UV." [24:193]

2.G.2. CONTROL OF UV

All light is damaging, so lights should be turned off as much as possible in the stacks. In a situation where study carrels or desks are located in the stacks, each carrel should have its own lamp. The stack ranges should have timer switches or, at least, switches with signs that remind people to turn off the lights when they are not needed.

Beyond the need to control the levels of visible light reaching materials in the stacks, it is mandatory to eliminate as much of the ultraviolet radiation as possible. The percentage of ultraviolet radiation in natural sunlight is greater than in fluorescent lighting; incandescent lighting has virtually none.

"Daylight contains different kinds of light. Light from the sky (blue light) is higher in UV than light from the sun (yellow light). Reflected daylight is lower in UV than direct daylight since no surface, except snow, reflects UV. Thus, UV is most intense when it comes straight downward from a light source. Direct sunlight and skylights should be avoided since they permit so much UV radiation." [5:4]

Window glass, which absorbs short-wavelength UV, passes UV radiation in the range of 310 to 400 nm. Curtains or blinds can be hung and drawn over windows to prevent direct sunlight from reaching library materials. Blinds should be locked into position so they cannot be changed. Some libraries have built curtain walls (*brise soleil*) of decorative brick or concrete block to filter light through large expanses of ceiling-to-floor windows. Indirect light is always lower in UV because UV does not reflect. Much of the radiation coming in from windows and skylights can be removed by reflecting the light from walls painted with titanium dioxide or zinc white paint. Titanium dioxide paint absorbs all UV radiation, so the reflected illumination will be free of UV regardless of the UV content of the source of the light. Ceiling tiles also absorb UV light. Unfiltered fluorescent tubes can be used in libraries and archives if they are part of an indirect lighting system.

"Even better protection is obtained by the use of plastic filters which incorporate various organic compounds with ultraviolet absorbing properties. Plexiglas UF-1 is practically colorless and does not interfere with color rendering. The Plexiglas UF-3 is somewhat yellow but also a somewhat better ultraviolet absorber." [12:11] Plastic sheets made of this material can be placed in light fixtures to filter the UV radiation. Tubes or sleeves are also available that can be placed on regular florescent bulbs. The sleeves come with caps that enclose the bulb at each end and protect the environment from breakage and phosphor contamination. While the sleeves will filter 92 percent of the ultraviolet wavelengths from 0 to 385 nm, they may cause a problem during installation. The bulbs slip around inside the sleeves and make them very difficult to insert into their sockets. One building superintendent says it takes his people an average of 15 minutes per bulb to install this type of shield because the bulb cannot be easily held in place inside the tube. This type of filter also contains the heat of the bulb better than the Plexiglas™ sheets do. The UV coating doesn't break down, but the carrier (the Plexiglas™ jacket) does deteriorate over time. Another type of filter made of flexible plastic fits over a standard 48-inch tube without having to remove the tube from the socket. This filter transmits practically none of the harmful UV light.

All fluorescent lamps, both warm whites and cool whites, should be filtered. UV is so destructive that, especially for rare book rooms and display cases, the added costs for filters are well justified. In display cases, the filter should be built into the case.

It has not been possible to manufacture glass that is capable of filtering UV light. There are, however, glass laminates that incorporate a plastic film containing UV absorbers between two sheets of glass. These are suitable for glazing windows. There are also rigid plastic acrylic sheets containing UV absorbers [see above]. Thin acetate or polyester films and varnishes containing UV absorbers can be applied to windows and provide a relatively cheap and simple solution. [24:193]

UV filters are not permanent and should be checked about every six months. "There are no reported instances of the acrylic sheets failing, but plastic films and varnishes are usually guaranteed for no more than ten years. This is often because of failure of the film or varnish itself, rather than a reduction of the efficiency of the UV absorber. If condensation occurs on the windows to which these materials have been applied, the UV absorbers will have a shortened life span." [24:193]

There are a few other procedures that can lower UV and also reduce the effects of visible light. One involves taking a compass and checking the orientation of the stacks and shelving in the library or archive. If they are facing east, west, or south, they will receive much more light than if they were oriented toward the north. Thought should be given to changing the orientation of shelving so that it does not directly front an east- or west-facing window or, for that matter, any windows. Some libraries have installed automatic light turn-off switches in stack areas and/or reduced lighting levels in various sensitive areas where the collection is housed.

2.H. Monitoring

This section discusses in some detail the means of monitoring temperature, humidity, and light in the library. See Appendix A for a listing of various types of environmental monitoring equipment and their functions.

2.H.1. MEASURING UV AND VISIBLE LIGHT

If a light source emits more than about 75 µw/lm, it requires a UV-absorbing filter. A simple, effective means of determining the UV level of a fluorescent lamp (or any other type of light) is by using a device known as the Crawford UV Monitor Type 760. The monitor measures the proportion of UV radiation in the light as microwatts of UV radiation per lumen (of visible light). There are two windows on top of the instrument, one passing UV radiation and one visible to two photosensitive devices beneath. When a button is pressed, one of two red light-emitting diodes lights up. With the button depressed, a knob is turned until the light flicks between one and the other of these diodes. The pointer on the knob then gives the proportion of UV in the light source. [27:21]

Incandescent bulbs normally emit less than 75 µw/lm of UV, whereas sunlight is composed of about 400 µw/lm of UV. The light sources in museums and art galleries should emit less than 75 µw/lm; otherwise, UV absorbing filters should be used.

Unfortunately, most museums and libraries cannot afford to purchase a UV monitor. A table showing the UV output of most fluorescent lamps on the market in 1982 has been created, however, by the Canadian Conservation Institute. [10:9–11] As explained earlier, lumen output is the total amount of visible light given off by a source and varies considerably from one lamp to another.

UV light can also be qualitatively monitored by placing blue scales (textile fading cards) in the area of exposure. The scales, available from TALAS, are pieces of wool cloth dyed with blue dyes that are used as light fastness standards; they indicate the approximate effect of both UV and visible light by fading after exposure. [25:44] Blue scales can be used to monitor the net exposure to light and, through proper placement and observation, will alert librarians to rotate materials on exhibit or to reduce the intensity of the light. The object to be monitored should cover up to one-half of the scale so there will be an immediate comparison of fading. The card should be dated when it is placed, and the blue scales will give a rough indication of the amount of UV exposure they receive.

Light meters are necessary to ensure beyond any doubt that light levels are acceptable. If a meter is not available, however, a good photographic exposure meter can do the job if it is calibrated in footcandles. It must, however, be capable of accurately reading illuminance as low as 50 lux (five footcandles) if it is to be of any use. Care must be taken when using many such meters, because the 0 to 20 footcandle range is often compressed into the lower part of the scale and is difficult to read. [12:12] Lux meters are also available for about $100.

If a light meter calibrated in footcandles is not available, the readings on photographic light meters can be converted by translating the exposure readings into footcandle equivalents. The following method of measuring footcandles with photographic light meters, either a separate meter or one built into a camera, is taken from a 1975 *Conserve O Gram*, distributed by the National Park Service. [26]

> There are two basic types of photographic light meters: (1) an incident light meter, which measures light directly from the light falling on the object (bulb → meter); and (2) a reflectance light meter, which is pointed at the object, not the light source, and measures the light reflected from the object. Cameras with built-in light meters are of the latter type (bulb → object → meter). Many reflectance light meters have an attachment to take incident light readings.
>
> To convert readings to footcandles using an incident light meter:
>
> 1. Set the ASA film speed to 100.
>
> 2. Lay the meter next to the object or on it, if possible, and read the exposure value.
>
> 3. Set the meter to the observed exposure value and read the suggested exposure time for an aperture reading of f4.
>
> 4. Consult [Table 2.5].

TABLE 2.5. Incident light meters: converting at ASA film speed 100.

EXPOSURE TIME (SECONDS)	FOOTCANDLE EQUIVALENT	APERTURE READING
1	5	f4
1/4	15	f4
1/15	125	f4
1/125	375	f4

Source: Thomsen, Fonda, and Mike Whiltshire. "A Method of Measuring Light Levels in Exhibit Areas." *Conserve O Gram.* Washington, DC: National Park Service, July 1975.

To convert to footcandles using a reflectance light meter (it is much easier to do this if the camera is in manual mode):

1. Set the ASA film speed to 100.
2. Place two sheets of white bond paper on the object to be checked.
3. Point the light meter at the white paper and read the exposure value.
4. Set the light meter to the observed value and read the suggested exposure time at f4.
5. Consult [Table 2.6].

Footcandles can also be calculated with a 35mm camera:

1. Set the ASA film speed to 100.
2. Set the f-stop to 5.6.
3. Read the light reflected from a white card.
4. The shutter speed will equal the footcandles.

TABLE 2.6. Reflectance light meters: converting at ASA film speed 100.

EXPOSURE TIME (SECONDS)	FOOTCANDLE EQUIVALENT	APERTURE READING
1/8	5	f4
1/15	15	f4
1/60	125	f4
1/500	375	f4

Source: Thomsen, Fonda, and Mike Whiltshire. "A Method of Measuring Light Levels in Exhibit Areas." *Conserve O Gram.* Washington, DC: National Park Service, July 1975.

2.H.2. MEASURING RELATIVE HUMIDITY

2.H.2.a. Psychrometers

Psychrometers consist of two thermometers, somewhat like the dew point hygrometer. One measures the room temperature; the other is sheathed in cotton that must be kept moist. The moisture will evaporate and cool the thermometer below the indication on the dry bulb. If the environment is at 100 percent relative humidity, obviously no evaporation can occur, and both thermometers will show the same readings. The drier the environment, the more rapidly the water will evaporate, the cooler the wet bulb will get, and the greater will be the difference between the two thermometer readings. The instrument manufacturer provides a chart relating this temperature difference to the relative humidity.

Errors can occur in measurements made by a psychrometer as a result of small air movements causing differences in the evaporation rate from the wet bulb. To avoid these difficulties, it is necessary to maintain an air flow over the bulbs in excess of a critical value. In the Assman-type psychrometer, this air flow is accomplished by a small electrically driven fan. In the sling psychrometer, a flow of air is created by whirling the whole psychrometer assembly around a handle at a given rate for a given period of time. The accuracy of a well-constructed instrument of the Assman type is greater than that of the sling psychrometer, but sling psychrometers are cheaper. With a good Assman psychrometer, the relative humidity measurement can be accurate to within two units of percent. [13:9–10]

Sling psychrometers are simple and reliable but are not error free. The most common problem is too high a wet bulb reading, leading to a high relative humidity estimate. This occurs because of (1) insufficient swinging (bulbs must be swung around steadily for at least three minutes), (2) too long a pause before finding the wet bulb reading (which starts to rise as soon as the swinging stops), (3) hands and/or breath too near the thermometer bulbs, or (4) a dirty wick. Great care must be given to the wicks or sheaths, which should be closely fitted to the thermometer bulb, adequately wetted with distilled water, and kept free of salts. If the wick is even slightly soiled, the temperature reading will be inaccurate. For example, if the room temperature is 68 °F, and 2.5 is the difference between wet and dry bulb temperatures, the relative humidity is 88 percent. If the wick was soiled and the bulb read 2.7 instead, the relative humidity would be 87 percent. Thus a 0.2 error in determining the temperature difference will result in an error of 1 percent in the relative humidity measurement. [13:10]

When using the sling psychrometer, these guidelines should be followed:

1. Use only distilled water for the wick. Keep the wick clean and change it when necessary. New wicks must be soaked in at least three changes of distilled water (each overnight) before the first use and then handled only while wearing gloves.
2. Sling it well away from the body and near the area to be measured. Be careful not to sling it too near walls or other objects.
3. Keep hands and breath away from the thermometer bulbs; otherwise body temperature will affect the reading.
4. Keep the thermometer bulbs away from strong light.
5. Make sure the wet bulb wick does not dry out.
6. Since the wet bulb temperature falls during slinging, successive readings must be taken to find its true value.
7. Read the wet bulb first and quickly, before it starts to rise. The dry bulb can be read after the wet bulb reading is taken.
8. Read to $1/4\,°C$ or $1/2\,°F$. It is not practical to read much less than this, but in the middle of the range, a $1/4\,°C$ or $1/2\,°F$ error in either wet or dry bulb reading amounts to an error of 2 percent RH. Therefore, an accuracy of ±2 percent RH is all that can be expected. [27:72]

2.H.2.b. Electronic hygrometers

One recommended electronic hygrometer is the Beckman (Nova Sina Mik 3000) hand-held instrument that measures both relative humidity and temperature. Like other relative humidity measuring devices, the Beckman Mik 3000 should be allowed to become acclimated to its environment before use, particularly if it has just been brought in from outdoors. The instrument is held away from the body and switched on. Almost immediately, the percentage of relative humidity and the temperature will be displayed.

Like all other hygrometers, the instrument must be calibrated. This is done by removing the guard surrounding the sensors on the head of the instrument and replacing it with the Sensor-check. The Sensor-check carries a salt solution behind a semi-permeable membrane and, in effect, surrounds the sensor with a known relative humidity. If necessary, the instrument can be adjusted to this known relative humidity value after the reading with the Sensor-check in place settles down to a steady value. An advantage of the electronic hygrometer is that of the direct reading. It is not necessary to consult a hygrometric or psychrometric chart. [27:76]

2.H.2.c. Hair hygrometer

The principle behind hair or dimensional change hygrometers is that a hair element will lengthen as the relative humidity increases and shorten as the relative humidity decreases. This change in the length of the hair is transmitted to a pointer on a dial or to a recorder pen that marks a chart on a revolving drum. [13:10] Hair hygrometers are most commonly used when there is little or no air movement.

Hair hygrometers are not as accurate as psychrometers or dew point hygrometers and have severe calibration drawbacks. They should be calibrated once a week by using a sling or, preferably, an Assman psychrometer. They may take up to a half hour to fully respond to a change in the relative humidity. They are prone to rapid changes in their calibration after any event that either quickly raises or lowers the normal humidity. This effect is particularly noticeable after a rainstorm. Hair hygrometers are inexpensive, however, and are most accurate in the range of 30 percent to 80 percent relative humidity. [1:73]

The most practical instrument for a library is the recording hygrothermograph. This is a combination of a hair hygrometer and bimetallic strip thermometer. The two are connected to levers carrying pens that mark 24-hour or week-long charts on a rotating drum. The chart permits continuous recording of the temperature and relative humidity, overnight, on weekends, and on holidays. Changes in the environment are obvious by examining the chart; trends can be identified, helping to isolate the causes of relative humidity and temperature instability.

2.H.2.d. RH indicator cards

Various cobalt salts such as cobalt thiocyanate or cobalt chloride change color depending on the relative humidity. Paper that has been impregnated by such a salt can be placed in the environment to check relative humidity. The cards consist of nine separate small squares or particles in a vertical column. Each square responds to humidity changes in 10 percent steps. The color on the patches, which changes from blue (dry) to pink (damp), can be compared to a standard color chart devised for this purpose to indicate the approximate relative humidity. Readings, however, are not particularly accurate since the relative humidity cannot be determined to better than ±5 percent, and the salts do not lend themselves to measurements in large rooms. However, cards are inexpensive and can be used as warning devices in confined cases. [27:76–77]

2.H.3. RECORD KEEPING

Whenever monitoring takes place with manual devices, a record or log of temperature and relative humidity readings must be maintained. Several formats can be used, and the staff should choose one that fulfills the library's purpose. See Appendix B for examples of forms. Temperature, relative humidity, and so on should be recorded several times a day, at the same times each day, every day of the week. Recording must be consistent, accurate, and continuous in order to create a record of environmental conditions that can be useful in analyzing the library's HVAC and other systems. This is the only reliable way information can be developed that will be convincing and useful to decision makers.

2.I. Mold and Mildew

Much of the information in this section, except where noted otherwise, is based upon or taken, with permission, from SOLINET Leaflet Number 5. [14]

Mold causes a downy or furry growth on the surface of organic matter and is "a multi-cellular, microscopic vegetable plant which forms cobweb-like masses of branching threads from the surface of which tiny fertile threads project into the air, bearing the part of the plant from which spores develop. Mold may be of brilliant colors or black and white, depending on the type. Molds can develop on leather, cloth, paper, etc., especially in the presence of relatively high heat and relative humidity." [22:171] Mildew is any fungus, especially the families Peronosporaceae and Erysiphaceae, that attacks various plants or appears on organic matter, paper, leather, etc., especially when exposed to moisture, resulting in a thin, furry, whitish coating or discoloration. Both mold and mildew "derive their food from the substance on which they form, e.g., the materials of a book. During its growth, mildew produces citric, gluconic, oxalic, or other organic acids, that can damage paper, leather, cloth, etc. It also can produce color bodies, leading to staining, which is difficult to remove." [22:170]

Until recently, fungi have been classified with plants, but they are now considered a distinct group of organisms. Unlike plants, which produce their own food, fungi absorb nutrients from dead or living organic matter. [15:2] After the nutrients fungi feed upon are exhausted, or close to being exhausted, they create new spores that are launched into the air or carried by other means to new food sources. The creation and dispersion of new spores can cause a serious problem in libraries that are not environmentally controlled, particularly in subtropical or tropical climates. Mold results from the spores landing on a substrate that has the correct temperature and humidity for spore germination, i.e, above 70°F and 68 percent relative humidity. "The mold mycelia exude liquids that dissolve the substrate, and this food is then used in the production of more mycelia, and eventually, millions of spores." [17:117]

Every cubic foot of air contains thousands of mold spores that land on surfaces and objects in the library every day. Thus, attempts to kill mold and mildew through chemical means, while perhaps temporarily effective, are fruitless over the long run. Chemicals such as ortho-phenyl phenol (OPP) and paradichlorobenzene (PDB) kill some of the fungi spores on the surface and some of the mycelia. As soon as the chemicals have volatilized from the surface, however, the paper, books, or other materials are again vulnerable to new mold spores landing on them. If the temperature and humidity have not been lowered below 72°F and 68 percent respectively, germination and production of more mold and mildew will result. This is because these chemicals do not leave any residue to prevent mold from growing in the future. Fumigation will kill fungi but does not have any residual effect. Note also that molds that have begun to grow above these temperatures and relative humidity can continue growing even after the temperature and relative humidity have been lowered.

2.I.1. EFFECT OF MOLD AND MILDEW ON LIBRARY MATERIALS

Mold and mildew eat books and paper. The cellulose, adhesives, and starches in the sizing provide a source of nutrition that enables the fungi to excrete digestive enzymes that convert these materials into forms they can digest. Cellulose in paper is more difficult for mold to digest; but it, too, comes under attack, although not as often as the cloth coverings on books and the sizing used in paper. Mold will usually attack bindings before the text block, probably because it lands on the bindings first, the cellulose is more difficult to digest, and the text block is tightly closed. In the process of breaking down the nutrients in books, paper, and other library materials, mold and mildew can irreversibly stain them. The stains are often serious enough to destroy text and images. Books and paper can also be seriously softened and weakened by mold, making them difficult to handle. [15:2–3]

2.I.2. DEVELOPING A MOLD-PREVENTIVE ENVIRONMENT

As noted elsewhere in this work, humidity is the most important factor to control in the environment. Books and paper naturally contain a certain amount of water. They are hygroscopic, so that when relative humidity goes up, they absorb water to achieve equilibrium. At 50 percent relative humidity, the moisture content of paper is approximately 7 percent; at 70 percent relative humidity, it is approximately 10 percent. Moisture enables mold to absorb nutrients from book and paper substrates, so the more moisture a book contains, the greater are the chances for fungus spores to germinate at room temperature. The potential for mold or mildew development on wet books is one important reason for quick freezing of books damaged by water.

Relative humidities above 70 percent can easily lead to mold growth; for safety, it is generally recommended that libraries keep their relative humidity below 65 percent. Relative humidity below 35 percent, however, can cause books and paper to become fragile from dryness. Hence, the acceptable range is 40 percent to 65 percent. Some molds, however, can begin growing at 70 percent relative humidity or higher and then continue growing at relative humidities of less than 70 percent. Because of this, new acquisitions should be checked for mold and treated, if necessary, prior to storing them with the rest of the collection.

Most molds thrive at warmer temperatures. When combined with high levels of humidity, temperatures of 70°F to 75°F will allow mold to develop. Temperatures below freezing will not kill mold, but they do make it dormant. Few molds will be active at temperatures of less than 50°F. Mold can also grow in conditions of up to 140°F. High heat will kill mold, but it will also severely damage library materials.

Adequate air circulation in conjunction with humidity and temperature control will also help prevent mold growth. Air circulation helps to control moisture levels through evaporation. HVAC systems with humidity controls can solve all three problems of humidity, temperature, and air circulation, and they can also help control insect infestations.

If the library cannot install or improve an HVAC system, alternative remedies exist. Fans can be installed to improve air circulation. They should be placed near outside walls close to floor level. Fans and vents in attics will increase air circulation by pulling air through the building. Fans are particularly useful when it is necessary to keep the windows open.

Sunlight—in particular, ultraviolet radiation—generally inhibits mold growth. The Virginia State Library observed a direct connection between the rate of mold growth and the presence of light during several outbreaks in its collections between 1978 and 1980. It was found that more light correlated with slower growth rates. [15:3–5] [Note, however, that there is a trade-off because UV radiation degrades library materials; see section 2.G.]

2.I.3. OTHER ENVIRONMENTAL CONSIDERATIONS

1. Don't shelve books directly against an outside wall. Temperature and humidity differences between inside and outside environments may cause condensation on the walls or the backs of bookcases.
2. "Stacks should be arranged parallel to the air flow, so that the prevailing air movement is across the spines of the books as they stand on the shelves. Shelves should never block air flow from existing windows or ventilation created by fans." [11:30]
3. "Stacks should be open backed, particularly free-standing stacks which are joined at the back. This will improve the ventilation on all sides of the volume." [11:30] Use cross braces if stability or strength is needed.
4. Closed front cabinets or book cases should be avoided whenever possible. If microforms or other materials must be in locked cases or storage cabinets, both the front and the back of the cabinet or case should be ventilated. If this is not possible, a favorable microclimate should be created in the closed space to counteract high relative humidity. This can be done by using desiccants. [11:30]

5. Reduce the number of plants indoors. If possible, replace all live plants with artificial ones. Although the ambience may be damaged, artificial plants do not contribute moisture to the atmosphere. There should never be indoor planted areas in a library or archive.
6. Water-sealant paint should be used on floors and walls. Basement walls and other walls below grade should be waterproofed to prevent moisture from wicking through the walls and into the interior. Sealing walls will aid in reducing humidity in the building.
7. Check rain gutters and downspouts regularly; keep them clean and free of debris so they will not clog. Drains should be constructed to direct water away from the building foundation. Check to make sure water does not collect in areas against the outside walls or foundation.
8. Interior fountains or waterfalls should not be allowed in the building. (Drinking fountains, of course, are permissible.)
9. Inspect the collection regularly for any occurrence of mold or mildew. If any is detected, take the steps recommended for eradicating it, and continuously monitor the area until the environment is adjusted to the standard and stabilized.
10. Drains or trenches that are open to the air in mechanical rooms and near stack areas should be covered to prevent evaporation of moisture into nearby spaces. [17:118; 15:5–6]

2.I.4. CORRECTIVE PROCEDURES FOR MOLD AND MILDEW

2.I.4.a. The environment

1. Check the temperature and humidity. If the temperature is above 72 °F, lower it to between 68 °F to 72 °F. The lower the temperature, the better. If it can be set below 68 °F, do it. If the relative humidity is above 55 percent, bring it down to 50 percent. If the air-conditioning system merely lowers the temperature of the outside air prior to moving it through the building, turn it off, because cooling the air without removing the moisture will increase the humidity. Cold air cannot hold as much moisture as warm air.
2. Look for a source of water. Broken windows, air-conditioning, or water pipes should be repaired immediately. Roof leaks and water fountains are also sources of water that can raise the humidity.
3. Check for sources of fungus growth and spore production. In addition to the water sources mentioned above, heat-exchange

coils and water pans of air-conditioning units are prime sources of mold. If mold is found in the air-conditioning system, turn it off so spores will not continue to be distributed throughout the area and/or building. The mold must be killed and the unit cleaned as soon as possible. Household mildew eradicators or bleach can be used effectively for this problem.

4. Isolate the infected materials to minimize the spread of mold. If there are only a small number of books or other materials involved, immediately remove the books and papers infected with mold from the shelves or containers. Ideally, they should be taken out of the building; at a minimum, they must be isolated from other materials in the collection so the mold spores will not land on unaffected materials. Do not seal moldy materials in airtight plastic bags. The microclimate created by the bags encourages mold to grow more rapidly on the materials in the bags. If the infestation is large, quarantine the area so books and materials will not be taken to healthy stack areas. Wear rubber gloves and a filtration mask whenever handling moldy materials.

5. Increase air circulation. This will also help to lower humidity. If it is not raining outside and the exterior humidity is lower than inside the building, open windows to improve the circulation. Use fans and dehumidifiers to help lower the moisture content of the air, especially if the air-conditioning system is not able to handle the job.

6. Monitor the environment in the affected area continuously with a hygrometer, sling psychrometer, or hygrothermograph. If changes are needed in the environment, make them at once. [15:6–7]

2.I.4.b. Removing mold

There are both chemical and nonchemical means to kill mold. Effective treatments can be *fungistatic* or *fungicidal*. Fungistatic treatments are those that prevent the mold spores from germinating, but do not kill the mold. Freezing is one such method. Fungicidal treatments kill the mold and its spores. No safe large-scale treatment, however, imparts lasting, or residual, mold control. That is why it is important to change the environment so it inhibits mold growth. Furthermore, there is some evidence that books and papers treated with fungicides may be more susceptible to mold after treatment than they were prior to the outbreak. [15:7]

2.I.4.b.1. Treatments using little or no chemicals

1. The first and most effective treatment is changing the environment as described above, so it is no longer conducive to mold growth.

2. The best way to remove mildew from the cover of a volume that
has not been seriously damaged is by vacuuming it with a small
hand-held or canister-type low-power vacuum cleaner with a
flexible hose. The vacuum should not have more than one to 1-1/2
horsepower. Use the long, slender crevice tool and not the short,
round brush attachment. The brush will catch and hold the spores
and prevent them from being drawn into the vacuum. The crevice
tool is more effective because it concentrates the pull of the
vacuum on a small surface area. Use the vacuum only if the book
is reasonably dry; do not vacuum if the book is very wet. Do not
vacuum the surface of the pages. Do not use large shop or
wet/dry vacuums on individual items [11:48] When the vacuum
bag is full, seal it and dispose of it in a safe container. Plastic or
rubber gloves and filtration masks should be worn when handling
moldy materials.

If a small vacuum is not available and the volume is not
seriously damaged, fungus may be removed by brushing or
wiping the binding and text block carefully with a clean, soft
brush or cloth. Be careful not to brush the mold into air indoors
or on to other objects; this can be prevented by wiping books or
papers off outdoors or under a fume hood. Used rags should be
stored in sealed plastic bags until they can be washed in bleach
or discarded.

Rags moistened with isopropanol (alcohol) can be used to
wipe visible mold from the binding. "[Isopropanol] may cause
staining, changes in the color of the cloth, or loss of gilding. For
mold on the outside of volumes, vacuuming is preferable."
[11:49] Isopropanol should not be applied to paper (text blocks)
except by a conservator. Some suggest using Lysol™ because it
contains a very weak solution of ortho-phenyl phenol, a
fungicide [see section 2.I.4.b.3]. There are at least two problems
with using Lysol™. It will cause the binding and paper to
cockle because it is water based and its chemical formulation
may change without warning. The latter may happen with all
over-the-counter products. Whatever is used, the surface must
first be tested to see if moisture will make the colors run. After
wiping, the book must be allowed to dry thoroughly. [18]

An effective and safe way to remove mold from the spine of a
book with a hollow back is to use a cotton swab soaked in
isopropanol. The swab should be on a long stick such as a
wooden or bamboo barbecue skewer. Use the swab to remove
mold from the inside of the spine and the back of the book
block. "The book should then be placed upright in an open
position and allowed to dry thoroughly before the volume is
closed and returned to the stacks." [11:49]

The leaves of books and single sheets of paper are not strong
enough to withstand the pull of a vacuum cleaner without
damage. "Mini-vacuums designed for cleaning camera

equipment, electronics, and other delicate materials can be used to remove mold from the surface of pages and documents without damage to the paper. If mini-vacs are not available, a vacuum aspirator can be improvised." [11:50]

Both the front and the back of the leaves should be cleaned. After using the mini-vac or aspirator, clean the surface of the page, following the procedures described in surface cleaning of paper in section 4.F.2. *A very brittle item should not be surface cleaned.* See section 4.F.1 for information on how to conduct the brittleness test.

Works of art with pastel, chalk, or other friable pigments should *not* be vacuumed. In such cases the mold must be *lifted* from the surface of the item using a fine pointed, stiff bristled brush or very fine pointed surgical tweezers. [11:52]

If a large number of books are affected, the bindings may be vacuumed through a plastic or cloth mesh, using low suction. Use a wet/dry vacuum cleaner with a 10 percent solution of sodium hypochlorite in the tank. If the inside of the book is damp, it may be stood on end with the leaves fanned open to allow them to dry. The volume should then be removed to a dry room with good air circulation. If the humidity is below 65 percent, the book can be placed outdoors and fanned open in the sunlight for a day or two. Don't leave books and papers out overnight because dew may appear on them. [15:8]

3. Blast freezing books and papers at a temperature of -40°F (-40°C) results in an 11 percent survival rate of fungi. A second blast freezing treatment at the same temperature kills all but 1 percent. [7; 8:7] Therefore, treatment by freezing is problematical since some of the mold will probably survive.

4. Gamma radiation has been used with success in killing mold; thus, it is a fungicide. There is evidence, however, that it can damage leather and adhesives by softening them and, at high radiation levels, it breaks down the internal structure of paper. The folding endurance of paper also decreases with higher levels of radiation. Mold can be killed at lower levels when heat is applied, but the heat can also damage paper. Special equipment and skilled technicians must be available for this procedure, and since it does harm materials if not carefully used, it is generally not recommended. [15:8]

5. Ultraviolet light, although destructive to paper [see section 2.G], inhibits mold growth and may kill mold. It is not recommended as a full-scale treatment for mold on books and papers, because the amount of exposure necessary to kill mold would induce fading and accelerate aging. However, it has been suggested as a possible step in treating small, localized outbreaks. Again, consult a competent book or paper conservator. [15:8]

2.I.4.b.2. Treatments using chemicals

Many chemicals can be used to kill mold. Those discussed here do not harm books or paper, but they do have toxic effects on humans and other living things. After chemicals are used (and preferably before), the environmental conditions that produced the mold still must be modified in accordance with the criteria outlined above in order to prevent any recurrence of the problem.

1. *Ethylene oxide* (EtO) was used widely in museums, libraries, and archives. "In 1984 the Occupational Safety and Health Administration (OSHA) released a new standard for exposure to ethylene oxide of 1 ppm. Based on animal and human data, OSHA has determined that exposure to EtO 'presents a carcinogenic, mutagenic, geotoxic, reproductive, neurologic, and sensitization hazard.' Safety requirements for use of the gas include methods of exposure control, personnel protective equipment, measurement of employee exposure, training in use of the gas, medical surveillance, signs and labels, regulated areas, emergency procedures, and record keeping requirements. [11:42] It is a highly dangerous substance and must be applied by competent, licensed personnel.

2. *Ortho-phenyl phenol* (OPP) is a phenolic chemical that has been used for nonresidual mold control on library materials. **This chemical is not registered for use for mold control in libraries in the United States,** but has been used in the past for extensive mold infestations brought about by flooding and fires. Repeated applications of the diluted material in alcohol were made by spraying or fogging this solution onto the library materials. These types of applications are usually performed by professional pest control operators or those who are thoroughly trained in the use of this chemical. Although it is a phenol (like thymol), OPP is not absorbed through the skin. It may cause some skin irritation with prolonged contact. It can cause eye irritation, and inhalation of the powder can cause upper respiratory irritation. Repeated and long-term exposure could lead to kidney damage. An article by Sandra Turner in the August 1985 issue of *The New Library Scene* describes the use of OPP in a library environment. [29]

   Paradichlorobenzene (PDB) is crystalline at room temperature and can be used in an enclosed space as a mild fumigant for mold control. It is not a proven fungicide, but seems effective as a fungistat. PDB fumigation will take up to three weeks to be effective unless the crystals are volatilized by heat. Use one pound of PDB crystals per one hundred cubic feet of space for a period of at least two weeks. This application will kill surface mold and spores.

   PDB seems to be most useful as a method for preventing mold growth, especially in small, enclosed spaces. It is hazardous if inhaled, ingested, or absorbed through the skin. Exposure can cause dizziness, headaches, skin and eye irritation, respiratory problems, and loss of coordination. Long-term effects include dermatitis and possible liver and kidney damage.

Before fumigation, remove visible mold from the bindings [see section 2.I.4.b.1]. Fan the books open and stagger flat paper on the shelves in the fumigation cabinet. The cabinet should be airtight (similar to a refrigerator). Some institutions have designed small chambers for fumigation purposes. PDB crystals are placed on a metal tray and heated with several 15 to 20 watt light bulbs. The cycle is two hours of heating with the light bulbs on, 22 hours with the light bulbs off, for three consecutive days. The space within the enclosed chamber becomes saturated with PDB molecules, fumigating the materials inside. The same precautions apply for the operator as previously discussed. The cabinet is kept closed for the entire cycle to allow the vapor to penetrate. Upon completion, the cabinet is opened, and books/papers are aerated for several hours. Some cabinet designs incorporate exhaust systems, which make aerating safer and easier at the end of the cycle. Goods fumigated in such a way should be aerated thoroughly in a fume hood or outdoors to volatilize any remaining PDB before the materials can be safely handled. After the materials have been aerated, there will be no PDB left on them to provide protection against subsequent mold development.

3. *Thymol* has been used as a mold-control chemical on books, paper, and other library materials. Paper will yellow after treatment with thymol if exposed regularly to light. **Thymol is toxic to humans and is not registered by the Environmental Protection Agency for use as a mold-control chemical in the United States.** Thymol can be absorbed through the skin, by inhalation, or by inadvertent ingestion. Symptoms of overexposure include gastric pain, nausea, vomiting, and central nervous system hyperactivity. Very high levels of exposure could result in convulsions, coma, and cardiac or respiratory arrest. Long term effects from repeated exposure include liver and kidney damage and dermatitis. [21:121] Thymol will kill some species of mold spores and mycelia upon contact, but its use either as a mist, spray, or fumigant volatilized by heat does not impart residual mold control to the library materials. Taking materials out of the thymol atmosphere will leave them vulnerable to mold spore deposition and possible germination.

There are a number of other fungicides that have been used for controlling mold in libraries, archives, and media centers. Most require licensed technicians for their application and must be used with caution. It is always preferable to use fungistatic methods if there is a choice.

Appendix C contains an outline of factors to consider when pricing the cost of hiring an outside contractor to remove mold and mildew in a media center. The same factors apply to libraries and archives.

2.I.5. CLEANUP ACTIVITIES

Mold infected areas in the library or archive must be cleaned before books and papers are returned to them. Shelves, floors, walls, ceilings, and windows can be cleaned with a mold and mildew killing solution such as household bleach, Lysol™, or X-14™. The area must be properly ventilated while it is being cleaned. It may also be necessary to clean carpets and draperies if the infestation was serious. Filters and heat-exchange coils in HVAC systems should be checked and replaced or cleaned with a mold killing household cleaner.

Charcoal and/or baking soda can be used to remove the odor of mold if cleaning has not done so. Place briquettes and/or bowls of baking soda in the area to absorb the odor. Do not wipe the books or paper with the charcoal or baking soda. If a small number of books needs deodorizing, charcoal briquettes may also be put in a *clean* metal outdoor barbecue, with the books placed on the (*clean*) cooking grill. Close the lid and wait two or three days or until the smell can no longer be detected.

The area and the materials in it should be monitored for six months to a year after fungicidal treatment for any signs of mold growth. Books seem to be more susceptible to mold after they have been treated. The environment must be checked and changed in accordance with the recommendations in section 2.I.4.a before returning the materials to the shelves. For additional information, see sections 2.H.2 and 7.B.

2.J. Pest Control

A single approach to pest prevention and control will not eradicate insects, rodents, and other biological pests from the library. "Instead, a combination of techniques is usually required to maximize the effectiveness of any pest control program. The term 'integrated pest management' (IPM) has been coined to embody this concept: That all pest control programs must rely on several approaches working in concert to effect the desired result. An IPM approach must be considered when addressing the problems of pests in libraries." [17:103] IPM goes beyond simple prevention and control to include monitoring and use of cultural, mechanical, and chemical control techniques. Most of the information in this section is based upon Thomas Parker's article "Integrated Pest Management for Libraries." [17]

2.J.1. INSECTS

Cockroaches, silverfish, various beetles, and book lice are the major causes of insect damage to library materials. The following IPM procedures are outlined for controlling the insects found most commonly in libraries. One of the most effective measures for controlling insect infestation is to maintain relative humidity between 50 and 60 percent at all times and to use the air-conditioning system or fans to circulate air in the stacks.

2.J.1.a. Book lice

Book lice (psocids) feed on microscopic mold that grows on paper. They do not damage the books themselves, except if their bodies are crushed when books are closed upon them. They prefer warm, damp, undisturbed environments, and therefore their presence is a good indicator of high humidity. They are most numerous during spring and summer when humidity is high and fungi is more likely to grow. Their control is difficult and is best accomplished by keeping relative humidity within 50 to 60 percent and the temperature from 68 °F to 72 °F.

2.J.1.b. Carpet beetles

The adult carpet beetle may be found in light fixtures and on window sills. The larvae feed on materials high in protein, such as the carcasses of insects (their primary food source) or rodents; thus their presence is a good indication of infestation by other pests. When the larvae pupate and emerge as adult flying beetles, they seek out other proteinaceous materials on which to lay their eggs. Rarely do the larvae attack leather-bound books, but they may eat the felt lining of storage boxes for rare books, and attack herbarium collections, tapestries, and woolen goods.

IPM procedures for controlling carpet beetles include:

1. Vacuum all library areas, especially in rooms where dead insects may be found, since adult carpet beetles will deposit their eggs on them.
2. Use sticky traps or glue boards where carpet beetles seem to be a problem. The traps can help determine the presence of carpet beetles and other insects. The traps must be removed regularly due to the carpet beetle eggs deposited on other insect carcasses caught in the traps.
3. Screen all windows and doors. Around the building, avoid planting shrubs such as crepe myrtle and spirea that have white or blue flowers and contain high amounts of pollen. (Adult carpet beetles also feed on pollen.)
4. Eliminate all bird nests on and around the building, since carpet beetles feed on debris in the nests. Eliminate rodents and their nests for the same reason.

2.J.1.c. Cigarette beetles

The cigarette beetle is a small, round, cinnamon-colored flying beetle whose larvae infest dry leafy materials including books. It and the drugstore beetle are commonly called "bookworms" because their eggs are laid on the spines of books and along the edges of book covers. When the larvae hatch they tunnel immediately beneath the book cover in order to eat the glue. They will tunnel about three to four inches, pupate, and leave the book through a round hole, often leaving a fine powder the color of the book cover upon which they were feeding. Piles of this powder can be easily seen on shelves by using a flashlight.

The IPM control approach is:

1. Screen all windows and doors.
2. Ban all dried flower arrangements (real flowers) from the library. The eggs and larvae are often found on such arrangements.
3. Spices and leafy vegetable matter should not be stored in the library.
4. Do not store or display botanical collections in the library.

2.J.1.d. Cockroaches

The American cockroach, the Oriental cockroach, and the Australian cockroach are responsible for most of the cockroach damage done in American libraries. Cockroaches like starchy materials such as book covers, and they easily destroy paper, paper products, bindings, and other materials covering books, pamphlets, recordings, etc. Damage done by chewing can be recognized by the ragged edges of the areas fed upon. Fecal pellets and smears are very often seen in association with feeding. The smears blemish materials.

IPM procedures for controlling cockroaches include:

1. Lay a six-foot-wide gravel barrier around the library to discourage access.
2. Remove all vines, ivy, debris, leaves, etc. from around the building.
3. Clean out dirt and debris from gutters.
4. Caulk and seal all small holes and cracks on the outside of the building.
5. Screen windows and doors.
6. Install sodium vapor (not mercury vapor) outdoor lights so they shine on the building, but are not attached to it.
7. Place sticky glue boards on insect pathways in false ceilings, basements, elevator shafts, and closets to monitor the existence of cockroaches.
8. Use 2 percent Baygon Cockroach Bait sparingly throughout the interior of the library in areas not open to the public. This bait

is bran mixed with molasses and 2 percent Baygon. It looks like sawdust, and large cockroaches are attracted to it. It is effective, but some cockroaches are becoming resistant to it. Products containing ortho boric acid are also effective but should only be used in cracks and crevices. Boric acid is highly poisonous to children. Silica gel is less toxic and just as effective. **Note: Always follow the manufacturer's directions when using these products.**

9. Install thresholds, weather seals, and rubber flaps on exterior doors.
10. Place steel wool in holes and openings around pipes.
11. Spray residual insecticides in cracks and crevices around the perimeter of rooms. Pay particular attention to areas around pipe chases, elevator shafts, storage areas, and mechanical rooms.
12. Exterior power spraying of walls, eaves, and overhangs may be required for control of American and Australian cockroaches.
13. Do not apply aerosol or fog insecticides inside the building. They are oil-based and the small droplets will eventually settle on the entire collection, causing irreversible damage.

2.J.1.e. Drugstore beetles

The drugstore beetle infests books and manuscripts; like the cigarette beetle, it is sometimes called a bookworm. This beetle's larvae often tunnel through the text block of the book, emerging through the fore edge, cover, or spine (it may even bore through an entire shelf of books). It may be found in storage areas that tend to be damp. This insect can do a great deal of damage to books and must be dealt with expeditiously. Only books that have small, round exit holes with powder drifting onto adjacent books and shelving need to be treated.

Procedure:

1. Do all the things listed for the cigarette beetle that are appropriate to the situation.
2. Caulk all cracks, holes, and areas around windows.
3. Pigeon nests may harbor drugstore beetles and should be eliminated from around the building.
4. Relative humidity should be maintained between 50 and 60 percent at all times. Use fans to circulate air in the stacks and keep the books from becoming damp.
5. Use a flashlight and inspect the stacks regularly for piles of fine powder.

2.J.1.f. Silverfish

Silverfish are very fond of sized paper, particularly sizing made with starch, dextrin, or casein. They also like rayon, cellophane, and papers made from pure chemical pulp. They eat the microscopic mold that grows on plaster walls and drywall. They are a problem year-round in cool, moist basements and poured-concrete buildings. They tend to migrate into cooler, moister areas of buildings in the summer and to attics and higher levels in the fall and winter. They are very common in cardboard box and drywall manufacturing plants. Since silverfish lay their eggs in the corrugated walls of boxes, every box coming into the library is likely to carry silverfish.

Silverfish control procedures include the following:

1. Vacuum perimeters of rooms, especially around baseboards and toe moldings.
2. Use sticky traps or glue boards for monitoring where silverfish seem to be a problem.
3. Silverfish like moisture. Use finely powdered silica gel in void spaces beneath bottom shelves and in cabinets. The silica gel will kill them by drying them out.
4. Apply residual, liquid insecticidal sprays to room perimeters, stack bases, and the backs of cabinets where the latter are attached to walls.
5. Silica gel/pyrethrum insecticidal dust should be used in voids where pipes enter walls and floors.
6. Repair leaky plumbing fixtures and eliminate moisture in lavatories, staff rooms, and workrooms.
7. Caulk and patch cracks and holes.

2.J.2. VERMIN

The mouse or house mouse is the most common rodent found in libraries. It causes damage to library materials by chewing on paper in order to make nests and by urinating and defecating on books, papers, and other materials. When mice die, their bodies attract and are eaten by carpet beetles. Mice also like the insulation on electrical wires, chewing it off and thereby causing shorts and electrical fires. They have a very small range, and the males are very territorial. The ranges often are not more than 12 to 30 feet from the nests. Gnaw marks, small stained holes in floors and walls, and a pungent urine odor are signs of their activity.

Control procedures:

1. Caulk all cracks and holes ¼ inch or larger in the exterior of the building. Stuff steel wool into larger holes.
2. Mechanical traps are preferred to toxic baits. If the latter are used, mice will die in the walls or other inaccessible places and provide food for carpet beetles. Traps can be baited with cotton balls or peanut butter. Glue traps, snap traps, or multiple-catch live traps can be used.
3. Two or three weeks after the extermination program has begun, all droppings should be removed in order to determine the success of the program.

4. Sonic devices are not recommended for permanent control.
[17:115–116]

2.J.3. FREEZING

Freezing has recently been advocated as an attractive means of eradicating insects from library materials. This technique has been used with success at the libraries of the University of Miami (Florida) and Yale University. At the latter institution, each insect infested book was placed in a plastic freezer bag and sealed with a hot iron so water would not condense after it was brought out of the freezer. The books were then blast frozen at -40 °F (-40 °C) for 72 hours, acclimated to room temperature over a 24-hour period, and returned to the shelf. The objects to be placed in the freezer must be at room temperature (above 65 °F), and the freezing must be done very quickly before the insects become acclimatized to the cold. [18] The University of Miami uses a household chest freezer for this purpose very successfully.

Freezing does not affect library bindings, paper, or colors, although the bonding action of adhesives will decrease when frozen. Every new book for the Beinecke rare book library at Yale goes through the freezer before being added to the collection.

Wei T'o Associates is marketing a mechanically and electrically modified supermarket freezer that dries wet books and exterminates insects. The unit functions as a vacuum freeze-dryer and exterminates insects by exposing them to subzero temperatures at which their body fluids crystalize. According to the manufacturer, 400 to 600 volumes can be treated per three-day extermination cycle. Insects are exterminated in their adult, pupa, larva, or egg life forms. [30]

REFERENCES

1. "The Accurate Measurement of Relative Humidity." *Conservation Materials Catalog.* Sparks, NV: Conservation Materials Ltd., 1982.

2. Banks, Paul N. "Environmental Standards for Storage of Books and Manuscripts." *Library Journal* 99 (February 1, 1974): 339–343.

3. Cressman, A. W. "Control of an Infestation of the Cigarette Beetle in a Library by the Use of Heat." *Journal of Economic Entomology* 26 (February 1933): 294–295.

4. *Environmental Specifications for the Storage of Library & Archival Materials.* SOLINET Preservation Program Leaflet, No. 1. Atlanta, GA: Southeastern Library Network, Inc., April 24, 1985.

5. *Environmental Specifications for the Storage of Library Materials.* Carbondale, IL: Midwest Cooperative Conservation Program, University of Illinois at Carbondale, n.d.

6. *Fact Sheet.* Alachua, FL: Dinh Company, Inc., 1988.

7. Florian, Mary-Lou E. "Freeze Drying." A lecture given at the Cryobibliotherapy Conference on April 3, 1987 at the School of Library Service, Columbia University. New York: Columbia University, School of Library Service, April 3–4, 1987.

8. Florian, Mary-Lou E. "The Freezing Process—Effects on Insects and Artifact Materials; A Literature Review and Recommended Procedures for Freezing Insect Infested Artifacts for Insect Eradication." *Leather Conservation News* 3 (Fall 1986): 1–13, 17.

9. "Heat Pipe Assisted Air Conditioning." *Windows of Opportunity: NASA Applications Engineering Program.* Washington, DC: Technology Utilization Division, NASA, [1985?].

10. Lafontaine, Raymond H., and Patricia A. Wood. *Fluorescent Lamps.* Revised ed. Technical Bulletin, No. 7. Ottawa: Canadian Conservation Institute, 1982.

11. Lee, Mary Wood. *Prevention and Treatment of Mold in Library Collections with an Emphasis on Tropical Climates: A RAMP Study.* Paris: UNESCO, 1988.

12. Macleod, K. J. *Museum Lighting.* Technical Bulletin, No. 2. Ottawa: Canadian Conservation Institute, April 1975, reprinted May 1978.

13. Macleod, K. J. *Relative Humidity: Its Importance in Measurement and Control in Museums.* Technical Bulletin, No. 1. Ottawa: Canadian Conservation Institute, May 1978.

14. Morton, Bernard W. *Humidification Handbook: What, Why and How.* Hopkins, MN: Dri-Steem Humidifier Co., 1986.

15. Nyberg, Sandra. *The Invasion of the Giant Spore.* SOLINET Preservation Program Leaflet, No. 5. Atlanta, GA: Southeastern Library Network, Inc., November 1, 1987.

16. Padfield, Timothy. "Climate Control in Libraries and Archives." In *Preservation of Library Materials: Conference held at the National Library of Austria, Vienna, April 7–10, 1986,* edited by Merrily A. Smith. Vol. 2. IFLA Publications, 41. Munchen: K. G. Saur, 1987.

17. Parker, Thomas A. "Integrated Pest Management for Libraries." In *Preservation of Library Materials: Conference held at the National Library of Austria, Vienna, April 7–10, 1986,* edited by Merrily A. Smith. Vol. 2. IFLA Publications, 41. Munchen: K. G. Saur, 1987.

18. *Preventing the Growth of Mold and Mildew on Books.* Chapel Hill, NC: Rare Book Collection, University of North Carolina, n.d.

19. Remington, Charles. "Freezing and Insect Mortality." A lecture given at the Cryobibliotherapy Conference on April 3, 1987 at the School of Library Service, Columbia University. New York: Columbia University, School of Library Service, April 3–4, 1987.

20. Research Libraries Group. *RLG Preservation Manual.* 2d ed. Stanford, CA: The Research Libraries Group, Inc., 1986.

21. Ritzenthaler, Mary Lynn. *Archives & Manuscripts: Conservation: A Manual on Physical Care and Management.* SAA Basic Manual Series. Chicago: Society of American Archivists, 1983.

22. Roberts, Matt T., and Don Etherington. *Bookbinding and the Conservation of Books: A Dictionary of Descriptive Terminology.* Washington, DC: Library of Congress, 1982.

23. Smith, Merrily A. "Care and Handling of Bound Materials." In *Preservation of Library Materials: Conference held at the National Library of Austria, Vienna, April 7–10, 1986,* edited by Merrily A. Smith. Vol. 2. IFLA Publications, 41. Munchen: K. G. Saur, 1987.

24. Staniforth, Sarah. "Environmental Conservation." In *Manual of Curatorship: A Guide to Museum Practice,* edited by John M. A. Thompson, et al. London: Butterworths, 1984.

25. TALAS. *Catalog.* New York: Technical Library Service, Inc., 1986.

26. Thomsen, Fonda, and Mike Whiltshire. "A Method of Measuring Light Levels in Exhibit Areas." In *Conserve O Gram.* Washington, DC: National Park Service, July 1975.

27. Thomson, Garry. *The Museum Environment.* 2d ed. London: Butterworths, in association with the International Institute for Conservation of Historic and Artistic Works, 1986.

28. *Treatment of Wooden Shelving for Books.* Andover, MA: Northeast Document Conservation Center, 1986.

29. Turner, Sandra. "Mold . . . the Silent Enemy." *The New Library Scene* 4 (August 1985): 1, 6–8, 21.

30. *Wei T'o Book Dryer-Insect Exterminator.* Matteson, IL: Wei T'o Associates, Inc., May 25, 1988.

3.
CARE AND HANDLING OF LIBRARY MATERIALS

3.A. Introduction

This chapter covers the storage, care, handling, exhibit, and security of books. Similar information for audio-visual materials, i.e., audio and video disks, film, magnetic tape, and photographs is discussed in Chapter 6.

3.B. Care and Handling of Books

The procedures discussed in this section will be of no value if the staff and public are not made aware of the necessity of handling books and other library materials with care. Education of the staff and patrons in preservation will help prolong the life of collections. This can be accomplished "by including preservation information in staff orientation programs, by mounting exhibitions about preservation or conservation, by including articles on preservation in staff and student newspapers [and by inviting reporters from city newspapers to do stories on preservation], or by preparing" [20:45] audio-visual programs, book bags, bookmarks, demonstrations, handouts, manuals, posters, and signs.

Preservation of books in general collections begins by selecting and using proper shelving and bookends, then learning how to remove, store, and replace books on shelves; how to use book trucks properly; how to handle books in ways that will prolong their lives; and how to utilize good circulation and photocopying techniques.

3.B.1. SHELVING

Library bookcases should be constructed of steel with a baked enamel finish. Wooden shelves should never be used in an archive or library because of the possibility of the wood outgassing harmful compounds [see section 2.E.2]. The shelves should be smooth and solid, without rungs or slots, and free of jagged edges and protruding screws. The bottom shelf should be no less than four inches above the floor in order to avoid problems from rising water and splashes from cleaning. Shelves and their bracing should be checked annually for looseness. If the shelf is braced by diagonal guy wires, the wires can be tightened to correct looseness or sag. [See section 8.C.1 for a discussion of bracing shelves against earthquakes.]

Bookends should also be made of steel, with a baked enamel finish. They should be free of sharp edges and rust, and high enough to support over half the height of the book. A properly designed bookend should be thick enough to be easily seen on the shelf and constructed so it won't "knife" a book when it is pushed onto it. Wire bookends that hang from the shelf above should be avoided, because books tend to slip under them and slide into a leaning position. Bookends that are too short and/or made of thin metal can be economically modified by gluing cardboard to the upright part of the bookend and covering the cardboard and the metal with buckram. [2]

Similarly, map, blueprint, or poster cases should be constructed of steel with a baked enamel finish. Drawers should not be more than two inches high and should be fitted with hoods or dust covers to protect the contents from slipping or being caught up under the drawer above. Drawers more than two inches high can hold too many items, causing overloading problems such as bunching, tearing, or wrapping during removal and replacement.

3.B.1.a. Shelving, removal, and replacement of normal-sized books

Books should be shelved upright, resting square on their bases. They should not be placed on their fore edges, allowed to lean, or packed too tightly or too loosely. Most bindings are weakest at the joint or hinge area. When a book is shelved fore edge down, gravity will eventually and inevitably pull the text block from the case at the hinge. Bookends should always be used for shelves that are not full. Do not stack volumes on top of each other or on top of other upright volumes.

When removing a book from the shelf, gently push the books on either side of it farther back on the shelf. If this is not possible, place an index finger firmly on the top edge of the book (not on the headcap) and tilt the book out of the shelf. With the whole hand, grasp the desired volume by the sides at midspine and remove it. Then readjust the bookend, if necessary, and straighten the shelf. Removing books in this manner will save fragile headcaps from becoming frayed and breaking. Use a step stool to reach high shelves.

Before reshelving, dust books to remove damaging dirt and set aside volumes needing repair. Securely fasten all portfolios and boxes protecting fragile materials. To replace a book on the shelf, loosen the bookend and move the books on the shelf to create a space for the volume. Reinsert the book into the space and readjust the bookend. As noted above, do not shelve the book fore edge down. If the book is too high for the shelf, it can be shelved spine down, and an acid-free slip with the call number can be placed in the center of the text block. This approach, however, can cause problems of its own, such as the slip being lost and the book jutting out into the aisle. A better solution is to adjust the shelf height or provide special shelving for oversized and folio volumes. [2]

3.B.1.b. Shelving, removal, and replacement of oversized books

"Oversized books . . . frequently have bindings that are weak in proportion to their size and weight [and] . . . cannot be stored safely on ordinary vertical shelving." [10] Broad, fixed shelves or roller shelves should be provided for oversized volumes. Sometimes double-width shelves can be used for this purpose. Ideally, folios should be stored flat, one to a shelf. If this is not possible, they should be stored flat with no more than three or four volumes on top of each other. There should be no protrusion of books into the aisle. Empty shelves should be interspersed throughout the stack area so volumes that are being removed to get access to another book can be transferred to them. If space does not permit the use of empty shelves, a table should be provided nearby upon which to place the volumes. Another possible solution for shelving oversized books is to designate special stack areas for vertical shelving where they can be shelved together. Volumes of like size can provide better support for each other, but over time, gravity will pull them away from their spines.

Use *both* hands when removing an oversized volume from a shelf. If it is not the top volume on the shelf, and the books are stored flat, transfer the upper volumes to a free shelf or a nearby table or book truck. Do not pile them on top of each other. Do *not* pull the book out from between other volumes, because the chances of damage and falling are great. If the transferred books are being placed on a book truck, make sure they are neatly stacked, do not hang over the edges, and are low enough on the truck to maintain its stability. After the desired book has been removed, transfer the upper volumes back to the shelf.

Unbound materials, such as maps and broadsides, are often oversized and stored in piles. The procedures described above should be used to remove a desired item from the stack. Do not drag the wanted material out of the pile, as such handling increases the possibility of tearing. [2]

To return an oversized book to a shelf, repeat the procedure above. If the volumes are stored flat and stacked on top of each other, move the volumes with *both* hands to a free shelf, book truck, or table. Replace the volume on the shelf with *both* hands and transfer the upper volumes back onto the shelf. [2]

When accessing materials in map cases, the pieces on top of the required item should be removed and placed on top of the map case following the procedure described above for oversized volumes.

Pictorial signs can be placed throughout the stacks depicting how to remove and replace books. This will remind both patrons and staff of the fragility of the materials they are handling.

3.B.2. CLEANING AND MAINTENANCE

Whenever sections are being shifted, dust each volume before placing it on the new shelf. Books should be vacuum cleaned at least twice a year, and the book shelves wiped with a 2 percent formalin solution. This thorough cleaning should include removal of every item, cleaning shelves, and cleaning each volume. If possible, use a small vacuum cleaner with soft brush attachment and use cloths impregnated with End Dust™. Wash the cloths as they get dirty, since particle dust is abrasive and conducive to the growth of mold. If vacuuming books, extreme care must be taken so brittle books are not harmed. Use a cheesecloth filter on the vacuum tube to catch any stray paper. "Dust-Witch 2000 is a device that fits onto the hose of [a] . . . vacuum cleaner and works by blowing out air, then drawing it in again. It is said to be good for brittle books because bits and pieces are less likely to go up the tube. It is available from Garnet Projects, Calgary, Alberta, Canada." [18:75] When cleaning shelves, whether dusting or vacuuming, work from the top shelf down, exercising extreme caution in handling brittle items. In any event, a regular cleaning cycle designed to work through the entire library every three to eight years should be established, with the length of the cycle depending on the size and value of the collection, local dirt conditions, and use patterns.

Eliminate foreign materials from the stack area. (Eating, drinking, and smoking should never be permitted around shelves.) Shelf labels should be of the type that fit into brackets on the front edge. If tape must be used to label shelves, be sure it does not extend above or below the edge of the shelf; this is necessary to keep the adhesive from coming in contact with the books.

If books are haphazardly sprawled on shelves, users are likely to be casual about handling them. If they are upright in neat rows, users will tend to keep them that way, and may even straighten up a toppled row if it is a conspicuous exception to general neatness. If enough time is given to straightening and cleaning to create an overall impression of care for the books, readers will be inclined to perpetuate the arrangement.

During the cleaning process, damaged or deteriorated volumes can be identified for treatment. Bindings that are broken or weak should be tied with white, flat, cotton twill tape to keep the covers and spine pieces from being separated from the text blocks. The volumes should be tied so that the bow or knot is positioned across the top or fore edge (opposite the spine) rather than on the front or back cover, so the resulting bump will not interfere with good shelving practices.

Boxing is an alternative that provides greater protection than tying damaged volumes, depending on the value and condition of the bound materials. A variety of phase and drop-spine boxes can be purchased or constructed, if trained personnel are available [see Chapter 4 for more information].

One person should be given specific responsibility for the appearance of the shelves; in a large stack area, this responsibility may be divided, by area, among two or more assistants. A crash program of straightening up may be easily combined with reshelving, shelf-reading, weeding, etc. The responsible person(s) should be encouraged to suggest major shifts, rearrangement of shelves, requests for more bookends, and so forth, as appropriate. [3:5.2.2] See Appendix G for additional information about shelf maintenance.

3.B.3. TRANSPORTING BOOKS

3.B.3.a. Book trucks

Book trucks should be used to move books to the stacks from processing, circulation, patron tables, or other places in the library. Book trucks should be in good condition, easily maneuverable, and wide shelved, and they should be equipped with protective rails and rubber bumpers on all four corners.

Materials on book trucks should be shelved upright, resting square on their bases with their spines parallel to each other and perpendicular to the shelf bottom—as they are on the shelves. They should not be placed on their fore edges, be allowed to lean, or be packed too tightly or too loosely. They should *not* be placed on their fore edges because this tempts the shelver to do the same when placing the book on the shelf if it is too high. If a book truck shelf is not full, either a bookend or a pile of similar sized books laid flat can be used to support the others. These procedures should also be used for book lifts. Unbound materials that can stand by themselves should be placed in Princeton files or between bookends for support. Those that have little or no rigidity should be placed flat in small, neatly stacked piles in order to prevent them from falling off the truck. [17:1.2]

Overloaded book trucks are difficult to maneuver, and books are likely to fall off. Keep the center of gravity low so the truck remains stable. Large books, however, should be placed flat on the top shelf so they don't slide off or damage the heads of other books. If the building has an elevator that stops out of alignment with the floor, it will be difficult to lift the book truck into the elevator successfully. If this situation occurs, use the emergency stop button to keep the door open while moving the book truck into the elevator compartment. [2]

3.B.3.b. Mailing books

When mailing books, use "reinforced boxes fitted with adjustable Velcro™ straps to provide firm support. Such boxes are sturdy, reusable and excellent for inter-library loans." [2] If such a box is too expensive or not practical, heavy mailers may be purchased from library supply houses. Whatever is used, "the material should be protected from environmental damage, primarily water; it should be protected against damage from handling, e.g., shock from impact, abrasion from friction, distortion from pressure; [and] the packaging should provide a means of labeling for address or shipping instructions." [5:22] Sandwich pamphlets and other flexible materials between cardboard so they will not be damaged. Use glassine, jiffy bags (envelopes padded with pulverized paper), or bubble wrap to cushion and protect materials in transit. Unfortunately, there are "no custom-made containers for shipping books available on the market today. What is available are general use containers such as corrugated cardboard cartons" and the cushioning materials mentioned above. [6:23]

3.B.4. CIRCULATION OF MATERIALS

3.B.4.a. Date slips

Date due slips should be placed inside the cover on the endpaper next to the text block, not on the verso of the front or rear cover. If the charge slip is on the verso of the cover, the force of stamping the book out for circulation bends the board and strains the weakest part of the binding—the hinge where the cover and text block meet. If the slip is already pasted on the inside cover, circulation clerks should be trained to place the book on the counter so the cover is fully supported by the counter surface before stamping the book out. [2]

3.B.4.b. Inclement weather

On rainy or snowy days, provide plastic bags to protect materials that will be leaving the library. The gesture will not only protect the books and other materials but will impress the public with the seriousness of the library's intent to protect its collection.

3.B.4.c. Book drops

Many libraries have book drops for patrons' convenience when the library is closed. Since even the best designed book drops contain the potential for damage to books, they should be available for use only when the library is closed. Book returns should be routinely emptied at the beginning of each work day and locked while the library is open. A well-designed book drop will have its floor fixed on springs just below the return slot, minimizing the distance a book will fall after it is pushed through the slot. As more books are put into the return, the floor depresses slowly under their weight. Book drops that are built into the wall of the library invite trouble. There are countless reports of fire, floods, and other problems (such as insect infestation) occurring because vandals placed fire bombs, hoses, or other items in the slot of returns that opened into the library. If the return must be built into the wall, it should be protected by a secure fire- and flood-proof enclosure.

3.B.5. PHOTOCOPYING

A major problem in copying bound materials, especially those that are oversewn or sidesewn, is the damage done to spines and paper when the books are pressed down in order to copy all the way to the inner margin. The pressing action places a serious strain on the thread and adhesive in the binding, often causing the thread to rip through the pages and the adhesive to fail. Brittle pages crack and separate from their attachments or simply break and fall from the volume. The eighth edition of the Library Binding Institute's *Standard for Library Binding* contains alternatives to the old oversewn method of leaf attachment for library materials that help reduce damage when photocopying. Librarians should familiarize themselves with the new standards and request their binders to avoid oversewing volumes except where such methods are appropriate. [13] [See Chapter 4 for an explanation of the new standard.]

In the 1970s there were a few electrostatic copying machines available that minimized damage to books being copied. They were designed to copy deep into the inner margin without harming the volume, usually by extending the glass copying surface to the edge of the machine. This enabled the operator to place the page to be duplicated on the copying surface and the facing page down over the side of the machine, thus avoiding the problem of squashing the spine down to copy as far into the inner margin as possible. During the 1980s, these machines disappeared from the market. Today, however, there are again a few new machines that can be used to copy material from books and bound periodicals without damaging them. Four currently available are the Archivist face-up copier (Total Information Group Ltd.), the BookMaster Selectric 1700 (University Copy Services, Inc.), the Océ copier (Océ-Business Systems, Inc.), and the Xerox 5042 (or BookSaver Copier) (Xerox Corporation). Inclusion in this list does not imply endorsement of these products.

Archivists and librarians should look for certain minimum characteristics in a copying machine before leasing or purchasing:

The surface adjacent to the copying surface should be sloped to help when copying bound volumes.

Copying controls should be conveniently located so they do not interfere with handling material.

The copying platen should be fixed so that all material is photocopied in a stationary position—outside of the copier. Image quality should be clear, readable, and acceptable to users. The exposure control should permit varying shades of dark or light copies to compensate for the clarity of the original. [22:37]

When copying materials, support the covers and pages of the volume. Avoid forcing the book flat on the copying surface of the machine. Identify materials whose size, structure, or physical condition prevents them from being easily copied. For example, brittle books should not be copied because they are quite likely to be damaged, perhaps beyond retrieval. Such materials should be microfilmed and the patrons given copies from the film. [10] [See sections 5.E and 5.F for more information on preservation microfilming and photocopying.]

3.B.6. GENERAL HANDLING OF BOOKS

3.B.6.a. Cleanliness

Cleanliness should be enforced in the library. Hands should be clean. Food, drink, and smoking materials should not be permitted. These items can not only damage books and papers, but they will also attract insects and other pests.

3.B.6.b. Opening new books

"Careless opening of a new book, or a newly bound volume, can crack its spine. Books bound in plastic are especially prone to having tight spines and should be handled carefully. With the book on its spine on a flat surface, and the text block held upright, open the front cover and run the fingers gently along the hinge. Do the same to the back cover, followed by both front and back end sheet pages. Then, alternating front and back until the entire text block is completed, open small sections of pages, applying the same gentle pressure along the hinge while holding the remaining text block in an upright position." [17:1.6]

Many new (or even older) books will not lie flat while being cataloged. During the cataloging or other processing activities, a book snake, book stand, or sheet of Plexiglas™ should be used to keep the book open. Never use a heavy weight or another book because the stress may damage the spine. [17:1.9]

3.B.6.c. Inserts and enclosures

Acidic paper inserts, such as place markers or newspaper clippings, are often left in books for many years, with the result that text pages can become stained and damaged. When found, inserts should be evaluated to determine whether they are important to the work at hand. If they contain important information, they should either be reproduced on acid-free paper and tipped into the book, or pamphlet-bound and placed with the item on the shelf, as appropriate.

Avoid excessive use of enclosures. Often the staff will insert various kinds of enclosures or processing instructions into books as they travel through technical services. Thick, bulky packs of information placed inside the cover next to the hinge can strain or break the hinge. A thin packet of information can be safely placed in the center of the text block away from the inner margin. Thick or bulky packets should be placed either on top of the book or in envelopes attached with white cotton tape passed around the sides of the book. [17:1.8]

3.B.6.d. Paper clips, rubber bands, and staples

Paper clips and rubber bands should never be used to attach materials to books. Metal paper clips will rust, tear the pages, or leave a wrinkled impression. If something must be clipped, use a plastic clip. Rubber bands bend or rip pages and covers. Over time, rubber bands rot, leaving a sticky acidic residue on the book. Rubber bands and staples should never be used on books.

3.B.6.e. Uncut pages

Bone folders should be used to cut pages in books that will not be sent to the bindery. The book should be held partially open. Use a bone folder to cut the top and fore edges with very short strokes, taking care not to saw back and forth through the foldings. Holding the text block flat with a free hand will help avoid uneven cutting of pages. [17:1.10]

3.C. Exhibits

"Putting items on display presents many opportunities for abuse. By the very nature of their uniqueness, the objects shown are often the ones which can least afford the exposure." [1] Much avoidable damage is inflicted by careless staging of exhibits. Even with the greatest care, most materials will suffer some damage.

The Research Libraries Group published guidelines for exhibiting materials. A few of its recommendations are excerpted here:

Restrict display of materials to no longer than three months to avoid fading or permanent distortion/damage. Exhibit conditions for an item that must be displayed for a longer period must be stringently controlled. Watercolors and some other colored items are particularly sensitive to damage by light and should not be displayed or, if they must be exhibited, should not be subjected to lighting levels of greater than five footcandles, or 50 lux . . . ten footcandles, or 100 lux should be the maximum level.

Levels of lighting should be carefully controlled to limit damage by fading. . . . UV radiation and temperature/humidity monitoring devices, and blue wool cloth test cards to detect fading, are available to monitor conditions inside cases. . . . Lighting outside the cases may need to be dimmed for the materials to be viewed adequately. [See section 2.H.1 for a full discussion of the ways to measure the effects of light.]

If fluorescent lights must be used in exhibit cases and display areas, filter them to stop UV radiation. Filters can be special plastic sleeves or sheets. Curtain or filter all windows providing direct sunlight. [See section 2.G.2.]

Stabilize the environment within an enclosed exhibit case at 50 percent relative humidity and not above 70°F. . . . In cases without temperature control, the relative humidity can be controlled with preconditioned silica gel." [19:140]

Use a dial hygrometer to monitor the humidity inside the case. [19:140] [See section 2.D.3.d.]

When books are displayed, special care must be taken to avoid putting strain on bindings. If a title page or the front pages are shown, support the elevated cover from the back so the binding is not stressed.

Supports can be made of covered bricks, cut cardboard, or book board. Be sure to use an acid-free barrier to separate acidic materials from the book. When a book is displayed at an angle, an easel or book support is appropriate. Library suppliers offer various styles made of acrylic, Plexiglas™, or metal. Hardware stores or gift shops sometimes carry cookbook stands that are suitable.

As a book is displayed more vertically, it becomes important to support the page bottoms to prevent them from sagging. If a large volume is displayed, showing it at a very low angle rather than upright will lessen stress on the binding. Easels with a ledge can be made of plywood (covered with paper or polyurethane).

Book cradles can also be made of book board, mat board, or even cardboard lined with acid-free paper. One of the best arrangements is to make a set of half-cradles or wedges of varying sizes and angles. The librarian can then select the most appropriate one to fit the lay of the book. The cradle should fit the book, not the other way around.

Once the book is on the cradle, cut 1/2- to 3/4-inch-wide bands of clear polyester film (Mylar™), loop the bands around the fore edges and cover, and fasten the ends together with tape or Velcro™ coins. The bands should be snug, but not tight enough to crease or damage the pages. Turn the pages at least weekly to limit the exposure of the paper to harmful ultraviolet light. While doing so, examine the display for any changes such as sagging pages or covers that might cause physical damage to the exhibit. [1]

3.D. Security

Archives and libraries increasingly face problems from vandals, thieves, and thoughtless individuals who damage and otherwise diminish collections. The Association of College and Research Libraries' "Guidelines Regarding Thefts in Libraries" [9] covers in detail the security procedures libraries should implement to protect collections from a variety of problems.

Electronic theft detection systems, however, are not covered in the Guidelines. These systems require insertion in library materials of specially treated detectable targets that trigger alarms as they are passed through sensing screens. These devices are effective and should be considered in libraries experiencing theft. They are treated in detail in various issues of *Library Technology Reports*, a periodical publication of the American Library Association.

The remainder of this section contains checklists and guidelines that are helpful in reducing security problems in all types of libraries. It closes with a discussion about special collections, covering in more detail many of the points on the checklist.

3.D.1. COLLECTION SECURITY CHECKLIST

Adherence to the following security checklists will reduce vandalism, mutilation, and theft opportunities. The checklists are based upon "Library Crime and Security: An International Perspective" by Alan J. Lincoln and Carol Zall Lincoln. [14:147–152]

3.D.1.a. Entrance/exit point control checklists

General Security
Consider a monitoring contract

Develop a "lock-up" procedure

Electronic security system installed

Guards, exit attendants, book checkers used

Intrusion detection system installed

Entrances
Break-resistant materials in door glass

Dead bolt or sequential combination push-button locks

Door hinges should be on inside

Door locks that are difficult to pick or damage

Entry monitoring system

Entry points with adequate alarms

Improve control of emergency exits

Patrons cannot enter or exit undetected

Reinforced door frames

Reinforced exposed hinges

Secured roll-down doors

Fire Escapes
Fire escape alarm to indicate use

Fire escape secured

Locks and Keys
Install a sequence lock system

Keys marked "Do not duplicate"

Lock exchanges to maintain integrity of system

Multi-level master key system

Windows
Break-resistant windows

Security screens on windows

Skylights secured

Windows have security locks

Other
Air conditioners secured from inside

Fireproof receptacle for return

Turnstiles slow and control exiting

Vents and ducts secured

3.D.1.b. Interior space control checklist

Monitoring
Adequate interior lighting

Alarms for areas housing rare materials

Avoid or eliminate hidden areas in building

Closed circuit TV/"dummy" cameras

Closed stacks for valuable items

Mirrors to improve visibility

Monitor reserve rooms

"Peepholes" in book stacks

Posters and displays should not block vision

Reading areas visible from desk

Stacks arranged for maximum visibility

Staff

Staff circulating on floors

24-hour deployment of custodians

Other

Reserved shelves for items in demand

Staff/patron access to rare materials restricted

3.D.1.c. Collection controls

General

Consistent application of policies

Convenient library hours

Coordinate assignments with public schools

Learn names of patrons

Library policies written and available

Limit carrying by patrons of bags and parcels

Participate in theft clearinghouse [see section 3.D.3]

Circulation of Materials

Actual value charged for "lost" rare items

Adequate parking to encourage returns

Amnesty days

Change is available

Close book drop if being misused

Deposits on selected checkouts

Few restrictions on number of items checked out

Mailgrams or collectors for overdues

No fine/low fine policy

Overnight circulation of reserves

Periodic renewal of cards

Procedure to assess damage after use

Provide secure book drop for after hours

Reasonable loan and renewal policies

Require picture I.D. before issuing card

Simple registration procedures for new users

Some reference and nonbook titles circulate

Development and Maintenance

Back issues of some periodicals on microfilm

Bind pamphlets and clippings in vertical files

Collection that strongly supports the curriculum (for academic or school libraries)

Inventory often enough to notice theft

Maintain current inventory of rare items

Multiple copies of high demand items

Properly mark library materials

Rare materials identified

Repair/remove mutilated materials

Reserve system for demand items

Stripe unbound journals with various colors on four edges including spine as visual check to door checkers

Publicity

"Give away" file

Inexpensive photocopying services

Post notice of laws and penalties for book theft

Post penalties for mutilation

Provide "free" copy card as part of fees

Publicize problem by displaying mutilated material

Publicize theft problem and cost

3.D.1.d. Security checklist for school libraries

School libraries should adhere to the following checklist in addition to those listed in the collection controls checklist [16:54].

Adequate holdings of both current and back-issue periodicals

Circulation of curriculum reserves at least overnight

Flexible and adequate scheduling for individual and class use

Interlibrary loan policy for titles not available

Long-range classroom loans

Multiple copies of high-demand items

Paperback editions in popular subject areas

Quick and efficient checkout

Renewal of all items, except those on reserve

Selection policy that reflects users' needs

Typewriters (or word processors, if possible) for student use

3.D.2. SPECIAL COLLECTIONS

As the value of books and documents rises, especially those in rare and special collections, many items are smuggled out of collections under the raincoats or in the briefcases of thieves. Security for general library collections depends on two things: electronic devices that can detect the removal of material, and the care and vigilance of library employees. In rare book and archival collections, however, the staff alone bears the responsibility for security, since rare items cannot be tagged. Technological innovations have had, as yet, little effect upon archival and special collection security procedures. Instead, improved security means implementing and refining procedures that have been in place for at least 60 or 70 years. [11]

3.D.2.a. Evaluation of security

To assure security for items that cannot be protected electronically, existing security arrangements must be evaluated. Suggestions on improving security should be elicited from all staff members. They will be the ones to implement changes, and each can contribute from his or her own experience. [23:2, 4] The librarian or archivist may also choose to bring in a security consultant. An interested staff member can be appointed as a security officer to assume responsibility for periodic assessments and to attend workshops. Once security has been evaluated, the security officer should write up a security policy. The policy should list procedures for preventing, detecting, and reporting thefts, and the steps to be taken in recovering items, as well as the names and phone numbers of those to be notified when a loss is discovered. This could be part of the disaster preparedness and recovery policy, if the resulting product is not too unwieldy [see Chapter 8]. The security officer should contact local law enforcement agencies and book dealers, giving them information about the collection.

3.D.2.b. Theft prevention policy

A policy for theft prevention must consider four areas: the physical surroundings, the collection itself, reader policies, hiring and other personnel policies. Usually, a theft occurs in the same manner as shoplifting—the book is smuggled out. If items are particularly valuable, however, a more ambitious break-in might be planned and carried out. Therefore, anyone responsible for rare books or documents must protect them from burglars. The rare books area should be located, if possible, away from the exterior of the building. Ideally, there should be only one door, and it (in fact, any door in the area) should be solid core and have fixed-pin hinges and mortise locks or a vertical-bolt auxiliary. If a vault is not available, store books in a closet whose door meets all these requirements. [23:11–12] Keys should be distributed only to those who need them. Janitors are not included among those who need keys. In rare book or special collections areas, cleaning people should work only during operating hours, while the staff is there. Master keys should be avoided, and keys should be assigned to avoid duplication.

3.D.2.b.1. Environment

An alarm system should be installed. Alarm systems serve to detect intrusion and to frighten the intruder away. Perimeter alarms are triggered when an electric current, passing through foil tapes on windows or across the narrow gap between a door and its frame, is broken. Interior alarms detect motion in a variety of ways—for instance, by photoelectric beams, pressure sensitive switches, vibration detectors, or microwaves. [23:13] No alarm can function unless it is protected from tampering. Alarms should be away from public traffic, and when power is interrupted, a backup system should come into operation. If the system is running on batteries, an alarm should sound in the monitoring station when the batteries are low. [4:9] A burglar alarm, like a low temperature, water, or fire alarm, works best if its warning is transmitted somewhere where it will receive an intelligent response. A local alarm that is nothing but a conversation piece for passersby is often useless.

3.D.2.b.2. Collection

After the environment is secure, the collection itself must receive attention. A fundamental step in providing security is to know exactly what to protect: items that may be tempting to thieves must be identified. The first step is to establish tight bibliographic control. It has been suggested that curators not accept items if they cannot process them within a reasonable length of time. [12:123] When material is accepted, it should be evaluated and described as thoroughly as possible. Identification and other unique marks on rare books should be noted in the cataloging description along with the imprint and a description of the binding. Manuscript descriptions should include physical dimensions and the first word of the second page, if any. Contents should be noted in detail. Not only will such descriptions aid in identifying stolen items, but if contents notes are included in finding aids, they will help preserve rare items from excessive handling and save both the librarian and the user unnecessary trouble. [12:130]

Photocopies of valuable and/or fragile items should be supplied for public use. If a photocopy is not practical, precious items can be stored in a separate folder that is checked before and after use to insure that a reader returns all that was received. Marketable items are probably best individually appraised and insured for current market value. Appraisers are available from the SAA and the Antiquarian Booksellers Association of America. Truly priceless books and documents may as well be left uninsured, and the money spent on better security. [23:10]

It is impossible to mark all the items in a collection; but once valuable holdings have been identified, they should be marked in some way. A document can be embossed or marked with micro targets or invisible ink, but these methods are usually either too inconspicuous to function or too easily reversed. The Association of College and Research Libraries (ACRL) "Guidelines for Marking" suggest using indelible ink on a small stamp. [7:400–401] The Library of Congress provides fast drying, nonfading, stable, ineradicable ink to archivists and librarians.

The formula is kept a secret in order to make removal of the mark difficult. [23:9] A document should be marked on its verso, if it is blank, or in the margin. Composite texts, those whose components can be separated, should be marked on each division. [7:400] If a marked item ever leaves the collection, it is better to leave the mark as evidence of the item's provenance rather than try to conceal it.

Most rare book and document collections are in a department within a larger library, and the head of special collections will often be responsible for security within the general collection as well. Especially in large research libraries, old or valuable books may remain unnoticed within the circulating collection. The ACRL suggests that a library set up a program to identify and remove valuable books from open stacks. [8:349] Once responsibility for this task is defined, authority delegated, and procedures established, valuable books can be sorted out as part of routine collection management, e.g., when books are considered for binding, weeding, or interlibrary loan. If the library's automated systems are capable of it, machine-readable cataloging (MARC) records can be searched by imprint date. Circulation, shelf-reading, and interlibrary loan requests are generally handled by staff who (while recognizing vellum or a broadside) may not recognize a publisher's binding, decorated endpapers, or significant provenance when they see it. Therefore, librarians should know their collection themselves, and should also encourage patrons to point out valuable books (to the librarian, not to their friends).

Transferring a rare book to special collections or to closed stacks will necessitate changing all the catalog records and perhaps leaving a dummy book at the old location. Preservation treatment may also be necessary. [8:350–351]

3.D.2.b.3. Use

After the physical facilities and the collections are secured, use policies must be developed. Policies should be written, printed, published, and explained to both staff and patrons. A use policy should include detailed instructions about who is permitted to use a special collection and how the collection should be protected. Details of the latter should not be explained to the public, however.

Readers using rare book rooms should be required to complete an identification form. If especially rare or fragile materials are to be used, patrons should be asked to supply letters of recommendation attesting to their experience in using sources and to the genuineness of their research need. After the patron has filled out the identification form, he or she should be asked to provide photo identification. Some libraries supply a reader's card to serve as identification in the future, but the card should either have a photograph or an inkless fingerprint on it, or the reader should register each day. Registration should include reading and signing a short statement of collection policies and rules. [15:481–485] One of the last steps in registration is to have the reader sign a statement that he or she has read the special collection reading room policies. These policies are generally standard and familiar to most researchers. They include placing outerwear, briefcases, notebooks, umbrellas, or any other receptacle that could conceal a document, in lockers outside the reading room or at the desk. Readers are also reminded to handle materials carefully, to leave papers in a file in order, and to obtain the legal right to publish from private collections. [12:132]

Some archives and libraries provide marked paper upon which to take notes, preferably in pencil, so that it will not be necessary even to bring notebooks in. Each reader is provided with his or her own station in the reading room. Requests for material are made on a signed call slip; the slips are saved, both to help identify the collection's holdings and to identify the last user. Only one box or file of documents should be allowed on the reader's table at a time. Other boxes the reader requests can be kept at a truck by the table or at the desk. There should never be so much paper around a reader that the observation of the reading room attendant becomes confused. When a reader leaves, all materials must be returned to the desk, where each box or folder is checked. If an item is in a slip case, the slip case should be kept at the desk. [23:3]

3.D.2.b.4. Staff

Regardless of how good the alarms, no matter how extensively items are marked, and no matter how stringently readers are identified, security for archives and rare books depends ultimately on the staff. Employees should be trained to observe by dividing the room into quadrants, observing each quadrant in turn, and moving occasionally to get a different perspective of the scene. [23:5–6] All tables should face the attendant's desk. Cubicles should not be permitted. Closed circuit television and/or mirrors act as deterrents and should be installed in appropriate areas.

The reading room attendant who observes a theft, however, is in an uncomfortable position. Staff have neither the training nor, in most instances, the legal right to *forcibly* detain a suspected thief. Such an attempt may lead to tragedy and should never be permitted. It is important, therefore, to write careful and explicit instructions to be followed when theft is detected. For example, when a person is detected concealing material, the staff member should immediately get another staff member to watch the suspect and then call the police. The patron should be approached, told (with suitable tact) there is a problem, and asked if he or she would step into an office to discuss it. If the patron complies, a staff member should stay with him or her until the police arrive. If the patron leaves, the second staff member should follow and get a description of the automobile, while the first staff member immediately writes a description of the thief and the theft, away from any questions or comments. [21]

A draft of model legislation for theft and mutilation of library materials is included in the 1988 [ACRL] Guidelines Regarding Thefts in Libraries. [9:161–162] The model places library thefts on the same statutory basis as shoplifting, by including two important legal elements. First, the concealment of material is taken as prima facie evidence of intent to steal. The library need not prove then that someone intended to steal, i.e., the defendant must prove that he did *not* intend to steal when he put the document in his pocket. Second, the librarian has civil immunity from suits for false arrest if he or she had probable cause to detain a patron. The guidelines also state that reasonable force may be used when detaining a suspect, the police must be notified immediately, and the suspect may not be detained for more than one-half hour (but note in the paragraph above the caveat against using force). The patron should not be searched, nor should an attempt be made to obtain a signed confession. [9:161–162]

Unfortunately, a significant proportion of major thefts are by library staff members. All employees should be checked before they are hired. It should be noted if applicants are collectors in an area where the archives or library has holdings. Employees should be bonded against theft. [23:5] After an employee is on the job, emotional changes or signs of mental stress may be indications that theft is taking place and should be noted.

3.D.3. REPORTING THEFTS

Thefts must be reported as soon as they are detected. Reports should be made to the security officer, the local authorities, and to the Bookline Alert: Missing Books and Manuscripts (BAMBAM).

BAMBAM is an online database, with periodic updates printed in *Library and Archival Security*. Archives and libraries that are missing material send detailed descriptions of the items to the database. BAMBAM is consulted by dealers and librarians who may doubt the provenance of newly offered or acquired materials. BAMBAM is especially helpful in catching the thief-for-profit. Thefts can also be reported to *AB Bookman's Weekly* (which runs a column on missing books), local dealers, and others. Names and addresses of organizations that can help when thefts occur are listed below.

AB Bookman's Weekly
P.O. Box AB
Clifton, NJ 07015
201-772-0020

Bookline Alert/Missing Books and Manuscripts (BAMBAM)
Daniel and Katherine Leab
P.O. Box 1236
Washington, CT 06793
212-737-2715

The Security Committee
Association of College & Research Libraries (ACRL)
Rare Books & Manuscripts Section
50 East Huron Street
Chicago, IL 60611-2795
800-545-2433
800-545-2444 in Illinois

REFERENCES

1. Boydstun, Jim. *Technical Notes.* Illinois Cooperative Conservation Program. Carbondale, IL: Southern Illinois University at Carbondale, Morris Library, n.d.

2. *Care and Handling of Books.* Slide/tape program produced by the Conservation Department of the Yale University Libraries with a grant from the National Endowment for the Humanities. New Haven, CT: Yale University Libraries, Conservation Department, 1980.

3. Columbia University Libraries Preservation Department. *The Preservation of Library Materials: A CUL Handbook.* 4th ed. New York: Columbia University Libraries, 1987.

4. Currie, Susan, et al. "Cornell University Libraries Security Checklist." *Library and Archival Security* 7 (1985): 3–31.

5. DeCandido, Robert. "Out of the Question: Part I." *Conservation Administration News* 43 (October 1990): 22–23.

6. DeCandido, Robert. "Out of the Question: Part II." *Conservation Administration News* 44 (January 1991): 22–23.

7. "Guidelines for the Security of Rare Book, Manuscript, and Other Special Collections: A Draft." *College & Research Libraries News* 50 (May 1989): 397–401.

8. "Guidelines on the Selection of General Collection Materials for Transfer to Special Collections," *College & Research Libraries News* 46 (1985): 349–352.

9. "Guidelines Regarding Thefts in Libraries." *College & Research Libraries News* 49 (March 1988): 159–162.

10. *Handling Books in General Collections.* Slide/tape presentation. Washington, DC: Library of Congress, National Preservation Program Office, 1984.

11. Haugh, Georgia C. "Reader Policies in Rare Book Libraries." *Library Trends* 5 (1956–57): 467–475.

12. Land, Robert H. "Defense of Archives against Human Foes." *American Archivist* 19 (1956): 121–138.

13. *Library Binding Institute Standard for Library Binding,* edited by Paul A. Parisi and Jan Merrill-Oldham. 8th ed. Rochester, NY: Library Binding Institute, 1986.

14. Lincoln, Alan J., and Carol Zall Lincoln. "Library Crime and Security: An International Perspective." *Library & Archival Security* 8 (Spring/Summer 1986): 147–152.

15. Mason, Philip. "Archival Security: New Solutions to an Old Problem." *American Archivist* 38 (1975): 477–492.

16. Paris, Janelle A. "Internal and External Responsibilities and Practices for Library Security." *Security for Libraries: People, Buildings, Collections,* edited by Marvine Brand, 51–82. Chicago: American Library Association, 1984.

17. "Preservation Guidelines for Processing Staff." *Preservation of Library Materials: A Manual for Staff,* Module 1 (draft), 1.11–1.16. Austin: University of Texas, The General Libraries, 1986.

18. "Products & Services." *The Abbey Newsletter* 13 (July 1989): 75.

19. Research Libraries Group, Inc. "Exhibits." *RLG Preservation Manual,* 140–142. 2d ed. Stanford, CA: RLG, 1986.

20. Smith, Merrily A. "Care and Handling of Bound Materials." In *Preservation of Library Materials: Conference held at the National Library of Austria, Vienna, April 7–10, 1986,* edited by Merrily A. Smith, 45–53. Vol. 2. IFLA Publications, 41. Munchen: K. G. Saur, 1987.

21. "Steps To Follow in Case of Observed Reading Room Concealment of Material." University of Virginia Libraries. In Association of Research Libraries, *Theft Detection and Prevention.* SPEC Kit No. 37. Washington, DC: Association of Research Libraries, Office of Management Studies, 1977.

22. Sung, Carolyn Hoover. *Archives & Manuscripts: Reprography.* SAA Basic Manual Series. Chicago: Society of American Archivists, 1982.

23. Walch, Timothy. *Archives and Manuscripts: Security.* Chicago: Society of American Archivists, 1977.

4.
BINDING AND
IN-HOUSE REPAIR

4.A. Background

Books were originally sold in signatures. Buyers then had each book individually bound to their own tastes. The growth of the printing industry forced booksellers to stop this practice, and publishers began producing trade and then edition bindings. The latter were an outgrowth of mechanization in the industry. Bindings became less durable as book publishing became more automated, and librarians found they had to rebind books in order to extend their usable life. The usable life of a volume (in library binding terms) may be defined as the number of circulations it can sustain before the binding becomes non-functional. For example, the LBI has stated that a hardcover book will sustain 26.7 circulations on the average before falling apart. If it is given an LBI standard library binding, it will last for an average of 92.4 circulations, an increase of 346 percent. [15:23]

The library binding industry grew slowly during the early years of the twentieth century as a small group of companies independently developed their own specifications for library bindings. As early as the 1920s, they began coming to an agreement on the specifications for Class A Library Binding, which was formulated in 1934 and accepted by the Library Binding Institute (LBI) in 1935. (*Class A binding* and *Class B binding* are archaic terms and no longer used.) The LBI was founded in June 1935 as the successor to the Library Binding Division of the Book Manufacturers' Association and was the primary force in bringing rationality into the industry. Prior to that time there had been "price-wars, quality chiselling and labor sweating." [2:4] The Institute promoted communication, education, and the development of technical standards that have been accepted by most library binders. In 1958 it promulgated a set of standards for certification of its members. Today the eighth edition of the *Library Binding Institute Standard for Library Binding* [14] is a testament to the close cooperation of the industry and librarians. For the first time it recognizes the importance of strengthening and preserving library materials, while taking into consideration everyday use by patrons, such as photocopying. It also describes the options that are now considered acceptable for leaf attachment. The *LBI Standard* was a joint effort of a committee of library binders and librarians who worked together under the auspices of the American Library Association and the Library Binding Institute. The Institute inspects library binderies and checks the quality of materials and level of workmanship in the books they bind. A library bindery whose binding meets the Institute's standards can be certified by the Institute as being in compliance with all of the Institute's requirements. Libraries should consult the LBI list of certified binders or ensure that candidates adhere to the *LBI Standard* for Library Binding when choosing a binder. The *LBI Standard* and a list of certified library binders is available from the Library Binding Institute in Austin, Texas.

The specifications approved for Class A binding in 1934 addressed durability and provided a solution for easily manufactured bindings. The oversewing machine, which was developed shortly after World War I, made this possible. It created an inexpensive and strong text block that often outlasted the paper in the book and that, ironically, was the ultimate downfall of the Class A binding. Oversewing results in a very tightly secured text block at the binding margin. It is so stiff that an oversewn book will often snap shut after being opened. The thread can rip through weak paper at the inner margin when the book is opened and pressed flat on a copying machine. The strain on the text block caused by extensive copying led to damaged volumes and the need for a new standard that was compatible with today's library needs. This chapter discusses book structure, the eighth edition of the *LBI Standard*, and simple repairs that can prolong the usable life of a book.

4.B. Book Structure

4.B.1. BACKGROUND

The vast majority of books in libraries today were produced since 1800. The modern book is the product of centuries of change. Its advantage over earlier versions of recorded information is that it is compact, portable, an efficient way of organizing information, and easy to use. Its table of contents, chapter headings, and indexes enable the reader to quickly move to the desired section and begin reading immediately—a quality the modern computer, for example, often does not possess. All in all, the modern book is an admirable invention. The challenge to the librarian and the binder is to maintain its advantages, protect the text block, and enable the book to continue to meet the needs of the user.

Before the nineteenth century, booksellers had two options: to sell the book in signatures or in small bound runs. If they were bound, the signatures were usually sewn outside the spine or in grooves sawn into the spine. Endpapers were invented to bear the strain caused by opening the covers. They saved wear and tear on the first and last sheets or leaves of the text block. The text block was rounded into an arc and backed so the shoulders could accommodate the boards of the covers or case [see Figure 4.1].

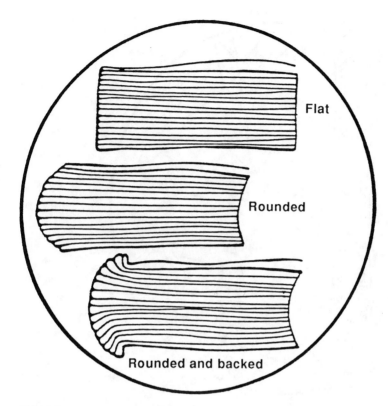

Flat

Rounded

Rounded and backed

FIGURE 4.1. Back/backing. Reproduced, with permission, from *Library Binding Institute Standard for Library Binding*. 8th ed. Edited by Paul A. Parisi and Jan Merrill-Oldham. Rochester, NY: LBI, 1986, p. 13.

Through the late fifteenth century the boards were made of wood. During the sixteenth century, binders began using boards made from multiple sheets of paper pasted together. Early headbands were wrapped around a cord and used to attach leaves or signatures together at the head and tail of the text block. This method of attachment prohibited trimming, so after the sixteenth century, headbands were attached after trimming.

Pressure to bind books as fast as printers produced them forced binders to change their traditional methods and take shortcuts. Built-up boards gradually gave way to paper covers and the creation of the edition binding. Edition binding became economically attractive in the nineteenth century when many copies of the same title were printed. Since all the copies were exactly the same size and shape, they could be rapidly bound in assembly line fashion. Thus case binding appeared. In this procedure, the cover or case is made separately from the text block. Tapes or sewn-in cords were used originally because they produced a smooth spine or back [see Figure 4.2]. Headbands were glued on after the book had been rounded and backed and thus became merely decorative. Spines were lined with lightweight muslin cloth or paper, and the boards and spine of the case were glued to the endpapers. [24]

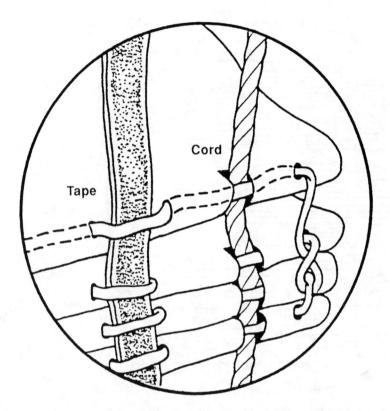

FIGURE 4.2. Sewing on sewn-in cords and sewing in tapes. Reproduced, with permission, from *Library Binding Institute Standard for Library Binding.* 8th ed. Edited by Paul A. Parisi and Jan Merrill-Oldham. Rochester, NY: LBI, 1986, p. 16.

4.B.2. BOOK CONSTRUCTION

Most of the information in this section is taken from or based on Robert J. Milevski's *Book Repair Manual.* [23]

Modern hardcover books are case-bound. The case, or cover, and the text block are constructed separately, and the two pieces are brought together and attached to each other through an adhesive on the endpapers. [23:9]

The text block of a book is a block of pages that are bound together. The block is made up of either a group of folded sections or individual leaves. The sections or leaves are formed from large sheets of paper, called press sheets, on which a sequence of pages are printed. Each sheet is then folded so the pages are in correct order. This makes up a section. Individual leaves of text are formed when the folded edges of each section are cut off. [23:9]

Sections and leaves are sewn and/or glued together along the folded edge of a section or the fold-cut edge of the individual leaves, which have been roughened by machine to more readily accept an adhesive. This edge is the spine of the text block. Endsheets are then tipped on to the front and back of the text block at the spine edge. Next, the spine can be rounded and sometimes backed to form the convex spine and concave fore edge typical of most books [see Figure 4.3]. Following this, a headband and a tailband and one or two spine linings are glued down to reinforce the spine. The endsheets and spine linings attach the text block to its case. [23:9]

How the pages of a book's text block are held together as a unit is vital to how well the text block will open and hold its shape. Until just recently, books whose sections are sewn through the folds and to each other have been much superior to and have operated more effectively than leaves of text held together with a layer of adhesive. Adhesive bindings, also commonly called perfect bindings, are hardly perfect when the adhesive doesn't hold. The leaves of a perfect-bound book can sometimes be removed almost as readily as sheets from a pad of paper. The use of better adhesives and double-fan adhesive binding, however, is enabling binders to produce adhesive bound books that have much of the same strength (in fact, some binders say more) and most of the desirable attributes of fold-sewn volumes. [23:10]

Also important are the method and materials used to attach the text block to its case or cover once the casing-in process is completed. The case is constructed of two pieces of heavy board, a heavy paper or bristol spine strip that will hold the rounded shape of the book spine, and a covering material of book cloth, buckram, or paper, etc. [23:10]

The boards and spine strip are cut to specific measurements and glued onto the covering material at predetermined distances from each

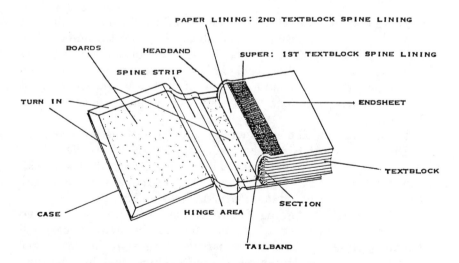

FIGURE 4.3. Major components of a typical modern book. Reproduced, with permission, from Robert Milevski, *Illinois Cooperative Conservation Program Book Repair Manual.* Carbondale, IL: Illinois Cooperative Conservation Program, Morris Library, Southern Illinois University, 1984. Reprinted by the Illinois State Library, Springfield, IL, 1988, p. 11.

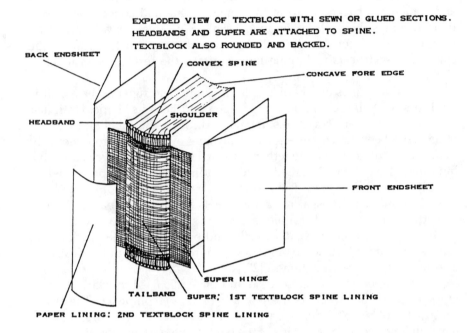

EXPLODED VIEW OF TEXTBLOCK WITH SEWN OR GLUED SECTIONS. HEADBANDS AND SUPER ARE ATTACHED TO SPINE. TEXTBLOCK ALSO ROUNDED AND BACKED.

BACK ENDSHEET

CONVEX SPINE

CONCAVE FORE EDGE

HEADBAND

SHOULDER

FRONT ENDSHEET

SUPER HINGE

TAILBAND   SUPER: 1ST TEXTBLOCK SPINE LINING

PAPER LINING: 2ND TEXTBLOCK SPINE LINING

FIGURE 4.4. View of a textblock. Reproduced, with permission, from Robert Milevski, *Illinois Cooperative Conservation Program Book Repair Manual*. Carbondale, IL: Illinois Cooperative Conservation Program, Morris Library, Southern Illinois University, 1984. Reprinted by the Illinois State Library, Springfield, IL, 1988, p. 11.

other. These distances are critical because the case must cover the text block precisely. The cover boards should lie flat and also hinge freely around the shoulder of the text block. The cover spine should fit snugly over the text block spine. The cover boards should form a one-eighth-inch square on the top, bottom, and fore edges of the text block. The result is a cover that functions properly and both encloses and protects the text block. [23:10]

The points of attachment between text block and case are the hinge areas. These are critical. Hinges have several purposes: The covers move or open or turn on them (more specifically, the shoulder of the text block), and they serve to hold the text block into its cover. If quality materials are used and are properly glued into place, the book will function very well, and the hinges will be strong. If proper materials are not used and workmanship is poor, the hinge areas, which are inherently weak, will fail. Combine this weakness with ordinary use during circulation, and the book may develop loose hinges, and/or the text block may become loose in its cover. [23:9–10]

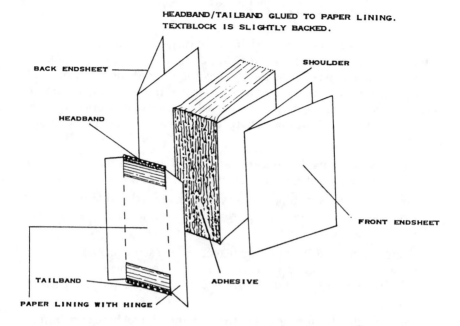

FIGURE 4.5. Exploded view of an adhesive bound book. Reproduced, with permission, from Robert Milevski, *Illinois Cooperative Conservation Program Book Repair Manual.* Carbondale, IL: Illinois Cooperative Conservation Program, Morris Library, Southern Illinois University, 1984. Reprinted by the Illinois State Library, Springfield, IL, 1988, p. 12.

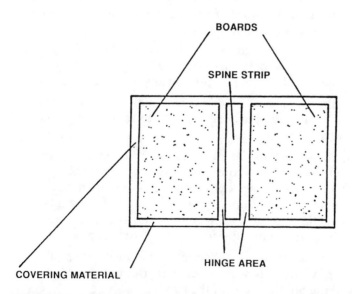

FIGURE 4.6. Case before covering material is turned-in. Reproduced, with permission, from Robert Milevski, *Illinois Cooperative Conservation Program Book Repair Manual.* Carbondale, IL: Illinois Cooperative Conservation Program, Morris Library, Southern Illinois University, 1984. Reprinted by the Illinois State Library, Springfield, IL, 1988, p. 12.

4.C. Leaf Attachment

The process by which the leaves of a text block are connected to each other is called leaf attachment. Adhesive, staples, or thread are usually used to secure leaves together at the inner or binding edge. Binders and conservators often use the term *leaf attachment* when discussing the means a library binder will use in preparing a text block for a library binding. There are at least 12 methods of leaf attachment:

Adhesive binding: loose leaves are milled and secured into a solid text block with adhesive rather than sewing or stitching.

Single-fan adhesive binding: leaves are clamped and fanned once over the glue roller where approximately .00001 inch of adhesive penetrates between the pages.

Double-fan adhesive binding: leaves are passed over the glue roller twice in opposite directions, so the adhesive, usually polyvinyl acetate (PVA), is placed on both sides of each leaf.

Mekanotch adhesive binding: the Mekanotch machine cuts thin slits into the spine of the text block. Adhesive is then forced into all of the notches as well as on the ends of the leaves. It can be used with the double-fan process.

Sewing through the center fold by hand: thread is sewn through holes in the center fold of each section and around tapes or cords that provide additional support. Each section is joined, one to the other, by kettle stitches and/or overcasting.

Sewing through the fold by machine: like sewing through the fold by hand, except tapes or cords are not usually used; there are many more holes, and the thread links one signature to another.

Side sewing: the leaves of the sections of a book are secured with thread through the binding edge from front to back through the entire thickness of the text block.

Cleat lacing: the spine must be milled to separate the text block into separate leaves; then parallel slits or cleats are cut about one-eighth inch into the spine by saws set at opposed angles. Thread is then laced in a figure eight pattern around the cleats, holding thin sections of the text block together. The spine and thread must be coated with adhesive to stabilize the spine.

Oversewing: thin sections are milled into separate sheets and sewn together by thread passing at an angle through the edge of the spine and the binding edge of the leaves.

Saddle sewing: a periodical issue or pamphlet is sewn through the center fold with thread. This allows the signature to open fully and lie flat.

Saddle stitching: the leaves of a section are fastened through the center fold with staples in two or more places. It has the same advantage as saddle sewing, but is much stronger.

Side stitching: similar to side sewing except the sections are secured with staples from front to back through the entire text block.

This list does not exhaust the possible methods (posts, rivets, ring binding, etc.), but librarians are most interested in the types of leaf attachment that are used by library binders to prepare the text block for a library binding. The next sections point out which methods these are and describe their advantages and disadvantages. They are discussed in order of preference, i.e., beginning with those treatments that cause the least amount of damage and ending with those that cause the most. [26]

4.C.1. RECASING

This is not actually a method of leaf attachment; instead, it involves replacing the case or using the old case if it is still in good condition. Both sewn or adhesive bound volumes may be recased.

Sewn materials will be addressed first. For a book to qualify for recasing, the text block must have been sewn, the original thread still in good condition, and the text block intact, i.e., each section still firmly attached to those beside it. The sewing thread may be broken at the first and/or last signature. A wobbly or loose (but not broken) text block is still a candidate for recasing, because it is lined and will be firmed up when new adhesive is applied. The thread that is visible along the center of each signature should take up at least 40 percent of the length of the fold. Anything less will require either removing the original thread and resewing through the fold, or double-fan adhesive binding. "Recasing . . . involves replacing the original case with a new one without altering the existing method of leaf attachment." [18:23] Loose leaves should be hinged in or tipped in before the volume is recased. "The text block is removed from its case, old lining material and adhesive are removed from the spine; new endpapers are attached; the spine is coated with new adhesive; a strong new spine lining is applied, and a new case is made and attached to the text block." [18:23] If the bindery discovers that the book selected for this treatment cannot, or should not, be bound this way, the library and the binder must discuss what type of binding, if any, should be applied.

The binder should remove all of the old spine lining and old adhesive from text blocks that are to be recased. This may be done by heating and softening the adhesive, then scraping it and the old lining off. Some binders brush a thick paste on the spine, and the moisture softens the adhesive so it can be removed more easily.

The purpose of recasing is to minimize the amount of damage rebinding inflicts on the text block and to preserve, as much as possible, the flexibility and openability of the book. Therefore, any process that interferes with this purpose should be avoided by the binder. The librarian should be aware of the method the binder uses to attach the endpapers to recased text blocks, because some techniques, such as whip stitching, will prevent the book from opening fully and lying flat. Three styles of endpapers are described in the *LBI Standard* and should be used by the binder, although none is fully satisfactory. They are (1) a single leaf hinged with reinforcing cloth to a single folded sheet, (2) a single folded sheet with a reinforcing cloth hinge that is adhered along the binding edge of the endpaper and extends beyond the fold, and (3) two folded sheets, nested. The fold of the inner sheet is reinforced with a reinforcing cloth strip that is three-fourths inch wide. [14:5] Unfortunately, no economical procedure has yet been developed for attaching endpapers in a structurally sound and aesthetically pleasing way.

Advantages of recasing:
Since the spine does not need to be milled during the procedure, the entire binding margin remains intact.

Openability of the text block either remains the same or is improved. The latter may be true because the stiff adhesive applied by the book manufacturer has been removed from the spine during the recasing procedure.

The sewing structure remains unchanged from the original. [18:26]

Disadvantages of recasing:
It is more expensive than either double-fan adhesive binding or oversewing, because the binder must remove the original spine lining and adhesive, in some cases manually round and back misshapen text blocks, sew new endpapers on through the fold, and hand trim them. The binding is only as good as the original sewing. [18:26]

Adhesive bound text blocks may also be successfully recased if they are first double-fan adhesive bound. The old adhesive must be removed, because it is usually inflexible and doesn't secure the leaves to each other as well as the PVA adhesives used by binders. The only time an adhesive bound text block should not be recased is when the gutter margin is so narrow the milling procedure would cut into the text.

4.C.2. SEWING THROUGH THE FOLD

If the text block is not intact (i.e., it is composed of separate sections that are not sewn together, but the folds of the sections are intact, such as the issues of popular magazines), then the text block may be sewn through the fold. A volume cannot be sewn through the fold if the signatures are entirely or partially attached by sewing thread or adhesive from a previous binding. [18:13] A volume is a candidate if significant illustrations bleed across binding margins, a condition that precludes a binding method requiring milling of the spine and oversewing. Monographs that were sewn through the fold by publishers are rarely resewn by binders. Most, though, can be recased or double-fan adhesive bound. Usually the library must prepare the volume for center fold binding by removing the original spine lining, glue, and thread, separating the signatures, and repairing all damaged folds. It is expensive for the library to do this, but it may be necessary if there is no other way to satisfactorily bind the volume, for example, if it is a rare or valuable art book. [20:16]

Sewing through the fold may be accomplished by hand or machine. The technique has been used for centuries and is considered the best way to bind separate and complete sections together. However, if done by hand, it can be very expensive and time-consuming. Consequently, it is not usually done manually by library binders; there are machines that can sew through the fold adequately at less expense and higher speed.

Hand sewing is done by passing a threaded needle through a hole in the center of the folded section of leaves, starting from the outside (or back edge) of the signature. The thread is drawn through a hole near the end of the section, then drawn parallel to the spine to the next hole and through it to the outside once more. Tapes are used to anchor and strengthen the sewn sections one to the other, and they run perpendicular to the text block across the spine. They are completely external to the text block and do not restrict its ability to open. The thread is drawn around the tape through a hole immediately on the other side and into the center of the section once again. It is then drawn down the gutter, parallel to the spine, to the next hole, and the procedure is repeated until the full length of the spine is sewn. Usually there are about three to five tapes used on a text block, depending on its height. The beginning and end of each signature are tied off with a kettle stitch to attach the signature just sewn to the one previously sewn. The entire process is repeated for each section. The first and last sections are the endsheets, which are made up of two or more folded sheets with a cloth reinforcing strip at the inner or outer fold. After sewing, the tapes are cut off approximately one inch beyond each side of the spine and glued down securely. [26:10]

Advantages of hand sewing are:
No spine milling is necessary.

The volume will open completely, lying flat on the reading surface.

Very little damage is done to the spine.

Disadvantages of hand sewing are:
Since it is a slow process, it is expensive.

Very few books are published in signature form these days, thus hand sewing will slowly be eliminated as an option. [26:10]

Cords can also be used to provide a framework around which the sewing structure is built. In contrast to tapes, cords are recessed in cuts sawn perpendicularly into the spine of the text block. The recessed cords restrict the openability of the volume and should be substituted for tapes only with the permission of the customer.

Machine sewing is done on the same type of machines used by edition binders, except library binders use better quality thread. The same type of text block preparation is required for machine sewing as for hand sewing, except tapes and cords are not usually used. A National or Martini sewing machine is usually used by library binders for this process. These machines can handle volumes up to 15 inches wide and 17 inches tall. Signatures must be hand-fed into the machines one by one. Publishers' binders also use the Smyth sewing machine, which can accommodate volumes only up to 11 inches wide and 14 inches tall. [18:16] The operation of these machines is similar to that of hand sewing. The major difference is that the text block is sewn with multiple sewing heads that simultaneously sew each folded section. The machine sews through the folded section, producing a stitch like the chain stitch made by household sewing machines, only larger. The stitches run along the fold of the section about one stitch every one-half inch, and because the paper will tend to break or split along the sewing line, this technique can create a problem as the paper ages. Each stitch connects the section on either side to it vertically by means of a loop through which the thread on the adjacent section is drawn. After the sewing operation is completed, the text block may or may not be trimmed, according to the customer's specifications. Adhesive is then applied to the spine prior to rounding and backing in order to fix the sewing structure.

Advantages of machine sewing are:
It costs less than hand sewing.
It has the same advantages as hand sewing.

Disadvantages of machine sewing are:
Most of the machines have constraints not encountered by hand center fold sewing. For example, the machine cannot sew folded sections that are less than three folded sheets or more than one-quarter inch thick.
A machine cannot sew a combination of single sheets and folded sections. [26:10]

4.C.3. DOUBLE-FAN ADHESIVE BINDING

If the text block is two inches thick or less, the paper is not extremely stiff, coated, or glossy, or the book fails to meet other criteria for sewing through the fold, then the volume may be considered for double-fan adhesive binding (for example, if the book is already adhesive bound or sewn through the fold, but the thread is not intact). This form of adhesive binding should not be confused with perfect binding. The latter involves the application of a hot-melt adhesive to the binding edge of the clamped text block, without fanning, so there is little, if any, penetration of the adhesive between the sheets. It is a fast and inexpensive form of binding, subject to failure, often after very little use. Double-fan adhesive binding, on the other hand, involves milling the binding edge of the sections to produce separate leaves, if they are not already separate, and fanning the clamped leaves in both directions (single-fan is in only one direction), so that the cold adhesive, usually a polyvinyl acetate, is applied a slight distance onto the leaves, forming a good bond on both sides of the sheets. [30:6] After the leaves are fanned and adhesive applied, the text block is consolidated by applying a stretch cloth back lining to the spine. The text block is then removed from the clamp and allowed to dry for several hours. An adhesive bound volume gets two spine linings: A second one of heavy cotton mull is applied over the back lining for additional strength. The binder has to be careful that all the leaves have received adhesive and will successfully bond together. If the leaves are not jogged flush to the surface of the spine, some may not touch the glue roller and will be loose in the text block. Some binders increase the surface area of the spine with notching, so greater contact is made between the paper and glue, which strengthens the bond between the leaves. However, not all binders agree that this is necessary, and the process does remove more of the inner margin, thus partially negating the advantage of adhesive binding. When the processes are properly controlled, the finished product, notched or not, will be stronger and less expensive than a sewn-through-the-fold binding.

Advantages of double-fan binding are:
The volume will open completely flat with the leaves opening to their innermost edges, thus allowing for easy reading and photocopying.

Except for a small amount of milling, only about one-sixteenth inch of inner margin is used for binding.

Rebinding can be done with little loss of additional inner margin. [18:22]

The binding is very strong, except in books with heavily coated paper.

Disadvantages of double-fan binding:
Volumes in signatures must have their spine folds cut before they are fanned. If the sections are large, this can result in a significant loss of inner margin.

Without proper care, leaves may be left unattached.

Occasionally, adhesive will flow between leaves and tip them together. This is a problem when stiff or thick leaves are interspersed throughout the text block, as with the individual issues of a serial.

Adhesive will not penetrate into the fibers of heavily coated papers, leaving them with a weak bond. [18:22]

4.C.4. OVERSEWING

When a volume does not meet the criteria for recasing, sewing through the fold, or double-fan adhesive binding, it should be considered for oversewing. The text block must have binding margins of at least five-eighths inch and the paper must be sturdy. Oversewing was used for most library binding from the 1920s to the late 1980s. It is extremely strong, economical to produce, and popular with library binders. The binding of an oversewn volume will probably last longer than the paper in the text block, and that is part of the problem with the technique. Books and periodicals with weak paper tend to lose their leaves when used heavily by library patrons after oversewing. That is not to say that other types of leaf attachment would prevent leaves of poor quality paper from breaking or detaching from the binding, but the mechanics of oversewing put too much stress on the paper at the binding edges. Oversewing requires that each book be separated into small sections of 15 to 20 individual leaves. In most cases this means that folded signatures must have the folds milled off and the original glue and thread removed. Normally, this is done by machine and results in a loss of up to one-eighth inch of inner margin. This is why volumes being considered for this process must have an inner margin of at least five-eighths inch. The sections, along with specifically manufactured endpapers, are then clamped at a 45° angle into an oversewing machine before the first and after the last sections. Vertically placed punches make holes about one inch apart through the sections. Threaded needles pass through the punched holes, entering through the spine and exiting the sections about three-sixteenths inch from the back edge of the section. Horizontal shuttle needles then pass through each of the separately formed thread loops and complete the stitch. Each section is sewn by means of successive lock stitches to the section before and after, on up the spine. [26:9] If the text block has narrow inner margins, the *LBI Standard* specifies that it be oversewn on a machine that has been modified by adding a narrow sewing plate. Since the product will be less strong than regular oversewing, it should be used only as a last resort. [14:3]

Advantages of oversewing:
A book of unlimited width, up to 15 inches high and 5 inches thick, can be oversewn even if the paper is stiff or coated.

If the paper in the text block is in good condition, the leaf attachment is very secure because the lock stitch is extremely strong.

Disadvantages of oversewing:
The spine of the volume must be milled unless it can be separated into sections less than one-eighth inch thick. The milling removes part of the binding margin.

Oversewing causes the thread to perforate at least three-sixteenths inch into the margin, which inhibits the openability of the volume, often causing it to snap shut.

Another one-fourth inch will be lost if the text block must be oversewn again, since one-fourth inch of the margin has already been lost during the original milling and sewing process.

The paper is weakened in the binding margin because of the multiple perforations of the oversewing punches and needles.

As the paper ages, it will tend to break along the line of sewing. [18:12]

4.C.5. OTHER METHODS OF LEAF ATTACHMENT

Other methods of leaf attachment are available, although they are not recommended for binding library materials meant for permanent retention. Side sewing is described in the *LBI Standard* as an option for leaf attachment that is acceptable to the Library Binding Institute. Holes are usually punched through the binding margin, and then the section or sections are stitched. The *LBI Standard* states that any side sewn volume cannot be more than one-half inch thick or have a binding margin less than three-fourths inch wide. [14:6] The sections do not have to be milled, which keeps the signatures intact for any future rebinding, but side sewing severely inhibits the pages of a volume from opening all the way to their inner margin. Almost any volume that can be side sewn can also be double-fan adhesive bound for a more flexible binding. [18:27] The leaves of side sewn volumes are very securely connected, and for this reason the method is often used for children's books. It is not recommended for other types of library materials.

If no method of leaf attachment is suitable, the item should be boxed. Boxes come in a variety of sizes, shapes, and styles. They may be open at one end or completely enclosed. The preferred approach is to design an enclosure specifically for the item in hand in order to provide the best protection possible [see section 4.G.2.a].

4.C.6. DECISION TREES

Jan Merrill-Oldham's decision trees for leaf attachment clearly summarize the criteria required for deciding how to repair both monographs and serials. A number of decisions must be made, however, before deciding about the type of leaf attachment to use. Is the paper in the book brittle? Does the volume have artifactual value? Should it be treated in-house? [These questions are examined in more detail in section 5.E.1 and Appendix J.] The following charts illustrate steps for deciding whether to commercially bind or take other action.

Once the questions have been answered, the criteria for leaf attachment (if appropriate) can be applied to the volume. Note that these charts are only models; each library must develop a system for its own particular needs. As Merrill-Oldham points out, "It would make little sense . . . for a public library to spend extra money recasing a volume that will eventually be discarded, when a less expensive binding would serve as well. The openability of [the] volume is important, but preservation of the original sewing structure is probably irrelevant." [17:7]

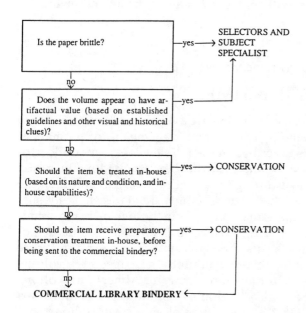

CHART 4.1. The decision to commercially bind. Reproduced, with permission, from Jan Merrill-Oldham, "Flow Charts for Library Binding: A Reassessment." *The New Library Scene* 8 (February 1989): 7.

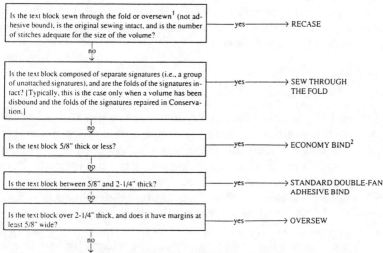

CHART 4.2. Decision tree for library binding—monographs. Reproduced, with permission, from Jan Merrill-Oldham, "Flow Charts for Library Binding: A Reassessment." *The New Library Scene* 8 (February 1989): 8.

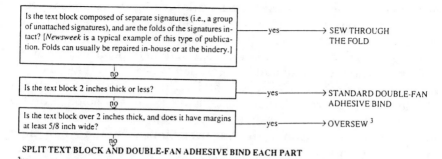

Is the text block composed of separate signatures (i.e., a group of unattached signatures), and are the folds of the signatures intact? [*Newsweek* is a typical example of this type of publication. Folds can usually be repaired in-house or at the bindery.] ——yes——→ SEW THROUGH THE FOLD

no

Is the text block 2 inches thick or less? ——yes——→ STANDARD DOUBLE-FAN ADHESIVE BIND

no

Is the text block over 2 inches thick, and does it have margins at least 5/8 inch wide? ——yes——→ OVERSEW [3]

no

SPLIT TEXT BLOCK AND DOUBLE-FAN ADHESIVE BIND EACH PART

[3]Whenever possible, an attempt is made to limit the size of text blocks to 2 inches thick or less, regardless of margin width. In this way good openability and photocopying is ensured.

CHART 4.3. Decision tree for library binding—serials. Reproduced, with permission, from Jan Merrill-Oldham, "Flow Charts for Library Binding: A Reassessment." *The New Library Scene* 8 (February 1989): 8.

4.D. Quality Control

The library has a vested interest in ensuring that the volumes it sends to the bindery are competently bound or repaired according to the *LBI Standard*. The library binder is very aware that the product returned to the library is an advertisement of the company's ability to deliver quality goods and will determine whether the company continues to have the library's business. All binders that subscribe to the *LBI Standard* have quality control procedures established as part of their ongoing routine of production. Each step in the binding procedure, from inspection and preparation to casing-in and packing, will be under scrutiny to ensure that the volume is bound correctly.

The library, too, has a responsibility for quality control if it expects to have its volumes consistently well bound according to the agreement between it and the binder and in accordance with any special instructions for particular volumes. Quality assurance begins at the point the library inspects the materials that need attention, before they are sent to the bindery. It begins with the decision about what type of treatment the item should receive—a library binding and particular type of leaf attachment, a box or protective enclosure, or perhaps the withdrawal of the book or leaving it alone.

The library's ability to implement effective quality control for library binding involves four key factors: (1) knowledge and understanding of the LBI standards for library binding; (2) ability to apply those standards to each item in the collection, as appropriate; (3) communication of the library's general and specific binding and treatment needs to the library binder; and (4) knowledge and understanding of binding materials and techniques. [5] Library staff must become familiar with the LBI standards and be trained in their application to the materials in the collection. The Preservation of Library Materials Section (PLMS) of the Association for Library Collections and Technical Services (ALCTS), a division of the American Library Association, frequently holds institutes on issues concerning conservation and preservation. In cooperation with the Library Binding Institute, the American Library Association recently published a librarians' guide to the *LBI Standard*. [18] The guide examines in detail each of the treatment options of the standards. Every staff member who is involved with library binding should attend the appropriate institute or other training programs, read the guide, and practice applying Merrill-Oldham's criteria to volumes that are candidates for binding. A tour of a library bindery is a must for staff involved in these operations. Most library binderies are happy to conduct staff and administrators through their plants and give them instruction in how books and periodicals are bound.

4.D.1. BINDING PROBLEMS

There are a large variety of problems that can befall a commercially bound library volume. These can be categorized into three areas: mistakes, cosmetic problems, and structural problems. [3] Any one of these can happen, singly or in combination, even at the best of binderies, and most should be corrected by the binder without hesitation.

Mistakes:
Library's instructions not followed.

Covering material is a different type and/or color from that specified.

Parts of the text or periodical issues out of order.

Spine lettering and/or numbers are incorrect.

Text block cased-in upside down.

Text block does not belong to the case.

Wrong edge of text block bound.

Cosmetic problems:
Covering material flawed.

Dirt on case, text block, and/or pages.

Edges of leaves stuck together by adhesive (usually seen on head or tail of text block), or excess adhesive showing.

Spine lettering crooked, improperly positioned, or wrong size.

Spine lining crooked or extends beyond text block at head or tail.

Squares too wide or too narrow.

Text block nicked or burred by dull or damaged knives or sloppy hand-trimming.

Turn-ins uneven in width or not turned in smoothly.

Structural problems:

Adhesive applied poorly at head or tail of double-fan adhesive bound volumes, causing leaves to be loose.

Board thickness inadequate for width or size of volume.

Endpapers not adhered smoothly to boards.

Endpapers not attached properly for method of leaf attachment (e.g., not sewn through the fold for recasing, but tipped on, whip-stitched, or stab-sewn).

Joints uneven in width and depth, not parallel, or not firmly impressed.

Leaf attachment method inappropriate for the text block; or specifications for type of leaf attachment or other options not followed (e.g., covers in or out, no trim, etc.).

Sewing done incorrectly or poorly (e.g., too few stitches, broken threads, sawn-in cords).

Spine lining extends less than one inch onto front and back boards.

Spine lining not smoothly and completely adhered.

Spine not shaped properly.

Spine of recased volume not adequately cleaned before application of new spine lining.

Text along binding margin invaded by adhesive, notching, or sewing.

Text block cased-in crookedly.

Text block not flush with bottom of case (if that was specified).

Text covered by adhesive portion of binding slip.

Text, illustrations, or foldouts have been trimmed.

Text obscured by sloppy application of adhesive.

4.D.2. INSPECTION GUIDELINES

Jan Merrill-Oldham has also developed a set of guidelines for inspecting library bound volumes after they have been returned from the bindery [see Appendix D]. After some practice, it takes about one minute per volume for the inspection. This procedure must be practiced regularly, and each volume, not just a random sampling, should be inspected.

A number of the aforementioned problems might be expected now and then with volumes returned from the bindery. Occasionally, every binder has turnover in trained staff or other difficulties that can lead to lapses in quality control. There are, however, at least four volume problem situations that will require communication with the binder—and the sooner, the better:

The work is not being done in accordance with the *LBI Standard*.

Workmanship is consistently sloppy.

The library's instructions are not being followed, and the binder offers no explanation.

There is a marked change (for the worse) in the quality of the work.

On the other hand, the binder will appreciate being told about significant improvements in the product. Everyone—and a binder is no exception—likes to know when the quality of work is good. Binders should be informed when they are doing consistently good work over a period of time. Positive communications are as important as those that must be constructively negative, and they will help maintain good relations and improve understanding of each other's problems.

4.E. Binding Contracts

Every library, archive, media center, or information center that has materials needing binding should carefully select a certified library binder and write either a detailed contract or letter of agreement that addresses the binding needs of the institution.

A good contract is not easy to draw up, but it is worth the trouble, especially if the materials to be bound have permanent value. The librarian, and not the institution's or agency's purchasing agent, should determine the specifications, and they should be reviewed yearly. The contract can be modeled on that of a larger library or library system, but should be made appropriate to the library using it.

Library binders, or someone familiar with the capabilities of library binderies, should participate in the discussions leading to the creation of a contract. Although it would be inappropriate for binders to take part in actually formulating a contract on which they might later bid, their contributions to a general discussion can be quite valuable. [9:13–16] Contracts are discussed in more detail in section 4.E.4. A model contract is in Appendix E.

4.E.1. SELECTING A LIBRARY BINDER

"Selection of a library binder can be a difficult and uncertain process, unless the only criterion is low price, in which case the official can simply accept the lowest bid or cheapest price list." [28:754] In "The Library Binder," Matt Roberts covers most of the points the librarian must keep in mind when going through the selection process. If the librarian is interested in the highest quality, regardless of cost, the problem can become complicated, because the highest bid or the binder with the highest price list may not offer the highest quality.

A successful "library binding program must be built on mutual understanding and cooperation between the librarian and the binder." [28:754] A good library binder must know something about the library the work is to be done for, for example, the mission and goal of the library, its clientele, and how the books will be used. The librarian's responsibility is to "become informed about bookbinding in general, and good binding in particular, in order to be able to communicate the library's needs intelligently and accurately." [28:754] Librarians responsible for binding operations must know what the binder is capable of offering: the state of the technology, the experience of the bindery staff, the quality of materials, new materials that may have been developed or identified, the level of training, and the abilities of the bindery supervisory personnel. All these must be known if the library is to receive the product desired. [28:754–755]

Because it takes several years for both parties to work out the many details involved in a successful binding program, some experts believe that once a competent library bindery has been found, its services should be retained permanently, assuming it continues to do good work. It is very difficult to maintain a mutually satisfactory binding program if the library changes binders every year, or even every few years. Binderies would like to endorse such an arrangement, but to do so would appear to be stifling competition. It makes a great deal of sense, nevertheless, to stay with one company, so long as it does competent work and its prices remain competitive.

The librarian can get a list of bindery names from the Library Binding Institute. Such an approach, however, excludes binders who may be highly qualified but are not members of the Institute. Many librarians visit several binderies, inspect their facilities, look at their work, and judge for themselves whether or not the work is good. Library binderies are few in number and widely scattered, so this approach can be expensive and time-consuming. An alternative possibility, and one that several libraries (or groups of libraries) have found worthwhile, is to request that interested binderies submit samples of their work for inspection and evaluation.

4.E.2. BINDING SAMPLES

"The purpose of viewing binding samples is to eliminate from further consideration those binders who cannot produce binding that meets the library's needs or specifications. It is important, therefore, for the library to have some statements of specifications, even if they are purely eclectic in nature and draw heavily on the LBI's own standard." [28:755] The library should require that the binder provide representative text blocks that have been double-fan adhesive bound, fitted with a new case only (original sewing structure retained), oversewn, sewn through the fold by machine and by hand, and economy paperback bound. The samples fulfill two purposes: The library binder demonstrates his capability to deliver a quality product conforming to the LBI standards, and the samples can be examples of good binding practice (if they adhere to the LBI specifications) and can be used as a staff training tool. Librarians need to study good examples of volumes bound in accordance with the standards and to become familiar with specifications for fold-sewing, trimming, and margins, as well as the procedures for handling special format materials and brittle paper. They need to learn about the adhesives and chemicals used in the binding process and, last but not least, when not to bind.

"Sets of samples should be as uniform as possible, so that all binderies work with the same problems. The samples should also consist of books representing the normal work the library expects to have done during the course of the contract. It is pointless, for example, for the library to ask for an example of binding a Braille book if the library does not acquire books in Braille. The same may be said for newspapers, portfolios, slipcases, etc." [28:755–756]

According to Roberts, a typical set of samples might include the following: [28:756–757]

1. A *periodical volume made up of thick issues with relatively narrow margins or even center spreads.* Such a sample will demonstrate the ability of the binder to sew through the folds, and its thickness will show skill (or lack of it) in proper rounding and backing.

2. A *monograph 1.5 to 2 inches thick, with an inner margin of at least three-fourths of an inch.* This type of sample will indicate whether the binder is capable of binding a book according to the LBI standard.

3. A *monograph 1 or more inches thick, having an inner margin of less than 3/4 inch, which the binder is instructed to tape-sew.* This will indicate whether the binders have the personnel to sew a book by hand on tapes.

4. A *monograph approximately 1/2 inch thick, which is to be adhesive-bound using a hot-melt adhesive.* The binder should be instructed not to round and back this book, and to cover it in a cloth lighter than buckram, such as "C" cloth. Some library binders do not have the equipment for this style of binding, and adhesive-binding can be expensive when done by hand.

5. A *very thin publication, e.g., a single periodical issue, to be covered in a light cloth, as above, and without rounding and backing.* Casing-in a thin book can be a troublesome operation, especially when trying to obtain a proper joint.

6. A *monograph of any thickness more than* 1/2 *inch, containing foldouts, maps, etc., as well as pocket material.* This will indicate how well the binder can make both a pocket and a compensation guard. It will also determine whether the bindery checks for foldouts, etc., before trimming the fore edge.

7. A *publisher's binding with instructions to rebind.* The original sewing should be weak in all samples, or strong in all, so that each binder will have to decide whether to resew or retain the original sewing.

Each prospective binder should be sent a sample package, a copy of the library's specifications, a list of instructions, and a deadline beyond which the sample will not be accepted.

Judging of the sample should be demanding and based on the problems outlined in section 4.D. The least confusing and fairest way to evaluate the sample is to prepare a chart listing the pertinent aspects of a binding. Prospective binders should be warned that no work on the samples may be subcontracted; instructions must be followed, and there should be no excessive trimming. After evaluating the samples, the library should inform the binders if their samples passed inspection.

4.E.3. THE CONTRACT

Having gone through this procedure, the library is now in the position to select the binder that best meets its needs in terms of the type of bindings it can produce; its ability to meet the requirements of special provisions, such as double-fan adhesive binding, no trimming, and sewing through the fold; and its commitment to execute the contract or letter of agreement. The model contract in Appendix E is a good place to begin the process of developing one's own approach. It is based on contracts developed by the libraries at the University of Southern Illinois at Carbondale, the University of Connecticut at Storrs, and the University of Virginia.

Certain essential specifications must be written into every contract, regardless of the size or type of library. The following are the minimum to include. [29:29–30]

1. *Collation,* i.e., putting the issues in order and making sure that no parts are missing, is an important part of serial binding. The library may do the collating itself or have the binder perform this task. Binders, in general, do a good job of collating, and assume responsibility for errors, but they do charge handsomely for it. If your staff is well-trained and motivated, it may be cheaper to do the collating in the library, but it may not be worth the risk.

2. *Mending* torn pages, damaged folds, etc. Japanese tissue should be specified for tears through the print; acid-free bond paper

for other places and for reinforcement. The type of paste should also be specified. If the library has skilled staff, it could do the mending in-house. [See section 4.F for instructions on various aspects of the procedures for mending.]

3. *Sewing,* the method to be used. This will depend largely on the format of the book, its use, value, inner margins, and the condition of the paper.

4. *Preparation for sewing,* which includes the treatment of double leaves, inserts, folded sheets, and if the volume is to be oversewn, how much of the back is to be milled off.

5. *Sewing details,* closeness of the sewing to the head and tail of the volume if it is oversewn, and the number of tapes (no less than three) that will be used when sewing through the fold.

6. *Maximum thickness* of the volume will depend on the criteria discussed in Merrill-Oldham's leaf attachment decision tree [see section 4.C.6] and the LBI standard.

7. *Endpapers,* including the number of free fly leaves, the joint, and how the endpapers will be attached.

8. *Trimming,* covered in the LBI standard, but the library may not want some volumes trimmed at all. Also, it may have to be specified that no printed material will be trimmed away at all.

9. *Gluing, rounding, backing, and lining,* bindery use of approved flexible glue, rounding and backing the book properly, and lining it with approved lining material.

10. *Covers,* cloth or buckram, and their quality. The type, quality, and thickness of binder's board to be used.

11. *Casing-in,* the quality of paste, and general method of pressing the volume.

12. *Lettering,* if other than standard, the type and type size to be used, e.g., Serif, Gothic, 18 pt., 24 pt., etc. One size and style for all leads to better results.

13. *Records of sets,* i.e., rubs or other records for serials.

14. *Quality control,* bindery inspection of all volumes for defects before they are shipped to the library.

15. *Brittle paper.* Volumes printed on poor paper should be sewn through the folds. Books whose paper is brittle should not be bound and returned to the library. The library should catch these items before they are sent to the bindery, but this covers the institution in the event they are missed.

As noted earlier, a representative contract is included in Appendix E. It contains most of the provisions any library might wish to include in its own written agreement. A library should carefully study its provisions and modify, add, expand, or delete those sections or provisions that do not reflect its own needs. The contract should be written with the library's unique needs in mind and should not be taken verbatim from another institution.

There are, of course, some materials in any collection that should be retained in their original format and should not be altered under any circumstances because of their rarity, value, or aesthetic nature. The guidelines in section 5.E.1, developed by the RLG Preservation Committee, are useful in identifying candidates that should not be sent to the binder or altered in any way. These materials should have appropriate protective wrappers or cases made to prolong their lives and keep them available for the use of future generations.

4.F. In-House Repair

During the process of examining a volume or periodical issue and while going through the leaf attachment decision tree, the staff should be alert to any problems requiring repair, either by the binder or by the library before the item is sent to the bindery. A number of simple repairs that the library can make before the volume is sent to the bindery will save money for the institution. Staff can be easily trained to make these in-house repairs, which also apply to other items not under consideration for binding. At a minimum these are (1) mending torn pages, (2) tipping in loose leaves, and (3) simple cleaning of light soil, such as pencil marks on pages. Any library can undertake these simple mending tasks with a modicum of staff training, supplies, and equipment. A number of treatments should be left to the experts, however: deacidification, removal of pressure-sensitive tape, removal of stains, and mending of very fragile, brittle, or thin paper. [8:1]

4.F.1. BRITTLENESS TEST

The paper to be mended should first be tested for brittleness (this should also be done for any volume that is a candidate for the bindery). The standard test is to fold a small corner of a page (or leaf) about three-eighths inch from the tip of the corner to the fold; crease it; fold it forward, and press the fold firmly. Fold the corner backward along the same crease, and press firmly again. Repeat the process again for a total of four folds, i.e., two forward and two backward. If the tip of the page breaks off easily, at or before the fourth fold, the paper is too brittle and fragile to withstand a library binding, and other means should be found to conserve it. [18:3]

4.F.2. SURFACE CLEANING OF PAPER

This procedure should be used only with paper that is in good condition with a *surface* accumulation of dust and dirt. Grease and ink spots cannot be removed without using sophisticated techniques and should not be attempted by nonconservators. **The techniques described here are not suitable for cleaning fragile or brittle paper or most works of art on paper.**

There are three fundamental points to remember when surface cleaning: (1) always begin with the gentlest cleaning method possible, (2) stronger methods may be used only if it is necessary and safe to do so, and (3) when in doubt, it is best not to do anything. [6:6–7]

Cleaning is important in the conservation of paper. Not only does it improve its appearance, but it removes microscopically small particles of dirt and dust that have rough, sharp edges that may cut paper fibers and accelerate their deterioration. Such practices may also carry harmful gaseous pollutants.

4.F.2.a. Preparation for cleaning

Hands should always be clean, so oils and grease will not contaminate the paper. To ensure that finger and hand marks will not get on the item, a clean white glove should be worn on the hand holding the volume or leaf. The work surface must always be clean and, if possible, white, so it will be obvious when the work area has become dirty and needs cleaning. The products described below have all been tested by conservators and are safe to use for the procedures described.

All these procedures should begin in the center of a page and radiate outward from that point; this will help to prevent any edge tears from increasing. [6:6]

4.F.2.b. Kneadable cleaner

The first cleaning method described is also the gentlest. Absorene™, a commercial wallpaper cleaner, is very effective for removing dust and loose accumulations of dirt, especially on large surfaces. One advantage of this product is that it can be used over pencil marks. It is kneadable, and if it dries out and forms a crust, kneading should restore its pliability. If necessary, a few drops of water may be sprinkled on it; if it is too sticky, it can be left to dry out for a few hours. It should be stored in an airtight container.

Remove dirt and debris by blotting the Absorene™ lightly over the surface of the paper, starting in the center and moving outward. When a portion of the Absorene™ becomes soiled, knead it again until the area disappears into the gob. When it becomes uniformly soiled, discard it. Crumbs of Absorene™ should be removed from the item being treated by blotting them with the larger piece. Don't leave the crumbs on the paper because they can become hard and abrasive, and they also may cause the pages to stick together. When dirt and debris no longer are being picked up by the Absorene™—and there is still dirt on the paper—the next technique should be tried. [6:6]

4.F.2.c. Powdered erasers

Opaline™, Dandy Rub™, and Skum-X™ are recommended for this procedure. The erasing substances in these products have been ground into powder and placed in small porous bags or pads. The bag is held a few inches over the item to be cleaned and the bag is kneaded until powder is sprinkled on a small area on the paper. The bag itself should never be used to clean the paper. The powder is then removed by careful brushing with a clean, white, wide, soft brush, such as a Japanese utility brush. If dirt remains on the paper, more powder is sprinkled on the page and is then gently rubbed in by the fingers in a circular motion. Any damage being done by this action will quickly be detected by the fingers and thus signal that the procedure should be halted. The powder becomes darkened as it absorbs dust and dirt from the surface of the paper. It should be carefully brushed away from the paper and the work surface so crumbs will not soil or abrade the item. The process should be repeated until the powder is no longer soiled. [6:6–7]

4.F.2.d. Solid erasers

"For more stubborn soil, a stronger eraser may be needed. One acceptable brand, Magic Rub™, comes in both block and pencil form. The block eraser has a larger surface area, which helps to prevent cleaning lines. The pencil-type eraser, however, is useful for working in small areas and for cleaning around areas that should not be disturbed." [6:7]

"Magic Rub™ is a soft vinyl eraser, but it is abrasive and should always be used with a very light touch." [6:7] Do not use this method with coated paper because it will cause streaking or remove the surface coating. It will also cause abrasion on soft, felt-like papers and those that have been damaged by mildew. [6:7]

The paper should be held firmly in the gloved hand, because if it slips during this procedure it may tear. The cleaning motion of the eraser is very important. Use short, light strokes from the center of the page outward. Never rub back and forth with an eraser; this can wrinkle and tear the paper. Do not erase over a tear or a weakened fold line because that might cause further damage. If the dirt persists, it may not be surface soil, so stop the procedure before the surface of the paper is abraded. Be sure the eraser remains clean by periodically rubbing it over a clean piece of wastepaper. Brush the eraser particles away from the paper and the work area with a soft, clean brush. [6:7]

4.F.3. MENDING TORN PAGES

There are two acceptable methods for mending paper tears: (1) with Japanese paper and starch paste and (2) with heat-set tissue. Books and periodicals that will not be kept in the collection permanently may be mended with archival quality pressure-sensitive tape, but this method should never be used on any item that the library deems to be of any permanent value.

4.F.3.a. Mending with Japanese paper

4.F.3.a.1. Materials

Materials needed for this procedure are [see chapter 9 for a list of suppliers]:

acid-neutral blotting paper

assortment of Japanese papers in a variety of weights and colors, e.g., Kozo, Sekishu (natural or white), Tengujo

awl or needle

bone folder

cheese cloth or nylon mesh

cooking thermometer

cork-backed metal ruler

double boiler

hot plate

light weights, e.g., paper weight, beanbag, small blocks of steel (2 inches x 1 inch x 3 inches)

measuring cup

micro-spatula or tweezers

Oriental watercolor brush or ruling pen (or Q-tips™)

polyester web

rubber spatula

sharp knife or small scissors

small glue brush (1/2 inch to 1 inch)

small pieces of glass (2 inches x 1/8 inch x 4 to 6 inches)

tablespoon

tiny whisk, long-tine fork, or wooden spatula

two or three bricks wrapped in clean unprinted paper

two or three small jars with airtight lids

waxed paper

wheat or rice starch paste

All mending should be done on a clean work surface and with clean hands. There is no sense in adding to the problem by accidentally putting the volume or leaf to be mended into a mess of sticky paste or water left over from a previous task. The first step is to select a piece of Japanese tissue that will be compatible with the paper to be mended. Handmade

Japanese paper is available in a variety of weights and colors and may be purchased from a number of suppliers [see chapter 9 for a list of suppliers].

4.F.3.a.2. Paste preparation

Wheat or rice paste is often used with Japanese paper to mend paper tears. Rice starch is more flexible than wheat paste and can be made using the same formula, but it must be cooked five to ten minutes longer.

4.F.3.a.2.a. *Wheat starch paste*

"Wheat starch paste is a strong, tacky adhesive that dries clear and is reversible with a small amount of water." [28:100] Wheat paste is packaged as a dry powder and comes in either a cooked or precooked form. Both forms are suitable for mending paper.

Cooked wheat paste is preferred by many conservators for mending materials. These pastes are reversible with a small amount of water and therefore are especially good for repairing valuable books and manuscripts. Wheat paste is prepared by putting two tablespoons or about 20 grams of Aytex-P wheat starch in one-half cup of distilled or filtered tap water. Use a glass, enamel, stainless steel, or Teflon™ double boiler, put the cool water in the top half, then slowly add the wheat starch and let it soak for about 20 minutes. The water should not be heated during this period, but should be stirred occasionally. After the starch granules have absorbed the water, put more water in the bottom half of the double boiler and cook the mixture over a medium heat, stirring constantly with a clean wire whisk or wooden spoon for about 20 minutes. The gel temperature range of the Aytex-P wheat starch is between 65 °C and 90 °C (149 °F to 194 °F). The paste will thicken and become translucent. The temperature of the paste at the end of the cooking cycle should be between 85 °C and 90 °C (185 °F to 194 °F). The paste is finished cooking when it reaches the consistency of cake mix batter and flows off the spoon in sheets. Transfer the hot paste into a clean, airtight container made of glass, stable plastic, or ceramic. Cover the container immediately to avoid the formation of a skin of paste on the surface upon cooling. The paste sets up as a semisolid mass as it cools, and needs to be strained before use. Strain the paste through a very fine (and strong) cheesecloth or nylon mesh. The straining procedure can be facilitated by using a rubber spatula to push the paste through the cloth. Scrape the strained paste off the other side of the cloth, and put it in a clean jar to use. A lower concentration of powder can be used to produce a thinner, creamier paste. The concentration needed will vary according to the experience of the mender and the task to be done. For example, a thinner solution could be used for soaking and removing the old adhesive from the spines of books. To dilute stock paste, transfer the amount needed to a second container with a clean spoon. Gradually stir in water to obtain the consistency wanted. [27:100–101]

During the last five minutes of cooking, add 20 ml (two or three drops) of a 7 percent solution of ortho-phenyl phenol in ethanol to the paste and continue to stir well. This will inhibit the formation of mold. A stock solution of the fungicide can be prepared by using 60 ml of ethanol and 4 grams of ortho-phenyl phenol, or multiples thereof, in the ratio of 15 ml of ethanol per gram of ortho-phenyl phenol. **NOTE: The solution should be stored in a dark glass bottle and labelled "Poison."** An alternative to adding a fungicide to the paste is to cover the cooked, cooled paste with an inch of tap water every day after using. Pour the water off the paste when it is to be used, and always replace the fresh water when storing it. Watch the paste closely for the growth of mold. If any is evident, either through the appearance of small dark spots or a sour smell, discard it immediately. It should last about three or four weeks. Wheat paste loses its adhesive strength as it decomposes.

Store the paste in an airtight container in a cool, dark place. Do not refrigerate because that will cause the paste to retrograde more rapidly. [27:101]

Precooked wheat starch paste is also available from conservation supply houses and is easy to prepare. It is very satisfactory for use on archival materials, provides a good bond, and, of course, does not require cooking. It also is reversible with a small amount of water. Use two tablespoons of No. 301 dry wheat paste to one-half cup of distilled or filtered tap water. Slowly add the powder to cold water, stirring constantly until smooth. It may be helpful to sift the powder through a small flour sifter into the water in order to avoid the formation of small lumps. If lumps are formed, the paste can be strained through a cheesecloth or nylon window screen to remove them. As with the cooked wheat paste described earlier, store the paste in a cool, dry place in a clean jar that has a tight-fitting lid and discard at the first sign of mold. Since this paste is so easy to prepare, a fungicide such as ortho-phenyl phenol need not be added. Make up the paste in small batches as needed, and stir occasionally while using, otherwise the water will tend to separate out of solution. [27:101]

Precooked wheat paste tends to be slightly acidic, and its pH should be checked with EM Laboratory colorpHast™ Indicator Strips [see section 1.D.1.c for instructions]. If found to be acidic, add "a small amount of calcium carbonate to the mixture (10 percent by weight of the dry wheat powder). Thus, about two grams of calcium carbonate would be added to the above recipe." [27:101]

4.F.3.a.2.b. *Methyl cellulose*

Another type of adhesive is methyl cellulose. It is a synthetic adhesive that comes in a dry, powdered form and is mixed with water to make a paste. It does not spoil like natural adhesives and can be stored almost indefinitely in an airtight container at room temperature. It is not as strong as the wheat and rice pastes, so it should not be used to tip in, hinge, or back other materials unless it is mixed with a stronger adhesive. To prepare methyl cellulose paste, slowly pour one and a half tablespoons of methyl cellulose into a cup of water and beat it in until it is smooth and completely absorbed. Stir until the mixture is like runny cream of wheat. Let it stand for 20 to 30 minutes while the methyl cellulose granules swell. If the mixture is thick enough to hold the imprint of a spoon or the beater, add more water to loosen it up. If the paste thickens over time because of evaporation, it can be thinned with water with no loss of quality until it is all used. Store in a clean jar. Since methyl cellulose is not susceptible to mold infestation, it is not necessary to add ortho-phenyl phenol as an inhibitor. As with all pastes, pour what is needed into a smaller dish or jar instead of using the paste directly out of the storage container. This will keep the paste clean and uncontaminated for a longer period of time. [27:101–102]

These are the only pastes to use for valuable books and materials. They are completely reversible, strong, and transparent when dry.

4.F.3.a.2.c. *Polyvinyl acetate adhesive (PVA)*

Commercial preparations such as PVA are considered nonreversible and should never be used on materials that are to be retained permanently in the collection. PVA is a thick, nonflammable, synthetic emulsion adhesive. It is water soluble in its liquid state but difficult to remove from materials, tools, or clothes when dry. It should be used and stored at room temperature and can be kept for about a year without loss of quality. It dries very quickly straight from the bottle. PVA can be thinned with methyl cellulose to slow down the drying speed and make it more flexible. Mix about one part paste with two parts PVA. Thinning is a good idea when using PVA in repairs with almost anything because, not thinned, it drys so quickly it may cause accidents for the unwary. Many conservators dilute PVA with water (four parts PVA to one part water and mixed thoroughly) for most book repair procedures. An exception would be when tightening the hinges of a case bound book: then use seven parts PVA to three parts water until the solution runs like thick cream from the end of a spoon. [23:69] "PVA is recommended for use on materials in general circulating collections [and] should not be used on rare, special, unique, valuable, or local interest/history materials." [23:69]

4.F.3.a.3. Mending papers

The next step in mending paper is to choose an appropriate Japanese paper and make some mending strips, the number of strips depending on the number of tears in the volume. As noted earlier, Japanese paper is handmade and comes in a variety of weights and colors. A library that plans to do much in-house mending should stock a number of different papers in order to be able to have the right paper for the task at hand. The paper selected for the mend should be unsized and close in color and weight to the paper to be mended. Sekishu (natural or white) and Kozo are good medium-weight mending papers; Tengujo is suitable for lightweight documents. Be sure the paper used is not acidic.

Tears must be properly aligned before mending to avoid misalignment of text or cockling of the leaf. The repaired page should lie flat without any wrinkles. Many tears have overlapping edges, and it is possible to reinforce them by applying a small amount of adhesive on the two surfaces that will overlap before applying the Japanese paper. In fact, in a few cases this may be all that is necessary. Straight tears may be mended with thin strips of Japanese paper torn to the proper length and width. They generally should not overlap the tear more that one-sixteenth to one-eighth inch on either side or at the ends. Curved tears must have tissue torn to match the tear, except in very long tears, where it is better to mend with several slightly overlapping strips. [27:102]

4.F.3.a.4. Grain direction

Before the tissue is torn, its grain must be determined. There are several ways of doing this, and each will be described in turn.

If the tissue has chain lines, hold the mending sheet up to the light. The chain lines should be visible, lighter than the rest of the paper, and about one inch apart [see Figure 4.7a]. The grain runs parallel to them. If there are no chain lines, the tissue can be torn in one direction and then the other. The tear that was made more easily and is approximately a straight line will be in the direction of the grain.

Another approach is to slightly wet (licking a finger will sometimes do it) two edges of the sheet: one will curl, the other will wrinkle [Figure 4.7b].

a. **Visually.** Some papers have lines, called chain lines, lighter than the rest of the paper and about 1" apart, visible if the paper is held up to the light. The grain is always parallel to these lines.

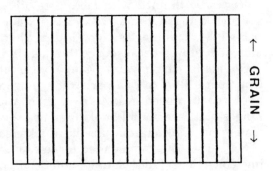

GRAIN

b. **Wetting.** This will determine the grain direction of papers that do not have chain lines.

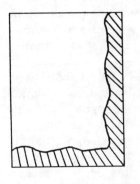

One will wrinkle.
One will curl.

(This drawing is exaggerated.)

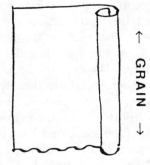

GRAIN

Wet two edges of a piece of paper.

The grain runs parallel to the curl.

c. **Bending.** Bend first in one direction, then in the other. Press down gently with the palms of your hands. You will feel less resistance in one direction than in the other. The direction of the least resistance is the direction of the grain.

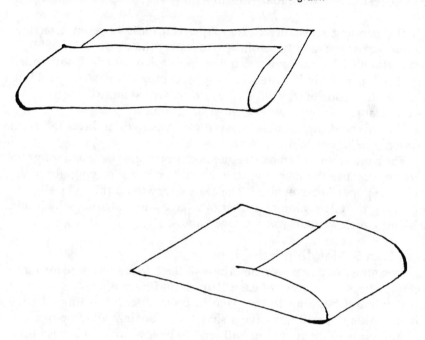

d. **Tearing.** Paper will tear approximately in a straight line in the direction of the grain, but not across it.

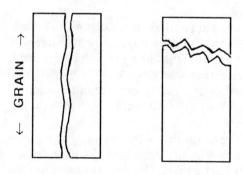

FIGURE 4.7. Determining grain direction. Reproduced, with permission, from Jane Greenfield, *Tip-Ins & Pockets*. New Haven, CT: Yale University Library, 1980, p. 8.

The grain runs parallel to the curl. A small square of the tissue can also be cut from a corner of the sheet and immersed in water (or licked) for the same result. Be sure to mark the direction of the sheet before snipping it off.

The bending resistance of the paper can indicate grain direction. Without creasing it, gently bend the paper over in one direction while it is on a flat surface, and push it down with a hand to feel how much resistance is in the fold [Figure 4.7c]. The procedure is repeated by folding the paper the opposite way (90°). One fold will resist more than the other. The one that resists the most is against the grain.

Finally, the straightest tear in a piece of paper will indicate the grain direction [see Figure 4.7d].

The page in the volume to be mended should also be tested for grain direction, because the mending strip should be in the same grain direction as the paper to be repaired. The easiest way to do this is by slightly moistening the edges along a corner of a page and watching which side curls and which wrinkles, as explained above.

4.F.3.a.5. Mending technique

Once the grain has been determined, the tissue should be torn into mending strips. The edges of each strip should be feathered in order to gain maximum bonding to the page to be mended. A feathered edge provides strength, will not have a sharp edge against which paper can bend and crease as it ages, and will tend to be less noticeable because it blends into the page. Strips can be dry torn or water torn. To dry tear the strip, run the point of a needle or awl along the edge of a ruler set on the tissue. The needle will slightly perforate the tissue without cutting the fibers and will enable the strip to be pulled or torn away from the sheet. A strip near the edge of the sheet should be torn off first, and then the needle run along the ruler or straight edge at an appropriate width for the size of the mending strip on the sheet. Thus, both side edges of the strip will be feathered. All the strips needed for one mending session should be done at once in order to have them at hand.

The water tear is done either by using a small brush dipped in water, running it along a straight edge, and then tearing in the manner described for the dry tear, or by using an India ink ruling pen (the type used in drafting). The latter makes a smoother tear line. A Q-tip™ or cotton swab can also be used if small brushes or a ruling pen are not available. Before moistening the tissue to be torn, place it on a sheet of blotting paper to absorb any excess moisture.

Curved strips can be torn to the shape of the tear by placing a piece of glass over the page or leaf, then putting the mending tissue on top of the glass and tracing the outline of the tear with the needle or wet brush. The glass protects the paper beneath from becoming wet. After the outline of the mend has been scribed or formed, carefully tear the strip away from the sheet and gently fan out the fibers on each side.

The mend is now ready to be pasted into place. Put a piece of silicone release paper or waxed paper under the sheet or page to be mended. This is done so any paste that seeps through to the other side of the page will not adhere to the sheet beneath. The mending strips should be pasted on a waste sheet that is thrown away immediately after the strip has been taken from the sheet. This step is important because the waste sheet will be covered with paste, and anything touching it (such as the volume being mended) will adhere and become stuck with adhesive. A polished marble sheet is an excellent pasting-out surface and can be cleaned up very nicely after use. Local monument companies will often give away small scraps of marble that can be used for this purpose.

The paste should be as thin and dry as possible, while still being tacky and workable. If it is too wet, the excess moisture will increase the drying time and the likelihood that the document will cockle. The strip should be pasted from the center out to each end with smooth, even strokes, pasting over the edges onto the waste sheet or pasting-out surface. Use a pair of tweezers or a micro-spatula to carefully pick up the strip and lay it on the aligned tear. Make sure that the feathered edges of the mending strip extend evenly across the full width of the tear. Be careful to not stretch the strip as you lightly tamp it in place with a bone folder or brush, working out the feathered edges perpendicular to the strip so they are smooth and don't bunch up. If the tear extends to the edge of the paper, wrap a few fibers around the edge of the leaf to the other side for a reinforcement. After the strip is tamped in place, cover it with a small piece of polyester web (on both sides of the sheet), and then cover the web with blotting paper. The blotting paper will absorb any excess moisture, and the web will prevent the pasted mending strip from adhering to the blotting paper. The patched sheet should then be placed under weight to dry. The easiest way to do this is to wrap a clean brick in paper, close the book, and place the brick on top of it. Let the patch dry overnight.

Small weights can be made of clean and grease-free metal blocks wrapped in paper or cloth. The blocks are then placed on small, narrow pieces of glass. The glass distributes the weight evenly across the tear.

All mending must be done in a completely clean environment and with clean tools and supplies, otherwise the task could turn into a disaster instead of a solution. Staff should practice mending on discarded books or sheets before attempting to repair library materials.

4.F.3.b. Mending with heat-set tissue

Coated papers can be mended more successfully with heat-set tissue than Japanese paper. Heat-set tissue can be purchased from a variety of library and conservation supply houses. Although it is more expensive than Japanese paper, it may be the only solution for some coated papers. Heat-set tissue is a lens tissue especially prepared for use in mending tears in paper, strengthening margins, and laminating weak or badly torn leaves. It is not acidic and is coated on one side with an acrylic resin. It is applied with an iron at about 190°F to 200°F (88°C to 94°C). To apply the tissue, place it over the tear area, shiny side down, and draw a very light pencil line on the dull side of the tissue about one-eighth inch on each side of the tear. Cut out the piece following the pencil marks and erase the marks. If a feathered edge is desired, perforate the tissue with a needle and tear it in the same manner as Japanese tissue. Do not make a water tear; this will inhibit the tissue's ability to make a bond. Place a small piece of Mylar™ under the tear (the polyester acts as a heat sink) and lay the heat-set tissue, shiny side down, over the aligned tear. Cover the heat-set tissue with a silicone or polyester release sheet (the tissue often comes with this material as a backing) and tack it down with a pre-heated iron set at medium (180 °F or about 91 °C). Apply light, even pressure (for about five to ten seconds) until the mend becomes almost invisible. Trim off excess tissue at the edge of the sheet, if necessary, and tack it with the iron (or bend the excess tissue over the side of the page to reinforce the patch). You need not mend a torn sheet on both sides of the leaf or page, so before mending, check the text on both sides of the page and place the mending tissue on the side that obscures the least amount of text. [16]

4.F.4. TIPPING IN

Materials and supplies needed for tipping and hinging are [see chapter 9 for a list of suppliers]:

acid-neutral blotting paper

bone folder

cork-backed metal ruler

map folder stock

micro-spatula

paper cutter

paste brush (one-half to one inch)

polyester web

pressing boards

PVA adhesive or methyl cellulose or wheat paste

scalpel and blades or X-acto™ knife

scissors

Sekishu paper

wastepaper

waxed paper

weights (wrapped bricks)

Use four parts PVA to one part water [23:69] (or one part methyl cellulose or wheat paste to two parts PVA) [10] for the adhesive to use for these procedures.

Tip-ins are loose pages or groups of pages that must be inserted into volumes. Often they are errata slips, replacements for misprinted pages,

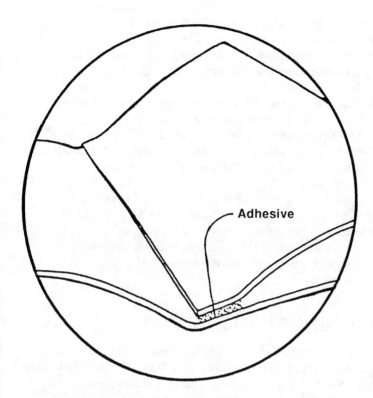

FIGURE 4.8. A tipped-in leaf. Reproduced, with permission, from *Library Binding Institute Standard for Library Binding.* 8th ed. Edited by Paul A. Parisi and Jan Merrill-Oldham. Rochester, NY: LBI, 1986, p. 17.

an index or table of contents, or photocopied replacements for pages missing, torn, or cut out of books. Photocopied replacement pages must have margins of at least three-eighths inch; if not, they will have to be recopied or guarded* with a strip of Japanese paper. If replacement pages are copied on both sides, text should line up. A thin line of adhesive is applied along the binding edge (usually) of the leaf, page, or sheet to be tipped in. The leaf is then attached at the gutter to the leaf or to the page next to it.

Single sheets are easily tipped-in; however, good judgment must be used when tipping-in a number of pages. If the inserted material is too thick, it will put a strain on the binding and damage its structure. Thick materials should be sent to the binder with instructions to bind them in the appropriate place. In some cases it may be appropriate to bind the material separately and shelve it next to the book. [22]

    1. First determine if the item to be tipped in is the same size as the pages in the volume. If not, it should be recopied and cut to

---

* A guard is a strip of paper pasted onto the replacement page or leaf to reinforce and/or extend it, if necessary.

size, remembering to keep the textual material as close to the size of that in the volume as possible for a good match.

2. Place the tip-in sheet face down on a piece of clean wastepaper; then place another piece of scrap paper (with a straight edge) about one-eighth inch from the binding margin, i.e., the edge to be tipped.

3. Brush the adhesive along the exposed edge, always brushing from the center out, toward and over the tip-on edge.

4. Remove the top waste sheet and throw it away; lift the tip-on sheet from the bottom waste sheet (throw it away also), and gently set the sheet into place along the gutter of the proper page of the volume.

5. After the sheet is in place, rub it down with a finger or bone folder and place a sheet of waxed paper on either side of the tip-in to prevent the moisture from spreading.

6. Close the book and allow the adhesive to dry completely, usually overnight, before removing the waxed paper.

4.F.5. HINGING SINGLE LEAVES

Generally, hinging is better than tipping because the hinge allows the leaf to swing freely, creating less strain on itself and the page to which it is attached. Figure 4.9 illustrates a hinged-in leaf. See section 4.F.4 for a list of supplies.

1. Cut a hinging strip of Sekishu paper five-eighths inch wide by approximately one-half inch longer than the height of the leaf. Hinging strips should always be cut with the grain running in the same direction as that of the item to be hinged. Cut several waste strips about three inches wide by several inches longer than the height of the leaf to be hinged.

2. Lay the hinge strip on a piece of wastepaper and lay another piece lengthwise halfway over it to mask the part that will not be pasted. Paste out the hinge strip with smooth brushing motions from the center outward, away from the wastepaper.

3. Remove the top waste sheet; throw it away, and gently pick up the hinge and place it pasted side up on another piece of clean wastepaper. Place the sheet to be hinged on the half of the hinge that has been pasted. Be sure to place the right edge of the sheet over the hinge, i.e., the margin that goes in the gutter of the volume. The hinge strip should extend beyond the top and bottom of the sheet. Along the area pasted, rub the leaf firmly with a bone folder through a piece of clean wastepaper. Remove the wastepaper, turn the leaf over, and place it on a new waste sheet; put a clean waste sheet over it and rub again. This will absorb some of the excess moisture, help avoid wrinkling, and reduce drying time.

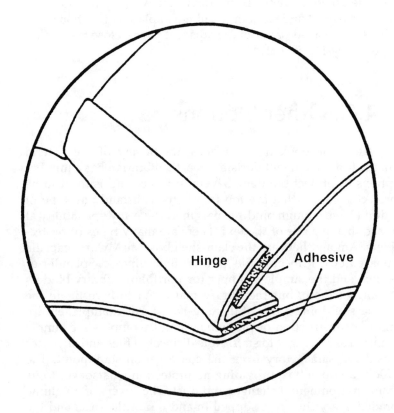

FIGURE 4.9. A hinged-in leaf. Reproduced, with permission, from *Library Binding Institute Standard for Library Binding.* 8th ed. Edited by Paul A. Parisi and Jan Merrill-Oldham. Rochester, NY: LBI, 1986, p. 14.

4. Place the hinged leaf between two strips of polyester web, which, in turn, are covered respectively by two pieces of blotting paper. Place this sandwich between two pressing boards. Weight the boards down with a brick and let the leaf dry for one to two hours.

5. After the hinged leaf is dry, trim the ends of the hinge to match the leaf.

6. Fold the unpasted part of the hinge back on itself and crease it with a bone folder.

7. Place a clean piece of waxed paper in the fold of the hinge next to the leaf and a clean piece of wastepaper in the fold and over the waxed paper. The wastepaper should be next to the hinge. Paste the outer side of the hinge and remove and throw away the waste sheet. Keep the waxed paper in the fold.

8. Take a piece of map folder stock (longer than the height of the hinged leaf) and place it into the fold under the waxed paper. Use the map board to push the hinged leaf all the way into the gutter of the book. Be sure the leaf is in the proper page and

right side up. Remove the board (leave the waxed paper in place in the fold) and smooth the hinge in place with a bone folder. Place waxed paper in the adjacent pages, close the book, and let it dry. [13:59–62]

4.G. Other Options

When the book in hand does not fit any of the criteria described in the leaf attachment decision tree, the librarian has a number of other options to protect the item. Several types of enclosures can be made to protect volumes that are too fragile to withstand any type of binding or don't have enough binding margin to leave any openability at all without sacrificing some of the text. There are many types of protective containers. Among them are the clam-shell box, the Mylar™ capsule or sleeve, phased box, Princeton file, pull-off box, slipcase, Solander or drop-spine box, and the simple wrapper (or portfolio). Library binders can make many of these, but the library may want to investigate the cost-effectiveness of doing a few of them in-house. For example, encapsulation and the construction of phase boxes and wrappers are simple tasks that can be easily taught to staff. Note: Princeton files and slipcases are not considered satisfactory from the conservation standpoint. The Princeton file is an open box, providing no protection whatsoever to its contents from environmental changes and dust. The covers of a volume may be abraded every time it is slipped in and out of the case, and the spines are not protected from dirt or light.

4.G.1. GOALS

Whatever protection is selected, the goals of the library in regard to the item to be protected, both in the present and the future, must be assessed before deciding what protection to use. Some factors to consider are listed below: [7:50]

Where will the item be housed, and who will use it? If it will be shelved in an area closed to the public, where only library staff will be handling it, a complicated design might be considered. If the material will be handled by a wide variety of patrons, emphasis must be placed on simplicity of design. It is useful to predict the number of persons who will be using the material for the first time, as the order in which to close the flaps of a wrapper can be confusing, seem unimportant, and thus be ignored or carelessly handled. The protection should be selected and designed to meet the user's needs as well as those of the object.

Who will make the wrapper? Does the library have trained staff to handle a complicated design? Does the staff have the time to spend on wrapper or protective cover construction? If either of these are problems, perhaps an outside supplier should be contacted.

How much does the wrapper cost? What financial resources are available? How much time is available? How many wrappers are needed? If money or time is scarce and a large number of wrappers are needed, a simple design that takes little time and less expensive materials should be selected.

How much use will the item receive? Heavy use materials should be housed in a sturdily designed cover.

4.G.2. CONSTRUCTION OF PROTECTIVE WRAPPERS

The purpose of a protective wrapper is multifold. A well-made wrapper will not only protect its contents from dirt and the destructive rays of ultraviolet light, but it will also provide a microenvironment that will resist the changes of temperature and humidity fluctuations of the area in which the item is housed. A tightly fitting, custom-made wrapper will have its own interior environment that will change only very slowly in response to the outer changes in the atmosphere. There are several designs for protective wrappers. Most are acceptable for a variety of uses, but the four-flap portfolio is almost universally satisfactory.

4.G.2.a. Construction of the four-flap portfolio (phase box) [4]

It is very important that the portfolio be an exact fit for the book it is to protect. If it is too big (wide, high, or long), the book will slip around inside, and air, light, and dust will gain access to the volume. An easy way to measure each dimension of the volume is to cut a long, narrow, paper strip (make it longer than the book is high) and place it on the work surface under the book, parallel to the spine, with each end of the strip sticking out from the head and the tail of the volume. The strip should be approximately equidistant from the fore edge and spine of the book. Firmly place a right angle triangle perpendicularly against the head of the volume, with its 90 degree corner squarely on the paper strip. Make sure both the front and back cover of the book touch the triangle. Use a sharp pencil, and make a mark on the edge of the paper strip where the triangle meets the book. Hold the book in place as you switch the triangle to the tail of the book and repeat the procedure on the same edge of the paper strip, making a mark on the strip where the triangle meets the tail of the book. Label the two marks "H" for the height of the volume. Turn the strip over and place the book on it so the ends of the strip are parallel to the head and tail of the book (about in the middle of the volume). Carry out the same procedure as you mark the width of the volume on the edges of the paper strip. Label those marks "W" for width. Set the book up on its tail. Place it over the paper strip so the strip is parallel to the spine and fore edge; hold the covers closed, and mark the thickness along the edge of the strip. Label those marks "T." An even easier method is to purchase a measuring box. The MEASUREpHASE™ measuring box may be purchased from The Bridgeport National Bindery, Agawam, Massachusetts.

The phase box, portfolio, or wrapper is made of two strips of map folder stock fashioned together in the form of a cross. The book to be protected is placed in the center area where the two strips cross, and the strips are folded around it and fashioned shut with Velcro™ dots (Velcoins™) [see Figure 4.10].

1. Using the method described above, measure the book for length, width, and thickness.
2. Determine the grain direction of a piece of .020-inch map folder stock.
3. Mark the folder stock with the paper strip, using the width measurement of the book to determine the width of the vertical board strip and the length measurement of the book to determine the width of the horizontal strip. The grain of the stock should be perpendicular to the long dimension of each strip. This allows the stock to fold easily.
4. Cut the board strips to these measurements.

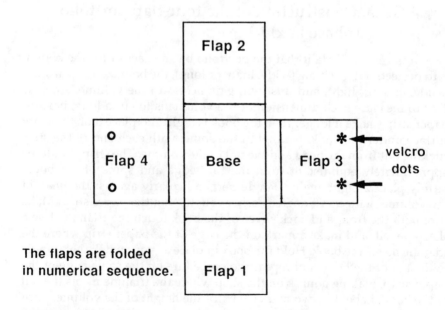

FIGURE 4.10. Phase box.

Vertical Board Strip

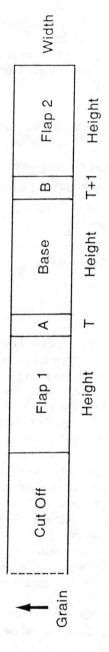

Grain

| Cut Off | Flap 1 | A | Base | B | Flap 2 |

Height | T | Height | T+1 | Height | Width

Horizontal Board Strip

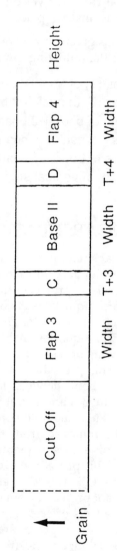

Grain

| Cut Off | Flap 3 | C | Base II | D | Flap 4 |

Width | T+3 | Width | T+4 | Width | Height

FIGURE 4.11. Phase box board strips. Source: Robert Espinosa. "Instructions to Accompany the Videotape. Number Six: Protective Enclosure: Portfolios and Wrappers," pp. 52–53. In *Instructions to Accompany Videotapes Illustrating Simple Conservation and Repair Procedures for Library Materials. Washington, DC: Library of Congress, National Preservation Program Office, July 1987.*

5. Mark the board strips for creases. Note that extra thickness must be allowed for each flap that folds over another [see Figure 4.11].
6. Trim off the excess end of the strips.
7. Score and crease the strips.
8. Round the corners, using a corner rounder or toenail clipper.
9. Glue or use 3M Scotch Brand #415 one-quarter–inch double-sided tape to adhere the vertical strip to the horizontal strip. If glue is used, press the strips under weight until dry.
10. Mark the portfolio for Velcoins™.
11. Stick the Velcoins™ in place.

The dimensions given above are for .020-inch map folder stock. For .040-inch stock use the following dimensions:

A = Thickness (T) of book + 1 board thickness (~$\frac{1}{16}$ inch).

B = Thickness (T) of book + 2 board thicknesses (~$\frac{1}{8}$ inch).

Base = Length of book + 2 board thicknesses (~$\frac{1}{8}$ inch).

C = Thickness of book + 4 board thicknesses.

D = Thickness of book + 5 board thicknesses.

Base II = Width of vertical strip + 2 board thicknesses.

4.G.3. ENCAPSULATION [6]

Polyester encapsulation is a method of providing physical support to single sheet documents and manuscripts, although the procedure is also used occasionally to protect entire books that are very fragile and of great value. The technique consists of placing the item in a "sandwich" between two sheets of polyester film and sealing the edges with 3M Scotch Brand #415 one-quarter–inch double-sided tape. The sealing can also be done by sewing or with a very sophisticated (and expensive) sonic sealing machine. This procedure is not the same as lamination, which uses heat to form a bond between the cellulose acetate sheets and the paper fibers of the item. Lamination is very difficult to reverse and is no longer considered an acceptable conservation procedure. An encapsulated item may be removed from the polyester wrapping simply by cutting the tape or other closure material away from the edges. In fact, the main advantage of this procedure is that it is fully reversible.

Encapsulation will protect the enclosed leaf from gases in the atmosphere, but it will not protect it from light or changes in temperature, nor will it inhibit the effects of acid degradation in the paper. A document being considered for this procedure, therefore, should be deacidified before it is encapsulated; an acid-free label, so stating, should be placed in the capsule with the item. Many people take for granted that an encapsulated document has been deacidified, so it is important to have a positive indication that it has (or has not) been treated. It is virtually impossible to test an encapsulated sheet for its pH level without removing it from the capsule and destroying the protective covering. Some tests seem to indicate that an encapsulated document will deteriorate more rapidly than if it is left in the open air; however, the tests are inconclusive, and if it has been deacidified and buffered it will be in far better shape than if not treated at all. The effects of encapsulation can be reduced by placing a sheet of alkaline paper in the sandwich along with the document. [6:8]

The polyester capsule enables a document to be handled without danger of its being torn or soiled. It also provides protection from dust particles in the atmosphere. The electrostatic attraction between the two sheets of plastic helps to hold paper fragments in place so that extensive mending of tears is usually not necessary, although long tears should be repaired with "bridges" of Japanese tissue at intervals across the tear. [27:106–107]

The polyester used for encapsulation, i.e., Mylar™, Melinex™, or Scotchpar™, is inert and chemically stable when formulated with no coatings or additives. The chemical stability of the paper, therefore, will not be affected by the plastic. The procedure does have some disadvantages, however, in that encapsulation increases the weight and volume of the document. If many items require this treatment, it can add considerable bulk to the collection. Because of its glossy appearance, many researchers do not like to use encapsulated materials. The process must not be used with pencil, pastel, or charcoal drawings, or any document that has a loose or flaky surface, because the electrostatic attraction of the plastic might lift the media from the surface of the paper. Storage areas with very high humidity or severe fluctuations in relative humidity may cause moisture to condense on the inside of the capsule.

4.G.3.a. Encapsulation procedure

The item selected for this procedure should be extremely fragile or be expected to have heavy use, such as a map, poster, or a brittle print that has many tears and is in great demand.

1. Examine the document for surface soil and clean it, following the procedures for surface cleaning described in section 4.F.2.
2. Deacidify, if possible. If the library does not have the ability to do this in-house, send it to a reputable binder or other agency. Whether deacidification is an option or not, prepare an appropriate acid-free label to place in the capsule, i.e., "Deacidified," or "Not Deacidified."
3. Cut two pieces of polyester film at least an inch larger on each side than the item itself.
4. Wipe the film clean with a soft, lint-free cloth to remove any dust that may have accumulated. This also sets up a static charge.
5. Align one of the sheets on a grid on the workbench.
6. Place the document in the center of the aligned polyester sheet. Hold it in place with a clean, smooth weight.

7. Apply a strip of double-coated tape around each edge, leaving a margin of one-eighth inch between each side of the document and the tape. The margin will lessen the possibility of the document coming into contact with the tape. Leave a small gap of about one-eighth inch between the tape at each corner of the sheet. This will allow the document to breath and let any gases escape that might be generated by the document.
8. Remove the weight and place the second sheet of polyester on top of the document. Smooth the film down, and force the air out from between the sheets with a clean, lint-free cloth. A rubber brayer or squeegee can also be used for this.
9. Replace the weight, and remove the backing paper from each piece of tape. Press along the tape line to ensure adhesion with the bottom polyester sheet. Keep smoothing the excess air out of the sandwich.
10. Trim the outside edges of the polyester with a paper cutter, knife, or scissors, leaving about one-sixteenth inch of margin outside the tape line. This helps prevent the tape from attracting dirt and dust. Round each corner with a corner rounder, scissors, or clipper. Sharp corners can damage unencapsulated items. [6:8–9; 27:106–107]

For materials that some patrons may want to examine more closely, i.e., by taking them in hand without the polyester barrier, a capsule can be constructed with one end open. The opening allows the document to be removed and replaced without harming the film. A capsule may also be made that will facilitate hanging the item on a wall for display by using one piece of film and folding it at one end, then taping the other three sides. Gravity tends to pull the protected item down; by folding instead of taping the lower end, the material will not come in contact with the double-sided tape.

Damaged or deteriorated books for which rebinding or full conservation treatment is inappropriate or unfeasible, but which require better protection than that offered by the phase box or wrapper, are candidates for the more substantial rigid walled box. So are loose-leaf manuscripts and prints or other unbound items that must be protected but cannot or should not be bound. Larger libraries may have the facilities, equipment, and trained staff to make clamshell, double-tray, and Solander boxes, but most libraries will have to purchase these protective cases custom-made from a binder.

REFERENCES

1. Association of Research Libraries. *Preservation Planning Program Manual and Resource Notebook,* compiled by Pamela W. Darling, edited by Wesley L. Boomgaarden. Revised ed. Washington, DC: Association of Research Libraries, 1987.
2. Barr, Pelham. As quoted by Brian J. Mulhern in *50 Years of the Library Binding Institute.* Rochester, NY: Library Binding Institute, 1985.

3. "Binding Problems Which May Occur." *New Directions in Library Binding: Life After 'Class A.'* A program planned by the Preservation of Library Materials Section of the Resources and Technical Services Division, American Library Association; September 16–17, 1988, Atlanta, Georgia. Chicago: ALA, 1988.

4. Espinosa, Robert. "Instructions to Accompany the Videotape, Number Six: Protective Enclosure: Portfolios and Wrappers." In *Instructions to Accompany Library Preservation: Fundamental Techniques; A Series of Six Training Videotapes Illustrating Simple Conservation and Repair Procedures for Library Materials*, 51–60. Washington, DC: Library of Congress, National Preservation Program Office, July 1987.

5. Eyler, Carol. "Quality Control." A paper presented at the RTSD conference, *New Directions in Library Binding: Life After 'Class A,'* in Atlanta, Georgia, on September 17, 1988.

6. Fortson-Jones, Judith. "Instructions to Accompany the Videotape, Number One: Surface Cleaning, Encapsulation, and Jacket-Making." In *Instructions to Accompany Library Preservation: Fundamental Techniques; A Series of Six Training Videotapes Illustrating Simple Conservation and Repair Procedures for Library Materials*, 5–18. Washington, DC: Library of Congress, National Preservation Program Office, July 1987.

7. Frieder, Richard. "Designing a Book Wrapper." *The Abbey Newsletter* 9 (May 1985): 50–52.

8. Greenfield, Jane. *Paper Treatment*. New Haven, CT: Yale University Library, 1981.

9. "Guide to Drafting of Contracts." *The Abbey Newsletter* Special Supplement on Binding 9 (February 1984): 13–16.

10. Harry Ransom Humanities Research Center, The University of Texas at Austin. A formula developed in the Conservation Department.

11. Jackel, Karl. "Traditional Preparation of Leather and Vellum for Use in Bookbinding." *The Abbey Newsletter* 8 (February 1984): 17–19.

12. Jones, Lynn. "Instructions to Accompany the Videotape, Number Five: Protective Enclosure: Simple Wrappers." In *Instructions to Accompany Library Preservation: Fundamental Techniques; A Series of Six Training Videotapes Illustrating Simple Conservation and Repair Procedures for Library Materials*, 44–50. Washington, DC: Library of Congress, National Preservation Program Office, July 1987.

13. Kyle, Hedi. *Library Materials Preservation Manual: Practical Methods for Preserving Books, Pamphlets, and Other Printed Materials*. Bronxville, NY: Nicholas Smith, 1983.

14. *Library Binding Institute Standard for Library Binding*, edited by Paul A. Parisi and Jan Merrill-Oldham. 8th ed. Rochester, NY: Library Binding Institute, 1986.

15. *Library Binding Manual: A Handbook of Useful Procedures for the Maintenance of Library Volumes*, edited by Maurice F. Tauber. Boston: Library Binding Institute, 1971.

16. Library of Congress. Publications on Conservation of Library Materials. *Conservation Workshop Notes on Evolving Procedures. Series 300. No. 1. Heat-Set Tissue Preparation and Application, May 1977*. Washington, DC: Library of Congress, 1977.

17. Merrill-Oldham, Jan. "Flow Charts for Library Binding: A Reassessment." *The New Library Scene* 8 (February 1989): 7–9.

18. Merrill-Oldham, Jan, and Paul Parisi. *Guide to the Library Binding Institute Standard for Library Binding*. Chicago: American Library Association, 1990.

19. Merrill-Oldham, Jan. "Guidelines for Inspecting Library Bound Volumes; University of Connecticut Libraries, March 1985." Association of Research Libraries. *Preservation Planning Program Manual and Resource Notebook*, compiled by Pamela W. Darling, edited by Wesley Boomgaarden. Revised ed., 587–588. Washington, DC: Association of Research Libraries, 1987.

20. Merrill-Oldham, Jan. "Method of Leaf Attachment, A Decision Tree for Library Binding; University of Connecticut Library at Storrs." *The New Library Scene* 4 (August 1985): 16.

21. Merrill-Oldham, Jan. "State of Connecticut Binding Contract, As Applied to the University of Connecticut Libraries at Storrs." Association of Research Libraries. *Preservation Planning Program Manual and Resource Notebook*, compiled by Pamela W. Darling, edited by Wesley Boomgaarden. Revised ed., 589–601. Washington, DC: Association of Research Libraries, 1987.

22. Midwest Cooperative Conservation Program. A handout in its *Preservation Workshop Packet*. Carbondale, IL: Morris Library, Southern Illinois University at Carbondale, 1984.

23. Milevski, Robert. *Illinois Cooperative Conservation Program Book Repair Manual*. Carbondale, IL: Illinois Cooperative Conservation Program, Morris Library, Southern Illinois University, 1984. Reprinted by the Illinois State Library, Springfield, IL, 1988.

24. Montori, Carla. "Book Structure." Paper presented at the RTSD conference, *New Directions in Library Binding: Life After 'Class A,'* in Atlanta, Georgia, on September 16, 1988.

25. Morrow, Carolyn Clark. *Conservation Treatment Procedures: A Manual of Step-by-Step Procedures for the Maintenance and Repair of Library Materials*. 2d ed. Littleton, CO: Libraries Unlimited, 1986.

26. Parisi, Paul A. "Methods of Affixing Leaves: Options and Implications." *New Library Scene* 3 (October 1984): 9–12.

27. Ritzenthaler, Mary Lynn. *Archives and Manuscripts: Conservation—A Manual on Physical Care and Management*. Revised ed. SAA Basic Manual Series. Chicago: Society of American Archivists, 1983.

28. Roberts, Matt T. "The Library Binder." *Library Trends* 24 (April 1976): 749–762.

29. Roberts, Matt T. "The Role of the Librarian in the Binding Process." *The Library Scene* 2 (Summer 1973): 26–30.

30. Roberts, Matt T., and Don Etherington. *Bookbinding and the Conservation of Books: A Dictionary of Descriptive Terminology*. Washington, DC: U.S. Library of Congress, Preservation Office (Government Printing Office), 1981.

5.
ACID PAPER AND BRITTLE BOOKS

5.A. Introduction

The authors of the Office of Technology Assessment publication entitled *Book Preservation Technologies* note that the problem of paper deterioration has been recognized for nearly a century. In fact, as early as 1898 an international conference was organized to discuss the poor quality and lack of permanence of wood pulp paper. [24:1]

The deterioration of modern paper is accelerated by the acids that accumulate in it through the papermaking process and through its contact with the environment. The acids attack the cellulose, breaking the molecular chains into smaller and smaller strings until the paper has lost all of its durability. The use of alum as a sizing agent, and in particular, alum-rosin sizing, caused the acid content of paper to rise dramatically [see section 1.D]. As the demand for paper rose, the supply of rags and linen used in papermaking could not keep up with the demand for more and more pulp. In the mid-nineteenth century, wood replaced these materials as the major cellulose feedstock. "Wood pulp contains lignin and hemicellulose that easily break down in air, causing discoloration and forming acidic compounds." [24:3] Acidic processes were developed to remove the lignin because it discolored paper. [27]

Wood pulp paper, however, can be very stable if maintained under the correct environmental conditions discussed in Chapter 2. Books published during the last 100 years and housed in libraries in Western Europe are in much better shape than copies of the same editions in American libraries, probably because they were subject to cooler and more stable conditions than their counterparts in North America. [22:8]

Nevertheless, the cumulative effect of all the acid in paper produced since about 1870 is devastating. A study conducted by the William J. Barrow Research Laboratory in 1959 determined that 39 percent of a sample of 500 books published in the United States between 1900 and 1949 had already become very weak. The pages were cracking after moderate use and would probably become too brittle to handle in another 25 years; an additional 49 percent were less durable than newsprint, the weakest paper for printing.

5.B. Acid-Free Paper Production

"The most obvious solution to the acid book problem is to make and use alkaline (acid-free) paper." [24:3] The technologies to produce alkaline paper have been developed since the 1930s. Europeans have been using them, and they are slowly gaining acceptance in the United States. University publishing houses now require the use of alkaline paper, and librarians are actively lobbying papermakers and publishers to adopt such paper for use in the publication of books, in particular. Printing books on alkaline paper eliminates the problem of paper deterioration at its source and has more direct impact on preserving knowledge than any other single effort. It behooves all librarians, archivists, scholars, and other concerned individuals and groups to continue the effort to make durable, alkaline paper widespread in publishing in this country. Such paper is the least expensive and most practical way yet devised of extending the useful life of publications (with the possible exceptions of chiseling inscriptions in stone). Section 1.F discusses in more detail the production of alkaline papers and the measures librarians, archivists, and others can take to encourage their use.

There are other ways of dealing with the acid book problem—preserving materials that are becoming or have already become brittle, and preserving the information in those materials that are already brittle and not worth saving. A recent report by the Commission on Preservation and Access sums up the dilemma librarians and archivists face when deciding upon the means and format for preservation when materials are not on permanent paper.

The practical message for the librarian is that the most expensive parts of most preservation activities are (1) selecting the materials to preserve and (2) turning the pages of the selected book for item-by-item chemical treatment, filming, or digitizing. Whether what is done at each page is to spray alkaline buffering solution, make a microfilm image, or digitally scan, the major cost is the time required to gain access to each page. Thus, each book should be handled only once. Chemical paper preservation done sheet by sheet is expensive, must be done on each copy, and does not help alleviate any scarcity of the book. Bulk deacidification, which does not require page-turning, holds out the promise of lower-cost preservation, but also does not increase the number of copies, leaves the original item in its fragile state (except for experimental processes that claim to strengthen the paper), and is not yet at a full production stage. Microfilming and digital memory, by contrast, make surrogates for the book that are inexpensive to copy. Moreover, conversion between microfilm and digital imagery is much less expensive than conversion to either form from paper. [11:2]

There are, nevertheless, major obstacles to converting to digital memory. The remainder of this chapter discusses these alternatives.

5.C. Strengthening

In cases where it is desirable to maintain the original format, embrittled materials can be strengthened by laminating or mounting. An early technique for laminating brittle paper was to sandwich it between finely woven silk, using starch or paraffin as an adhesive. During the 1930s, the National Bureau of Standards developed a lamination technique that sandwiched brittle paper between two sheets of cellulose acetate; the cellulose acetate was bonded to the paper by heating and pressing. Because it is not reversible and the heat required ages the paper, lamination is no longer recommended. The Library of Congress, however, has developed a procedure for encapsulating paper between two sheets of polyester film (e.g., Mylar™). The film is bonded around the edges but not to the paper, thus maintaining its reversibility. [24:4] This procedure is described in section 4.G.3.

Although these techniques can be automated to some extent, they can only be done a single sheet at a time. Encapsulation entails unbinding the book, taking the signatures apart, individually encapsulating each leaf or page, resewing the signatures, and then having the book rebound. The costs for this labor-intensive process are high, so it is rarely used for books.

Other processes have been developed that actually strengthen the paper through polymerization or during the deacidification procedure. Polymerization basically reverses the breakdown of cellulose by forming physical links between the broken cellulose fibers, thus restoring the paper's flexibility. Of course, this is a short-term solution for acidic papers unless deacidification is also part of the treatment. [24:4]

The most promising of these processes is the Parylene method where monomers polymerize into a clear film on book pages, thereby strengthening them. Parylene is a generic name for the various members of a polymer series (para-xylylenes) manufactured by Union Carbide and developed in Clear Lake, Wisconsin, by Nova Train, a Union Carbide subsidiary. It is stable at room temperature and pressure, but under a vacuum it sublimes into a vapor. When the vapor is heated, its molecules split into monomers that polymerize as a clear film onto the colder books in the treatment chamber. The bond is mechanical, and no thermal or chemical stress is placed on the paper. The process is irreversible. The Lithium Division of the FMC

Corporation has developed a process for strengthening paper while it is being deacidified. The process is described in section 5.D.4.e.

5.D. Deacidification

For materials that have not yet become brittle, deacidification processes have been developed to neutralize the acids that cause the paper to deteriorate. These processes also deposit an alkaline buffer that acts as a reserve to neutralize any acids that may continue to form. The objective is to extend the life of the paper; the treatment will not reverse previous damage or restore the paper to its original state.

Deacidification was originally developed by the late William J. Barrow in the 1950s and 1960s. His aqueous deacidification process effectively neutralizes the acid in paper and leaves an alkaline buffer that neutralizes acids that may form in the future. Each sheet is individually immersed in the deacidifying solution and then air-dried. The Barrow method has been widely used, especially in archives, where most of the materials needing treatment are not in bound form. A popular nonaqueous method employs either a liquid bath or spray. Sheets of paper are either dipped in or sprayed with a solution containing one or more alkaline compounds. The compounds precipitate out of solution, neutralizing the acids. Excess precipitate is deposited as a buffer. The alkaline compounds are normally magnesium or calcium carbonates, and the solvents can be aqueous or nonaqueous. Entire books can be sprayed with the solution, page by page, without being disbound. These two methods, while effective, are very labor intensive and not suitable for the treatment of the millions of bound volumes that are being destroyed by acid in libraries today. Another approach, and one that holds great promise for treatment of library books, is the mass deacidification process. A variety of technologies are either in place or being developed to treat large quantities of books simultaneously without disbinding or presorting, lowering the cost per volume and speeding up the process significantly.

In this chapter, the volume by volume, sheet by sheet processes will be discussed first, followed by discussions of mass deacidification.

Note: The following procedures should be undertaken only by qualified technicians who fully understand the effect on the paper, inks, and pigments to be treated. Irreversible damage can occur to materials that have not been tested for sensitivity to both the carrier (aqueous or nonaqueous) and the chemicals used for deacidification.

5.D.1. AQUEOUS DEACIDIFICATION

There are several aqueous deacidification techniques available for neutralizing the acids that cause papers to become brittle and eventually disintegrate. Probably the most widely used is the Barrow method mentioned above, where the paper to be treated is dipped in a magnesium bicarbonate solution that (1) neutralizes the acids in the paper, (2) washes out the poly-glucuronic acids and stains resulting from the oxidation of cellulose, and (3) deposits buffering salts in the fibers to inhibit any further acid contamination. [4]

The Library of Congress uses a modification of the Barrow method to deacidify materials in its conservation laboratory. The goal of this treatment is to neutralize the acid in the paper and leave a 2 to 3 percent alkaline buffer. The actual amount of buffering will depend on the ability of any one type of paper to absorb the magnesium carbonate deposit. Depending on the age, condition, and type (amount of alum-rosin sizing, etc.) of paper, this procedure will raise the pH to about 7.5 to 7.9.

The procedures in this section are based upon or extracted from the Library of Congress publication *Conservation Workshop Notes on Evolving Procedures, Series 500. No. 1. The Deacidification and Alkalization of Documents with Magnesium Bicarbonate. Working Draft, July 1978.* [13] The Library of Congress encourages those who are considering the use of the magnesium bicarbonate method "to seek the help and advice of a competent paper or book conservator before embarking on any program of treatment. The Library of Congress Preservation Information and Education Office will gladly supply more specific details on request about the treatment described, as well as about other aqueous and nonaqueous treatments which can be used with the supervision or guidance of a professional conservator to deal with specific problems." [13:15] "Deacidification of valuable or irreplaceable items should *not* be considered a do-it-yourself process. The following information about magnesium bicarbonate treatment should not be considered a substitute for the judgment and experience of a trained conservator." [13:1]

The chemicals used in magnesium bicarbonate deacidification are nontoxic, relatively inexpensive, and uncomplicated to prepare and apply. Used as recommended by the Library of Congress, the process described here substantially lengthens the useful life of many library and archival materials. [13:1] The treatment should not be used, however, without carefully selecting and testing the item to be deacidified. Aqueous deacidification using magnesium bicarbonate, while safe for many materials, can darken, change the color, or roughen the surface of some papers, and bleed, fade, or change the color of some inks, dyes, and paints. *Photographic prints should never be deacidified and alkalized by any method.* Photographic chemistry is complex, and alterations in the pH of prints may damage the emulsion or cause the image to become unstable.

5.D.1.a. Selection of materials to be deacidified

"Most white papers can be safely immersed in both water and magnesium bicarbonate." [13:2] Soft, unsized paper will absorb more magnesium carbonate than hard, sized paper, however, and for this reason solution strengths should be adjusted for the paper to be treated. Coated and filled papers are seriously altered by aqueous immersion. The surface of calendered papers and some other smooth surface papers may seem rougher upon drying after treatment. Paper containing groundwood pulp and large amounts of lignin will darken from any magnesium treatment. pH sensitive compounds mixed with the pulp of some papers made in the latter half of the nineteenth century will change color when the pH changes; however, the reaction is rare and unpredictable. [13:2]

Printed images based on black linseed oil, as well as many pre-nineteenth century manuscripts, are almost always stable when immersed in water or magnesium bicarbonate. Black inks, colored inks, dyes, and paints that are not based on linseed oil can bleed, fade, or change their colors. "Fresh inks, less than one year old, may smudge or feather during treatment. [Therefore,] it is extremely important to test any image prior to immersion." [13:2]

5.D.1.b. Testing

Careful, systematic examination of an item must always be done before treatment. The pH of the paper, the effect of both water and magnesium bicarbonate on the paper, and the stability of any images in the piece must be established before deciding to proceed. [13:3]

The surface pH of an item can be determined nondestructively by placing a drop of distilled water on the surface of the paper in an unobtrusive area. A nonbleeding pH indicator strip or a glass flat head electrode attached to a pH meter is pressed into the drop. After two minutes to a half hour (depending on the porosity of the paper) the reading is made. A surface reading is a simple, rough indicator of the pH but not as accurate as the extraction method, which requires the destruction of the paper [see section 1.D.1 for explanations of how to determine pH]. [13:3–4]

Water and magnesium bicarbonate solutions may change the appearance of some papers. Before the item is treated it is important to determine if this is likely to happen. Testing is done by using a sable brush to apply a very small drop of water to the paper in an inconspicuous place and then observing the reaction. If golden stains form at the edge of the drop, they indicate that the water is moving discolored matter in the paper, and the drop should be quickly blotted. If further testing is done in the area of the drop, it may cause a stain that will be difficult to control. If aqueous treatment is later found to be suitable for the item, however, immersion will brighten the paper and remove the discoloration. If there is no stain or other visible change with the first drop of water, wait for a minute, blot the spot, and repeat the test procedure several times, each time using more water. Write down your observations and keep a record of all testing procedures and results. [13:4–5]

After the spot has dried, check to see if the area appears different from the rest of the paper. If it does, then aqueous treatment may alter the surface texture of the item.

After testing with water, repeat this procedure with magnesium bicarbonate. Note that these tests do not duplicate the conditions of immersion but do serve as a fairly accurate guide to what may happen if the paper is wetted. [13:5]

Each ink and color must be tested separately with both water and magnesium bicarbonate. Select an inconspicuous spot, like the dot on an "i," and apply a very small drop of water. If the color starts to move, blot immediately; otherwise wait about a minute. If no color moves either on the paper or onto the blotter, repeat the procedure several times, each time using more water and recording your observations. Repeat the procedure with magnesium bicarbonate. [13:5]

After the magnesium bicarbonate solubility test, when it is certain that no color will move, apply a large drop of magnesium bicarbonate to each color and allow it to dry. If there is a color change, it means the color is pH sensitive (because the pH of the dried area will be higher) and will be altered by the magnesium bicarbonate treatment. [13:5]

After careful selection and testing, materials and images that have not been altered in any way may be treated with the magnesium bicarbonate solution.

5.D.1.c. Solution preparation [13:7]

A deacidification and alkalizing solution suitable for the immersion of single leaves may be made by suspending *light* magnesium carbonate in water in the proportions illustrated in Table 5.1:

TABLE 5.1. Aqueous deacidification solution.

PROPORTION OF MAGNESIUM CARBONATE PER MEASURE OF WATER

TAP, DISTILLED, OR DEIONIZED WATER	LIGHT MAGNESIUM CARBONATE (NF OR CP GRADE)[a]
One liter	8.5 grams
One quart	8.0 grams
One gallon	32.0 grams

[a]NF = National Formulary, CP = chemically purified

Source: Library of Congress. *Conservation Workshop Notes on Evolving Procedures, Series 500. No. 1, The Deacidification and Alkalization of Documents with Magnesium Bicarbonate, Working Draft, July 1978.* Washington, DC: Library of Congress, Preservation Office, July 1978.

Carbon dioxide (CO_2) is then bubbled through the mixture until a saturated solution of bicarbonate is achieved. The source of the carbon dioxide may be a cylinder of CO_2 gas purchased from a commercial supplier or the combination of a seltzer bottle and carbon dioxide sparklet ampules. Carbon dioxide is usually available in 4.4, 35.0 and 210.0 cu. ft. cylinders.*
Aluminum seltzer bottles can be purchased from restaurant supply houses

*Consult the Yellow Pages for local suppliers of gases in cylinders.

in one-liter and five-liter sizes. Those sold in hardware and department stores are usually marked and sold as one- or two-quart bottles.

5.D.1.c.1. CO_2 unpressurized method

1. Chill tap water to about 39°F (4°C) and measure into a glass or polyethylene jar or bottle. If local water contains high concentrations of dissolved iron or other heavy metals, use distilled water. The water should be well chilled before the light magnesium carbonate is added, because the reaction by which the latter is converted to the bicarbonate occurs most readily under pressure and the temperature noted.
2. Connect the cylinder of carbon dioxide to the bottle with a rubber or plastic tube, either through an aperture in the bottom of the bottle or through its neck. If the tube is inserted through the neck, it should extend all the way to the bottom of the magnesium carbonate solution. Bubble the gas through a porous glass at the end of the tube, mixing for approximately one and a half hours at a pressure of approximately 12 p.s.i.
3. At the end of this period, remove a sample of the concentration and check it by titration [see section 5.D.1.d for titration instructions). If the solution is not strong enough, continue bubbling the CO_2 gas for approximately 30 more minutes. The magnesium bicarbonate solution is ready for use when it requires at least 18 ml of reagent to reach the end point of titration.
4. Refrigerate the mixture for at least two hours before use. The solution should be clear or only slightly cloudy before using; if it is not clear, allow the excess magnesium carbonate to settle out, and then siphon off the clear solution into another bottle for use. [13:7–8]

5.D.1.c.2. Seltzer bottle method [13:9–10]

Seltzer bottles are less expensive to use when only small quantities of the solution are needed.

1. Use a one-quart or one-liter aluminum seltzer bottle (or other convenient size) and a supply of carbon dioxide sparklet ampules for charging the bottle with carbon dioxide.
2. Use the same grade of basic magnesium carbonate, No. 3, N.F., or C.P., in the proportions noted in Table 5.1.
3. Prepare the water as described for the CO_2 unpressurized method.
4. Mix the light magnesium carbonate with approximately 200 ml of the refrigerated water, and pour the slurry into a seltzer bottle. Add the water to the appropriate level marked on the bottle.
5. Secure the cap on the bottle and shake well.
6. Place a carbon dioxide sparklet ampule in the charging holder of the seltzer bottle, and slowly admit all of the carbon dioxide into the bottle, shaking vigorously until all of the carbon

dioxide is expelled from the capsule. Continue to shake the bottle strongly every five minutes for about half an hour.

7. Refrigerate the seltzer bottle for at least one hour before use. When the magnesium has dissolved, the solution should be clear or only slightly cloudy. Check the concentration by titration as described below. If the solution is cloudy, filter it through a fine grade of cotton wool until it becomes clear.

8. Keep capped in the seltzer bottle or another container.

The Library of Congress has modified these methods slightly to meet its own changing needs and requirements. For information on their present techniques and aqueous deacidification in general, contact the Preservation Office of The Library of Congress [13:9–10]. The National Archives and Records Administration also has information on aqueous deacidification procedures [see chapter 9 for addresses].

5.D.1.d. Titration

It is important that the solution be at the correct strength before using it for deacidification. If it is too weak, the pH will not be neutralized and buffered; if too strong, the paper it is meant to protect may be damaged. A magnesium carbonate drop test kit can be purchased from Taylor Technologies, Inc., in Sparks, Maryland. The kit can be used to titrate the solution as follows.

1. Filter the specimen to be titrated through filter paper from one cup to another until the solution is clear.
2. Place 5 ml of the filtered solution in a graduated eyedropper (or put ten drops in a small test tube or glass container).
3. Add one drop of EBT (Eriochrome Black T) for a hardness buffer.
4. Add one shallow dipper of Taylor Technologies, Inc. powder to turn the liquid red.
5. Add EDTA (ethylenediaminetetraacetic acid) drop by drop until the solution turns sky blue. It should take between 16 to 19 drops.

If the specimen turns blue before 16 drops, bubble or stir the solution for an additional hour or two. If too much CO_2 had been used or it had been added at too high a rate, the specimen may turn blue too soon. This is because carbonic acid has been formed; it will bubble off in a day or two and the solution will probably be fine. If it turns blue after 19 drops, add equal parts of water (i.e., take out one cup of solution and add one cup of water) to the batch until it falls within the 16- to 19-drop limit. Once it goes into solution, that's all it will take, so it can be cut with equal parts of water without changing the amount of CO_2.

5.D.1.e. Application

Single sheets of paper can, in most cases, be deacidified by immersion. The effectiveness of aqueous methods of deacidification and alkalizing, however, depends upon the paper's receptivity to water. If the paper will not absorb the aqueous solution, the 2 to 3 percent* alkaline buffer will not be achieved, and the paper will not be protected against future acid attack, particularly from atmospheric pollutants.

If the paper needs to be dry cleaned, it should be done before being deacidified, because dirt particles may be more firmly bound to the paper as it becomes deacidified.

Preliminary washing, though not absolutely necessary, reduces latent acidity and removes other water soluble degradable products. Use iron-free water, air-dry (be sure the paper is dry before treating it in the bicarbonate solution), then immerse the paper for 30 minutes to one hour in the deacidification solution and air-dry again. Shorter immersion times are possible when treating absorbent papers. Air-drying may be expedited if the paper is placed on flat screens that allow the air to reach both sides of the sheet.

To reduce cockling it may be desirable to place the damp (not wet) sheets between clean blotting or filter paper or oil-free felts and under a very light weight. Ambient air-drying is the preferred method, however. [13:13]

5.D.2. NONAQUEOUS DEACIDIFICATION (WEI T'O PROCESS)

The Wei T'o process, named for an ancient Chinese god who protects books against destruction from various calamities, was described in "Paper Deacidification, Part 3," by Richard D. Smith, the inventor of the procedure. "Methanol and trichlorotrifluoroethane (the organic solvents used in Wei T'o solution) dissolve the deacidification agent—a magnesium methoxide mixture with carbon dioxide—and carry it into paper. Initially, the excess magnesium methoxide mixture, introduced to protect against future acid attack, forms magnesium carbonate and magnesium hydroxide (dried milk of magnesia). These two chemicals react further to form basic magnesium carbonate. . . . Magnesium sulfate (Epsom salt) is the principal chemical deposited when the acids in the paper are neutralized." [21:40–41] These chemicals are the same ones introduced into paper by the aqueous processes. Wei T'o solutions can be applied by brushing, dipping (immersion), or spraying, using equipment available from Wei T'o Associates or its distributors.

According to the manufacturer, the treatment will neutralize the existing acidity, impregnate the material with an alkaline reserve to prevent future acid attack, protect against oxidation, sanitize the paper, and prevent brown stains caused by fungal attack. [8] The pH levels achieved by the Wei T'o system range from 8.5 to 9.5 on the pH scale. [3:15] All Wei T'o solutions are nonpoisonous, nonflammable, and nonexplosive. They should, however, be used in well-ventilated areas or with a fume hood, with the concentration of solvent vapors in workroom air

* Two to three percent of alkalizing salts per 100 grams of paper.

kept within OSHA limits. [8] Technicians should wear a respirator and goggles.

The materials to be treated must first be checked to ensure that inks, pigments, and so on will not be affected by the solution (e.g., run, fade, or feather). This is done by spraying a teaspoonful of the solution into the spray can cover, dipping a cotton swab into the solution, and rolling the tip over each different ink or color on the material to be treated. If a change of color appears or color or ink appears on the swab, the material to be treated is too sensitive for the Wei T'o solution. If no changes occur, dampen another cotton swab with water and carefully dampen and examine each tested area for pH color sensitivity. If a color change occurs, stop the process and obtain advice from Wei T'o Associates or a paper conservator. If no changes occur, then the solution can be used to deacidify the material. [8]

Brushing is done with a soft bristle brush, painting the solution onto the backs, if practical, of the leaves of books, documents, and works of art. [26:2–3]

Dipping, used for archival records and when no special attention must be given to each article, is a more efficient technique. Folded leaves, four-page pamphlets, leaves of unbound books, or works of art can be treated using this method. The document is quickly, carefully, and evenly slid through the solution in a dip tank in order to thoroughly wet it in one pass. Afterwards, the document is dried either on a flat support, such as cheesecloth stretched over a frame (so air can reach both sides), or it can be hung up to dry. [26:3]

Spraying is both faster and safer than brushing or dipping, and it can be accomplished using aerosol cans, airless spraying equipment, or compressed air guns. The latter is less efficient than the first two. The object is held upright and wetted thoroughly by the spray from about six inches away and then dried as described above. Slightly different procedures are recommended for each of the three spraying techniques, and complete instructions, equipment, and supplies are available from Wei T'o Associates.

5.D.3. VAPOR PHASE DEACIDIFICATION

This process uses a dry, volatile, gaseous alkali that vaporizes to penetrate the material being treated. It has implications for mass deacidification since books do not have to be disbound to be treated. Cyclohexylamine carbonate (CHC) mixed with small quantities of alpha naphthol ($C_{10}H_7OH$) is placed in interleaving envelopes. The envelopes are inserted about every 100 pages in the books to be deacidified. The gas neutralizes acid in books and boxed documents. Alpha naphthol is a complexing agent that reacts with and makes inactive the trace metals usually found in paper. The trace metals speed up the reaction between sulfur dioxide and the oxides of nitrogen in polluted air and the oxygen in the atmosphere, forming destructive acids in the paper. Interleaf, Inc., the distributor, maintains that since the trace metals are made inactive by the alpha naphthol, the paper is immune to future acid attack in polluted atmospheres, i.e., the paper is buffered. That claim has not been substantiated in laboratory tests.

The deacidifying envelopes are placed between the text pages of books for several weeks. Since CHC emits a mild ammonia-like smell, Interleaf is now making available envelopes containing activated carbon that absorbs most of the unused CHC and eliminates most of the odor. The carbon envelopes are placed between the covers and the text block of the books being treated. [6:28] Since no calcium carbonate or other buffering agent is added to the pages, there is no buffering effect.

5.D.4. MASS DEACIDIFICATION

Mass deacidification of books, papers, and other items is the only practical way to deacidify the millions of deteriorating materials housed in libraries around the world. It is simply too expensive and time-consuming to disbind, disassemble, individually treat each page, reassemble, and rebind the mountains of books published on acid paper. Certain deacidification techniques can neutralize the acid in books, and, in some treatments, deposit an alkaline buffer, without taking the book apart. These techniques not only increase the number of books that can be treated, but also lower the cost of treatment per book. According to Cunha [6:5], the Wei T'o system at the National Library and Public Archives of Canada was the only mass deacidification facility in operation in North America in 1987. An additional system using ammonia/ethylene oxide came into operation in 1988 and is available through Book Processing Associates (BPA) in Carteret, New Jersey. FMC's Lithco process came online in 1991 and the diethyl zinc (DEZ) system originally under development by the Library of Congress may be ready for production in 1992.

Several mass deacidification systems are in use throughout the world. The following sections briefly describe those in the United States and Canada that may have promise for archives and libraries. These systems are not harmful to books and paper, other than leaving some papers slightly brown in color after treatment, a condition affecting some papers with a high lignin content. The projected cost of such systems in the early 1990s is estimated to be between $5 and $10 per book. Most of this information is taken from Cunha's articles and the Office of Technology's *Book Preservation Technologies*, which should be consulted for more detailed and specific information. [5; 6; 24]

5.D.4.a. Diethyl zinc system

The Library of Congress has been developing the diethyl zinc (DEZ) process since the 1970s in an attempt to solve its almost overwhelming deacidification problem. Diethyl zinc gas, a vaporized metal alkyl, permeates paper in a vacuum chamber in a process that takes 50 to 55 hours and consists of three phases: preconditioning, permeation, and passivation. [5:385]

During *preconditioning* [Figure 5.1a] books are placed in a processing chamber, and the air is removed through a vacuum pump, lowering the pressure inside the chamber. The chamber is kept at a low pressure while the books are heated to 40 °C. Water migrates out of the books, evaporates, and is removed through the vacuum pump. The books are dried until the moisture in them is reduced to 0.5 percent of the initial weight of the paper. After the desired amount of water has been removed, the chamber is purged with nitrogen gas to ensure that no air remains in the chamber [Figure 5.1b]. Preconditioning takes from 18 to 20 hours. [5:385, 387]

Permeation involves introducing small amounts of DEZ vapor into the chamber [Figure 5.1c]. The vapor is continually fed into the chamber as it permeates the books, until all the acid in the book paper is neutralized. DEZ vapors react with the acids and water in the books, generating both heat and ethane gas. The DEZ reacts with the residual moisture in the books, creating zinc oxide, which is deposited in the paper fibers as an alkaline reserve. The ethane gas is vented to the atmosphere; any unreacted DEZ is recycled until no more heat or ethane are produced or until the desired amount of zinc oxide has been deposited [Figure 5.1d]. The reaction of the moisture with the DEZ takes about four hours. The ethane gas and any remaining DEZ are purged by a nitrogen gas sweep to ensure the removal of all remaining vapor [Figure 5.1e]. The entire permeation phase requires eight hours. [5:387]

Passivation and postconditioning consist of removing excess DEZ and returning moisture to the books. Water vapor is injected into the chamber to rehydrate the books to at least 75 percent of the library stack equilibrium moisture content [Figure 5.1f]. The chamber pressure rises slightly when the water is added; the amount of water absorbed by the books is indicated by book weight gain on the load cells. After a 24-hour soak, the chamber is vented to the atmosphere, and the deacidification process is complete. Passivation takes about 25 to 30 hours. After deacidification the books are removed from the chamber and returned to library stacks or humidity controlled postconditioning rooms for final moisture replenishment. Preselection of books based on size, binding, paper type, inks or colors, or condition is not necessary in the DEZ process. [5:387]

After neutralization is complete, the pH of the treated paper is from 7.0 to 7.5 and an alkaline reserve of 1.5 to 2.0 percent is established. The cost is estimated to be about $4.50 per book (in 1988), based on a run of 500,000 volumes. This figure includes capital cost amortization and $1.70 for operating costs. [6:23–24] A DEZ deacidification pilot plant designed and built by Texas Alkyls is currently in operation in Houston.

The Library of Congress believes that the DEZ process will meet its particular needs better than any other, but in September 1990 issued a

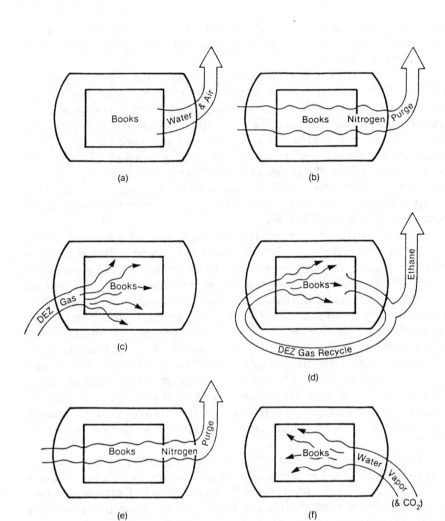

FIGURE 5.1. Key steps in the DEZ treatment process. Source: U.S. Congress, Office of Technology Assessment. *Book Preservation Technologies, OTA-0-375.* Washington, DC: U.S. Government Printing Office, May 1988, p. 24.

Request for Proposal (RFP) "To Provide Deacidification on a Mass Production Level of Paper-Based Books in the Collections of the Library of Congress." [10:97] Bids are expected in early 1991 and a plant should be operational in 1992 or 1993 (depending on the speed of the bid selection process through the federal bureaucracy). The RFP is very specific about the outcomes expected for the books to be deacidified. DEZ may or may not be the deacidification process selected, however, since the RFP does not specify a particular chemical or procedure. The plan is to contract the system out to a firm that will build a treatment center using private capital and pay that contractor a fixed price per book to operate it. The Library's goal is to deacidify one million books annually over a period of 20 years. [10:98]

5.D.4.b. Wei T'o

The mass deacidification process developed by Wei T'o Associates is a nonaqueous liquid process that uses the same basic chemistry as the manual Wei T'o processes currently in use in many libraries. A mass deacidification pilot plant was built for the Canadian National Library and National Archives in 1979. The plant was designed to treat 30 books at a time. Since 1981, the Canadian Library and Archives have been operating the system on a semi-production scale basis, treating about 120 to 150 books per 8-hour day. The process uses methoxy magnesium methyl carbonate dissolved in methanol and mixed with Freon 12 and Freon 113. These freons are liquid gases, normally used as refrigerants,

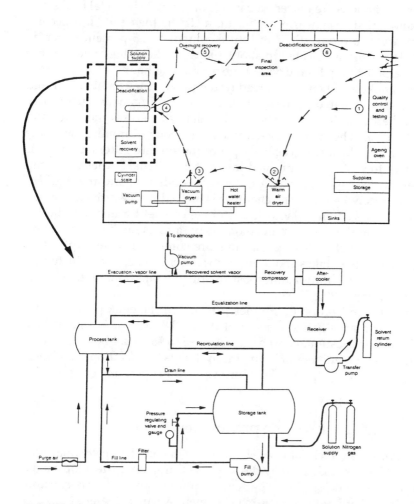

FIGURE 5.2. Wei T'o process (steps in sequence). Source: U.S. Congress, Office of Technology Assessment. *Book Preservation Technologies, OTA-0-375.* Washington, DC: U.S. Government Printing Office, May 1988, p. 88.

that allow the methoxy magnesium carbonate/methanol solution to penetrate into the paper. Books are immersed in the solution and the methoxy magnesium methyl carbonate reacts with moisture in the books, theoretically forming magnesium carbonate, magnesium hydroxide, and magnesium oxide. These compounds react with acids in the paper to form stable, neutral salts. Excess amounts of the compounds will join to form a mixture (called basic magnesium carbonate) that acts as the alkaline buffer. [24:87]

Books must be preselected for their suitability for treatment. The Wei T'o solution causes some feathering of alcohol-soluble inks and smudges some colors in book illustrations. The Wei T'o solvents clean book paper during the deacidification process, but they also detrimentally affect the paper sizing, increasing the wettability of the book pages. [5:436]

Selected books are placed in batches of about 30 in metal baskets or crates and dried in a warm air vacuum dryer, then put in a second vacuum dryer to reduce their moisture content to 0.5 percent water by weight. The books are heated to about 100°C and held there overnight at a pressure of 0.2 torr. Total drying time is about 36 hours.

The books are then transferred to the processing chamber. Air and moisture are evacuated from the chamber; the environment must be dry because the deacidifying solution will react with excess moisture and turn into a gel. The tank is pressurized for about 40 minutes with the solvent vapor, which wets the book pages thoroughly. After treatment is completed, the solution is drained into a storage tank. A vacuum pump removes excess vapors, sending them to a condenser, and the liquid is stored in a receiving tank. The chamber is purged with warm air, and the crates are removed and placed in a storage cabinet for about 16 hours. Here any remaining solution or freon evaporates as the books warm up and regain some of their original moisture content. The deacidification and buffering phase takes about one hour; the entire treatment, including pre-drying, deacidification, and post-treatment conditioning, takes a little over two days. [20:87–89]

After neutralization is complete, the pH of the book paper is from 8.5 to 9.5, and an alkaline reserve of 0.7 to 0.8 percent is established. [24:91] The cost is estimated to be about $3.95 to $6.50 per book (in 1987), depending on the number of hours the system is in operation each week. This figure includes capital cost amortization and operating costs. [5:421]

5.D.4.c. Bookkeeper process [6:35]

Preservation Technologies, Inc., of Sewickley, Pennsylvania, now has the patent formerly held by the Koppers Company to develop a mass deacidification process. Other systems require costly and time-consuming predrying of books, which may accelerate paper degradation. The Bookkeeper process deposits a suspension of fine (submicron) particles of magnesium oxide (MgO) dispersed in trichlorotrifluoroethane (Freon

113), a fluorocarbon. The alkaline agent (MgO) is deposited directly on the paper fibers so that no chemical reaction is necessary to accomplish the transfer. Because the submicron particles are smaller than the fiber dimensions, they thoroughly impregnate the paper and adhere to the fibers when they are flooded with the dispersion.

The treatment of bound volumes is carried out in a closed chamber. The books are loaded spine down into wire metal trays. The trays are then loaded into the chamber, the door closed, and the magnesium oxide dispersion pumped in, filling the chamber completely. The book trays are gently raised and lowered mechanically in order to cause the pages of the books to separate and fan out, providing access of the dispersion to each page. The motion is continued for several minutes until the treatment is complete; then the liquid dispersion is pumped back into a storage tank. The freon is vaporized from the books, and they are dried during the vacuum recovery phase. After the chamber is opened, the books are dry to the touch and show no visible effects of the treatment. [9:168] The entire cycle time from loading to removal of the books is under three hours, although it is possible to deacidify bound volumes in five minutes. [6:36]

The process does not immediately neutralize the acids present in the paper. Rather, when the books are immersed in the mixture, the magnesium oxide particles are implanted into the paper, and deacidification occurs later as the acids migrate to and react with the particles over time.

The system can be designed as either a batch or a continuous process. Figure 5.3 illustrates the design for continuous processing.

After treatment is complete, the surface pH of the book paper is from 8.0 to 9.0, and an alkaline reserve of 2.0 percent is established. [24:91] The cost is estimated to be about $4.00 to $6.00 per book (in 1988),

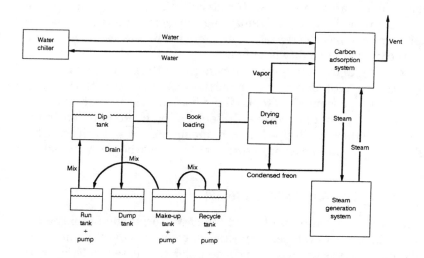

FIGURE 5.3. Bookkeeper process. Source: U.S. Congress, Office of Technology Assessment. *Book Preservation Technologies, OTA-0-375.* Washington, DC: U.S. Government Printing Office, May 1988, p. 90.

based on treatment of over 1,000 books. It includes all operating costs, raw materials, labor, maintenance, and depreciation, but not the cost of handling the books in the library before or after treatment. [6:39]

The Bookkeeper process may be an in-house option for libraries because of the simple equipment, relatively low capital cost, and lack of hazards. If the system were installed in a library it would eliminate the costs of packing and transportation to an outside facility.

5.D.4.d. Book Preservation Associates process

Information Conservation, Inc. (ICI), of Greensboro, North Carolina, in association with Book Preservation Associates (BPA) of Carteret, New Jersey, are offering a mass deacidification process to libraries. [6:47–55]

Ammonia and ethylene oxide react to form ethanolamine, which permeates the cellulose fibers in book paper and neutralizes acids by forming neutral crystalline salts. A side benefit is the destruction of mold and insects by the ethylene oxide, a powerful fumigant. Thus the process sterilizes the books in addition to deacidifying them.

Books are packed and sealed in corrugated boxes (15 to 25 books per box, depending on their size). The boxes are placed on metal pallets and moved into the treatment chamber. Air is removed from the chamber, a partial vacuum created, and the climate in the chamber is adjusted to 70 percent RH and 100 °F. Preheated aqueous ammonia is introduced into the chamber, followed by ethylene oxide gas. The ammonia becomes a gas and is drawn into the cellulose. The ethylene oxide reacts with the ammonia to create basic ethanolamines with the cellulose matrix of the books; this process neutralizes the acids. Surplus ethanolamines create the equivalent of an alkaline reserve and act as buffering agents against future acid contamination. The remaining unreacted ethylene oxide and ammonia are removed by repeated vacuum and air washes. Turnaround time at the treatment facility is 36 hours.

According to the company, treatment raises the pH to a range of 7.0 to 9.0. Treatment cost, depending on the number of books in the boxes, is estimated to range from $3.00 to $5.00 per book (in 1988) if the boxes are picked up by the company. [6:49–50] Books to be treated are left in the boxes in which they are shipped, thus reducing the cost to the library. No preselection is required except to sort out old leather-bound volumes.

5.D.4.e. Lithco process [6:56]

The Lithium Division (Lithco) of the FMC Corporation of Bessemer, North Carolina, has developed a process whereby two deacidifying compounds, one magnesium-based and the other zinc-based, interact with cellulose and deacidify, buffer, and strengthen paper. The process comprises three steps: preconditioning, impregnation, and postconditioning. Books and materials to be deacidified are deposited in sealed treatment containers

TABLE 5.2. Description of deacidification process.

PROCESS	DEVELOPED BY	VENDOR	DEACIDIFICATION AGENT/PROPELLANT IF APPLICABLE	STRENGTHENING PROPERTIES	DEGREE OF PRESELECTION REQUIRED	CYCLE TIME	DEVELOPMENT STAGE
DEZ	Library of Congress	Akzo Chemicals, Inc.	Diethyl zinc gas		Heavily coated paper, as in serial runs, may need to be treated separately	60 hours	Pilot plant
Wei T'o	Richard Smith/ Wei T'o	Union Carbide Paper Preservation Services	Liquified gas methoxy magnesium methyl carbonate dissolved in methanol and mixed with Freon 112 and Freon 113		Preselection required as some colors bleed, certain inks run, and plastic covers cannot be treated	48 hours	Facility at National Library of Canada. Similar plant at BN de France.
Book Preservation Associates		Information Conservation, Inc.	Ethylene oxide and ammonia	Said to strengthen some materials	Leather materials not suitable for treatment	36 hours	Available commercially
Bookkeeper	Koppers	Richard Spatz, Preservation Technologies, Inc.	Magnesium oxide in Freon 113	Said to strengthen some materials	Minimal	Under 3 hours	Laboratory
Lithco	Lithium Corporation of America	Lithium Corporation of America	MG-3, a Lithco proprietary compound + Freon 113	Said to strengthen some materials	Minimal	Under 8 hours	Pilot plant

Source: Reproduced, with permission, from Karen Turko. *Mass Deacidification Systems: Planning and Managerial Decision Making.* Washington, DC: Association of Research Libraries, 1990, p.6.

at the library. The containers remain closed and locked throughout the process and are returned to the library with seals intact.

During preconditioning, the books are dried, using dielectric heating, to a moisture content of approximately two percent by weight. The acids are neutralized.

After preconditioning, the books are impregnated with magnesium butoxy triglycolate (MG-3) solution. During this stage, the buffer and strengthening ligands (negatively charged groups of atoms) in MG-3 are deposited at the molecular cellulose level using a solvent. The ligands, which are attached to the magnesium and zinc atoms in the compounds, interact with the cellulose and strengthen the paper. Laboratory tests indicate that the paper is strengthened by a factor of 10 to 12. No cosolvents such as methanol are required.

In the postconditioning stage, excess solution is drained and the solvent is removed and recovered under vacuum. Books are removed from the treatment unit at room temperature. Total processing time is under three hours. [7:1–2]

The company says pH is raised by about 7 to 9 percent, and the alkaline reserve deposited is 1.5 to 1.7 percent for the zinc compound and 2.1 to 2.3 percent for the magnesium. [6:56] Cost of treating a volume is estimated to be from $5.00 to $8.00, including transportation. A demonstration plant with a capacity for deacidifying and strengthening 300,000 books a year began operation in May 1990. The company plans to build four operating plants with a total capacity of from one to four million books a year. [17:1]

Table 5.2 briefly summarizes the five mass deacidification processes and their basic chemistry.

5.E. Preservation Microfilming

Many library and archival materials should not be deacidified and/or strengthened because of their fragile condition, but converted instead to another medium in order to preserve the information they contain. Preservation microfilming is the process of microfilming the intellectual content (the written or printed matter and illustrations) of archival and library materials, following the standards and specifications necessary to provide optimal bibliographic and technical quality. The specifications include preparation of materials prior to filming, processing of the microfilm, and storage. [18:2]

Microfilm (roll film housed on a reel) or microfiche (a flat sheet usually 4 x 6 inches in size) can be used for this application. Microfilm has traditionally been used for serial publications, and microfiche for monographs, reports, and pamphlets.

Microforms can be produced in-house or contracted out to micro-form service bureaus or companies. However it is done, it is very important that all applicable technical standards and bibliographic spec-ifications are followed to ensure the microform's quality, consistency, and permanence.

Preservation microfilming may be a viable alternative for protecting the information the item contains when the item itself does not have any intrinsic value. The concepts of artifactual, intrinsic, historic, and bibliographic value emphasize the special status of the original and the caution with which decisions to microfilm and/or discard should be approached. These terms are often used interchangeably, even though they are defined differently, but understanding their meaning is important in determining what should and should not be microfilmed. The following definitions are taken from interpre-tations in Gwinn's book on *Preservation Microfilming*. [18:55]

Intrinsic or artifactual value: "the value of a single book, (or other library item) alone, without consideration of the aggregate value when a book is considered part of a collection of great worth" [16:182] *or* "the archival term that is applied to permanently valuable records that have qualities and characteristics that make the records in their original form the only archivally acceptable form for preservation. Although all records in their original physical form have qualities and characteristics that would not be preserved in copies, records with intrinsic value have them to such a significant degree that the originals must be saved." [25:1] [See also appendix J.]

Bibliographic value: "the importance of information to be gathered from a book through a study of its physical parts, structure, format, and printing." [16:179]

Historic value: "the interest that a book or binding has beyond the information transmitted by the printed words; the integrity of a book in terms of the original production details and accidents of time." [16:182]

5.E.1. SELECTION OF MATERIALS FOR MICROFILMING

Some materials have physical or intellectual qualities that may be totally or significantly lost in their reproductions. "It is the physical *and* informational nature of an item—its age, its rarity, its historical or technological or bibliographic importance, its close connection with an event, etc.—that should prevent it from being discarded, even if it is reproduced in some fashion." [18:55–56] Guidelines have been developed by the profession to help identify the attributes of an item that will enable decision makers, those persons having curatorial responsibility, to come to the correct conclusion in regard to its disposition.

5.E.1.a. Materials suitable for microfilming

Many libraries consider the following types of materials suitable for this procedure:

—books, monographs, and pamphlets on brittle paper
(usually published after 1870)

—newspapers

—long serial runs on poor paper

—statistical materials

—scrapbooks

—vertical files (clippings, etc.)

—letter books and manuscript materials

—ledger books and account books

—certain types of atlases or maps

—government reports, foreign and domestic

—carbon copies, stencil-mimeograph, thermofax, verifax, and other reproductions of correspondence [18:34]

5.E.1.b. Items not acceptable for microfilming

Other types of materials may not be suitable for preservation microfilming because of the difficulty in satisfactorily reproducing them or because of the nature of the item itself.

Many items are important largely or entirely because of their format, and there are often clear reasons to maintain those titles in their original states. In other cases, the reasons may not seem so clear, but there may be certain physical elements that should be weighed carefully before contemplating either withdrawal or a conversion to another format for any reasons, including deterioration, space saving, superseded editions, or duplication. The Research Libraries Group, Inc., has published a number of justifications for the retention of items in their original format. [20:82–84] They are reprinted here with permission.

Considerations in the Retention of Items in Original Format

1. Evidential value

a) Physical evidence associated with the printing history of the item, such as registration pin marks, cancels, printing techniques, paper, and typographic errors

b) Evidence of the binding history of the volume such as original sewing stations, binding structure, printed wastepapers used in the spine lining, and cover materials

2. Aesthetic value

a) Bindings of unusual interest/technique/artistry

—Historical/developmental interest of structure/materials

—Signed/designer bindings

—Early publishers bindings

b) Other book decorations of interest (e.g., gilding, gauffering, decorated endpapers, fore-edge paintings)

c) Illustrations not easily reproducible or meaningful only in the original

—Color

—Original woodcuts/etchings/lithographs, etc.

d) "Artists' Books" where the book is designed as an object

e) Original photographs

f) Maps of importance

g) Pencil, ink, or watercolor sketches

3. Importance in the printing history of significant titles

a) First appearance

b) Important bibliographic variants

c) Important/collected fine press printings

d) Indications of technique important to the printing history

e) Examples of early local imprints

4. Age

a) Printed before [specific dates] in [specific countries]* (e.g., all titles printed before 1850 in the U.S., or, all books printed before 1801)

b) Printed during the incunabula period of any area (the first decades)

c) Printed during specific later periods, such as war years, in specific countries

---

*Each library or archive should insert its own set of dates and/or countries. For a list of cutoff dates for rare books, see Swara, Tamara, and Bohdan Yasinsky. *Processing Manual,* Mono-11. Washington, DC: Library of Congress, Preservation Microfilming Office, 1981. The same list can also be found in: American Imprints Inventory. *Manual of Procedures,* 46. 5th ed. Chicago: Historical Records Survey, 1939.

5. Scarcity
   a) Rare in RLG/NUC [Research Libraries Group/National Union Catalog] and major European libraries
   b) Less than 100 copies printed
6. Association value of important/famous/locally-collected figures or topics
   a) Notes in the margin, on endpapers, within the text
   b) Bookplates and other marks of ownership of such figures; other evidence of significant provenance
   c) Inscriptions/signatures of importance
7. Value: Assessed or sold at more than *specific cost* (Each library or archive should assign the latest selling cost as it sees fit.)
8. Physical format/features of interest
   a) Significant examples of various forms as evidence of technological development
   b) Unique or curious physical features (e.g., watermarks of interest, printing on vellum, wax seals, etc.)
   c) Certain ephemeral materials likely to be scarce, such as lettersheets, posters, songsters, and broadsides
   d) Manuscript materials
   e) Miniature books (10 cm or less in height)
   f) Books of questionable authenticity where the physical format may aid in verification
   g) Representatives of styles/fads/mass printings that may now be rare
9. Exhibit value
   a) Materials important to an historical event, a significant issue, or in illustrating the subject or creator
   b) Censored or banned books

Appendix J contains the National Archives and Records Administration staff information paper defining intrinsic value of archival materials. It is a useful decision-making guideline for the retention of archival materials, and can be used in conjunction with this list.

5.E.1.c. Preservation options

An excellent source of information that outlines in detail the selection procedures, techniques, and criteria to be followed in selecting materials for preservation microfilming is Nancy Gwinn's *Preservation Microfilming*. [18] Her book also examines the administrative decisions, production planning and preparation of materials, microfilming practices and standards, bibliographic controls, and cost controls, and includes a sample contract. It should be consulted when gathering information about the implementation of a preservation microfilming program. Gwinn covers the preservation options available for the average librarian or archivist to consider when deciding just what action to take to either preserve the individual item or the information it contains. The following is taken, with permission, from chapter two of *Preservation Microfilming*. [18:27–30]

Preservation Options
Generally speaking, the most crucial decision to be made regarding an individual item is this: Must this book (or map, letter, scrapbook, document, etc.) be preserved and retained in its original form?

The "yes," "no," or "maybe" answer to this question will give you the necessary guidance for the review of the menu of preservation/conservation options currently available. Only if you are aware of the full range of preservation options can you make wise decisions about which items are suitable for preservation microfilming. Here is a brief comment on the advantages and disadvantages of each. Some are obviously more relevant to library collections than to those in archives.

1. Options to repair items in order to retain the original format

   a) Minor repairs: repairing book bindings, mending tears in flat paper materials, etc.

   Positive aspects: original format retained; usually low unit cost, depending upon condition.

   Drawbacks: not suitable for materials that have sustained significant loss of paper strength and are, therefore, too fragile to benefit from simple repair.

   b) Commercial rebinding of hard-cover books.

   Positive aspects: relatively inexpensive method of providing primary protection for text block.

   Drawbacks: usually cannot be used for brittle papers; not a long-term solution to unstable or brittle papers; generally not suitable for rare materials.

   c) Full conservation treatments, including aqueous/nonaqueous deacidification with polyester encapsulation and/or conservation rebinding.

   Positive aspects: retains the original item in a stable format.

   Drawbacks: high labor cost of treatments; lack of skilled personnel/resources to take on such treatment; cannot be expected to make an impact on large-scale masses of brittle materials.

   d) Protective enclosures/phase wrapping of books.

Positive aspects: maintains all bibliographic pieces together in original format at a relatively low cost; provides a micro-environment to buffer storage environment.

Drawbacks: does not stop ongoing deterioration; is only a "phase" of preservation, a step to keep all parts of a volume together until other treatments become available or affordable.

e) Protective enclosure of single sheets by encapsulating with polyester film.

Positive aspects: retains original format and protects with a stable material.

Drawbacks: ideally, is preceded by a deacidification process, which is specialized and expensive; encapsulated item is heavier and bulkier than the original; cost of polyester is significant.

f) Mass deacidification processes.

Positive aspects: large quantities of materials can be safely stabilized at low unit cost, and thus retained in original format.

Drawbacks: not all types of materials can be deacidified in existing processes because of effects upon inks, leather, etc.; capital cost of facility is high and unavailable to most institutions at this time; neither restores strength to weakened papers nor repairs binding structures.

2. Options to replace items with hard (paper) copy

a) Replace with hard copy—from out-of-print market.

Positive aspects: collection receives exact or near-exact duplicate of deteriorated/damaged item.

Drawbacks: high expense for some items; lack of availability of rare, scarce, or unique items; exact replacement copy unlikely to be a permanent/durable copy and will require treatment in the future.

b) Replace with hard copy—new in-print copy.

Positive aspects: collection receives near-exact duplicate of item, usually at reasonable cost.

c) Replace with hard copy—reprint edition.

Positive aspects: collection receives exact or near-exact duplicate.

Drawbacks: reprint edition may not be permanent/durable; cost of reprints often high.

d) Replace with hard copy—create a photocopy in-house or purchase one and bind.

Positive aspects: exact text replacement in similar format of original; can use permanent/durable papers.

Drawbacks: cost of duplication and binding can be considerable for materials in bulk; only one copy made, so inexpensive copies not available for scholarly use generally.

3. Option to replace item with commercially available microform

Positive aspects: often the least expensive method of preserving an item; with reader-printers, microforms can be relatively easily enlarged in the form of paper copies for users; space reduction can be significant, especially with longer serial runs, because of the space efficiency obtained with full 100-foot reels of microfilm (at approximately 1500 frames per 100 feet) or with microfiche.

Drawbacks: not all materials are appropriate for, nor available in, microform; often, commercial sources do not make monographs available individually; parts of serials and series might be commercially available in microform, but, if acquired, could present difficulties in circumstances where part of the title is found in hard copy at one place and part in microform in another place within the library; not all commercially available microforms are produced in compliance with archival standards (e.g., they are not produced on silver-gelatin film); microforms require somewhat more extensive recataloging than other replacements; microforms require equipment and facilities for reading and service.

4. Option to discard/deaccession with no replacement

Positive aspects: since preservation selection decisions function like acquisition decisions, decision to discard indicates lack of value to the collection; decision "not to preserve" reserves funds for items in the collection that warrant preservation treatment.

Drawbacks: has limits in research collections where all materials acquired can often be assumed, for the most part, to have long-term research value in some format; use of the discard/deaccession option in research collections may result in significant loss to the collections.

5. Option of no action, i.e., reshelve as is

Positive aspects: if this option is used conscientiously with a plan of priorities for preservation treatment, it has an effect of "benign neglect," one that frees resources to preserve more important items in the collection.

Drawbacks: as in the discard/deaccession option, this option has limits in a research collection where materials are acquired for their permanent research value; use of the "do-nothing" option will result eventually in permanent loss to the collection.

6. Option of providing preservation by storage environment (placing items in controlled temperature, relative humidity, light, air quality conditions)

Positive aspects: by slowing down rate of deterioration, preservation in original format for many types of materials is possible; long-term storage of items can be maintained at a low unit cost.

Drawbacks: major capital outlay required to build and equip a facility that maintains cool temperatures, moderate relative humidity, appropriate light levels, and purified air; materials that have significantly deteriorated in physical strength or have damaged structures are not restored in this method; deterioration is considerably slowed, but not stopped altogether in this option; if storage is in a remote location, there is the added expense of selecting and changing catalog records of items to be moved.

7. Option to preserve intellectual content in microform by using an in-house facility or a filming service agency

Positive aspects: intellectual or informational contents of materials are captured and preserved on a very stable medium; after initial filming service, copies are easily and cheaply produced for wider dissemination to other institutions; space reduction, especially for serial publications, is significant; for certain materials this is the only viable option for preserving content; hard copy (e.g., Copyflo*) can be created for appropriate items (music, dictionaries, etc.).

Drawbacks: strict adherence to technical standards for the selection of film stock, processing procedures, and storage of master negatives is necessary; microforms require more extensive recataloging than other replacements; not all materials that are damaged or deteriorated are suitable for this type of preservation; it can be at times an irreversible process, because damage may occur in filming certain types of materials (e.g., tightly bound volumes with very brittle paper), and others must be disbound to be properly filmed.

This broad menu of preservation/conservation options recognizes that different situations and problems require a variety of solutions. As a knowledgeable librarian or archivist, you will have access to as many of the methods

---

*Copyflo is a registered trademark of the Xerox Corporation for the equipment and process that creates paper copy from negative microfilm in a continuous roll. The equipment is no longer manufactured or serviced by Xerox, but the service is available from some commercial microfilm agents and older library photographic service departments.

and techniques available as your institution can reasonably provide, but be wary of indiscriminate or wholesale applications of any option in the management of the collection.

5.E.2. TITLE SEARCHING

Production of microfilms is time-consuming and requires trained staff and expensive equipment. Therefore, titles that are candidates for reproduction should be searched in a variety of tools before they are filmed or otherwise reproduced to ensure that they are not already available on film or in hard copy from other libraries, archives, or commercial publishers. *Preservation Microfilming* and the *Preservation Planning Program Resource Notebook* provide a list of useful tools and a suggested searching sequence [see below]. Additional search sources are listed in both publications.

Search sources are arranged in a ranking, based on institutional experience, of those that most frequently contain citations for replacements, with the most comprehensive tools first.

Suggested order for searching replacement tools: [18:49–53; 19:371–378]

FOR MICROFORM REPLACEMENT
Monographs

Online bibliographic databases:

Online Computer Library Center (OCLC) online database (available through OCLC, Dublin, Ohio).

Research Libraries Information Network (RLIN) online database (available through the Research Libraries Group, Mountain View, California).

Bibliographies:

National Union Catalog: Books. (NUC) Microfiche. Washington, DC: Library of Congress, 1983– . Starting in 1983, includes entries for microforms of monographs that formerly went to the *National Register of Microform Masters.*

National Register of Microform Masters. (NRMM) Washington, DC: Library of Congress, 1965–1975 cumulation, annual volumes for 1975–1983.

New York Public Library Register of Microform Masters: Monographs. Microfiche. New York: New York Public Library, The Research Libraries, 1983.

Books on Demand. (BOD) Hard-copy or microfiche. Ann Arbor, MI: University Microfilms International, 1977–.

Guide to Microforms in Print. (GMIP) Westport, CT: Meckler Publishing, 1978–. Annual edition and supplement.

Serials

Online bibliographic databases:
[see above under monographs]

Bibliographies:

Serials in Microform. (SIM) Ann Arbor, MI: University Microfilm International, 1972–. Annual.

National Register of Microform Masters. (NRMM) Washington, DC: Library of Congress, 1965–1975 cumulation, annual volumes for 1975–1983.

Guide to Microforms in Print. (GMIP) Westport, CT: Meckler Publishing, 1978–. Annual edition and supplement.

Microforms Annual: An International Guide to Microforms. Elmsford, NY: Microforms International Marketing Corporation and Oxford Microform Publications, 1980–. Biannual.

Newspapers

Online bibliographic databases:
[see above under monographs]

Bibliographies:

Newspapers in Microform: United States. (NIM) Washington, DC: Library of Congress, 1948–1983 cumulation.

Newspapers in Microform: Foreign Countries. (NIM) Washington, DC: Library of Congress, 1948–1983 cumulation.

Serials in Microform. (SIM) Ann Arbor, MI: University Microfilm International, 1972–. Annual.

Guide to Microforms in Print. (GMIP) Westport, CT: Meckler Publishing, 1978–. Annual edition and supplement.

FOR PAPER COPY REPLACEMENT

Monographs

Books in Print. New York: R. R. Bowker, 1948–. Annual edition, supplements, and international editions.

Paperbound Books in Print. New York: R. R. Bowker, 1955–. Spring and fall editions.

Forthcoming Books. New York: R. R. Bowker, 1966–. A bimonthly updating of *Books in Print.*

Guide to Reprints. Kent, CT: Guide to Reprints, Inc., 1967–. Annual edition.

Books on Demand. (BOD) Hard-copy or microfiche. Ann Arbor, MI: University Microfilms International, 1977–.

Serials

Guide to Reprints. Kent, CT: Guide to Reprints, Inc., 1967–. Annual edition.

5.E.3. FILM SELECTION

Only one film base is acceptable for preservation microfilming: silver gelatin, previously referred to as silver-halide. Images recorded on this type of film, when manufactured, processed, and stored in accordance with national standards, will last centuries longer than the same information recorded on acidic or brittle paper. Silver film scratches easily and is susceptible to mold and water damage, however, and must be handled according to ANSI and AIIM standards in order to ensure its permanence. Master copies should be stored off-site in environmentally controlled, fire resistant, and secure areas. Duplicates, or service copies, should be made as needed for sale or use, but in no case should a master negative be used more than five times before a second-generation negative is made. Duplicates can be produced on either silver or nonsilver film, such as diazo or vesicular, with these more durable nonsilver types preferred for titles expected to receive very heavy use. [18:xxiv] There is no national standard for vesicular film, but both vesicular and diazo are fairly durable and inexpensive to produce and can be easily replaced if damaged. There is disagreement in the profession about the use of these two types of film, however. The American Library Association's Association for Library Collections and Technical Services Division, Resources Section, Micropublishing Committee, and the Standards Committee of the Reproduction of Library Materials Section have recommended that silver gelatin be used for *all* microforms intended for a library's permanent collection.

Preservation microfilming is an extremely complex activity requiring skilled operators and expensive, specialized equipment to be carried out successfully. It is not simply a matter of mounting a 35mm camera on a pylon over a lighted desk and snapping pictures. Operators must be well trained; the film must be constantly checked for quality and the images for clarity. Libraries and archives seriously interested in preservation microfilming as an alternative to other options for preserving acidic and/or brittle materials should consult with experienced, competent professionals. Organizations that can supply further information are listed in Chapter 9.

5.E.4. BIBLIOGRAPHIC CONTROL

The expense of creating a usable copy or preserving a disintegrating book in microform can be wasted if a record does not exist, both locally and nationally (and even internationally), indicating the existence of the new copy. The creation and distribution of the bibliographic record not only provides access to the item by the user, but also will help other libraries prevent costly and wasteful duplication of effort. Consequently, it behooves every library and archive participating in the creation of microform records to ensure that these records are fully cataloged and the bibliographic record entered into national databases. [See section 5.E.2 for sources of bibliographic information about the existence of materials in microformat.]

Bibliographic control will not be addressed here, but the latest guidelines and rule interpretations can be found in the *Anglo-American Cataloguing Rules, Second Edition, 1988 Revision* and the *Library of Congress Rule Interpretations.* [1:58–59, 257–273; 2; 12] An explanation of the MARC fields applicable to microforms are in *MARC Formats for Bibliographic Data,* the *RLG Preservation Manual,* OCLC's *Bibliographic Input Standards,* and *Preservation Microfilming.* [14; 15:57–79]

5.F. Photocopying

Hard copies can be made of fragile materials, permitting their use without requiring a reader or reader/printer to read them. Two systems are currently being used by libraries to reproduce materials for use by patrons and to save wear and tear on originals: photocopies (i.e., the electrostatic process) and the Photostatic process (Photostat is a trademark of the Itek Corporation).

5.F.1. PHOTOCOPIES

Photocopying materials that do not lend themselves to microfilming or Photostatic reproduction may be a viable alternative for some libraries or archives. Photocopying, as used in this context, is a general term applied to copies produced directly on paper through the electrostatic process, i.e., xerography. The copies are usually about the same size as the original; thus the term does not normally include microimages. Most often photocopying is limited to items for which a hard copy is preferred instead of a microform, to reduce wear and tear on the original, and because the material is not available from a commercial publisher. Photocopying provides the same information as the original, but in a long-lasting format that is close to the actual item and requires minimal effort on the part of the reader to access and use. It is particularly appropriate for high-use monographs (particularly those of fewer than 100 pages), current reference sets, serial volumes needed in hard copy to complete a set, and items requiring reference to extensive notes, indexes, or graphic materials. At present, it does not work well for oversize materials, color, newspapers, or those items that are heavily illustrated with halftones, though this may change in the future. [28:43]

Since there are no national standards for photocopying, each library or archive must write its own guidelines.* For every purpose noted above, procedures used by the Research Libraries Group, Inc., for

---

* The Association for Library Collections & Technical Services (ALCTS), a division of the American Library Association, did, however, publish *Guidelines for Preservation Photocopying of Replacement Pages* in 1990. This free four-page pamphlet covers procedures for making copies for tipping-in, binding, and preservation microfilming.

photocopying provide guidelines for producing usable products: [20:16, 118]

1. Everything in the original text should be copied, with the exception of extraneous material laid in or tipped on to the original text. A reasonable effort should be made to complete partial items before copying.
2. Photocopies should be copied onto acid-free, alkaline-buffered, 20-pound permanent paper. "Suitable papers include Xerox XXV Archival Bond, Howard Permalife, and University Products Perma/Dur." [20:16]
3. Equipment should be maintained to ensure: (a) that the contrast control can be set to capture all text and illustrations as clearly as possible while minimizing the gray cast or streaking of the background; and (b) there will be strong bonding of the print to the paper. Maintenance of the correct fusion temperature is critical to permanent copying.
4. All preservation copies, whether for binding or microfilming, should be made one page per exposure. For binding, double-sided copying that maintains the original format and size should be provided unless otherwise specified.
5. "Every page of the original should be aligned on the platen consistently, straight and parallel to the edge of the paper. Recto and verso of double-sided copying should be lined up so they are in register, i.e., back-to-back. A mask on the platen will help center the image, eliminate dark borders, and allow for consistent alignment." [20:16]
6. "A minimum border of three-fourths inch should be allowed on the left margin of the recto of photocopies for binding. Copies should also be made so that the recto of the original is also the recto of the photocopy." [20:16]
7. "Foldouts should be copied in sections if they are larger than the largest available size of photocopy paper. Sections should align well so that they may be reassembled into a single flat sheet. The binding margin of three-fourths inch is required for photocopies for binding." [20:16]
8. "The photocopy should be of high quality, complete, and in the order of the original. Recopy if necessary." [20:16]
9. The photocopy should be bound properly with a margin wide enough to facilitate future copying from the copy [see above]. Double-fan adhesive binding is one recommended option.

Photocopiers using both heat and pressure to fuse the image produce more permanent copies. Photocopying is more limited than large-scale microreproduction because photocopies may lose their resolution and legibility when recopied.

5.F.2. PHOTOSTATS™

A Photostat™ is a right-reading negative paper photocopy. The camera produces a silver gelatin paper copy in a single step. The machine includes both optical and developing systems and can enlarge or reduce a document up to 50 percent of its linear dimensions. The system produces high-quality, large-sized prints and is useful for reproducing maps and newspaper pages. The equipment and the photographic paper is expensive, so the cost per page of any item, large or small, will be high, causing its use to be limited to single documents of high research value that have poor image quality and cannot be reproduced satisfactorily by photocopying. [23:36]

5.G. Digital Techniques

Deacidification and/or strengthening of books published on acid paper ensures the continuing existence of the treated item only, not the supply of copies. A microfilmed book or paper is easy to copy and distribute to libraries and archives, and it has a long life if maintained in a controlled environment.

"Digital imagery, where books are scanned into computer storage, is a promising alternative process. Storing page images of books permits rapid transfer of books from library to library (much simpler and faster than copying microfilm). The images can be displayed or printed, much as film images, although with greater cost today. Additionally, digital imagery permits considerable reprocessing: adjustment of contrast, removal of stains, adjustment of image size, and so on. At present the handling of these images still requires special skills and equipment few libraries possess, but there is rapid technological progress in the design of disk drives, displays, and printing devices. Imaging technology will be within the reach of most libraries within a decade." [11:1]

5.G.1. DIGITAL IMAGERY

Digital imagery permits the preservation of the original book in its exact format and appearance. Bound volumes and individual documents can be scanned with resolutions comparable to most laser printers. A normal book can be scanned for 13 to 28 cents a page, compared to filming for 10 to 15 cents a page. Each page would consume about 0.1 to 0.5 megabytes (Mbyte) of compressed or uncompressed storage. "Since a typical book is 300 pages long, if uncompressed, six books would fit in a gigabyte [Gbyte, equal to 1,000 Mbytes]. If compressed, perhaps 30 books would fit in a gigabyte." [11:4] A CD-ROM (Compact Disc-Read Only Memory) stores a little over 0.5 gigabytes, thus a CD could hold from 3 to 15 books. [11:6] The disadvantages of this technology are that the text cannot be searched for specific information and the shelf life of CD-Roms and other digital storage media is currently much less than that of microfilm [see sections 6.E and 6.F].

5.G.2. ASCII (NONIMAGE)

ASCII (American Standard Code for Information Interchange) files produced by OCR (Optical Character Recognition) scanners produce computer-readable versions of text. "The words are preserved, but not their exact format and appearance. With an ASCII file, it is possible to search for names, specific terms, phrases or, with suitable software, to do various kinds of subject searches. . . . ASCII storage is also much more compact; a page of text that will use a few hundred Kbytes in image will contain only one to two thousand bytes of ASCII, or 1/100th of the space." [11:4] ASCII also has the advantages of being easily reformatted and reprinted, and can be displayed on a wider variety of equipment than digital imaged texts. A disadvantage of nonimage digitizing is that non-standard typefaces and faded images, such as found in many brittle books, often cannot be read by present OCR programs. Rekeying, costing $1.00 to $2.00 or more per page, may then be necessary. "For any illustrated book, ASCII conversion still leaves behind the question what to do with the pictorial or graphical material." [11:8]

Both forms of digital conversion require special equipment and software programs that rapidly become obsolete. Thus, files that are created in the 1990s may be unreadable in the 2010s. Nevertheless, since this technology is improving very quickly and permits wide access to computer-based files (a major disadvantage of the other systems), it should be closely watched and implemented as appropriate.

5.H. Additional Consideration

Finally, the selection for preservation and conservation decisions should not be limited to paper-based materials, whether they be books, letters, manuscripts, or photographs. As Margaret Child points out, we should apply these (or similar) criteria to sound recordings, magnetic tape, videotape, film (both photographic and movie), video discs, and other information-bearing media. [2:1] Scholars and others will want to have access to these materials in the future, just as they have to paper records in the past. The wide and ever changing variety of media makes these decisions even more difficult than those that must be made for paper; not only must the format be preserved, but also must the means of accessing the information contained therein, i.e., the projectors, viewers, computers, disc drives, and the programs required to run them.

REFERENCES

1. American Library Association. "Chapter 11, Microforms." *Anglo-American Cataloguing Rules*. Second Edition, 1988 Revision. Chicago: American Library Association, 1988.

2. American Library Association. "Rule 1.11, Facsimiles, Photocopies and Other Reproductions." *Anglo-American Cataloguing Rules*. Second Edition, 1988 Revision. Chicago: American Library Association, 1988.

3. Banks, Joyce M. "Mass Deacidification at the National Library of Canada." *Conservation Administration News* 20 (January 1985): 14–15, 27.

4. Cunha, George Daniel Martin, and Dorothy Grant Cunha. *Conservation of Library Materials: A Manual and Bibliography on the Care, Repair, and Restoration of Library Materials*. Vol. 1. 2d ed. Metuchen, NJ: Scarecrow Press, 1971.

5. Cunha, George M. "Mass Deacidification for Libraries." *Library Technology Reports* 23 (May-June 1987): 362–472.

6. Cunha, George M. "Mass Deacidification for Libraries: 1989 Update." *Library Technology Reports* 25 (January-February 1989): 5–81.

7. FMC Corporation. *Paper Preservation Process*. Chicago: FMC Corporation, April 1990.

8. *How Do Wei T'o Sprays and Solutions Stabilize Paper?* Matteson, IL: Wei T'o Associates, Inc., n.d.

9. Kozak, John J., and Richard Spatz. "Deacidification of Paper by the Bookkeeper Process." In *TAPPI Proceedings, 1988 Paper Preservation Symposium, Capital Hilton, Washington, D.C., Oct. 19–21*, 167–171. Atlanta, GA: TAPPI Press, 1988.

10. "LC Invites Proposals for Deacidification Service." *The Abbey Newsletter* 14 (October 1990): 97–98, 100–102.

11. Lesk, Michael. *Image Formats for Preservation and Access: A Report of the Technology Assessment Advisory Committee to the Commission on Preservation and Access*. Washington, DC: The Commission on Preservation and Access, July 1990.

12. Library of Congress. "Chapter 11, Microforms." *Library of Congress Rule Interpretations*, edited by Robert M. Hiatt. 2d ed. Washington, DC: Library of Congress, Cataloging Distribution Service, 1989– .

13. Library of Congress. *Conservation Workshop Notes on Evolving Procedures, Series 500. No. 1, The Deacidification and Alkalization of Documents with Magnesium Bicarbonate Working Draft, July 1978*. Washington, DC: Library of Congress, Preservation Office, July 1978.

14. Library of Congress. *MARC Formats for Bibliographic Data*. Washington, DC: Library of Congress, 1980– .

15. "Microform Records in RLIN." *RLG Preservation Manual*, 57–79. 2d ed. Stanford, CA: The Research Libraries Group, Inc., 1986.

16. Morrow, Carolyn Clark. *Conservation Treatment Procedures: A Manual of Step-by-Step Procedures for the Maintenance and Repair of Library Materials*. Littleton, CO: Libraries Unlimited, 1982.

17. Murray, Toby. "FMC Dedicates Paper Preservation Demonstration Plant." *Conservation Administration News* 42 (July 1990): 1–2.

18. *Preservation Microfilming: A Guide for Librarians and Archivists*, edited by Nancy E. Gwinn. Chicago: American Library Association, 1987.

19. *Preservation Planning Program: Resource Notebook*, compiled by Pamela W. Darling, revised edition by Wesley L. Boomgaarden. Washington, DC: Association of Research Libraries, Office of Management Studies, 1987.

20. Research Libraries Group. *RLG Preservation Manual*. 2d ed. Stanford, CA: The Research Libraries Group, Inc., 1986.

21. Smith, Richard D. "Paper Deacidification, Part 3." *Art Dealer and Framer* (November 1976): 40–46.

22. Smith, Richard D. "Paper in Archives, Libraries, and Museums Worldwide." In *TAPPI Proceedings: 1988 Paper Preservation Symposium*, 7–12. Atlanta, GA: TAPPI Press, 1988.

23. Sung, Carolyn Hoover. *Archives & Manuscripts: Reprography*. SAA Basic Manual Series. Chicago: Society of American Archivists, 1982.

24. U.S. Congress, Office of Technology Assessment. *Book Preservation Technologies*, OTA-O-375. Washington, DC: U.S. Government Printing Office, May 1988.

25. U.S. National Archives and Records Service. *Intrinsic Value in Archival Material*. Staff Information Paper 21. Washington, DC: 1982.

26. *Using Wei T'o Deacidification Sprays and Solutions: Questions and Answers*. Matteson, IL: Wei T'o Associates, Inc., June 15, 1984.

27. W. J. Barrow Research Laboratory, Inc. *Permanence/Durability of the Book, Vol. VII: Physical and Chemical Properties of Book Papers, 1507–1949*. Richmond, VA: W. J. Barrow Research Laboratory, 1974.

28. Walker, Gay. "Preservation Decision-Making and Archival Photocopying." *Restaurator* 8 (1987): 40–51.

6.
PHOTOGRAPHIC, AUDIO, AND MAGNETIC MEDIA

Preservation of photographic, audio, and magnetic media is complex and often requires equipment and expertise not widely available. This chapter outlines the basic procedures for extending the life of these materials. For additional information and information concerning treatments and recommendations for specific types of photographs, recordings, and magnetic media not covered, consult the references for this chapter. Salvage of these media is discussed in sections 8.E.5 and 8.E.6.

6.A. Photographs

"The photograph is a composite of several different layers, each of which may react in a different way to the immediate environment and in some cases to each other, and generally includes a support, a binder, and an image-forming component." [28:3] The support may be ceramic, glass, metal, paper, plastic, wood, or a variety of other media. The binder carries the image and may consist of gelatin, gum arabic, albumen, collodion, or starch. Most images are based on organic dyes or silver-sensitive salts. Organic dyes, particularly of color materials, tend to vary in chemical stability from product to product and, in general, are not stable. [28:13] "The forms in which a silver image can be produced vary considerably. Silver is very sensitive to a wide range of pollutants, and is consequently particularly vulnerable to chemical degradation." [7:1] Silver is relatively stable, and silver-based images are used for the preservation of information on otherwise impermanent media such as acidic paper.

Modern photographs have a subbing/baryta or isolating layer between the gelatin binder and the base support. The purpose of the baryta layer is to reduce the textual interference of the paper fiber base so it doesn't show through the transparent binder layer. Prints without the baryta layer were produced prior to 1886. Initially baryta was formed from barium sulfate bound in gelatin; today it is made of titanium dioxide. Both are white pigments applied to the support base before it is

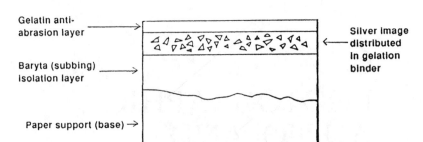

Gelatin anti-abrasion layer

Baryta (subbing) isolation layer

Silver Image distributed in gelation binder

Paper support (base)

FIGURE 6.1. Cross section of a modern black-and-white photographic print.

coated with the light-sensitive emulsion. The subbing layer is an adhesive designed to assist in coating and adhering the gelatin binder to the plastic support. Both the baryta and subbing layers are missing from earlier (before the 1880s) photographic processes. [28:14]

Figure 6.1 represents the laminated structure of a typical modern black-and-white photographic print.

6.A.1. HANDLING

"Handling photographic materials is a safe and simple procedure, provided that certain guidelines are followed. Photographic materials are delicate and may be easily scratched, torn, creased, or broken. Handling should be kept to a minimum, but when necessary, it should be done with care." [18:9]

Direct handling should be avoided because the oils and chemicals on human skin can cause permanent damage to photographs. Clean, lintless, white cotton gloves should be worn when working with prints, negatives, sleeves, and enclosures. The materials should always be handled by the extreme edges and supported underneath to prevent bending, which may stress and crack the emulsion.

Henry Wilhelm, considered one of the world's leading independent experts on color permanence in photography, states that "light fading—the damage that occurs when color prints are displayed—is the result of accumulated exposure to light and ultraviolet (UV) radiation; that is, light intensity multiplied by time." [32:38] [See section 2.G.] Color pictures on display are much more affected by light levels and exposure time than temperature and humidity. UV radiation is not a significant danger in normal indoor display because "all current chromogenic papers—the materials used for printing color negatives—are already well protected by built-in UV-absorbing filter layers." [32:39]

He also says that "black and white negatives and prints are virtually unaffected by light and heat. When properly fixed and washed—and additionally protected by selenium or sulfur toning—black and white images can actually be more stable than the paper or film base upon which they are coated." [32:38]

Always make a display copy and store the original in the dark. Order two copies when purchasing or making prints: one for display, one for dark storage. Make copies of Polaroid pictures or other instant photographs. Each print is unique, and if the original is of value, it should be protected [see section 6.A.3.d].

6.A.2. STORAGE

Much of the information in this section is based upon the Northeast Document Conservation Center (NEDCC) handout, *Storage Enclosures for Photographic Prints and Negatives*. [33]

6.A.2.a. Paper enclosures

All photographs, prints, glass and film negatives, etc. should be stored within individual permanent/durable paper or plastic enclosures. Paper enclosures should have a high alphacellulose content, not be highly colored, contain no lignin, groundwood, or alum-rosin sizing, and be of 100 percent rag. Cardboard made of groundwood should not be used. Paper and board should be acid-free (pH 7.0 to 7.5) and conform to the specifications outlined in ANSI Standard IT9.2-1988, *Photographic Processed Films, Plates and Papers—Filing Enclosures and Storage Containers* (although silver and dye gelatin photographs may be more stable when in a pH environment of 6.5 to 7.5). "The effect of direct contact of buffered paper on photographic emulsions is presently being questioned. Buffered storage enclosures are not recommended for color image, cyanotypes, or albumen prints. They *are* recommended for cellulose nitrate and early safety film negatives, brittle prints, and photographs on brittle acidic mounts. Research has yet to be conducted to determine the effect of buffering agents on many photographic processes. However, if the relative humidity of the storage environment is below 50 percent, buffered enclosures should present few, if any problems." [33]

Unfortunately, even good quality storage papers may harm photographs. The only way to know whether a paper product is safe is to run a photographic activity test against it. Information about the test can be obtained from the Image Permanence Institute [see section 9.E.1 for address]. [33]

Advantages of paper enclosures: [33:1–2]

1. They protect the image from light because they are opaque.
2. Since they are porous, they protect the object from accumulations of moisture and harmful gases. This is especially important for nitrate-based images [see section 6.B.2].
3. They are usually cheaper than plastic enclosures.
4. They are easy to write on.

Some disadvantages of paper enclosures: [33:1–2]

1. Since paper enclosures are opaque, the object must be removed from the enclosure for viewing. Handling is increased with attendant possibilities of damage to the photograph.
2. The photographic activity test is required to ensure they are safe for photographic images [see above].

Three varieties of paper enclosures are available: seamed envelopes, seamless envelopes, and folders. [33:2]

The *seamed envelope* has one open end and should have a protective flap. Recommended envelopes have the seam at the sides and across the bottom (not in the center of the envelope where the print or negative may come in contact with the seam and its adhesive). Adhesives should be non-acidic and unreactive with silver. There should not be a thumb notch. The negative or print should be stored in the enclosure, with the emulsion side away from the seam.

Seamless paper envelopes do not need an adhesive because the enclosure is formed by folding three or four flaps (which are attached to a back) over each other to form a pocket. The fourth flap folds down to form a protective cover. Its construction encourages the user to lay the folder flat on a surface before opening it, thus protecting brittle or fragile items. Since no adhesives are used in its construction, a four-flap paper enclosure design is most often recommended by photographic conservators.

Paper folders are made from sheets of paper folded in half. They are closed on one side only and must be housed in correctly sized boxes in order to adequately protect the image. If stored vertically, the photograph must be supported to prevent sagging or curling. Folders are used for large or mounted materials.

6.A.2.b. Plastic enclosures

Plastic enclosures should be chemically inert and nondestructive. Three types of plastics are suitable for archival purposes: polyester, polypropylene, and polyethylene. If plastic enclosures are used, be aware of the possibility of static electricity, especially with polyester and polyethylene. Plastic should not be used for photos that have flaking or lifting emulsions. "Polyester is the most inert and rigid of the three. It generates static electricity which can attract dust, and it is expensive. Polyester enclosures should be either DuPont Mylar D or ICI Melinex #516. Polypropylene is almost as rigid and strong as polyester when in a sleeve format, but is soft when used for ring binder storage pages. Polyethlene is the softest, most easily scratched, and least rigid of these plastics." [33:2] Kodak advises against nitrated and formaldehyde-based plastics, polyvinylchloride (PVC), and acrylics, including acrylic lacquer and acrylic enamel. PVC is chemically unstable and will cause photographic images to deteriorate. Unplasticized polymethyl methacrylate may be used if the item is not to be folded. [30:106, 109] (These plastic films are difficult to distinguish from each other. Appendix F describes several tests used to identify them.)

Advantages of plastic enclosures: [33:3]

1. The image can be seen without removing the object from the enclosure, lessening potential damage to the photograph or negative.
2. Objects are protected from moisture, sulfides, and other pollutants in the environment.
3. Most plastic envelopes have heat-sealed seams. Therefore, adhesive problems are eliminated.

Disadvantages of plastic enclosures: [33:3]

1. Moisture can be trapped inside plastic enclosures and cause ferrotyping (sticking resulting in shiny areas). This is a particular problem in areas with high humidity or in water-related disasters.
2. "Cellulose nitrate film and early safety film should not be stored in plastic enclosures. Such enclosures accelerate their deterioration." [33:3]
3. Enclosures with matte or frosted surfaces may scratch emulsions.
4. They are very difficult to write on.
5. They may "be flimsy and require additional support, such as archival-quality Bristol board. Any information which should accompany the image can be recorded on this board." [33:3]

There are several types of plastic enclosures: envelopes, folders, sleeves, encapsulation, ring binder storage pages, polyester sheet/matboard folders, and polyester sheets within paper folders. [33:3–4]

Polyethylene and *polyester envelopes* have heat-sealed seams and are marketed by archival product suppliers.

Plastic folders are usually made from polyester and may be used with paper envelopes. The folder protects the object when it is taken out of the envelope.

Sleeves are open at two opposite ends and are made from polyester or polypropylene. They are usually one piece with a self-locking fold on one edge.

Encapsulation consists of using double-sided tape or a polyester welding machine to seal all sides of a sandwich of two polyester sheets on either side of a photograph. Encapsulation is used for fragile or torn prints but not recommended for photographs on poor quality mounts or for contemporary color photos [see section 4.G.3].

Ring binder storage pages are good for high-use collections of slides, etc. They are made of all three types of plastic and come in a variety of formats and sizes.

Polyester sheet/matboard folders are used for oversized photographs or those on rigid mounts. They are made by attaching a sheet of polyester to a sheet of matboard of the same size, and joining them along one edge with double-sided tape. The board supports the photograph, and the plastic protects it while allowing the image to be seen. The folders are stored flat.

Polyester sheets within paper folders are useful for protecting small, fragile prints. They are made by attaching a polyester sheet to the inner edge of a paper folder, opposite the center fold, with double-sided tape. The polyester holds the object in place but permits easy viewing and removal.

6.A.2.c. Furniture and containers

Storage furniture should be constructed of noncombustible and noncorrosive materials such as anodized aluminum, stainless steel, or steel with a baked-on enamel finish. Surfaces should be smooth, non-abrasive, and durable. Cabinets or drawers should have no mechanical features such as spring clamps that could damage or place undue pressure on their contents. Select only those materials for storage containers that will not add to the chemical problems already existing in films and prints. Avoid wooden shelves, cabinets, or drawers, including those made with plywood, pressboard, and chipboard, because of the presence of lignin, peroxide, and formic acid, which can leach out and initiate damaging chemical reactions in photographic materials. Wood also absorbs and retains moisture, which causes swelling, warping, and mildew. If wood must be used, it should be sealed with several coats of polyurethane varnish. Epoxy paint is the safest finish for any other material, but allow any paint to cure for about two weeks (or until there is no noticeable odor, whichever is longer). [36:118–119] [See also section 2.E.2 for more information about wood shelving and testing of paint.]

Fragile images and those having brittle mounts should be stored flat in document cases or clamshell boxes conforming to the specifications outlined above, i.e., no lignin, alum-rosin sizing, or groundwood. Photographs that are in good condition and intact can be filed on edge, perpendicular to the shelf, in upright storage boxes. They should not lean to the side. "Boxes should be neither overfilled nor under-filled; the former condition will result in damage as photographs are forced in and out of tight boxes. Conversely, boxes that are not completely filled will encourage slumping and the natural tendency of photographs to curl. If photographs are to be stored in filing cabinets, hanging or suspended filing systems should be employed to avoid damage that would be caused by folders (and thus enclosed prints and negatives) slumping, moving about, and sliding under one another. Folders that can be scored to accommodate varying thicknesses of material should be used, rather than single-fold file folders." [29:101]

Best practice dictates a separate storage enclosure for every photograph and negative. If that is not possible, then original prints of high value and/or in fragile condition should be individually enclosed. As an interim measure, less valuable materials may be stored together, separated by interleaving them with sheets of neutral pH paper or polyester. Similar size photographs should be filed together. [29:101–102]

Neither rubber bands (which contain sulphur) nor pressure-sensitive tapes should be used to keep materials together or repair them. [29:99–100] Do not use a rubber stamp with stamp pad ink on any paper materials intended for use in storing photographs.

6.A.2.d. Storage areas and environment

Photographic collections should be stored in a cool, dry area away from overhead steam or water pipes, washrooms, or other sources of water. Acceptable temperature and humidity levels must be maintained. Try to give ventilation to the materials stored inside the containers. "The recommended temperature at which to store general collections is 68 °F with a daily fluctuation not to exceed 2.5 °F. For storage, as opposed to display, a temperature of between 40 °F and 50 °F can significantly reduce both chemical deterioration and biodeterioration of photographic artifacts. However, there is a danger of condensation on objects brought directly from colder temperatures [into warmer rooms]. For example, the dew-point in a room at 68 °F and 55% RH is 51 °F, so condensation will form on any object whose temperature is below 51 °F. Passage through a pre-conditioning zone is one way to avoid this problem. For most institutions, however, the benefit of colder temperatures does not outweigh the inconveniences of establishing a pre-conditioning zone and the time delay associated with allowing artifacts to adjust to room temperature. Therefore, because the range for human comfort is about 68 °F to 77 °F, the lowest point within that range has been chosen as the recommended temperature." [4:G6]

Patrons often ask for the best location in the home for storing photographs; it is in the dark on the top shelf of a first-floor closet. Never store photographs or slides in the basement, which may be damp, or in the attic, which is too hot. [31:84] "Don't store photographs on the floor, which in many houses becomes too humid during at least part of the year." [32:48]

The large number of different types of photographs, prints, and negatives, each having its own special problems and solutions, precludes any meaningful in-depth treatment in a book of this length. Eastman Kodak Company's *Conservation of Photographs* [8], Reilly's *Care and Identification of 19th-Century Photographic Prints* [26], and Ritzenthaler's *Archives and Manuscripts: Administration of Photographic Collections* [29] should be consulted for detailed information concerning photographic materials. Salvage procedures for photographs are discussed in section 8.E.5.

6.A.3. STORAGE GUIDELINES BY TYPE OF MEDIA

6.A.3.a. Negatives

Negatives on cellulose nitrate film should be duplicated onto safety film and the nitrate film destroyed if it is deteriorating [see section 6.B.2]. Nitrate film should be destroyed with great care, preferably by burning in the open air. If nitrate film must be kept, it should be stored separately in ventilated metal boxes at 21°C (about 70°F) or lower, with a relative humidity of 30 to 50 percent, preferably below 40 percent. See section 6.B.2.a for specific information on identifying and handling nitrate film.

Black-and-white negatives on acetate and polyester film base should be placed in individual enclosures that protect the film from dust and abrasion. For long-term storage, paper envelopes should be made of plasticizer-free, chemically stable paper, the edge seams held with a nondestructive adhesive according to ANSI Standard 4.20. The emulsion side of the negative should be positioned away from the seam. Plastic sleeves of triacetate, polyester (Mylar™) or polyethylene (Tyvek™) are acceptable. [30:110–113] Polyethylene enclosures may be used, providing the RH is kept well below 50 percent and surface pressure is avoided. [11:7]

Kraft paper and glassine envelopes are not suitable for long-term negative storage. There is no perfect negative envelope. Two types of materials thought to be safe for negative enclosures are the paper envelopes and folders as well as the plastic sleeves and envelopes described in section 6.A.2. The plastics act as barriers to prevent transmission of air and moisture, although this can be a disadvantage in high humidity conditions, since it can cause ferrotyping on a gelatin emulsion. [36:136–137]

A relative humidity of 30 percent is acceptable when various types of negatives are stored together in the same area. As noted elsewhere, the RH should be stable and cycling avoided. Maximum temperature for any extended period of time should not exceed 25°C (77°F) and should be kept below 20°C (68°F).

White cotton or nylon lint-free gloves should always be worn when handling negatives. Always handle negatives by the edges. In order to avoid scratching the emulsions, do not slide negatives in and out of sleeves.

Do not store diazo and silver gelatin negatives together. Always file different types of film in separate sleeves and boxes.

6.A.3.b. Glass-plate negatives

Glass-plate negatives should be separated from the picture collection, grouped by size, and stored on edge under slight lateral pressure in metal filing cabinets. The temperature should be kept below 21°C (about 70°F) and the RH between 30 percent and 50 percent, preferably below 40 percent. [30:113]

Use rigid metal baked enamel dividers at intervals depending on the type of separator and size of glass plate. Don't use typical office-type file drawer dividers that pivot forward and backward from a channel in the drawer bottom, because the leverage exerted will crack the glass. [36:118–119]

6.A.3.c. Black-and-white photographs

The storage area should be located toward the center of the building. Photographs should never be stored in a basement, on a top floor, or near exterior windows. If the collection is large, it should be stored in several rooms rather than one to reduce fire hazard. Paint on storeroom walls should not have an oil base, because oil base paint usually contains peroxides that contribute to the oxidation of silver images. [5:I2–I3]

Processed negatives, slides, and prints should be enclosed in envelopes, sleeves, file folders, or albums to protect them from dirt and mechanical damage and to facilitate identification and handling. The principal physical and chemical requirements for paper and plastic enclosures are outlined in ANSI Standard 1T9.2-1988 *Photography (Processing) Processed Films, Plates and Paper-Filing Enclosures and Storage Containers.* Paper enclosures should be chemically stable and have a slightly rough or matte surface to prevent sticking and ferrotyping. They should have an alpha cellulose content in excess of 87 percent; be free of groundwood; contain neutral or alkaline sizing chemicals; have a pH between 7.0 and 9.5 for black-and-white materials with a 2 percent alkali reserve; and be void of waxes, plasticizers, or other ingredients that may transfer to photographic materials during storage. [8:94]

Storage boxes should be constructed of a high-quality, acid-free board with an alkaline reserve. No artifact should be placed inside a storage box without first being put in an enclosure, sleeve, or envelope. Do not overfill the boxes. No more than three boxes should be stacked upon each other. The shallowest boxes available should be used. [5:I5-I6]

6.A.3.d. Color negatives and positives

Wilhelm believes the best way to ensure the permanence of color photographs is by creating them on the most stable films and papers meeting the user's needs. Unfortunately, many film repositories must preserve materials that are on unstable media. Wilhelm and his associate, Carol Brower, provide a few guidelines to help maintain color materials in good condition. [42:48]

1. *Light* is the great enemy of color photographs. It is visible light that does the damage. Ultraviolet radiation contributes little if any to the fading of most current color prints displayed indoors under average conditions—even under fluorescent illumination.

Invariably, color photographs last far longer when stored in the dark than they do on display.

2. *Color prints:* Extended display, especially under bright light, will destroy color prints. . . . if a photograph is important to you, make two copy prints (Fujicolor Super FA, Cibachrome, or Fujichrome Type 34 papers are recommended for this). Store the original and one copy in the dark and use the other copy for display. If the original negative or transparency is available and still in printable condition, use it to make the new prints. Because instant color prints are one-of-a-kind images that have no negatives, they should never be displayed for long periods. Use copy prints instead.

3. *Color slides:* Projection of original color slides should be minimized—especially if they were made on Kodachrome or older Agfa, GAF, or Ansco films. Valuable slides should always be duplicated (Fujichrome Duplicating Film is recommended) and the duplicates used for projection. Don't leave color transparencies on light tables or sitting on desk tops any longer than absolutely necessary. Any older transparencies that appear to have faded or suffered a noticeable shift in color balance should be duplicated promptly. With the notable exception of post-1939 Kodachrome, almost all of the color-transparency films manufactured until around 1980 had poor dark-storage stability.

4. *Color negatives:* Prior to the mid-1980s all color-negative films had poor dark-storage stability. Some are still very poor. . . . [Print] valuable older negatives . . . on Fujicolor Super FA paper, if it isn't already too late. But even if they are too far gone to make good prints, don't throw them away. Electronic image-enhancement systems are now becoming available, such as the Agfa Digital Slide Printer and the Kodak Premier Image Enhancement System, which will, at reasonable cost, allow substantial corrections to be made when printing faded negatives and transparencies. [See chapter 9 for addresses.]

Table 6.1 gives information about the longest lasting films and print materials for color pictures.

Paper that is in direct contact with processed color photographic material should have a similar composition to that used for black-and-white materials [see above], except that the pH should be between 7.0 and 7.5, and the **2 percent alkaline reserve requirement does not apply**. Alkaline sizing chemicals should not be present in excess, as is the case with some "acid-free" materials. [8:94] **Do not use buffered paper envelopes for stabilized color film.** [36:137]

Low-temperature storage in the dark is best. Archival collections of color materials should be stored at 2°C (35.6°F) at 25 to 30 percent RH. Moisture-proof heat-seal aluminum foil envelopes manufactured by Kodak help control humidity. [30:113]

TABLE 6.1. The longest-lasting [color] films and print materials

TRANSPARENCY FILMS	COLOR INTERNEGATIVE FILM
Best overall: Fujichrome films of all types, including Fujichrome Velvia and Fujichrome Duplicating films	Fujicolor Internegative Film IT-N
Best if projection can be avoided: Kodachrome films of all types	**COLOR NEGATIVE PAPERS** **Best overall:** Fujicolor Super FA Type II Fujicolor Professional Super FA
COLOR-NEGATIVE FILMS **ISO 25:** Kodak Ektar 25 and Ektar 25 Professional	**Best Process EP-2 Papers:** Konica Color Type SR Konica Color Professional Type EX
ISO 100-125: 3M ScotchColor 100	
ISO 160-200[a]: Kodak Vericolor Professional, Type L Fujicolor Super HG 200 Konika SR-G 200	**PAPER FOR PRINTING COLOR TRANSPARENCIES** **Best Overall:** Cibachrome II (glossy polyester base) Cibachrome-A II (glossy polyester base)
ISO 400: Kodak Vericolor Professional 400 Kodak Ektapress 400 Kodak Kodacolor Gold 400 Konica Super DD 400 Konica SR-G 400	**Best Process R-3 paper:** Fujichrome Type 34
ISO 1000-3200: Kodak Ektapress 1600 Kodak Kodacolor Gold 1600 Kodak Ektar 1000 Konica SR-G 3200 Professional	**MOST PERMANENT COLOR PRINT PROCESS OF ANY TYPE— BUT COSTLY** Polaroid Permanent-Color[b] Ultrastable Permanent Color[b]

[a] The four films listed in the ISO 160-200 group are intended for different applications, and . . . the most stable products of each type [are included]. Kodak Vericolor III Professional Film, Type S, is a daylight/electronic flash film intended primarily for professional portrait and wedding photography. Fujicolor 160 Professional Film, Type L, is a tungsten-balanced color-negative film generally used for studio portrait and product photography (this film is considerably more stable than Kodak's equivalent tungsten-balanced color-negative film, Vericolor II Professional Film, Type L). Fujicolor Super HG 200 and the pleasingly lower-contrast Konica SR-G 200 are daylight films intended for the general amateur market.

[b] Process may be used to make prints from color transparencies, color negatives, or already existing prints.

Source: Henry Wilhelm. "What's the Bottom Line: The Longest-Lasting Films and Print Materials." In Bob Schwalberg, with Henry Wilhelm and Carol Brower. "Going! Going!! Gone!!!" *Popular Photography* 97 (June 1990): 46.

Henry Wilhelm recommends the use of a frost-free refrigerator to store color materials at low temperatures and humidity levels without the use of vapor-proof packaging. In fact, this is the *only* simple way to store color materials without the use of vapor-proof packaging. The refrigerator compartment (not the freezer) can maintain a temperature of about 2°C (35.6°F) and relative humidity levels between 25 and 35 percent all year round. [41:32] These settings are close enough to the recommended levels to provide a satisfactory environment. A relative humidity of 30 to 50 percent is now the recommended level for photographic storage. Negatives stored in a refrigerator at 35°F will probably be able to be reprinted at least ten times longer than those stored at room temperature.

It must be noted that "only the refrigerator compartment can be used for unprotected storage. The freezer compartment has high humidity levels, especially during the daily automatic defrost periods. By the same token, 'frost-free' freezers, which have no refrigerator compartments, cannot be used for unprotected storage of photographs." [41:32]

Certain precautions should be taken when using frost-free refrigerators: [41:32–34]

1. Be sure the refrigerator is a true "frost-free" and not a "cycle-defrost" or one requiring a manually defrosted freezer compartment. The older manual defrost refrigerators normally have humidity levels between 90 and 100 percent. Before storing photographic materials, test the humidity level of the refrigerator compartment while it is running. A hygrometer should be kept in the refrigerator compartment permanently. It should be checked each time the refrigerator door is opened and/or at least weekly.

2. The unit must have separate refrigerating and freezing compartments. Cooling coils must be located ONLY in the freezer compartment. It should be impossible to see any part of the freezer or refrigerator that forms ice crystals.

3. The unit should be cooled by having air blown into the freezer compartment over the cooling coils through duct(s) in the freezer.

4. "ALL cooling in the refrigerator section [should come] from cold air blown in from the freezer section by a fan." [41:34]

5. Use only the refrigerator compartment for unprotected storage of photographs.

6. Cardboard boxes can be used to protect photographs from humidity fluctuations during the defrost cycle or when the door is opened. Slides can be kept in their original cardboard or plastic boxes. It is strongly recommended that all paper envelopes or boxes be placed in Ziplock™ bags before placing them in the refrigerator compartment. Large boxes should be wrapped in polyethylene. Tape the seams with freezer tape or masking tape. [40]

7. Do not open the refrigerator door more often than is necessary.

8. During a power failure, keep the door shut. If the power is out for more than two days, open the refrigerator door and leave it open until the power is restored.

6.A.3.e. Permanence of Polaroid instant prints

The following information is taken, with permission, from Schwalberg's article on permanence of color photographic images in the July 1990 issue of *Popular Photography*. [32:47]

The dyes in Polaroid instant prints are extremely stable in dark storage. However, when discussing the stability of Polaroid SX-70, Spectra, and Polaroid 600 Plus prints, dark-storage dye stability is only half the story. The problem with these prints is that in normal room-temperature dark storage they develop an objectionable yellowish overall stain in a relatively short period. . . . The stain is produced by slow migration of non-image dyes and/or other chemical constituents residing in the lower layers of the tightly sealed Polaroid print package.

Polaroid Spectra and 600 Plus prints also have poor light-fading stability. When displayed, these prints fade significantly faster than typical chromogenic papers. Polaroid color prints have no usable negative (like daguerreotypes, each exposure produces a unique image). If important pictures have been made on these materials, the best policy is to make two copies on a more stable print material (Polaroid itself offers good-quality copies made on chromogenic paper at reasonable cost). Keep one of these copies in the dark and use the other for display. [See section 9.E for addresses of labs offering Polaroid permanent color prints.]

Polaroid peel-apart prints (such as Polacolor ER and Polacolor 2) do much better in dark storage than Spectra and other Polaroid integral prints because with the peel-apart prints, the negative layer with its unused image-forming dyes and other chemicals is stripped away after processing. But these prints also have poor light-fading stability and should be displayed with caution. Copies should be made for long-term display.

6.B. Film

6.B.1. FILM STRUCTURE

Motion picture film is a relatively unstable and complicated product consisting of several layers of materials, each with different chemical and physical characteristics.

Black-and-white film has at least four and sometimes five layers [35:2-3]:

1. a clear gelatin antiabrasion layer that protects against mechanical damage;

2. the light-sensitive emulsion layer containing silver salts suspended in gelatin;
3. an adhesive substratum that binds the light-sensitive layer to the support;
4. the base or support, made of nitro-cellulose (nitrate film) prior to 1951, and now of acetyl-cellulose (triacetate or safety film); and
5. sometimes an antihalation layer, or a coating of gelatin to prevent curling, or both.

Color film has nine different layers:

1. the antiabrasion layer;
2. a blue-sensitive gelatin layer containing silver salts and color couplers;
3. a yellow filter layer that lets green and red rays pass through, but absorbs the blue light rays not absorbed in the blue layer;
4. a green-sensitive layer;
5. a gelatin barrier that prevents dyes from migrating from their own layer and spoiling the image during development;
6. a red-sensitive layer;
7. an adhesive substratum that binds the layers to the base;
8. the base or support layer made of cellulose triacetate or polyester; and
9. the antihalation or anticurl layer.

6.B.2. NITRATE-BASED FILM

Until the early 1950s 35mm movie film, both black-and-white and color, was produced almost exclusively on a nitrate base or support. Acetate or polyester bases were used for 8mm, 16mm, and 70mm film. Nitrate film decomposes even under favorable storage conditions and thus poses the most serious preservation problem for libraries and archives. It is highly flammable and has been known to spontaneously ignite at temperatures as low as 106 °F. [17:2] This problem seems to have been limited to motion picture film. There are no recorded instances of flat film (with the exception of X-ray film) causing fires or degrading in the same manner as roll film.

Cellulose nitrate progresses through five stages of decomposition: [25:4–5; 35:4]

1. the silver image begins to fade; the emulsion becomes amber or brown in color, and an acidic smell may become apparent;
2. the emulsion becomes sticky; negatives tend to stick together or to their containers; the acidic smell becomes stronger;
3. the film becomes soft in parts (formation of "honey"); blisters or gas bubbles form; the odor becomes strong and noxious;
4. the film is soft, welded to adjacent film, congealed to a solid mass, and is frequently covered with a viscous froth;

5. the film mass degenerates partially or entirely into a pungent, brown, acrid powder like gun-powder.

6.B.2.a. Film identification

Nitrate negatives are difficult to distinguish from acetate-based or polyester-based films. Cellulose acetate film should have "SAFETY" embossed on the edge of the film; some polyester based films have "ESTAR" on the film edge. There are two tests commonly used to help classify negatives as to the type of base or support used in their manufacture. The tests are taken from *The Care of Black and White Photographic Collections: Identification of Processes* by Siegfried Rempel. [27:6–7, 32] See Appendix F for additional tests to identify various types of plastic films.

The flotation test is a relative measure of the densities of the three different types of support. A sample punched from an edge or margin of the film (preferably in a transparent area) is dropped into a test-tube or small jar of trichloroethylene and trichloroethane. **NOTE: this test must be done in a well-ventilated area.**

The formulae for the test are:

1. Add 43cc of trichloroethylene to 25cc of trichloroethane for a total volume of 68cc. A pharmacist may be able to prepare this for you, if requested.

OR

2. Add 10cc of Kodak Film Cleaner to 40cc of trichloroethylene.

Either mixture (not both) should be put in a test tube. Small samples punched from the film should be inserted, the tube stoppered, and then inverted. Repeat the inversion three times.

Contemporary *acetate-based* films float to the top within ten seconds. Acetate-based materials, however, have been made from a number of compounds since their introduction. Earlier acetate will tend to stay in the solution and therefore will appear to be a polyester base.

Polyester-based film stays in the solution at various levels, neither falling to the bottom nor floating to the top during the ten-second test period.

Nitrate-based film immediately sinks to the bottom.

The second test consists of clipping (or punching) a small piece of film from the edge of the negative and burning it. This should not be done unless there is absolutely no other way to identify the base. Burning must be done in a well-ventilated room away from other nitrate and photographic materials. "The burning should **not** be conducted unless necessary, because cellulose nitrate film is self-sustaining once ignited. As it burns, this material generates its own supply of oxygen and **it cannot be extinguished until it has burnt itself out**. Cellulose acetate films will burn only with great difficulty and will not flame up or add to the combustion. Polyester film base burns with difficulty." [27:6–7, 19]

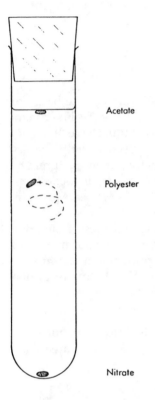

Acetate

Polyester

Nitrate

FIGURE 6.2. Flotation test. Source: Siegfried Rempel. *The Care of Black and White Photographic Collections: Identification of Processes.* Technical Bulletin No. 6. Ottawa: Canadian Conservation Institute, November 1980, p.7.

Any nitrate negatives that show signs of deterioration should be duplicated as soon as possible and the original film disposed of in an appropriate manner. Local fire departments should be contacted for disposal instructions. If local fire personnel do not know what to do, check with the Laboratory Services of the Motion Picture, Broadcasting, and Recorded Sound Division of the Library of Congress, the Northeast Document Conservation Center, Eastman Kodak customer service, or one of the preservation centers listed in Chapter 9.

6.B.2.b. Duplicating nitrate negatives

Quite often there will be legible photographic detail on the film into the third stage of decomposition. With careful handling many of the images can be saved with treatment and copying, especially if the film is in the first or second stage.

There are several options for making duplicates:

1. Either make a contact print from large-format original negatives or enlarge a smaller negative to standard size. Prints should be made on fiber-based photographic paper for maximum permanence.

2. Contact print the nitrate negative directly onto Direct Duplicating Film. If done correctly, this process will produce a stable negative that can be used to make high quality duplicate negatives with very little loss in detail.
3. Make an interpositive/duplicate negative. The nitrate negative is contact printed onto a sheet of film and processed. This produces a positive image, i.e., the interpositive. The interpositive is contact printed to produce a duplicate negative. The interpositive can be used as an archival copy to make as many duplicate negatives as needed.
4. Microfilm or video disc can be used to produce copies of complete collections, but neither approach creates high-quality archival copies.

The Northeast Document Conservation Center's *A Short Guide to Nitrate Negatives: History, Care, and Duplication* [25] contains guidelines for handling and treating nitrate negatives. This fact sheet should be in every library that has a collection of nitrate films.

6.B.2.c. Nitrate negative storage

Nitrate negatives should be stored separately from other negatives in a collection and, to minimize decomposition, should be placed in airtight enclosures and stored in a freezer set no higher than -5°C (23°F), with the relative humidity at 25 percent. The natural decomposition of cellulose nitrate is almost completely stopped at freezing temperatures. In any event, storage temperatures should not exceed 6°C (42.8°F), with the relative humidity between 50 and 60 percent. Storage cans should not be airtight; they should have holes punched in the bottom so the nitrate gases (which are heavier than air) can settle to the floor and be drawn off by an air-extraction system. Nitrate film should not be stored in buildings that contain living or working spaces. [35:6]

6.B.3. CELLULOSE ACETATE-BASED FILM

The combustible characteristics of cellulose nitrate-based film accelerated the efforts of the manufacturers of photographic materials to find a safe and satisfactory replacement. Although the first "safety film" based on cellulose acetate was reported in 1901, cellulose acetate was not used widely as a film base until 1923 when it became the support for 16mm amateur motion picture film. [1] "Cellulose acetate is manufactured by combining cotton linters or wood pulp (the sources of cellulose fibers) with acetic acid, acetic anhydride, and a catalyst such as sulfuric acid. The esterification process substituted acetyl groups for the hydroxyl groups on each glucose unit of the cellulose molecule. 'Fully esterified' cellulose has all three of its hydroxyl groups substituted, producing cellulose triacetate. A partially hydrolyzed acetate contains about 2-1/2 acetyl groups per glucose unit and this material is called cellulose diacetate." [15:4–5]

Cellulose diacetate, the first widely used acetate film base, was less than satisfactory. It was first manufactured by Eastman Kodak in about 1925. It was expensive to manufacture, had some degree of distortion, and was less resistant to moisture than cellulose nitrate. Kodak stopped making it in 1940, but Agfa/Ansco and Defender continued manufacturing it until they switched to polyester in 1955. [15:5]

Cellulose triacetate is tougher and more moisture resistant than cellulose diacetate. It gradually replaced cellulose nitrate as it became available in commercial quantities after World War II. Most professional motion picture film is still made from this material. Nitrate film ceased production in the United States in 1951. [15:5–7] "All 8mm and practically all 16mm, all 70mm, all magnetic films, and since the beginning of the 1950s, practically all 35mm films have been made on an acetate base." [35:7] See section 6.B.2.a and Appendix F for information on how to identify cellulose acetate.

6.B.3.a. Cellulose acetate film degradation

Although acetate film is much more stable than cellulose nitrate, precautions must be taken to ensure its preservation. The condition of some acetate negatives is deteriorating rapidly. Cellulose diacetate does not shrink, but it does warp. As the base degrades, it smells like vinegar, starts to channel (nitrate does not channel), becomes sticky, and distorts. Eventually the emulsion separates from the base, and the film is useless. The channeling seems to be random and can happen virtually overnight. All cellulose esters degrade over time, but procedures can be implemented to slow the aging process. Cellulose acetate negatives are extremely susceptible to high relative humidities and their fluctuations. Archival storage requirements recommend 30 percent relative humidity with little short-term recycling and a maximum temperature of 21 °C (about 70 °F). Acetate film should never be interfiled or stored in close proximity to nitrate film. Highly acidic kraft paper or glassine sleeves aggravate the degradation of acetate film. The paper sleeves or envelopes described in section 6.A.2.a should be used for containers and should follow ANSI PH1.53-1986 *American National Standard for Photography (Processing)—Processed Films, Plates and Paper—Filing Enclosures and Containers for Storage.* [15:56–57]

The date of manufacture, the manufacturer, and notch code can be used to identify film types. Notch codes were used to identify sheet film, both acetate and nitrate, by various manufacturers, at least up until 1971. They generally appear in the top right edge (holding the negative with emulsion toward the viewer) of the negative. They can be used to identify the name and approximate period of manufacture of the film. The National Center for Film and Video Preservation can assist in identifying the codes [see section 9.F]. "Negatives from some manufacturers made during specific time periods have a very high incidence of degradation. This is most evident in the Defender film manufactured between 1947–1955, and, to a lesser degree, some Kodak film in the 1930s." [15:54] David Horvath's report on acetate negatives in 1987 concludes "that every institution which contains a substantial quantity of safety film dating from 1925–1955 will find problems with degraded film base somewhere in their collection sooner or later." [15:55]

6.B.4. POLYESTER-BASED FILM

Polyesters are polymers formed by the condensation of polybasic acids with polyhydric alcohols that form polyethylene terephthalate. They are used as a film base because of their dimensional stability, strength, flexibility, transparency, and resistance to tearing and burning. They have the same requisite properties as nitrate and acetate bases, i.e., they are fully transparent and elastic. In addition, they have greater tensile strength, are unaffected by temperature changes or humidity, and do not release harmful gases. [35:9]

The emulsion layer of polyester film consists primarily of animal gelatin, a substance made by boiling collagen from cartilage, hide, and other connective tissue. Under good storage conditions gelatin is fairly durable, but it easily absorbs moisture, causing it to swell and become tacky, especially in warm conditions. Under favorable conditions, i.e., relative humidity of 60 percent or higher and above 70°F, mold and mildew will readily grow on gelatin. "Fungus growth on film emulsion mostly appears as a white, greenish, or grey covering. Fungus mold penetrates the emulsion, and if it is left to flourish undisturbed, the colors are altered and finally the entire emulsion is destroyed." [35:10]

Although there is some disagreement on the specific relative humidity and temperatures for storing film, a constant relative humidity of 30 to 50 percent and 68°F to 72°F is generally recommended. The cooler the better, but the RH should not be below 30 percent. Film stored at 20 percent RH or lower will become brittle. See section 6.A.2 for information about storage containers and Appendix F on how to identify polyester.

6.C. Fungus Removal
from Films and Slides

Surface fungus can be removed from prints, negatives, and slides by wiping them with a soft, plush pad, absorbent cotton, or a chamois moistened sparingly with Kodak Film Cleaner. Do not use water to remove fungus because mold will make the emulsion soluble in water; water then will damage the image. If the gelatin is degraded, e.g., localized stripping occurs, the fungus has permanently damaged the emulsion and restoration is not possible. "If the fungus attack is only slight and localized, the deterioration may be corrected by photographic reproduction, but retouching of the copy negative or print made from it will probably be necessary. Any enclosures or storage containers that have been in contact with the prints [slides or negatives] should be destroyed." [8:137]

Slides should be removed from their mounts before cleaning and inserted into new mounts after treatment.

Slides processed prior to 1970 may be coated with a film lacquer. Ektachrome films were never lacquered. "If the fungus growth has not penetrated to the emulsion of films that are protected by a film lacquer, the lacquer can usually be removed by soaking the film in a dilute solution of sodium bicarbonate (baking soda). Dissolve a level tablespoon of soda in a pint of water at room temperature. If the artifact is a slide on Kodachrome film, add about ½ fluid ounce of formaldehyde (15mL), 37 percent solution. Agitate the transparency for one minute, or a color negative for four minutes. Rinse for one minute in room temperature water. The film should then be bathed for about 30 seconds in KODAK PHOTO-FLO 200 Solution (diluted as stated on the bottle) or an equivalent, and hung up to dry in a dust-free place. The film can be relacquered after it is completely dry." [8:137]

If the fungus growth is extensive, the treatment described above should not be used.

A solution of eight ounces of denatured alcohol and one-half ounce of nondetergent household ammonia can be used to remove lacquer from films that have been damaged by fungus. The type of alcohol recommended for thinning shellac should be used; do not use rubbing alcohol. The negatives or slides can be dipped into and agitated in the solution, or they can be wiped with absorbent cotton saturated with the mixture. "The film should be supported, emulsion-side up, on a smooth nonporous surface such as a sheet of glass, to avoid scratching or marking the film base." [8:138] Dry the slides before remounting. Kodacolor film negatives can be treated by dipping and agitating them in the solution for no longer than two minutes. [8:138]

For more information on fungus removal see Kodak Publication AE-22 *Prevention and Removal of Fungus on Prints and Films*, [24] and Kodak Publication C-24 *Notes on Tropical Photography*. [20] Other salvage procedures are discussed in section 8.E.5. **Always consult a competent photographic conservator before treating photographic images.**

6.D. Phonograph Recordings

This section will deal with the storage and preservation requirements for phonograph recordings. A phonograph record "includes any format that consists of a turning surface with a wave-form groove which vibrates a stylus to produce sound." [16:236] The discussion in this work, however, will be limited to disc formats (not cylinders) and only to 12-inch, 33-1/3 revolutions per minute (rpm), long-playing (LP); 7-inch, 45 rpm, polyvinyl chloride; and 78 rpm shellac records. Magnetic tape formats are treated in section 6.E; compact discs in section 6.G.

According to Gerald Gibson of the Library of Congress, virtually no work is currently going on in the area of the preservation of sound recordings. [14] Most recordings were not designed and manufactured for long-term storage, and as Cunha wrote in 1971, "Sound recordings are made for play-back quality with emphasis on low manufacturing cost. Long life has never been a primary consideration." [10:41]

Most phonograph recordings housed in libraries are made of poly-vinyl chloride or shellac. These materials consist primarily of polymerized organic molecules linked together in long chains that, in turn, are often cross-linked to each other. "Identical substances are used in the manufacture of both sound recordings and books. For example, lampblack—a form of powdered carbon—is used to make records black (polyvinyl chloride is colorless) and to make printer's ink black." [19:23] Wood pulp ground into wood flour was sometimes used as a filler for shellac discs. Many laminated discs had paper cores. Sound recordings are often packaged and stored in paper products and have paper labels. Therefore, since they are made of virtually the same substances as books, storage requirements for most phonograph recordings are very similar to those for paper-based materials.

6.D.1. DISC STORAGE

For general storage conditions, a stable temperature of about 70°F with a relative humidity of 50 percent is acceptable. Lower temperatures are desirable, but it is more important to maintain environmental stability than to have low temperatures. Fluctuations should be limited to a maximum of 10 percent. [19:25] As noted in section 2.B, central air-conditioning systems should always have well-maintained dust filters to reduce problems from this source. Shelving areas should be regularly vacuumed and cleaned.

Dust levels should be kept as low as possible because sound information on recordings is contained in the disc grooves. Dust, lint, or other foreign matter collecting in the grooves will create distortion in the playback process. Most archives and libraries cannot afford to construct and maintain the ideal environment: a positive-pressure storage area where the air-conditioning system keeps the storage area air pressure higher than the outside pressure so dust cannot enter. An alternative is to store recordings in well-built steel cabinets with tight-fitting doors. Unfortunately, such cabinets usually must be custom designed and constructed. For most situations, however, the closed cabinets available from archival and library supply houses will help protect recordings from dust and other airborne contaminants.

The only practical way to shelve discs is vertically on end. They should be arranged on horizontal heavy-duty metal shelves (conforming to the same specifications outlined in sections 2.E.2 and 3.B.1) that are strong enough to support several hundred discs. The shelving should be wide enough to accommodate the widest discs in the collection. Discs can be damaged if they protrude beyond the shelf into an aisle. Discs *must be fully vertical* at all times and never slant or tilt against each other. The round shape of the disc is vulnerable to improper loading and can be easily deformed if subject to external stress. Such slanting causes serious warping, which adversely affects playback. In some cases warping can be corrected, but for many discs it is impossible to reverse satisfactorily. To avoid tilting, each shelf should be divided into vertical compartments or subdivisions by the use of semi-permanent spacing panels or dividers. Each divider should be spaced about 3-1/2 to 4 inches apart so no more than 20 discs can be stored in each subdivision. Each compartment should be filled completely with discs so they will not lean off the vertical. If metal subdividers or panels are not available or are impractical in a specific situation, acid-free cardboard containers have been used by some libraries to achieve the same result. Bookends should not be used because they cannot supply the correct support and will contribute to warpage. [19:30–33]

Most libraries and archives arrange shelving of discs by size. This simplifies shelf setup and is economical of space. Records should always be stored "in the inner sleeve and jacket, with the sleeve's opening up, to prevent the record from accidentally falling out and to deter airborne dust from getting at the record. Replace the inner sleeve in the jacket while the record is being played, again for protection from dust." [16:251]

6.D.2. DISC PACKAGING

LP records are usually packaged in a polyethylene, glassine, or paper inner liner or sleeve to protect the disc grooves; the liner is then placed in a paper box or dust jacket, which is shrink-wrapped. If shelved and housed according to the specifications outlined above, the original packaging is adequate if the shrink-wrapping is removed. Shrink-wrap must always be removed because it "is highly temperature-sensitive and can contract, causing disc warpage." [19:35] Even the paper and glassine inner linings should be removed and replaced with polyethylene liners, because most contain acid that can migrate to the disc and attack the vinyl surfaces. [19:35] Appendix F contains information on how to identify polyethylene.

Damaged or lost inner liners and jackets should be replaced, not repaired. Repairs will create uneven surfaces against the recording, and adhesives may bleed onto the record itself.

Shellac 78s should not be stored in their original packages. Each recording should be rehoused in acid-free liners made of 35 pound kraft paper. The original wrapping should probably be kept for the historical information it contains. A more sophisticated wrapping consists of four layers of different materials laminated together: the exterior layer is kraft paper, followed by polyethylene, aluminum foil, and a final layer of polyethylene. "The polyethylene and foil act as vapor barriers, while the polyethylene inner layer protects the surface of the record from abrasion and damage." [9:45] These are available from Conservation Resources International [see section 9.E.1].

6.D.3. CARE AND HANDLING

Do not touch the surface of the recording. To remove the disc from its enclosure, bow out the sides of the jacket and pull the disc out by a corner of the inner liner. Handle the disc by gently supporting it by the edge and paper covered center. Do not allow the recording surface of the disc to touch any surface except the inner sleeve and the turntable. Reverse this procedure when returning the disc to the jacket. [16:251–252]

Cleaning discs is a controversial subject. McWilliams covers the topic in some detail in his chapter on the preservation of sound recordings. [19:36–43] If debris is evident on the recording surface, a number of cleaning methods are available, but most involve washing. The Library of Congress employs a sonic cleaner that thoroughly cleans LP discs. Unfortunately, the cost of the equipment and the use of Freon as the primary cleaning agent removes this approach from use in most libraries. With the exception of the Keith Monks record washer, which vacuums the water and suspended dust particles out of the disc grooves, it is problematical whether washing does more harm than good. Several companies, however, have products that can improve sound quality over the life of the disc [see section 9.E.2].

Phonograph records can be cleaned with a soft, lint-free cloth or brush. Conduct the cleaning by circling in the direction of the grooves. Don't use alcohol—it breaks down the bond between the laminate and the base. If the disc is badly soiled it may be washed in cool (or room temperature) distilled water with a lint-free cloth. One that is recommended is the Selvyt cloth used for cleaning and polishing musical band instruments. It has a short, stiff nap, similar to a cotton chamois cloth, that helps remove debris from the grooves. The cloth is also useful for drying the disc. The cloth may be purchased in stores that sell band instruments. Clean the disc by using a slightly damp cloth in a circling motion following the direction of the grooves. If the disc is very dirty, use a drop or two of Joy™ dishwashing detergent in a quart of distilled water. If a large portion of the collection needs cleaning, contact the Laboratory Services at the Motion Picture, Broadcasting, and Recorded Sound Division of the Library of Congress for the latest information.

6.E. Magnetic Tape Media

6.E.1. AUDIO TAPE

The information in this section is reprinted, with permission, from "Increasing the Life of Your Audio Tape," by Jim Wheeler. [37] The information contained herein is based on theoretical investigations, accelerated tests, and Mr. Wheeler's experience as an audio engineer. By following the recommendations presented, the life of the information recorded on tape will be increased, but there is no guarantee that all information recorded on tape will be permanent.

6.E.1.a. The primary archival factors

All high-density data storage media must be treated with tender, loving care if they are to reproduce their information faithfully years later. . . . Magnetic tape is not perfect, but it will last for decades or centuries—if properly cared for. The main variables to control are:

Temperature	60°–70°F (15–20°C) or lower [39:2]
Humidity	20–40 percent relative humidity (RH)
Tape pack	Wind end to end before long-term storage
Dust	Store tape in a sealed container.

6.E.1.b. Potential problem tapes

Most tapes are iron-oxide coated on polyethylene terephthalate (PET) base film using a polyurethane binder. The iron-oxide and PET are very unstable. The polyurethane binder is hygroscopic and will deteriorate if stored at high temperature and/or high humidity (above 20°C/40 percent RH). [These factors are] the most critical concern for most archival tape.

Some tapes are made with chromium-dioxide (CrO_2) coated on PET. The CrO_2 particle has had a history of instability. The tape manufacturers using CrO_2 have been working on the stability problem, and some now have products that they believe are stable.

Acetate base film was used for audio tapes in the 1950s and into the 1960s and is still used for movie film. Acetate will deteriorate with age. Recordings made on acetate base film should be dubbed to polyester base-film tape.

Thin base-film tapes (90 min and longer on cassettes) are not good for long-term storage. Print-through is greater; tape packing is more critical, and tape stretching is more likely. A problem cassette may be "salvaged" by playing it on a professional tape deck.

6.E.1.c. Recovering from possible problems

Here are some possible problems and ways of recovering from them.

6.E.1.c.1. High temperature

Reel tapes can take up to 160°F (70°C) with no apparent problems, but cassettes can have warpage problems above about 130°F (55°C). The inside of a delivery van can reach 160°F (70°C) on a very hot day. If a tape has been subjected to a high temperature, cool it (under 20°C, if possible) for a couple of days. Then rewind it to relieve the stresses in the pack. [See section 8.E.6 for more information on the salvage of magnetic tapes.]

6.E.1.c.2. Water

If tape has been subjected to moisture, dry it before fungus starts. Place the tape in an oven at 120°F (50°C) for about a day. After it has cooled down to room temperature, shuttle it to the end and back on a tape recorder with few tape-contact parts. If the tape has been submerged in water, then repeat the heat-shuttle cycle a second time. To counteract the effects of the water, store the tape in a cold environment (not freezing) for a few days. After returning to room temperature, shuttle to the end and back to relieve stresses in the pack. [See section 8.E.6 for more information on the salvage of magnetic tapes.]

6.E.1.c.3. Loose pack

To determine whether a pack is loose, hold the reel by the hub and pull on the outer layer. If the pack rotates, the pack is loose and should not be accelerated or stored for very long. Play the tape to the end and then rewind. If the recorder tensions are set properly and the tape is not damaged, it will now be a tight pack. Carbon backed tape is less likely to have pack slippage.

6.E.1.c.4. Friction

In the early days of tape making, some tape manufacturers used lubricants which eventually migrated out of the coating. In such a case, the actual recording is still okay; the problem is the high friction. Such a high-friction tape can be "rejuvenated" for at least a few passes by applying Krytox™ to the oxide surface. This can be done by running the tape over a pad soaked in a solution of less than one percent Krytox™ and about 99 percent Freon TF.

6.E.1.c.5. Print-through

Most consumers are not even conscious of print-through, but the audiophile and the professional are well aware of it. There are six major variables that will affect print-through:

1. Temperature: High temperature is bad.
2. Tape thickness: Thin tape is bad.
3. Time: Print-through becomes worse with time.

4. Rewind: Rewinding the tape will reduce print-through.
5. Presence of a magnetic field.
6. Wavelength of recorded signals (low frequencies are worse).

To minimize print-through:

1. Use thick tape.
2. Store at low temperature (but not below freezing).
3. Ship in an insulated container to reduce temperature variations. Ship audio masters in a steel container (film can) to prevent any magnetic fields from affecting print-through.
4. Rewind every year or two.
5. Store tails out. This has two advantages:
   a. The tape must be rewound before being played, which will decrease print-through.
   b. An analysis of print-through shows that the pre-print signal is greater than the postprint signal (echo). So when replayed after tails-out storage, the echo becomes the louder signal (which seems natural). This gives the impression of lower print-through. (This is only effective for tapes recorded in one direction.)

Do not copy a tape with a print-through problem because that will only transfer the problem permanently. Rewinding the tape will reduce print-through.

6.E.1.d. Magnetic fields

Many people are concerned about tapes either self-erasing or being erased accidentally. The only legitimate concern about erasing tape is the "record" button on the tape recorder—it was designed to erase tape. If a valuable tape is to be safe, the tab on the cassette should be broken off or the tape recorder record circuit should be disabled (record lockout). Other forms of erasure to a tape are extremely unlikely. There is cause for some concern with audio mastering tapes being placed near a small magnetic field (about 10-20 gauss or greater) since print-through may be affected.

The National Bureau of Standards (NBS) [now the National Institute of Standards and Technology (NIST)] researched all possible forms of erasing tapes and concluded that it is not easy to erase tapes. Although the tests were performed on computer tape and are not directly correlatable to audio tape, the figures give an approximation. Some of the NBS findings are:

1. The largest hand-held magnet that could be found (2500 gauss) causes a five percent loss (about 0.5 dB, which is not noticeable) of signal when held two inches (51 mm) from the tape.
2. A tape held 16 inches (406 mm) from a large junkyard magnet had a five percent loss of signal. The magnet had a lifting capability of 800 lb (363 kg).

Airport security systems will have no effect on magnetic tape. X-rays do not affect magnetic devices, and hand-held detectors have too small a field to affect magnetic tape.

Motors, generators, and transformers are designed for efficiency, so their magnetic fields are contained internally. It is unrealistic to believe that any such devices can affect a tape kept more than about an inch away from the surface of such a device.

Television sets and loudspeakers have magnetic coils, but their fields are small and concentrated. Also, such devices are contained within cabinets, which makes direct contact with the coils impossible. Some microphones and earphones may have fields large enough to cause some second-harmonic distortion on audio tape.

The desensitizing and resensitizing equipment used in "full circulating" library electronic security systems (such as the 3M Tattle Tape system) can erase both tapes and floppy diskettes. The sensing screens, however, will not affect magnetic media.

6.E.1.e. Tape tension

The tension at which the tape is wound before storage is a very important factor. This can be measured by a special tension gauge, such as a Tentelometer. A low tension will cause a loose pack, which may result in pack slippage and possible folded layers of tape. Too high a tension can cause the tape to take on a different length and can also imprint the roughness of the backside onto the smooth oxide surface.

Some tape recorders wind tape at a constant tension, whereas others are designed to wind the tape at constant torque (force x radius is constant). Constant torque produces a preferred pack tension profile, but a constant tension is okay.

The ideal tension for the tape is proportional to the cross-sectional area of the tape—the width and the thickness. Figure [6.3] shows how these two variables relate to the tension. The total tape thickness can be determined by using a micrometer. Measure the thickness of 10 layers of tape; then divide by 10 to determine the thickness of a single layer. Now refer to Figure [6.3] to determine the proper tension. For a constant-tension tape recorder, use the nominal tension value.

If the tension decreases as more tape is wound onto the hub, then it is a constant-torque system. In this case the tension of the tape near the hub should not be more than the high value of Figure [6.3]. The tension of the tape as the pack approaches full diameter should not be less than the low value of Figure [6.3].

6.E.1.f. The tape recorder

Many tape problems can be traced to the recorder on which the tapes were recorded. It is very important that the recorder be properly maintained.

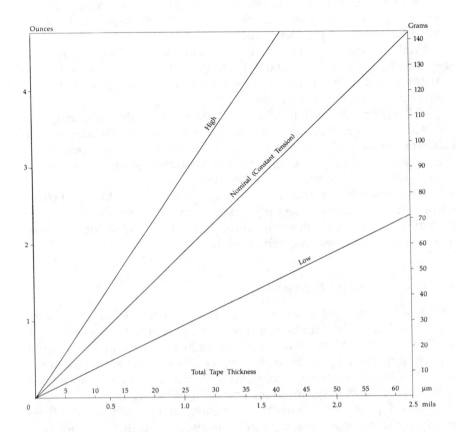

FIGURE 6.3. Tension per ½-inch (6 mm) width of tape. Source: Jim Wheeler. "Increasing the Life of Your Audio Tape." In *Journal of the Audio Engineering Society* 36 (April 1988): 235.

1. Always keep the tape path components clean.
2. Keep the recorder out of direct sun.
3. Cover the recorder with a dust cover.
4. Degauss the heads about every 100 hours. A magnetized record head will cause distortion in record.
5. Maintain the recorder as prescribed in its maintenance manual.
6. About every 1,000 hours of use, have the recorder checked for worn guides, worn heads, and proper tension.
7. Clean the recorder after a damaged tape has been used.

Using an inexpensive tape recorder (most consumer recorders) is more likely to create problems due to poor tape guiding, speed variations, poor tension control, and so on. The more expensive consumer decks and the professional decks are built with more precision and better parts.

6.E.1.g. The tape

1. Back-coated tape is preferable.
2. If possible, do not use thin base-film tape.
3. Try not to touch the tape with your fingers.
4. Cut off the end (reel tape) if it is damaged.
5. Do not allow the end to wrinkle or fold over while threading reel tape.
6. Before recording, fast forward to the end and back to relieve stresses.
7. Do not reuse old tapes whose environmental history is unknown.
8. Break off the tab on a cassette to prevent accidental record. Use record lockout on reel recorders.
9. Mark archival tapes with a large red *stop* or *do not erase* label.

6.E.1.h. The operating environment

1. A cool, dry, dust-free environment is preferred.
2. Do not leave tape in a hot place, such as near a heater or in the direct sun.
3. The floor should be covered with an anti-static carpet or made of a hard surface that can be mopped.
4. Airborne contaminants can best be eliminated with an air-conditioning system equipped with a 0.3 mm bag filter.
5. Dust from any nearby construction should be controlled or the tape recorder area should be sealed off.

6.E.1.i. Tape storage in a home environment

An uncontrolled environment is not recommended, but that does not mean that tapes stored in this manner will deteriorate. [Jim Wheeler] has audio tapes that have been stored 35 years at home and they still play back just fine (and they are acetate). Practicing the following helps ensure the longevity of your recording.

1. Before storing the tape, wind it to the end and back to relieve any stresses in the pack.
2. Secure the loose end of tape (if it is on a reel).
3. Expose the tape to a dry environment for a few days before sealing the tape inside a thick, quick-seal plastic freezer bag.
4. Store the tape in an area where the temperature stays under 70°F (21°C) and does not vary much. Avoid temperatures below freezing.
5. Keep the tape out of the direct sun.

6. Do not store the tape near combustibles, such as wood and cardboard.
7. Do not store tape in a room that may be flooded.
8. Rewind the tape every few years.

6.E.1.j. Archival tape storage

For that extra margin of insurance, the following should be practiced to increase tape life.

1. Leave the tape on the take-up hub after it has been in record or play.
2. Secure the loose end of a tape (if it is on a reel). Do not use any type of hold-down tape that will leave a sticky residue.
3. Store the tape at a cool, stable temperature (20 °C [68 °F] or lower is preferred).
4. A dry environment (preferably 30 percent RH) is necessary and can be obtained several ways:
   a. Use a humidity-controlled air system.
   b. Seal in an airtight container.
   c. Seal each tape in a metalized plastic bag.
   d. Seal each tape in a thick, quick-seal plastic freezer bag.

Note: Before sealing a tape, expose it for a few days to a dry environment (preferably 30 percent RH). This should be near the same temperature at which the tape will be stored.

5. Remove combustibles from the storage area. Steel shelves are good and will not affect magnetic tape. Wood and cardboard retain moisture, as well as create heat during a fire. Some cassette plastics may not have flame retardant in them.
6. Do not store tape in a room that may be flooded.
7. Rewind the tape every 5–10 years.

[For further information consult] H. N. Bertram, M. K. Stafford, and D. R. Mills, "The Print-Through Phenomenon," *Journal of the Audio Engineering Society* [3]; S. B. Geller, *The Effects of Magnetic Fields on Magnetic Storage Media Used in Computers* [13]; and J. Wheeler, "Long-Term Storage of Videotape," *Journal of the Society of Motion Picture and Television Engineers* [38].

6.E.2. VIDEO TAPE

Portions of this section on the care and handling of videocassette tapes are reprinted with the permission of the Ampex Corporation [39] and from Alan Calmes' article, "New Preservation Concern: Video Recordings," in the *Commission on Preservation and Access Newsletter.* [6] Calmes' article summarizes the current situation for the preservation of video tape [6]:

Video tape is not a long-lasting medium; each time it is played it loses some of the picture signal. Another major problem with the preservation of video recordings is not so much the life-expectancy of the tape but the obsolescence of the machinery necessary to read the tape. Once a format has been abandoned, machinery will rapidly become scarce and even spare parts will become difficult to find after a few years.

A particular video tape format requires a particular machine for playing. Since 1956 over 30 different formats have been used, each requiring a special machine. Most of these have been professional, educational, and industrial formats. There are only three consumer formats: Beta™, VHS™, and 8mm. The manufacturer will not stockpile spare parts for old machines; those out in service have a mean-time to failure of only about 2000 hours of playing time. Beta™ spare parts, for example, are already scarce.

Standards will not prevent the proliferation of incompatible formats. The many formats created during the past 30 years were produced according to standards. The new digital formats, however, may provide for re-copying of images without degradation of image quality, since the information will always be in some kind of digital code rather than in an analog signal as has been the case until today. Each time an analog recording is compiled there is an increase in ratio of noise to signal.

In the future, preservation of digital video pictures will become an activity closely associated with the complex world of computer data preservation, the use of computer storage devices, and constantly changing software. New tape formulations with unknown aging characteristics, such as metal particle tape, are likely to replace the more familiar magnetic tape, and new formats for high definition television will further complicate matters.

As it is known today, magnetic video tape for analog video recordings consists of a base of polyethylene terephthalate (PET), commonly called 'polyester,' and a recording layer of polyester polyurethane, referred to here to avoid confusion as 'polyurethane.' Some tapes are also back-coated. Polyester is dimensionally stable (which is important for consistent tracking), strong, and long-lasting. Polyurethane is durable, which is important for resisting wear by contact with the video-machine reading head. The polyurethane layer is called the 'binder,' for it binds in place the ferromagnetic particles which hold the signal which is the source of information to the machine for generating a picture. Lubricants also are placed in the binder to prevent friction. The back-coating, usually of polyurethane, prevents static. The chemical formulations for each layer vary from one manufacturer to the next; they are industrial secrets. It is a challenge to the professional and consumer alike to judge which tape is best.

The *U.S. Consumer Reports* have evaluated tapes for drop-outs, noise, dynamic range, and band width, but not for durability and longevity. There are differences in the performance of tapes and certainly there are differences in longevity. Higher quality tape may give better performance but not necessarily better life-expectancy. During the tape manufacturing process, despite industrial quality control procedures, some tapes will be flawed. Flaws can lead to difficulties, such as drop-outs. Some off-brand tapes may be manufactured with recycled polyester; some may even be reused tapes.

Accelerated aging of tape samples have been carried out by NIST, for the National Archives. NIST estimates the useful lifetime of digital computer tapes to be about 20 years when maintained in ambient environmental conditions. (Currently, video tapes and computer tapes are similar magnetic tapes.)

Considering the system as a whole—machine and medium—professionally produced video magnetic tape recordings may have a life-expectancy of 15-30 years under controlled storage conditions, careful handling, infrequent playback, and maintenance of a serviceable machine. [6:5-6]

"With present technology, the only way to guarantee the long term (100+ years) preservation of video images is to copy them to black and white motion picture film and store the film in a cool, dry, pollutant free environment. One can copy the video images to color film for medium-term (50+ years) preservation. In cold storage (0.0°C) color images can survive long term. A future method of preserving video recordings may be to copy analog video to digital video and thereafter copy the digital tape periodically to keep up with changing technology and to avoid being left with a tape that cannot be read by existing machines." [6:6]

6.E.2.a. VCR care

The Beta™ and VHS™ formats have both proven to be very reliable, and the VCRs require very little maintenance. [39:2]

The tape head and tape must be clean. The distance between the video head of the player/recorder and the tape itself is only about 0.02 mils. A fingerprint can leave as much as a 0.6 mils film on the tape, which can push the read/write head away from the tape, resulting in a loss of signal. Dust particles are huge in comparison with the reading gap and may gouge into the surface of the tape; this is called 'head crash.'

Normal library environment is likely to have high and fluctuating relative humidity, which is detrimental to tape, resulting in embrittlement of the tape. If care is not taken to wind the tape evenly, to keep the reading head clean and to wipe away residues from tape surfaces, the tape will become damaged and the system as a whole will become degraded: a damaged tape will damage the machine and a damaged machine, in turn, will damage tapes.

With consumer video products, it is difficult to control the tape guide, speed, and tension. A professional recorder/player, on the other hand, is designed specifically to provide for control over these variables. A professional video recorder, however, costs about 100 times more than a consumer VCR. [6:6]

Another VCR problem is tape misalignment while the tape is being recorded. Misalignment will create a nonstandard recording,

which will [appear] as a picture break-up when the tape is played back on another VCR. There are several possible causes of misalignment:

1. Cassette not seating properly.

2. Tape guides misaligned or worn.

3. Debris on the guides.

4. Tape recorded in an extreme environment.

These problems are more common on a consumer VCR than on a professional videorecorder because consumer VCRs are not ruggedly built and usually not properly maintained. Moreover, the Beta™ and VHS™ formats have very narrow recording tracks and the heads and tape run at very slow speeds compared to professional videotape recorders. [39:2]

To avoid these problems

a competent technician should perform the following procedures on the VCR after every 1000 hours of use. This technician should:

1. Clean all tape path components.

2. Visually check for loose or worn guides.

3. Use a tension gauge to check for correct tape tension.

4. Check for tape guide alignment by using a prerecorded test tape.

Tape guides are unlikely to become misaligned due to normal VCR use. The normal everyday culprits are dust, water and previously damaged tapes. Most VCRs are front-loading models which are designed to keep dirt and spilled water out of the critical mechanical mechanism. Cleaning a VCR tape path should not be attempted by an untrained person. Either have a professional person clean it or use a special cleaning cassette. A good quality cleaning cassette will not damage a VCR. Use it about every 100 hours or when a problem develops. [39:3]

Some experts, however, advocate waiting until the loss of picture quality indicates that head cleaning is clearly advisable. They contend that the less abrasion allowed to the head the longer the VCR will last. Store the VCR in a cool, dry, clean area and out of the direct sun.

6.E.2.b. Tape care

The following tips on extending the life of video recordings are taken from Calmes' article [6], with comments from Wheeler [39] as appropriate:

"Use professional 1 inch C format to generate a preservation master." [6:6] "The special consumer tapes that have extended playtime have a thinner basefilm than do normal tapes. These extended-time tapes are more susceptible to damage and should not be used for long-term storage. In addition, using tape with a carbon backcoat is preferred for long-term storage because layer-to-layer slippage is minimized. Some tape manufacturers sell carbon backcoated tapes as a standard product, while others sell it as an industrial-grade tape. It is also a good policy to use only known name-brand tapes because of the quality standards maintained by the companies that produce them." [39:3] Use a tape-certifying machine to weed out flawed tapes.

"Use a commercial VCR for the user reference copy. Do not use high compaction systems, because hardware precision increases with compaction, as the tape tracks are very close together.... Record at standard speed or the fastest speed available. Rewind at slow speed before storage and before playing. Rewind in the same environment as the storage environment before storage and the same environment as the operating equipment before recording or playing. Tape tension must not be too loose nor too tight." [6:6] The tape should be retensioned before playback and rewound evenly.

"Monitor the condition of tapes: look for edge damage and residues on surface. Recopy when deterioration is noted and/or when the format is obsolete. Differentiate between the master copy and use/distribution copies. Produce the master copy under controlled operations and environment. Designate a repository to be responsible for the preservation of the master copy. Only use the master to make distribution copies; ideally, this should be done rarely. Rewind the master on slow speed every few years. A special rewind machine should be used." [6:6]

"Most importantly, relative humidity (RH) should be kept stable and low, the lower the better, but not below 30 percent relative humidity (RH) and never above 55 percent RH. Once a relative humidity level has been chosen, say 40 percent RH, then it should not vary more than an average of plus/minus five percent RH during a 24 hour period. Tapes may be conditioned to 40 percent RH at storage temperature and sealed in foil-lined bags, in which case only the temperature need be maintained exactly." [6:6] "Tape kept in a metal-coated/sealed bag or sealed container will not be subjected to the moisture variations of the storage room. Two thick plastic quick-seal bags provide adequate packaging for most storage environments, but a metal-coated plastic bag is better, since the metal serves as a vapor barrier. Before tape is sealed into a moisture-proof package, it should first be exposed to a cool-dry environment for a few days. A cool-dry environment is below 68°F and 40 percent RH." [39:3]

"Temperature is equally important and should be stable and as low as possible, but not below freezing and never above 23°C (73°F). Minor fluctuations such as an average plus/minus 2.8°C (5°F) are permitted during a 24 hour period." [6:6]

Store the tapes in a cool-dry environment, in a sealed bag or container [see above] and in a fireproof area. Do not store them in a basement because of the possible flood hazard. [39:5]

"The tape and the machine should be conditioned to the same environment. The air must be clean and free of pollutant gases, especially those from oil-based paints, insecticides, perfumes, cigarettes, and chemical cleaners. There should be no dust or smoke present in the storage or operating environment. Even short term inappropriate environmental conditions can contribute to the degradation of the tape and its magnetic signal." [6:6]

"One must avoid subjecting tapes to shocks of rapid and extreme temperature/relative humidity changes, especially upon reading the tape on a reader. Before using tapes that have been shipped, re-equilibrate them 24–48 hours in the same environment as the video machine." [6:6]

"Magnets are not a problem, unless one is held within about an inch of the tape. Fields from devices like TV sets, microwave ovens and airport security x-ray detectors will not affect tape recordings." [39:3]

Break off the tab on the cassette to prevent accidental erasure.

[See section 8.E.6 for information concerning the salvage of magnetic tape.]

6.E.2.c. Cassette care

Wheeler's article also contains good advice for the care of video cassettes.

"Consumer videotape is packaged in plastic cassettes which sometimes have problems of alignment in the VCR. Also, these consumer cassettes sometimes have friction problems. Either of these factors can cause the tape to pack poorly when it is wound at high speed onto either the supply spool (left) or the take-up spool (right).

"Alignment is checked in the factory, but cassettes could warp if left inside a truck or on a loading dock in the hot sun during shipment. The cassette can take temperatures of up to 130°F (55°C) with no problem, but over 130 °F may cause permanent warpage. The inside of a truck or car can reach 160 °F (70 °C) on a hot day. If a tape has been exposed to high temperature, rewind it to relieve the stresses in the pack.

"Possible friction variation in a cassette and possible incorrect rewind tension of the VCR can be overcome by running the recorded tape in Play or Record mode before it is stored, because it is the low speed mode which produces the best tape pack. This is not necessary for tapes that will be stored for only a few months. Tapes intended to be stored for many years should be recorded at standard speed (SP). This is because standard speed is the fastest speed, and, hence, the lowest density recording. The lower density means the data has a better chance of being recovered in case of tape damage." [39:4]

6.E.2.d. Tape storage in a home environment

Follow the same recommendations as for audiotapes in section 6.E.1.i.

[See section 8.E.6 for information concerning the salvage of magnetic tape.]

6.F. Computer (Floppy) Disks

This discussion is limited to 5.25-inch personal computer floppy diskettes. ANSI standard X3.125-1985 specifies that the magnetic disk base be made of biaxially oriented polyethylene terephthalate or an equivalent. [2] The magnetic medium most commonly used is iron oxide (gamma-Fe_2O_3) mixed with carbon black to reduce static electricity, a lubricant, binder, and other materials. The medium is bound to the substrate to form a circular disk about 5.125 inches in diameter by .048 to .067 inches thick. The disk is housed in a protective jacket 5.25 inches square. The inner surface of the jacket is protected by a layer of lint-free lubricated liner.

Floppy disks are designed to perform within a temperature range of 50 °F to 125 °F. They can be shipped within temperatures ranging from -40 °F to 125 °F. They are very sturdy and are able to endure a wide variety of damage and still retain and release data. They are not designed for permanent retention of information, but should be able to store data for many years if housed in the same environment recommended for audio and video magnetic tapes. The same precautions should be taken for cleanliness, temperature, and humidity as outlined for magnetic tape media in sections 6.E.1 and 6.E.2.

In addition to the guidelines in those sections, certain special precautions must be taken for floppy diskettes:

Never bend a diskette.

Never touch the surface of a diskette (the part inside the oval shaped hole).

Never force a diskette into the slot of a disk drive.

Always replace diskettes in their envelopes when they are removed from a disk drive.

Never place another object on a diskette.

Always store diskettes vertically in an enclosed, dust-free container.

Never place diskettes near a heat source, in direct sunlight, or near magnetic fields like those found near electric motors.

Although the data on the diskettes should not be affected by security devices (such as those at airports), because of changing technology it is prudent to pass the diskettes around the devices instead of allowing them to be passed through.

If disks become wet or a foreign substance spills on them, their data may be salvageable if the magnetic media are not scratched. See section 8.E.6.d for a description of the salvage procedure.

6.G. Compact Discs (CD-ROM)

The compact disc (CD) read-only memory (ROM) is produced by injection molding polycarbonate plastic into a disc 120 mm (4.72 inches) wide and 1.2 mm thick. CD-ROMs are digital devices containing a spiral track of binary codes in the form of sequences of minute pits. The track is thinner than a human hair and is about three miles long, beginning at the center of the disc and spiralling out to the edge. The pits are 0.12 micrometers deep and 0.6 micrometers wide. The lands between the pits are between 0.9 and 3.3 micrometers long. Neighboring turns of the spiral are 1.6 micrometers apart, giving the CD-ROM an effective track density of 16,000 tracks per inch (tpi) compared to 96 tpi for floppy disks. The pits are burned into the bottom of the disc by a laser beam. After the information transfer is completed, a transparent layer of plastic is applied to the information side to protect the polycarbonate substrate, a reflective coating placed behind the information surface, and then a protective lacquer applied. [11:20]

Compact discs should be stored in their cases vertically on edge, perpendicular to the shelf. Environmental conditions recommended for other media are adequate for long-term storage of CD-ROMs.

Proper cleaning and maintenance will avoid unnecessary problems and loss of information when the disc is played. The following cleaning guidelines will help assure long life for the disc:

1. Open the case by placing the hinge (black bar) side on the left, holding the bottom sides of the case with the right thumb in the 3 o'clock position and the right fingers at the 9 o'clock position.

With the left hand on the top side, the fingers and thumb in the 6 and 12 o'clock position, lift the top open.

2. Remove the disc from its case by holding the disc by the edges with one hand while depressing the center-lock with the forefinger of the other hand.

3. Always hold the disc by its edges to help keep the surface clean.

4. Use a clean, soft, dry cloth to remove any loose particles of dirt, dust, oil, or fingerprints.

5. When cleaning the CD, never wipe it in a circular motion. Use a straight movement from the center outward to the rim.

6. Do not clean the surface with any cloth soaked in water, solvents (thinners, benzine), silicon cloths, antistatic sprays, or record cleaner sprays.

7. Do not use a hair dryer to blow dust off or to remove any moisture from the disc surface.

8. Clean the compact disc frequently, using a compact disc cleaning kit available at audio stores.

DO NOT:

1. Place pressure-sensitive tape, Velcro™, etc. on the disc.

2. Leave the CD in the drive overnight.

3. Bend the disc.

4. Write on or mar the surface in any way.

5. Make the center hole larger.

6. Scratch the surface of the disc while loading or unloading the player or storage case.

7. Store or place the disc in a heated area.

REFERENCES

1. Adelstein, P. Z. "The History of Film Base." Paper presented to the Society of Photographic Scientists and Engineers Symposium on the History of Photography, International Museum of Photography at the George Eastman House, Rochester, New York. Rochester, NY: George Eastman House, June 1986.

2. *American National Standard for Information Systems—Two-Sided, Double Density, Unformatted 5.25-Inch (130-mm), 48 tpi (1,9-tpmm), Flexible Disk Cartridge for 7958 bpr Use—General, Physical, and Magnetic Requirements (ANSI X3.125-1985).* New York: American National Standards Institute, 1985.

3. Bertram, H. N., M. K. Stafford, and D. R. Mills. "The Print-Through Phenomenon." *The Journal of the Audio Engineering Society* 28 (October 1980): 690–705.

4. Brooks, Connie. "Environment for the Storage of Black and White Photographs." In *Third Annual Seminar: Conservation of Archival Materials,* G1–G12. Austin, TX: Conservation Department, The Harry Ransom Humanities Research Center, 1984.

5. Brooks, Connie. "Housing for the Storage of Black and White Photographs." In *Third Annual Seminar: Conservation of Archival Materials,* I1–I15. Austin, TX: Conservation Department, The Harry Ransom Humanities Research Center, 1984.

6. Calmes, Alan, "New Preservation Concern: Video Recordings." *Commission on Preservation and Access Newsletter* 22 (April 1990): 5–6.

7. Collins, T. J. *Archival Care of Still Photographs*. Society of Archivists Information Leaflet. Vol. 2. Sheffield, UK: Society of Archivists, 1983.

8. *Conservation of Photographs*. Kodak Publication No. F-40. Rochester, NY: Eastman Kodak Company, 1985.

9. *Conservation Resources Catalogue*. Springfield, VA: Conservation Resources International, Inc., June 1988.

10. Cunha, George Martin, and Dorothy Grant Cunha. *Conservation of Library Materials: A Manual and Bibliography on the Care, Repair and Restoration of Library Materials*. 2 vols. 2d ed. Metuchen, NJ: The Scarecrow Press, 1971.

11. Dixon, Bradford N. "Making Miracles." *CD-ROM Review* 1 (October 1, 1986): 20–22, 24.

12. Fenstermann, Duane W. "Recommendations for the Preservation of Photographic Slides." *Conservation Administration News* 31 (October 1987): 7.

13. Geller, Sidney B. *The Effects of Magnetic Fields on Magnetic Storage Media Used in Computers*. National Bureau of Standards Technical Note 735. Washington, DC: U.S. Department of Commerce, National Bureau of Standards, July 1972.

14. Gibson, Gerald D. "Preservation and Conservation of Sound Recordings." Paper given at the Thirtieth Allerton Institute: Conserving and Preserving Materials in Nonbook Formats, November 6–9, 1988. Sponsored by the Graduate School of Library and Information Science, University of Illinois at Urbana-Champaign.

15. Horvath, David G. *The Acetate Negative Survey: Final Report*. Louisville, KY: University of Louisville, Ekstrom Library Photographic Archives, February 1987.

16. Jaffe, Lee David. "Phonograph Records." In *Nonbook Media: Collection Management and User Services*, edited by John W. Ellison and Patricia Ann Coty, 236–261. Chicago: American Library Association, 1987.

17. Karr, Lawrence F. "Film Preservation: Why Nitrate Won't Wait." Reprinted from the *IATSE OFFICIAL BULLETIN* (Summer 1972): 1–4.

18. Lawrence, John H. *Preservation Guide 2: Photographs*. New Orleans, LA: The Historic New Orleans Collection, 1983.

19. McWilliams, Jerry. *The Preservation and Restoration of Sound Recordings*. Nashville: American Association for State and Local History, 1979.

20. *Notes on Tropical Photography*. Kodak Publication No. C-24. Rochester, NY: Eastman Kodak Company.

21. *Picture Librarianship*, edited by Helen P. Harrison. London: Library Association, 1981.

22. *Polyester Film Encapsulation*. Washington, DC: Library of Congress, 1980.

23. *Preservation and Restoration of Moving Images and Sound*. Brussels, Belgium: Fédération Internationale des Archives du Film, 1986.

24. *Prevention and Removal of Fungus on Prints and Films*. Kodak Publication No. AE-22. Rochester, NY: Eastman Kodak Company, August 1985.

25. Puglia, Steven. *A Short Guide to Nitrate Negatives: History, Care, and Duplication*. Andover, MA: Northeast Document Conservation Center, 1986.

26. Reilly, James M. *Care and Identification of 19th-Century Photographic Prints*. Kodak Publication No. G-2S. Rochester, NY: Eastman Kodak Company, 1986.

27. Rempel, Siegfried. *The Care of Black and White Photographic Collections: Identification of Processes*. Technical Bulletin, No. 6. Ottawa: Canadian Conservation Institute, November 1980.

28. Rempel, Siegfried. *The Care of Photographs*. New York: Nick Lyons Books, 1987.

29. Ritzenthaler, Mary Lynn, Gerald J. Munoff, and Margery S. Long. *Archives and Manuscripts: Administration of Photographic Collections*. Chicago: Society of American Archivists, 1984.

30. Schrock, Nancy Carlson. "Preservation and Storage." In *Picture Librarianship*, edited by Helen P. Harrison. London: Library Association, 1981.

31. Schwalberg, Bob. "Color Preservation Update." *Popular Photography* 89 (January 1982): 81–85, 131.

32. Schwalberg, Bob, with Henry Wilhelm and Carol Brower. "Going! Going!! Gone!!!" *Popular Photography* 97 (June 1990): 37–49, 60.

33. *Storage Enclosures for Photographic Prints and Negatives*. Andover, MA: Northeast Document Conservation Center, January 1989.

34. *Third Annual Seminar: Conservation of Archival Materials*. Austin, TX: Conservation Department, The Harry Ransom Humanities Research Center, 1984.

35. Volkmann, Herbert. "The Structure of Cinema Films." In *Preservation and Restoration of Moving Images and Sound*, 1–11. Brussels, Belgium: Fédération Internationale des Archives du Film, 1986.

36. Weinstein, Robert A., and Larry Booth. *Collection, Use and Care of Historical Photographs*. Nashville: American Association for State and Local History, 1977.

37. Wheeler, Jim. "Increasing the Life of Your Audio Tape." *Journal of the Audio Engineering Society*. 36 (April 1988): 232–236.

38. Wheeler, Jim. "Long-Term Storage of Videotape." *Journal of the Society of Motion Picture and Television Engineers* 92 (June 1983): 650–654.

39. Wheeler, Jim. *Maximizing the Life of Beta™ and VHS™ Videocassette Tape*. Redwood City, CA: Ampex Corporation, April 20, 1987.

40. Wilhelm, Henry. *Important Notice*. Grinnell, IA: Preservation Publishing Co., August 1981.

41. Wilhelm, Henry. "Storing Color Materials: Frost-free Refrigerators Offer a Low-cost Solution." *Industrial Photography* 27 (October 1978): 32–35.

42. Wilhelm, Henry, and Carol Brower. "Going! Going!! Gone!!! What To Do with What You've Got" *Popular Photography* 97 (June 1990): 48.

7.
SURVEYING
THE BUILDING
AND COLLECTION

7.A. Introduction

One of the fundamental activities that must be performed in order to effectively implement a system-wide preservation program is to survey the condition of the collection as well as the building, facility, or space in which the library is located. The information gathered during these surveys will enable the librarian to develop the right protection plan for the collection and decide preservation priorities for upgrading the physical condition of the building, adjusting and stabilizing the environment, and improving the condition of the collections housed within. The results of such investigations can also be used as evidence to support funding requests, applications, or additional staff; to establish preservation priorities and aid in preservation decision procedures; and to make a comparison with conditions found in other libraries. The goals of such surveys are well expressed in the preservation planning document distributed by the Northeast Document Conservation Center:

> A survey should examine building conditions, collections, and storage and handling procedures. Each building should be inspected from roof to basement, outside to inside, and room by room. At the end of the survey, the surveyor should be able to:
>
> 1. Identify potential hazards to the collection (from the environment or from storage and handling procedures);
>
> 2. Prioritize areas of the collections for preservation action, distinguishing between artifacts [and informational or limited-lifespan circulating materials];
>
> 3. Identify preservation actions required to insure the long-term preservation of collections (e.g., boxing embrittled books or documents, improving housekeeping, installing fire detection devices, installing humidifiers or other climate-control equipment, conservation treatment);

4. Prioritize the needs of the collections and identify steps necessary to achieve the required preservation actions." [3]

The results of the survey should be used to develop a preservation plan with short-, medium-, and long-term goals. [3]

7.B. Building Surveys

Several organizations have developed surveys to examine the environment in which the collection is housed. For example, the internal and external hazards survey used by the Southeastern Library Network (SOLINET) is a good model to follow for checking the conditions around and inside a library facility for problems that could lead to disasters [see chapter 8]; it also ensures that the building is sound and capable of maintaining the proper environment for the materials housed inside.

The following areas should be checked for the conditions indicated. If any answers to these questions are unsatisfactory, the situation should be reviewed and appropriate action taken as soon as possible. [5]

1. Building site—Is it in a flood plain? Would it be damaged by a hurricane (is a hurricane likely in the area) or a tornado? Would it be damaged by an earthquake? If so, what precautions should be taken to minimize damage?
2. Outdoor hazards—Are railings, benches, planters, light/flag poles well anchored? Are overhanging trees or branches trimmed?
3. Roof—Is it sloped or pitched (i.e., not flat), and is the covering sound, without leaks and/or cracks? Are flashings present and intact?
4. Roof drainage (eaves, gutters, drains, downspouts, interior columns)—Is the roof draining freely, is it cleaned regularly, and are the drainage systems connected directly into the sewer system? Is there good drainage around the doors?
5. Windows and skylights—Are the caulking and sealants sound; are trees trimmed away?
6. Fire safety—there are a number of elements to consider under this heading:

   Are air passages between floors identified; are concealed spaces identified? Are there fire protection or suppression devices in those spaces?

   Electrical wiring—Is it in good condition and adequate for the load (i.e., not overloaded)? Are appliance cords (in the staff room and elsewhere) in good condition and unplugged nightly (if appropriate)?

   Fire marshall—Is his or her annual visit used wisely, e.g., are floor plans given to the fire department, high-priority collection areas noted, and appropriate follow-up taken on reports?

Detection systems—Are there smoke and ionization detection systems; are they tested regularly? Are they wired to an outside monitoring station?

Suppression systems (sprinklers, standpipes, portable extinguishers, Halon)—Are automatic systems present? Are the systems adequate and regular inspection and maintenance performed? Are the extinguishers the correct type and located appropriately?

Staff training—Can staff correctly interpret annunciator panels? Do they know how to sound alarms? Do they know when and how to notify the fire department and others? Do they know how to use the fire extinguishers; turn off the electrical power, heating, ventilating and air-conditioning (HVAC) system, sprinklers, and gas? Do they know how to close the fire doors?

7. HVAC systems—Are the temperature and humidity controls effective? Is there an automatic shut-off capacity? Is the furnace inspected annually? Is the air-conditioning system free from leaks and mold, is there effective drainage from pans, an adequate dehumidification capacity, and the ability to exhaust? Are air filters effective and changed regularly?

8. Water protection—Are pipes and plumbing (including toilets, icemakers, fountains, freezers, and other water sources) located away from collections and not above them? Are the pipes well supported and leak-free? Are pipe joints and valves in good condition? Are water detectors present, inspected, and functioning? Are sump pumps and back-ups available? Are appropriate dehumidifiers available? Are walls and ceilings water-tight and without any evidence of leakage or seepage? Are there protective enclosures for special materials (e.g., archives and rare maps) and fragile media (e.g., cassettes and diskettes)?

9. Stack areas—Are shelves well braced and the books shelved snugly? Is the shelving 4 to 6 inches off the floor? Are the water sources (pipes, etc.) above the stacks? Are there canopies on shelving units? Are all valuable collections away from water sources? Are important collections away from windows? Are all valuable materials on or above ground level (i.e., not in the basement)? Are stairways and pipe shafts enclosed and exits unobstructed?

10. Housekeeping—Are cleaning supplies and flammable materials safely stored? Is the staff room cleaned daily and well; is all trash removed nightly? Is smoking prohibited, and are food and drink prohibitions enforced? Are pest management strategies in place?

11. Security—Are book drops outside the building or in a fire- and flood-resistant room? Is the exterior of the building well lighted? Are there locks and alarms on windows and doors? Are there intrusion alarms and/or detectors? Are there effective closing procedures?

12. Insurance—Is there insurance in force, and is the policy up to date? Are "acts of God" covered? Are replacement costs specified for special materials? Are staff aware of the records required for claims, and are those records maintained [see section 8.G for a discussion of insurance]? Is there a duplicate shelflist and/or catalog, and is it stored off-site? Are staff aware of procedures for claiming federal disaster relief?

13. Construction projects—Is the responsibility for enforcement of fire safety precautions specified in the contract? Are fire guards used in all cutting and welding operations? Are fire-resistant partitions used to separate building areas, and are extra fire extinguishers on hand? Is debris removed daily? Are there procedures in place to cover openings in the roof in the event of rain, and to test water systems (including sprinklers) before collections are moved into the area?

7.C. Collection Condition Surveys

7.C.1. SURVEY GOALS

The Smithsonian Institution Libraries, Yale University, and other agencies have conducted physical condition surveys of their collections in order to ascertain the type and extent of problems affecting their materials. These surveys examined the three basic physical elements of the books in their collections: the text block, the binding holding the text block together, and the external cover. [7] The surveyors at the Smithsonian felt most books (in the Smithsonian collections covered by the survey) published since 1800 are not considered rare or intrinsically valuable, yet are important and worth preserving for their intellectual content. Of the three basic physical elements of a book, they decided the paper text block was the most important. "It is also, unfortunately, the element most obviously and seriously deteriorating in books today," [7:4] as noted in Chapter 1 and Chapter 5.

The goals of a typical survey could be "to yield a detailed description of the collections in the discrete units of the [library] system; to examine the complex relationships between the nature of materials, their condition, and the environment in which they are housed; and to estimate how many volumes require immediate attention, how many will need attention soon, and what kind of attention will be needed." [10:113]

To meet these goals, the collection survey should cover as broad a range of book materials, their construction, maintenance, and existing problems as possible. The information gathered can be used to analyze not only the physical condition of the materials, but also the conditions that may be causing deterioration. Decisions can then be taken to prevent or minimize problems in the future. Such a survey should investigate conditions in the following categories:

1. Nature of the materials—the kinds of paper, covers, and casing used; the presence of special elements like plates, tissue guards, foldouts, and supplementary materials;
2. Binding—the specific method of attachment used; the depth of the inner margin;
3. Date and place of publication;
4. Shelf maintenance, e.g., whether the collections are cleanly and properly stored;
5. Damage to the covers/casing, the spine/binding, and the paper;
6. The presence of extraneous materials in the books, e.g., adhesive tape and bookmarks; and
7. Both the acidity and the brittleness of the paper.

The survey should also include the location and call number of each book examined. This information will enable the library to develop collection profiles for individual subject areas and stack locations surveyed. [7:4] The Yale study provides a detailed explanation of the methodology used for examining the collections in a large and complex library system. [10] It should be read by anyone preparing to design a collection survey.

7.C.2. SURVEY METHODOLOGY

Several libraries have conducted collection surveys in the past few years and have produced reports or published articles describing their procedures and findings.* A perusal of their methodologies revealed that most of them used the same general approach. The following guidelines are a synthesis of those procedures.

7.C.2.a. Data gathering

A check sheet, rather than an open-ended survey form, should be designed in order to be sure that each surveyor gathers exactly the same data for each book, and to make the data gathering as simple and quick as possible. The limitations of such a format can be lessened somewhat

*See, for example, *Preservation Planning Program: Physical Condition of the Collections*, compiled by Task Force B. Evanston, IL: Northwestern University Library, 1986; *Preservation of Library Material: A Report of the Collection Preservation Committee*. Toronto: University of Toronto Library, 1984; *The Shakespeare Project*. Princeton, NJ: Princeton University Library and the Department of English, 1987; *Smithsonian Institution Libraries Preservation Planning Report of the Task Force on the Physical Condition of the Collections*. Washington, DC: Smithsonian Institution Libraries, 1986; Sarah Buchanan and Sandra Colemen. *Deterioration Survey of the Stanford University Libraries Green Library Stack Collection*. Stanford, CA: Stanford University Libraries, 1979; and last, but not least, Gay Walker, Jane Greenfield, John Fox, and Jeffery S. Simonoff. "The Yale Survey: A Large Scale Study of Book Deterioration in the Yale University Library." *College & Research Libraries* 46 (March 1985): 111–132.

by the inclusion of an area for additional comments and notes, if desired. The Task Force on the Physical Condition of the Collections at the Smithsonian Institution Libraries devised a form that could be used as a model. A modification of that form is included in Appendix G.

In the interest of speed and accuracy, most surveys followed a direct, objective data recording strategy. For example, publication information was recorded exactly as it was printed in the book to be examined (i.e., in Roman numerals, or city name only); the information was later translated into the appropriate number or country code for entering the data into the computer.

The survey form should also be on just one side of a single sheet for ease in handling during data gathering and data entry.

The forms, pencils, and other equipment should be kept handy and convenient for the surveyors to use as they gather data. The Yale surveyors were given a support jig for the survey form, thin cardboard strips for measuring gutter margins in the books, pencils for filling in the form, and an archivist's pen for checking pH [see section 1.D.1.d]. A short list of country name abbreviations was taped on the back of the jig. [10:130–131] Table G.1 in Appendix G contains a similar list.

7.C.2.b. Forms design

The format and arrangement of the information to be covered is determined by logical subject groupings and examination sequences. The Smithsonian survey recorded only the *presence* of problems, if any, and types of materials. The form in Appendix G has all the alphanumeric data that should be filled in first at the top of the form, followed by the present/not present data in two main groups, each subdivided: (1) external protection—materials, and problems; and (2) text block—materials, method of attachment, and problems. The use and contents of the survey form are explained in detail in Appendix G.

7.C.2.c. Sampling methodology and procedures

Unless the collection to be examined is a small one where each book can be examined individually, most surveys will require the drawing of a random sample from which inferences can be made to the entire collection. Simple random sampling means that every item in the collection has exactly the same chance of being included in the sample. A very close approximation to such sampling can be made if items are selected by choosing a random range, a random section, a random shelf, and a random item on that shelf.

The collection should also be examined to determine if the sample design should be stratified. A stratified sample takes into account any collection characteristics peculiar to each area (e.g., periodicals, government documents, reference) being studied. "The Sterling Memorial Library [at Yale] was subdivided so that each floor, and several of the special units (Periodical stacks, the Main Reading Room, and the Preservation Division) were studied as separate strata. Thus, the location, environment, reader access, and general level of maintenance within strata were similar, while the characteristics of one stratum could be quite different from those of another." [10:127] If a stratum requires less than 200 samples, however, it probably should not be analyzed separately.

The size of the sample is one of the first decisions to make when designing the survey. Sampling techniques have been highly refined and are very reliable when done by competent personnel, i.e., statisticians who know the methodology and are familiar with the goals of the survey and the idiosyncrasies of the collection. A competent statistician must be consulted if the results are to be reliable when a sample is taken. A test or pilot survey must also be conducted before the actual survey is undertaken. The pilot project will help to reveal deficiencies, misunderstandings, and other problems before expensive time and resources are wasted in the actual survey.

7.C.2.c.1. Sample size

Although formulas exist for determining sample size, it is usually easier to use sample size tables. Three elements of information are needed to determine the size, whether tables or formulae are used:

1. *Population size.* The total number of elements within the population, or the *size* of the population. The population in this case would be the size of the collection to be surveyed.
2. *Tolerance.* This denotes whether or not repeated sampling will produce the same results. A tolerance of 5 percent indicates a willingness to tolerate a 5 percent margin of unreliability in either direction of the mean or average value. It is a measure of the accuracy of the sampling result.
3. *Confidence level.* A confidence level of 95 percent is most commonly accepted in archive and library sampling. A confidence level of 95 percent indicates that a sample may be correct 95 times out of 100, i.e., the sample may have only five errors per 100 occurrences to be acceptable. Confidence can also mean that if a sampling study were repeated ten times (using the same sample size and tolerance but each time using a different sample), the results would be correct within the specified tolerance for nine of the replications. [1:120]

Mapping the collection can be helpful in estimating the number of volumes and their location in the collection, if this information is not known or is too old to be reliable. Floor plans identifying the location of ranges and sections can be developed by students or volunteers working under the supervision of a librarian who knows the stack areas at each site. The plans, or maps, should include all the ranges, sections and shelves, and should be annotated to indicate the number of sections in each range and the number of shelves in each section. Empty sections and shelves should not be included. Stack maps are useful for dividing the collection into strata. They can be used for differentiating regular monographs, periodicals, newspapers, reference materials, government documents, special collections, and so on. The maps are also useful in conducting the survey systematically with a minimum of confusion. [2:8] NOTE: Once mapped, the collection should be surveyed very quickly thereafter, since stack and shelving configurations tend to change rapidly.

A table published in an article by Carl Drott in *College & Research Libraries* [1] contains sample sizes that satisfy various levels of confidence and tolerance. It is reproduced in this book as Table 7.1. In addition to the three elements discussed above, however, one further piece of information needs to be developed before using the table. The actual sample size needed for a given tolerance and confidence is dependent on the relative percentages of a phenomenon observed during the study. Therefore a correction needs to be made to the figure in the table representing the sample size that corresponds to the desired confidence and tolerance. The correction is applied by estimating the percent of the sample that will be in the most important category to be studied: for example, the percentage of books in the collection needing some type of treatment.

The following example illustrates the use of the table and the application of the correction.

A survey is to be made of the collection of a hypothetical library of 35,000 volumes. A confidence level of 95 percent with a tolerance of 5 percent is deemed reasonable for the accuracy required. Drott's table will yield a sample size of 384 books at these levels. It is also estimated that

TABLE 7.1. Confidence and tolerance determine sample size

CONFIDENCE LEVEL	TOLERANCE	SAMPLE SIZE	CONFIDENCE LEVEL	TOLERANCE	SAMPLE SIZE
99%	±0.5%	66,358	90%	±0.5%	27,060
	1.0	16,590		1.0	6,765
	2.0	4,147		2.0	1,691
	3.0	1,843		3.0	752
	5.0	664		5.0	271
	7.0	339		7.0	138
	10.0	166		10.0	68
95%	±0.5%	38,416	80%	±0.5%	16,435
	1.0	9,604		1.0	4,109
	2.0	2,401		2.0	1,027
	3.0	1,067		3.0	457
	5.0	384		5.0	164
	7.0	196		7.0	84
	10.0	96		10.0	41

Note: Values in this table are based upon formulae derived in Report No. MG-ML-100, Community Systems Foundation, Ann Arbor, MI.

Source: Reproduced, with permission, from Carl M. Drott. "Random Sampling: A Tool for Library Research." *College and Research Libraries* 30 (March 1969): 124.

about 20 percent of the materials will probably need treatment, so a corrective formula is applied to the selected sample size. [1:124]

The correction is computed by taking the 20 percent of the books that are expected to be in need of treatment (e.g., that have brittle paper) and subtracting that percentage from 100 percent. These figures are then converted to their decimal equivalents and multiplied by 4, as follows:

a) 100% - 20% = 80%

b) .20 x .80 x 4 = .64

The figure from the table is multiplied by the result:

c) 384 x .64 = 246

If the percentage of occurrences cannot be predicted in advance, the sample sizes in the table may be used, because they represent the most conservative size estimates. [1:120]

Drott cautions that the figures in the table are valid only for sample sizes greater than 30 volumes but less than 10 percent of the total population to be surveyed. For example, in a library with only 25 volumes, the table could not be used; nor could it be used in a library with less than 663,581 volumes at the 99 percent, 0.5 percent, confidence and tolerance levels, or less than 3,841 volumes at the 95 percent, 5 percent, levels. Also, the sample size must be calculated *before* performing the survey. The table cannot be used for calculating the confidence and tolerance of a sample after it has been collected. [1:120]

There are other ways to determine sample size. Both the Smithsonian and Yale used consultants and statisticians to determine the size of their survey sample. Since the Smithsonian collection is in over 30 locations, it was decided the sample should consist of 0.5 percent of each library collection surveyed. This resulted in a sample consisting of the seventh book on every seventh shelf (0.5 percent equalled every two hundredth book at the Smithsonian, divided by approximately 30 books per shelf, equalled every seventh shelf; the seventh book was chosen to make the formula easy to remember in actual practice). [7:6]

Because of variations from library to library with regard to subject area, age of materials, degree of use, age of the library itself, and the different preservation problems that might be present, it is important that the survey cover as wide a range of these factors as possible.

The Smithsonian survey covered one location at a time, dividing into three two-person teams (one person to examine the books and one to record the information). The teams were positioned around the library according to the physical divisions of the stack areas, systematically working through the collection until every stack had been surveyed. Working collectively made it possible to consult each other when questions and problems arose, and improved the consistency and reliability of the data gathered. The presence of a staff conservator on one of the teams helped enormously in this regard. Where inconsistencies in the teams' data gathering did exist, the strategy of working collectively in one location at a time reduced the skewing of the data that might have occurred if each team had been individually responsible for a whole collection. [7:6]

7.C.2.c.2. Computer-generated random numbers

The size of the sample is only the first step in developing the observations for the survey. A set of random numbers must also be used to determine which volumes in the collection should be examined. A convenient way to select random numbers and place them in pulling order is to use a computer to do the work. James Divilbiss created a program for the University of Toronto Library to help its Collection Preservation Committee gather information about the physical state of the library collection. [9] The program is based on the assumption that a typical shelving area has several ranges; each range has several sections, and sections have several shelves. For example, a shelving area with 8 ranges, 16 sections per range, 5 shelves per section, and a maximum number of about 35 items per shelf would require a random number from 1 to 8, another from 1 to 16, another from 1 to 5, and finally, one from 1 to 35 to precisely locate a single item. Ranges having differing numbers of sections require the generation of sample locations based on the longest range in the area. Some generated samples would specify nonexistent locations, e.g., volume 34 on a shelf that has only 20 volumes. "No samples" of this kind do not introduce bias, but they do require that excess sample locations be generated. For example, it may be necessary to generate 300 random locations in order to identify 200 valid samples. As in the case of selecting any random numbers, however, before the numbers are generated and sorted, maps of the shelving arrangement must be drawn (as described earlier) so that any generated random number will unambiguously identify one specific item in the collection. This step is important because persons pulling the samples off the shelves must have absolutely no discretion whatsoever in selecting the samples; otherwise, the samples will be biased and any conclusions reached as the result of the study will be invalid. [9:7]

The program begins by interactively determining the dimensions of the area to be sampled. The "how many copies" parameter is useful for two reasons. First, if there are multiple floors with substantially identical floor layouts, this parameter eliminates the need to describe each floor separately. The "copies" generated in a run are not exact duplicates; each one has independently generated random locations. The second reason for producing copies is that it facilitates cross-checking when two or more people evaluate the same part of the collection. For example, if one person's observations show that 25 percent of the books in that area are brittle, and the second person's observations indicate that 80 percent are brittle, it would immediately alert the project director to a problem!

The program [see Appendix H for the program code] is interactive and is started by typing the command "RANDBK." The following then appears on the screen in response to answers to each of the questions (answers are supplied to provide an example):

Subject to a maximum of 4975

how many samples are to be generated? 5

how many copies? 1

how many areas are to be sampled? 1

how many ranges? 35

how many sections? 16

how many shelves? 5

books per shelf? 35

Do you want to change anything? N

Do you want output to the Printer or to the Screen (P/S)? S

The program then produces:

Copy: 1
Area: 1

R	S	S	B
A	E	H	O
N	C	E	O
G	T	L	K
E		F	

01	16	03	014
07	06	03	018
19	15	04	017
23	02	05	018
33	07	03	009

The original program was revised in order to permit it to run on an IBM-compatible personal computer using MS-DOS 3.20 and compiled under Turbo Pascal 3.01. This version will generate a maximum of 4,975 samples. The designation of more than one area was added to enable the system to identify more than one floor or the various branches of a library system. In the example above, one copy of five samples of one area were generated, for 35 ranges of 16 sections each, each section having 5 shelves with a maximum of 35 books per shelf. After generating the numbers, the program uses a standard shell sort and then separates them into range, section, shelf, and book numbers to aid in efficient data collection. [9:30]

7.D. Analysis

The information in this section and its subsections is based upon the material generated for the Smithsonian Institution Libraries report. [7:21–24]

7.D.1. PROBLEM CLASSIFICATION

Once the collection survey has been conducted, it is useful to rank the damage observed on a scale of one to four, as was done at the Smithsonian. Level 1 problems are ones that could be repaired or corrected on site or that will not affect the strength or use of a book. Level 2 would demand some attention to prevent further deterioration (e.g., the relatively simple solution of temporarily storing the item in an acid-free box or envelope). Level 3 requires active attention to save the book from disintegration or loss. Level 4 represents emergency problems that cannot be repaired on location, pose a threat to adjacent books, and/or should be sent to a conservator for professional treatment. [7:21]

"It is helpful to look at those problems ranked as 3 and 4. The highest ranking was given to mold/mildew damage and insect presence, conditions in which living organisms are attacking the books with the danger of further contamination throughout the collection. It can be assumed that once these conditions are treated, the books themselves will be available for use if they don't have additional problems in need of correction." [7:24]

Level 3 problems indicate actual or potential destruction of the text block, i.e., the intellectual content. They should be attended to soon in order to avoid more serious problems in the future.

First and second level problems should not be discounted, but are not as serious as the others. Treatment could be applied on-site or delayed. [7:24]

The survey form in Appendix G provides the framework for the following analysis.

7.D.1.a. Shelving [see also section 3.B.1]

Books shelved:

Flat and on spine (Level 1)—These are not considered problems to be corrected but often indicate space constraints and other storage problems. It should be noted, however, that books shelved on their spines are more subject to dust and warping problems over time.

Leaning (Level 1)—Because of the potential for cover and binding damage when a book is not shelved upright, this is a concern that should be addressed routinely in every library.

On fore edge (Level 2)—This should be corrected on site, to minimize the inevitable binding damage that will result from this situation. [7:24]

7.D.1.b. Cover problems

General:

Scratched (Level 1)—The appearance of a volume is degraded but the binding is unharmed.

Stained (Level 1)—Appearance is affected, but not the binding.

Red rot (Level 3)—Red rotted leather will rub off onto other books and stain or mark them. Requires attention because red rot weakens leather, causing covers and spines to break off from the book. Affected books should be placed in phase boxes or similar containers until they can be rebound or replaced.

Warped/misshapen (Level 2)—These books should be reshaped, if possible, because their hinges may become weakened and result in more serious damage.

Mold/mildew (Level 4)—Affected books must be segregated and treated immediately. [See section 2.I.]

Adhesive tape (Level 2)—Pressure-sensitive tape, which was often used to repair tears, will cause discoloration. Its adhesive will break down and become gummy, causing pages to stick together and stain. Its removal is difficult and time-consuming, requiring a trained conservator to do it successfully. An article describing various types of pressure-sensitive tapes and their removal was published in the *Journal of the American Institute for Conservation* in 1984. [6]

Front and/or back cover problems:

Loose (Level 2)—Books with loose covers should have some protection to prevent future detachment or loss of covers.

Torn (Level 2)—As with loose covers, tears should be repaired to prevent possible future detachment or loss.

Detached (Levels 2/3) and Missing (Level 3)—The text block lacks adequate protection and can lose shape, resulting in torn or lost pages and general deterioration.

Spine cover problems:

Damage (Level 1)—This usually refers to headcap damage, e.g., the headcap is torn, pulled loose, or missing. The book does not need immediate attention, but will probably suffer further deterioration.

Detached (Level 2)—A detached spine is likely to be lost, resulting in possible damage to the hinges, covers, and text block, and the loss of shelving information.

Missing (Levels 2/3)—The entire spine is gone. It should be repaired as soon as possible to minimize additional damage or loss.

7.D.1.c. Leaf (binding and paper) problems

End leaves:

Detached (Level 3)—Detached pages are a serious problem because they are easily lost, torn, or further damaged. They should be repaired quickly.

Loose (Level 2)—A potentially serious problem, requiring repair to prevent loss. They may have to be rebound.

Torn (Level 2)—Repair should be done soon to prevent further damage and loss of text.

Pages:

Acidity (Mild: Level 2; Extreme: Level 3)—This condition contributes to brittleness and deterioration of paper. The library should consider the preservation options listed in section 5.E.1.c.

Brittleness (Level 3)—Brittleness can result in loss of text from ordinary use; furthermore, it precludes rebinding. [See also 5.E.1.c.]

Foxed (Level 2)—Foxing in itself is not a serious problem. However, the book may be susceptible to mold, so books with this condition need further examination.

Gutter margin (Level 2)—Extremely narrow margins present problems in ordinary use, especially for photocopying, and can make rebinding impossible.

Insect damage (Level 2)—Repairs for such damage can be extensive.

Insect presence (Level 4)—Materials found with insects and/or eggs must be removed and treated immediately before the insects spread to other volumes. [See section 2.J.]

Marked or stained (Level 1)—These conditions will not usually affect the ultimate strength of the book, and the expense of removing stains is not justified.

Mold/mildew (Level 4)—This condition cannot be corrected on location. Affected books should be removed from the area and treated immediately. [See section 2.I.]

Stuck together (Level 3)—Since it affects the text, this is an important problem and cannot be handled on-site. Trained laboratory staff is required to release these pages.

Yellowed (Level 1)—Not considered of immediate concern except where it may be an indication of age and acidity.

Extraneous materials:

With the exception of adhesive tape and paper clips [discussed above], the other categories of extraneous paper materials (paper slips and additions) are of less concern. These can be dealt with on-site by removing slips and putting additions into acid-free envelopes.

7.E. Recommendations

These suggestions are synthesized primarily from the Smithsonian report. [7:26–28] The analysis provides the basis for a sound preservation program. In the context of the levels addressed by the survey outlined above, recommendations might include programs for the treatment of brittle materials, those that are moldy, those that have insect damage, and other types of damage.

7.E.1. BRITTLENESS

Brittle book programs should be put into effect to ensure that loss is prevented. Such programs should include identification and treatment of brittle materials, implementation of policies on retention and replacement, and measures to halt or circumvent the embrittlement of books. The elements listed below could be considered in the development of these programs. [See also section 5.E.1.c.]

Policies should be developed and implemented for:

1. The institution of a mass deacidification program.
2. An action procedure for damaged and/or deteriorated books—When to repair or replace, who is responsible for searching out and deciding on replacement formats, etc.
3. Books with the following Level 3 problems should not go out on interlibrary loan: detached or missing covers, missing spine covers, detached pages, pages stuck together, and brittle pages.
4. Brittle books should not to be photocopied in response to interlibrary loan requests.
5. The library may wish to consider restricting the purchase of books published prior to 1930 if they are available in alternative editions or formats. [7:26]

Staff should be trained in:

1. Identification of brittle paper. As these books reach the circulation desk, the Smithsonian considered the insertion of an acid-free strip with the following instruction printed on it: DO NOT PHOTOCOPY—BRITTLE PAPER.
2. Handling of books—correct shelving and photocopying methods, pulling paper slips and clips from books, removing pressure sensitive notes, prohibiting the use of adhesive tape.
3. Recognition that books with yellowed pages may indicate acidity. These books can be set aside for testing and evaluation.

Users should be educated through the development of instructional aids on how to handle and shelve books, how to photocopy correctly, how to use foldouts safely, and how to preserve books by avoiding the use of pressure sensitive slips and adhesive tape.

The book industry should be educated by librarians and others presenting the findings of tests on acidity and brittleness to publishers and by encouraging the use of acid-free paper in the future.

7.E.2. MOLD/MILDEW AND INSECT PRESENCE

These Level 4 problems are of urgent priority in relation to their potential for spreading. If the survey reveals their presence, policies should be developed and implemented for speedy identification and treatment. Staff should be trained and locations equipped to remove these books for treatment immediately. [See sections 2.I and 2.J.]

7.E.3. MATERIALS DAMAGE

The text block and intellectual content must be kept in good repair in order to provide access to them. To deal with existing problems both temporarily and permanently, and to prevent the development or aggravation of problems in the future, follow the suggestions presented below.

Well-trained technicians should undertake the following repairs (these are representative and not inclusive): reinforcing foldouts, tipping in pages, making spine corrections, repairing torn pages and hinges, inserting pockets for additional materials, and opening uncut pages.

Staff should be trained in:

1. Recognition and identification of missing pages, loose pages, and the need for rebinding.
2. Regular housekeeping, including the cleaning and vacuuming of books.
3. Handling of temporary external preservation, including tying books with acid-free cloth tape, putting books in acid-free envelopes or boxes, and measuring books for custom-made boxes.

Other policies that should be developed and implemented include:

1. Purchasing hardbound books when there is a choice, and avoiding leather-bound books. It may be worthwhile to study the cost differential and/or advisability of purchasing paperbacks and rebinding in a library binding.
2. Providing supplies of acid-free envelopes and tape.

The book industry should be educated to:

1. Encourage publishers to provide better quality in binding (i.e., sewn or better quality glue).
2. Make commercial binders aware of narrow margins when rebinding and to avoid oversewing on narrow margins.

7.E.4. USAGE

Librarians tend to assume that a brittle book must be treated or reformatted, regardless of its current usage status. The usage of a brittle volume, however, greatly affects its life expectancy. Utilization patterns of library materials by the users of research libraries suggest that fragile materials such as embrittled books may be at substantially lower levels of risk than previously thought.

"The findings of various studies indicate the interest of readers in the contents of materials often declines at a rate even more rapid than the rate at which their constituent materials deteriorate. This tendency toward obsolescence among older materials causes many documents to be handled with lessening frequency, thus affording such materials a modicum of inadvertent protection once their durability has reached dangerously low levels." [8:2] These studies indicate that many older materials may be in less danger than originally supposed and will probably last much longer on the shelves simply because they are not being used.

REFERENCES

1. Drott, M. Carl. "Random Sampling: A Tool for Library Research." *College & Research Libraries* 30 (March 1969): 119–125.

2. Merrill-Oldham, Jan. *Survey of the Condition of Three Medium-Sized Research Library Collections.* A research proposal submitted to the National Endowment for the Humanities. Storrs, CT: University of Connecticut at Storrs, Homer Babbidge Library, 1984.

3. Northeast Document Conservation Center. *Goals of a Preservation Planning Survey.* Andover, MA: Northeast Document Conservation Center, August 1987.

4. *Preservation Microfilming: A Guide for Librarians and Archivists,* edited by Nancy E. Gwinn. Chicago: American Library Association, 1987.

5. *Sample Checklist for Disaster Prevention & Protection.* SOLINET Preservation Program. Atlanta, GA: Southeastern Library Network, Inc., November 1988.

6. Smith, Merrily A., et al. "Pressure-Sensitive Tape and Techniques for Its Removal from Paper." *Journal of the American Institute for Conservation* 23 (1984): 101–113.

7. Smithsonian Institution Libraries. *Condition of the Collections.* Smithsonian Institution Libraries Preservation Planning Program: Report of the Task Force on the Physical Condition of the Collections. Typescript. Washington, DC: Smithsonian Institution, February 13, 1986.

8. Tomer, Christinger. "Selecting Library Materials for Preservation." *Library & Archival Security* 7 (Spring 1985): 1–6.

9. University of Toronto Library. Collection Preservation Committee. *Preservation of Library Material: A Report of the Collection Preservation Committee.* Toronto: University of Toronto Library, 1984.

10. Walker, Gay, Jane Greenfield, John Fox, and Jeffrey S. Simonoff. "The Yale Survey: A Large Scale Study of Book Deterioration in the Yale University Library." *College & Research Libraries* 46 (March 1985): 111–132.

8.
DISASTER PREPAREDNESS AND RECOVERY

8.A. Introduction

The best insurance for minimizing the effects of a disaster, whether it be from water, insects, fire, earthquake, or vandalism, is to be prepared in advance. Emergencies cause panic and shock, often immobilizing the library staff during the critical moments when effective action could be taken to reduce damage. A well-conceived disaster plan and a staff trained to implement it will aid in overcoming uncertainty in those first chaotic hours after a disaster has struck.

Disaster or emergency contingency plans must be written to fit the needs and situation of the institution they are designed to serve. No one plan can serve the requirements of all institutions; there are, however, generally accepted guidelines that can be adapted to cover the needs of any one library or archive. It is a truism that emergency planning is something every library should do, but few undertake it until after a disaster occurs. Potential disasters and their aftereffects may be averted and/or minimized by developing well-conceived and fully implemented plans. The planning process itself will help staff appreciate the need to prepare for possible problems.

The discussion in this chapter applies only to the protection and salvage of library, archive, and media center collections. It does not include procedures to be implemented in the event of bomb threats, building evacuation, health related problems, etc., involving patron and/or staff safety.

8.B. Disaster Preparedness Plan

8.B.1. DISASTER PREPAREDNESS AND RECOVERY TEAM

A plan does not come into being by itself. A disaster preparedness and recovery team should be appointed to investigate the needs of the library, archive, or media center, develop a plan to fit those needs, and implement it. The ultimate goals of the plan should be prevention and action: preventing foreseeable disasters and minimizing damage to the collection if one should occur. Some larger institutions have created two groups, a disaster prevention team and a disaster action team, to accomplish these goals. This discussion assumes one team can achieve both ends.

Conventional wisdom dictates that the team should be composed of a minimum of five full-time professional and/or support staff members with as diverse representation as possible within the institution. [3:3] Although a team of five may be the most efficient size, many libraries and archives simply don't have that many staff members. For those smaller libraries, a team of two or three would suffice. Whatever the size of the library (with the obvious exception of those that have only one staff member), more than one person, wherever possible, should be assigned to develop and implement the plan. The group should not have more than eight to twelve members; any more than that will inhibit the group's effectiveness because it will be difficult to schedule meetings and to achieve full participation. Each member should have an alternate so there will be as many competently instructed people as possible, and members should be chosen so each area in the library will have representation at meetings and someone available in the event of an emergency. Disaster preparedness and recovery responsibilities should be included in every appropriate job description.

The following personnel should be part of the team:

1. Public service personnel who know which services are most critical to get back in operation first. Staff in public services know how long the library can stay closed without jeopardizing its credibility with the community. Because of their knowledge of collection use, they are also qualified to decide which parts of the collection should be saved first.
2. Technical services staff who understand the impact on the system if the catalog (or other centralized functions) are destroyed or significantly reduced in effectiveness. For example, if centralized support is provided to branches and/or other systems by the main library and the main library is disabled for a significant time, technical services personnel should provide information (in both the planning and response stages) as to where and how those entities will be able to obtain the products and support needed to continue operating. A cataloger should also be included on the team. It would be the cataloger's responsibility to keep track of damaged materials as they are salvaged or discarded. Bohem suggests that the cataloger should also keep abreast of methods for accurate record keeping in a disaster situation and keep the team up-to-date on procedures for library disaster recovery. [3:4]

3. The preservation administrator or conservator. This person can identify the categories of material that should be saved because of the type of paper they are printed on, the rarity of their bindings, difficulty of salvaging them, etc.

4. The administrator in charge of building facilities. This should be a person with widespread contacts and authority who can commandeer assistance and cooperation from resource people and departments outside the library or archive and act as liaison with the library administration. He or she should also be able to approve the expenditure of large sums of money in an emergency. Normally, the director of the library should not be a working member of the team. Most library committees (in a sense, the team is a committee) are policy recommending and not policy setting bodies; the director will be taking the recommendations of the team and acting upon them. Therefore, the director's presence during the team's deliberations would be redundant and possibly inhibiting. If the director insists on a direct role, which may be appropriate, especially in smaller systems, he or she should act in an ex-officio capacity.

5. A representative from buildings and grounds or the maintenance department. This person's help can be invaluable. Often maintenance people are the only ones who can get into the building after hours and/or have keys and access to critical spaces. They know where important electrical switches and air-conditioning, heating, and water valves are located, and they may be the only ones who have special wrenches that will turn on or off a water line. They can also brief the staff on the configuration, condition, and operation of fire suppression systems.

   The maintenance crew must be alerted to the correct procedures to follow when cleaning up after a disaster, in order to minimize further damage to the collection. Maintenance people are a critical link in the library's ability to reduce damage to the collection.

6. The institution's risk manager and/or insurance claims adjuster should also be made a part of the disaster response team's planning phase. The risk manager's knowledge of the organization's emergency procedures, regulations, and resources will be invaluable to the team. The insurance representative can brief the team on coverage and requirements for filing claims. The team will also be able to alert both of these individuals to special requirements of the library for collection protection and recovery.

7. A representative from the local fire department should be included in planning. It will not be necessary for this person to attend every meeting, but involving him/her in one or two planning sessions will pay dividends. Fire departments are eager to help organizations reduce the effect of damage both

from fire and the means of putting it out—water. Their involvement will open communication between the library and the primary group it relies on to save the collection. The team will be able to brief the department on the location of high priority materials, show its representative which items should be covered with tarps, etc., during a fire, and encourage the use of misting instead of high-pressure nozzles on fire hoses.

8. A recovery director. This person could be one of the library staff members mentioned above who has knowledge of preservation principles, or an outside professional conservator with knowledge of disaster recovery. He or she should be vested with final decision-making responsibility during an actual emergency and should be released from all other duties during such a situation. It is important that all the recovery director's energy and time be concentrated on recovering from the disaster as soon as possible. In most cases, the latter requirement would preclude selecting the library director as the recovery director. The chief administrator of the library will have his or her hands full marshalling the resources for recovery, dealing with the community, and overseeing day-to-day operations of the library, with little or no time left to supervise on-site salvage and recovery operations.

In addition, a person should be designated to work with the media in order to keep the press fully briefed. A media liaison can minimize disruptive interviews and questions of the salvage team during critical periods of the operation. There should also be one person on the team who is a known skeptic. If that person can be persuaded that the plan is well conceived, necessary, and should be implemented, then the library staff will probably be more easily convinced to accept it.

One or more of the persons listed above could fill dual roles; for example, the recovery director could be an administrator from public or technical services. This will very likely occur in the smaller library. It is important to have a variety of people on the team in order to have wide representation from all affected departments. The old axiom, "two [or more] heads are better than one," is certainly true in this case.

8.B.2. CREATION OF THE PLAN

The first step to take in developing a contingency plan is to gather as much information about this type of planning process as possible. Contact organizations and/or libraries that either have plans or experience in developing them; their experience can be invaluable in helping to develop and critique the plan. A number of such organizations are listed in Chapter 9. Consult the growing number of disaster preparedness manuals now available. An excellent one, which covers all areas of disaster planning, is *An Ounce of Prevention: A Handbook on Disaster Contingency Planning for Archives, Libraries and Record Centres.* [20] Although it was produced for archives and libraries in Canada, the information is accurate, to the point, and applicable to all organizations that house information, whether in books, paper files, or on film or magnetic media.

The plan must be relevant to the library's own particular needs and should be tailored to the region being served. Procedures for incidents that are not likely to happen should not be included. Such instructions or precautions are superfluous and will detract from the credibility of the document. For example, the U.S. Gulf coast experiences hurricanes; therefore, one would expect library disaster plans written for the southern areas of Alabama, Louisiana, Florida, Mississippi, and Texas to include procedures detailing preparedness and recovery procedures for catastrophic storms, but not earthquakes or blizzards.

The plan should also be geared to the needs of the users. All too often policies are developed that address the library's needs and forget the mission of the institution. A disaster plan is written and implemented expressly for one underlying purpose: to provide the users *access* to the information in collections as soon as possible after the catastrophe is over. The objectives of the plan must be developed to meet this goal. For example, one of the first problems to be solved after the disastrous Los Angeles Central Library fire of April 1986 was how soon the system could resume providing business information to the community. Because of long-standing agreements among the libraries in the area, the Central Library housed the main business collection for the Los Angeles basin. After the fire, access to business information for many patrons was severely curtailed; much of the business collection was damaged or destroyed. One of the library's most important resources, the business reference staff, however, was intact. So the library administration solved the problem by sharing part of the staff with various other libraries in the basin. The collections in those libraries did not have the strength of the Central Library, but the relocated staff were able to provide support until the main collection was restored. [4] The disaster recovery plan must anticipate such situations and outline procedures that will enable the library to continue important services, even if on a limited basis.

The plan must reflect the goals of the institution. The priorities developed for saving the materials in a research library's collection would differ from those for a school library or media center. In the case of the former, rare and unique materials would probably have top priority, depending on the mission of the institution, while the media center specialist might wish to save only the catalog and, perhaps, *Books in Print*. In fact, some librarians may not wish to save anything, if their collections are very poor. During a disaster workshop in Florida, the director of one community college library refused to establish any priorities for the collection, saying that as far as he was concerned, the entire collection should be replaced. While this is an extreme case and not to be recommended, it does illustrate that each library must establish its own priorities based on its own situation and needs. It can be disastrous, or at the very least, embarrassing, if the staff has not agreed about which materials and/or records *must* be removed from the building or protected in the event of a potentially catastrophic situation. Recently, a national archive (not in North America) experienced a fire that appeared to be beyond the fire battalions' abilities to contain. The archives included in its holdings national treasures equivalent to the U.S. Bill of Rights, the Constitution, and other irreplaceable documents of incalculable worth. Because of the seriousness of the blaze, network television camera crews were at the scene to record what could be a national calamity. The battalion chief, on national live TV, told the staff that within 20 minutes or so the entire building would be lost. A national audience then witnessed the astounding sight of the several staff members arguing about which documents should be brought out of the building, while, behind them, the structure was being enveloped in flames. The story does have a happy ending. While the argument was going on, one staff member went into the building and brought out the most important documents, and fire fighters were able to save the building and its contents after all. Needless to say, if a disaster plan had been developed and implemented, such a scene would, in all likelihood, have been avoided. [4]

Congruent with knowing the goals of the institution is to know the collection of the library. Perhaps this should go without saying, but if the team does not have an in-depth knowledge of the materials in the library, it will not be able to develop an intelligent plan to save that collection.

Equipment protection and salvage is also part of a good preparedness plan. For example, if the library has an online system, what measures have been (or should be) taken to protect it and provide backup for the data? As noted earlier, if the system is providing service to other libraries or to branches, is there an alternative that can be used if the system goes down for any length of time? Backup is important not only for automated systems, but for any service the library provides, such as catalog card production. A large library must be concerned about a catalog that others depend on, even if they are not part of the system. Preservation is, after all, providing access.

The plan must be clear, concise, well organized, and easy to read, but not encyclopedic in size. It will most likely be consulted during a time of chaos, in poor light, by people who may not be very familiar with it. Even well trained personnel may have difficulty in sorting things out in a time of emergency. A document with large, easy to read type and easy to follow sequential steps can save much valuable time and help reduce confusion. The easier it is to use under poor conditions, the more valuable it will be, and the effort will have been worthwhile.

The plan must be practical. If it can't be implemented because of its sophistication, cost, or the impossibility of obtaining the required equipment and/or supplies, change it so that it is workable. For example, vacuum freeze-drying is the recommended way of drying wetted books and papers. If, however, there are only a few items damaged, e.g., 100 to 200, it may be more expedient to air-dry them. The plan must be flexible enough to cover options not known at the time of its creation.

The plan should be specific to the needs of the individual library, consortia, or group and not be general in nature. There is, however, no one right or wrong approach. The right plan is the one that actually works for the library or group it is written to help.

After the plan has been developed, approved, printed, and published, it must be distributed to those who will be implementing it during times of crisis, such as the staff and the local fire department. Finally, the library staff, maintenance workers, and any other appropriate group must be educated about the plan and why it is important.

8.B.3. STEPS IN THE PLANNING PROCESS

The Toronto Area Archivists Group developed a step-by-step approach to emergency planning that is helpful in developing a plan for any library or archive. The following outline is based on that model and modified, where appropriate, to reflect the needs of libraries. [20:169–170]

1. Designate the organizational structure of disaster planning by:
   a. appointing one person (e.g., the recovery director or the administrator in charge of building facilities) to direct planning and implementation efforts; and
   b. appointing a team to assist the disaster preparedness and recovery manager.

2. Educate the team in the specifics of disaster planning for libraries and preservation in general.

3. Establish liaison with local preparedness agencies:
   a. so the library's or archive's plan will be compatible with existing plans of local governments; and
   b. to obtain planning assistance.

4. Decide upon the scope of the plan:
   a. How broad it will be, e.g., will it cover one library or the entire system, be county-wide, include members of a consortium? Will it be limited to salvage procedures or will it embrace all aspects of preparedness and recovery of the collection including audio-visual, print, and computer materials?
   b. Will the plan be developed in toto or in stages, i.e., one step at a time over a period of years? (The latter is not the best way, but it is better than nothing at all.)

5. Establish realistic goals and timetables:
   a. The primary goal is access to the collection, and any plan must keep this foremost at all times.
   b. A date must be set for the plan's completion. Otherwise it will lose priority within the system and possibly never get done.

6. Establish a reporting schedule and lines of communication. The director must be regularly informed about what is going on and why it is being done. The staff must know why information is

being gathered about the collection, equipment, and facilities. When staff are kept fully informed, they often will volunteer information about problems threatening the collection that may not be obvious to others, e.g., flooding, fire hazards, mold, etc.

7. Conduct a vulnerability and needs assessment in order to:
   a. identify the emergencies that can occur and the hazards that exist;
   b. determine the probability and criticality of each; and
   c. assign priorities for planning and resources allocation.

8. Identify assets and assign priorities by:
   a. surveying collections, records, equipment, and other assets; checking for those items most apt to be damaged, e.g., film-based media, coated paper, and water soluble media such as pastels, artwork, manuscripts, magnetic media, and films; and
   b. prioritizing the assets according to their values and irreplaceability. These decisions must be based upon both the fragility of the material and the importance of the collection to the community. Such judgements are complicated because valuable materials may be imbedded in the collection, and it may be a temptation to try to salvage everything.

9. Formulate protection procedures (mitigation and response) for the:
   a. protection and reinforcement of facilities;
   b. protection of collections;
   c. relocation of collections within the building;
   d. relocation of collections from the library to a protected place; and
   e. restoration, salvage, or replacement of damaged collections.

10. Formulate recovery plans in order to:
    a. provide emergency supplies and equipment, and to house them in protected spaces;
    b. provide instructions for use following a disaster, i.e.,
       1) how to assess damage;
       2) how to assign priorities for recovery efforts;
       3) how to select recovery methods according to sustained damage; and
       4) how to request outside assistance.

11. Assess the fiscal implications of a disaster:
    a. Determine insurance coverage. If the library is self-insured, it may mean that there will not be any money for recovery if an area-wide catastrophe has occurred and caused heavy demands on limited resources. If that is the case, then the library should concentrate on preventing a disaster from happening and/or salvaging as much as possible.

If insurance has been written by a commercial firm, check for the type of coverage and whether it includes the cost of reacquiring and processing destroyed materials or renting temporary quarters so library services may be continued until permanent facilities are ready for use. Will it cover the cost of moving and salvaging materials or the expense of hiring an outside firm to salvage materials so the library need not use staff and volunteers? [See section 8.G for more information about insurance.]

b. Determine the cost-effectiveness of detection, prevention, and/or suppression systems versus recovery costs. While expensive to install, alarm systems tied into remote external monitoring stations or sprinkler systems can pay for themselves many times over by preventing or minimizing damage from fire. The library should budget for plastic sheeting, paper toweling, etc. [see section 9.E.2 for emergency equipment and supplies] to keep on hand in an emergency storage box. Readily available emergency supplies will help localize and reduce damage in the event of an emergency.

12. Write the emergency/disaster plan and place it in a loose-leaf folder for easy updating. [See section 8.B.4 for suggested plan components.]

13. Prepare the library or archive staff to implement the plan by:

a. training the staff to understand and use the plan. For example, the reason certain areas of the collection must be prioritized for protection against catastrophes and for early salvage is because many books are out of print and irreplaceable. A knowledgeable staff will understand the necessity of cooperation and will more readily accept that advance planning and preparation helps to protect not only the collection, but also themselves as professionals from charges of malfeasance, i.e., that they are not taking care of the collection.

b. encouraging (and in appropriate cases providing financial support for) staff to take outside courses in conservation of library and archival materials, disaster preparedness for libraries and archives, etc.

14. Test the plan by:

a. holding periodic exercises; and

b. revising the plan if the exercises reveal deficiencies.

15. Evaluate the plan by:

a. analyzing how well it works during exercises;

b. analyzing how well it works under actual disaster conditions;

c. maintaining good records of what happens during exercises and disasters, and encouraging thorough feedback from all involved persons on how well the plan did or did not work;

d. changing the plan as needed; and

e. KEEPING IT UP-TO-DATE.

8.B.4. PLAN COMPONENTS

The plan does not have to have all of the following elements, but all should be considered for inclusion and dropped only if they do not apply to the local situation.

8.B.4.a. Introduction

The introduction should include the why, who, and when of the plan as well as when it should be updated. Individual responsibilities should be designated by job position, not personal names of individuals. The revision date should be included in the introduction (or some other prominent place) to remind the staff the plan is not static and must be revised periodically.

8.B.4.b. Emergency information sheet

Every plan must include emergency response information. Brief instructions should be included on how to react to bomb threats, fire, water, or other emergencies. Content should be brief, explaining clearly and concisely the steps to follow. The sheet should be placed at the beginning of the plan and limited to one page, if possible, so it can be duplicated and kept at the circulation desk, reference desk, or other locations deemed appropriate and necessary. It must be easy to find, e.g., fastened to a wall near a telephone. If the library does not do this and does not train *all* staff in what to do in an emergency situation, staff are liable to exacerbate the problem. It is important not only to have instructions posted, but also to have staff trained in the specifics.

8.B.4.c. Telephone or reporting tree

When an emergency occurs, there is often confusion, uncertainty, and, occasionally, panic. A telephone reporting tree, in addition to an emergency information sheet, can go far in alleviating confusion in the first moments of an unusual situation. The tree displays, in calling priority, those needing to be notified in an emergency. It not only indicates who should be called first, but also relieves staff of having to call more than one, two, or three persons (depending on the institution's policy). In an emergency situation, the first person called calls two or three others on the tree, depending on the type of emergency, and they, in turn, call two or three others, and so on. The number of people called will be a factor of the size of the library and the magnitude of the situation.

Personnel who work in the area in the library or archive affected by the emergency should be called first. In the event of a fire or bomb emergency, however, security people are usually contacted first, then employees in the affected area. **Note: Each organization's regulations must be followed exactly as promulgated.** The library director should always be notified, unless he or she specifically requests that this not be done. Depending on the severity of the situation, the head of the disaster recovery team may be notified. He or she may then decide to call together the whole team. Other groups, such as maintenance, may also be notified as appropriate.

8.B.4.d. Collection priorities

This section of the plan outlines those areas of the collection that must be protected (or salvaged) first. The descriptions should be color keyed to floor plans of the facility in order to graphically illustrate where high priority materials are located. The floor plans should be simple graphics of each floor. Do not use copies of blue prints—they are usually too complex and too hard to see in poor light for quick and easy reading under stress. The local fire department should have a copy of this section and the floor plans and be invited to walk through the library or archive to see where the materials are located. Advance preparation will enable them to find their way more easily in the heat and smoke of a fire and will alert them to those materials that need the most protection. See section 8.E.1 for more discussion about identifying priorities.

8.B.4.e. Prevention and protection measures

Alarm and fire suppression systems need to be tested at least once a year. A form should be inserted in the prevention and protection section of the plan to note when inspections have been made, when the systems were tested, and what corrective action (if any) was taken. Internal and external surveys of the building and grounds should be made for hazards that could lead to disastrous situations or cause problems exacerbating existing conditions. Many of the items listed in section 7.B (Building Surveys) could be incorporated into a building security checklist. If there are any negative answers to the questions on the list, the situation should be reviewed and appropriate action taken as soon as possible. Both NEDCC and SOLINET have hazard checklists that are useful for this purpose.

This section should also be cross-referenced to the floor plan described above. In addition to showing the location of high priority materials, the plan should also show exits, emergency box locations, sprinkler system heads, and fire fighting equipment.

8.B.4.f. Response to an emergency situation

This section should contain clear and comprehensive instructions on how to initiate recovery activities for the library managers and/or head of the disaster recovery team. See section 8.D for more details.

8.B.4.g. Recovery

Full, up-to-date, detailed information about the procedures for salvaging materials in the collection is mandatory. It may not be practical to include all the instructions for recovery in the manual itself, but the information (not just references) should either be in this section or in appendices or attachments to the plan. Staff should be trained in the techniques through hands-on workshops and periodic updates as needed [see section 8.E].

8.B.4.h. Resources

This should contain a comprehensive list of needed supplies and equipment and where they are stored or can be obtained on short notice. The list should be checked twice a year. For example, deep freeze storage facilities may no longer be available as business conditions change. A list of sources of emergency equipment and supplies is in section 9.E.2.

8.B.4.i. Rehabilitation

Materials will almost always need to be cleaned, rebound, etc. They may need new labels or sorting. Once wetted, books and other paper-based materials will take up about 20 percent extra space on the shelves after they are dried, because of swelling. The library will need to box and repair materials. Procedures must be established for determining which materials should be kept and which discarded.

8.B.4.j. Appendices

Include basic information about the building, supplies, insurance, and reports of action taken in previous emergencies.

8.C. Disaster Mitigation

8.C.1. EARTHQUAKE

Fortunately, earthquakes are relatively infrequent in most parts of the United States, but if a library is located in an area that is earthquake prone, such as California, the consequences can be devastating.

While there is little that can be done in advance to totally prepare a library against the destructive effects of an earthquake, experience has taught librarians how to strengthen stacks against the sway caused by quakes. "Shelving is the most common earthquake vulnerability in libraries, and in nonstructural earthquake surveys of facilities, improperly braced shelving is much more commonly encountered than well-engineered earthquake restraint designs. Non-engineers have intuitively realized that tall shelving is among the most vulnerable of objects to earthquake shaking, and many times retrofits have already been implemented." [23:1] Tall and narrow library stacks are susceptible to overturning and exert large forces on the hardware anchoring them down. "There are a few good ways, and many bad ways, to brace shelving." [23:3] The collection of the Wardman Library of Whittier College largely withstood the temblors of the southern California earthquake of 1 October 1987 because of properly reinforced stacks. The library's double-sided steel shelving had the usual lateral bracing between the tops of the section posts, tying the sections together in each range. But, in addition, one-sixteenth-inch steel channel braces were bolted to the top of each range. The braces were fastened to each range with four bolts through steel plates on each range in parallel lines about six feet apart, and the braces at the end of each range were bolted to the walls at either end of the building. Very few books came off the shelves during the quake, unlike the situation in the California State University-Los Angeles library, just a few miles away, where thousands of volumes tumbled to the floor. The stacks were similarly braced, but with some very important differences. At California State-Los Angeles, the sway braces were about every nine feet apart, made of steel rod and fastened with a single nut to the exterior side of a fastening plate. It appears that the system at Whittier College—bolting the ranges to the floor, lateral bracing, the use of heavy channel or tubular steel braces spaced about six feet apart and securely bolted with several bolts to the top of the stack sections and wall joists— helped reduce the effect of shock. There is some disagreement about the wisdom of tying the ranges to walls, but the experience in California seems to show that it does help reduce sway. [5:2, 23–24]

Reitherman targets eight shelving components that are vulnerable to earthquake damage and offers suggestions on how each might be strengthened. [23:5–13]

1. Anchor bolts (devices that tie a shelving section to the floor). They should be properly sized expansion bolts installed according to the manufacturer's specifications and the International Conference of Building Officials (ICBO) 1988 [or later] Uniform Building Code. Explosively driven nails or lag screws in soft metal inserts should not be used.
2. Wall connections. Concrete or reinforced masonry walls, steel or reinforced concrete columns, or full-height stud walls may be

used. Note that stud walls are generally inadequate for anchoring more than one row of shelving. An unbraced partition (no brace at the top) is not strong enough. The connection should be made to wall studs with lag screws of at least the diameter of a pencil. Heavy sheet metal screws should be used for metal studs. Do not use toggle bolts or screws in plastic sleeves. Never tie the stack to plaster or sheetrock walls.

3. Overhead bracing struts. These may or may not be anchored to walls. Concrete or reinforced masonry walls or steel or reinforced concrete columns are good anchor foundations. Steel channel (U-shaped) or steel angle struts should be used. Do not use flat steel bars or wood strips. Overhead struts may be unnecessary if shelving is internally strong and anchored with good bolts.

4. Overhead strut-to-shelving connections. The strut should be connected to each shelving unit with two machine bolts. Do not use just one bolt or sheet metal screws.

5. Longitudinal or diagonal bracing. Most library shelves have open rather than solid closed backs; therefore some lengthwise bracing is needed. A double diagonal (X brace) should be made from a metal rod, threaded to take a turnbuckle, and connected to the upper and lower corners of the shelving frame by bolts or closed rings. Do not use open hooks on the ends of the rods, because they may bend or slip out under stress. The rods should be taut.

6. Connection of adjacent units. Adjacent sections should be connected together with machine bolts and washers at the frame or thickened edges of the panels. Do not connect through the thin sheet metal panels. Do not use sheet metal screws.

7. Shelf-to-frame connections. Shelves should be screwed to shelf brackets or bolted to posts. They should not be loose on the brackets or simply sitting on shelf tabs or pegs on the posts or section sides.

8. Shelf contents. It is impractical to restrain most books and periodicals on shelves. Rare and/or fragile books, however, may be restrained by screwing a clear plastic lip on the front of the shelf. The lip should be approximately one-third the height of the objects on the shelf. File folders should always be stored in cabinets.

All shelving should be checked for earthquake vulnerability by a well-qualified engineer. The California State Library recently published a manual of recommended practice for seismic safety standards for library shelving. [6] These detailed seismic standards are now required for book stacks in all California libraries whose construction is supported by the federal Library Services and Construction Act (LCSA), Title II, and/or California state bond funds. The California State Librarian is urging every library, public or private, to adopt the procedures detailed in these specifications. The manual "describes the practices to be followed for installation of, or modifications to, library shelving. . . . [The specifications are] limited to the support structures and bracing for [new or existing] library shelving" and do not treat the structure of the building itself. [6:1] Details of each standard are accompanied by drawings and installation instructions. The manual can be purchased from the California State Library Foundation [see section 9.E.1.].

8.C.2. FIRE

According to the A. M. Best Company, the leading causes of fires in libraries are incendiarism, malfunction of heating equipment, defective or inadequate electrical equipment (including the use of small-gauge extension cords), careless smoking, contractors' operations (especially welding and cutting), spontaneous ignition of oily rags, and exposures from adjacent occupancies. [1:105]

Therefore, compartmentalizing the building is essential to limit destruction to a single area. Compartmentalizing should be achieved by fire-resistive wall and floor construction, openings protected by self-closing fire doors, enclosed stairways, protected vertical openings, and air-handling systems designed to prevent the passage of smoke, heat, and fire. Boilers and furnaces, in particular, should be cut off from the remainder of the structure.

Towers and windowless areas present problems with fire-fighting access and smoke removal. Roof ventilation, knockout panels, emergency lighting, and automatic fire-suppression systems are desirable in such areas.

Sheet steel shelves are preferable to either wood or U-bar shelves; metal book trucks are preferable to wood. Interior finishes and furnishings should be fire resistant.

Perimeter lighting and clear space around the library are helpful where the risk of vandalism is high. Book drops leading to the interior of the building are very vulnerable to arsonists. Three ways to deal with this hazard are (1) to use freestanding book drops outside the library, (2) to use fire-resistive metal book carts to receive drop materials, or (3) to reinforce book drops and mail slots with fire-resistive materials to prevent fire spread. Because a set fire may flash almost immediately, a high risk of arson in a given area puts a premium on automatic extinguishing.

Fire and (usually) smoke alarms must be installed in public buildings in the United States. Since many emergencies occur at night or on weekends, alarms should be tied into remote monitoring stations that are manned continuously. If there is no one in the building when a local fire bell sounds, the alarm is virtually useless. There are several devices suitable for installation in libraries and archives, e.g., ionization detectors and photoelectric and linear beam smoke detectors. Ionization detectors are especially appropriate for libraries because they react to combustion gases—the first stage of a fire—and do not require heat, flame, or visible smoke to operate. Fire suppression experts should be consulted for the type of installation best suited for the library's needs.

Automatic sprinklers should also be installed because they can confine a fire to a small area. Even though sprinklers have often been resisted because of the possibility of water damage, experience with them in libraries has been good. Sprinkler systems that minimize water damage are available, e.g., hydraulically calculated systems that discharge less water, stop-and-go-systems (each sprinkler head goes on and off in reaction to a fire in its own area), rapid response sprinkler heads that open early over a small fire and thus require less water, and cross-zoned detection systems that require impulses from two well-separated circuits to trigger the system, preventing premature actions. At the least, libraries can utilize spot sprinklers in such high-hazard areas as janitors' closets and spaces containing substantial combustible contents.

Automatic sprinkler systems can be divided into two general groups: wet-pipe and dry-pipe. The lines in the standard wet-pipe system are always charged with water, which is then discharged through individual nozzles onto the fire. Most fires are controlled through the action of one, or a very few, sensor activated spray nozzles that must be manually turned off. A library can install a Flow Control system where the spray nozzle will automatically shut off when the temperature of the area falls below 95 °F, thereby limiting damage to books and restoring the system to full operation immediately. Dry-pipe systems operate the same way wet-pipes do, except air is in the lines from the feed pipe to the spray heads. The lines are empty until water is released into them by the action of a fire or smoke detector or the opening of a spray nozzle through a fusible link in the sprinkler head. Either type, wet-pipe or dry-pipe, is reliable and both are installed in libraries today. [7:1; 14:37–38; 15:53–54]

Nonaqueous suppression systems may be installed for the protection of special collections, rare books, or electronic equipment such as computers. Three systems are presently available: Halon 1301, high-expansion foam, and CO_2 (carbon dioxide). CO_2 is not recommended because of the high probability of persons suffocating in the area flooded with the gas. Halon 1301, although expensive, is the agent of choice of many libraries for protecting locations where values are high and can be confined to a compact space, and where water damage might create a severe salvage problem. Halon puts out a fire within seconds through the release of compressed halogenated hydrocarbon vapor ($CBrF_3$, bromotrifluoromethane). Through a chemical process, the gas interferes with the fire's chain reaction and immediately snuffs it out. The gas is stored in globe-shaped containers under high pressure; when needed, it is released explosively into the fire area. Fragile materials should not be stored or housed near the discharge duct of the system. Halon must be confined in the space where the fire is located for a minimum of 10 seconds at 5 or 6 percent of atmospheric concentration in order to be effective. No residue or moisture is released by its use, and it is harmless to people for up to five minutes of exposure.

Halon, unfortunately, harms the atmosphere and is being phased out as a primary fire suppressant.

High-expansion foam is a cheaper alternative, and since the foam contains very little moisture, most books and papers can be salvaged successfully. Both Halon 1301 and foam can be installed as fixed systems or be made available in portable extinguishers. [15:54, 81]

8.C.3. WATER DAMAGE

Most library disasters are water related, the result of flooding due to high water, leaks, storms, or from the water used to extinguish fires. As noted in the introduction to this chapter, the most effective means of avoiding or minimizing water-related emergencies is to prepare in advance by checking the building for leakage problems, fire hazards, and site location (the library may be situated in a flood plain). Air-conditioning systems are notorious for causing moisture problems. The ducts and water pipes for many systems are located above false ceilings out of sight and mind, but also forgotten in terms of preventative maintenance inspections. Leaky pipes above stack areas can wreak havoc and cause expensive damage. If pipes cannot be easily or immediately replaced or removed, rainspouts can be slung underneath them to duct the water from leaks away from book collections. Books and other library materials should not be stored in basements, but if they are and there is any danger of flooding, the bottom shelf in the book stack should be at least four inches above the floor.

The installation of a water detection alarm system should be considered if there is a chance of flooding, especially after hours or in areas not normally frequented by staff. There are at least two types of alarms available: a cable that precisely locates the intrusion of water, or a small turtle-shaped device that can be placed in the affected area (the latter cannot pinpoint the location of the problem). Both of these systems can be wired into remote monitoring stations. Such stations are preferable to local area alarms because they can be monitored continuously, and corrective action can be taken immediately when the alarm is activated.

8.D. Disaster Recovery: Initial Response [11]

There are three stages of disaster recovery: (1) the initial response; (2) short-term salvage procedures, such as packout and drying; and (3) long-term restoration programs that may take years, as is the case with the Florence flood of 1966, where restoration is still in progress. This section covers the initial response to an emergency situation, i.e., those actions that take place from the moment the disaster occurs to the time of packing and removal of materials. It concentrates primarily on water-related problems. The initial response may happen within an hour or two in the case of a broken water pipe, or it may happen days after a major disaster and may require permission from an outside agency before workers can enter the site.

Prime objectives in disaster recovery are to (1) stabilize the condition of the collection so no further damage occurs, and (2) salvage the maximum amount of material possible, whether it be in terms of number of volumes, high-priority items, or high-cost items. Time is almost always a critical factor in the development of response strategy, because mold and mildew will occur within 48 to 72 hours after materials are wetted. Access to the building should not deter the implementation of the response process, since actions can be taken to ensure an effective recovery before actually entering the facility. It is not necessary to implement these response operations in the precise order discussed, but many problems may be alleviated if this order is followed. Much will depend on when the staff is permitted to enter the disaster site.

The following list outlines the actions that should be taken by staff:

1. Assess the situation and make competent judgments on
   a. the nature of the damage,
   b. the number of items affected,
   c. the importance of materials affected,
   d. the type of material affected (e.g., books, manuscripts, magnetic media, photographs, etc.), and
   e. how much (if any) action and assistance is needed.

These are difficult, if not impossible, decisions for untrained staff to make accurately. That is why all staff, especially those who work at night and on weekends, must have knowledge of the collection and some training in recovery techniques.

2. Depending on the extent of the damage, notify and convene the necessary staff/experts and the recovery director, or the full team. Implement the telephone tree procedure if it has not already been put into effect.

3. Establish a command post. The recovery director takes this responsibility. It should be in a quiet place, preferably far enough away from the disaster area to avoid confusion and commotion, yet close enough for rapid communication with staff on the scene. At the post:
   a. brief the team on the situation,
   b. determine what action needs to be taken,
   c. develop a strategy, and
   d. assign/affirm responsibilities.

4. Activate plans for acquiring supplies, staff, and volunteers.
   a. Supplies. Be sure there is a prior understanding of payment terms, since it may be difficult or impossible to prepare purchase orders. This is when the establishment

of prior contacts and understandings with suppliers
will prove to be invaluable.
  b. Personnel (staff and volunteers).
    (1) Advance education of the community about disaster
        response needs will help the library gather volunteers.
    (2) Insurance policies should have been checked to
        ensure staff and volunteers are covered for emergency
        response situations.
    (3) Supervision. It is essential to have
        (a) clear cut lines of authority,
        (b) clear, simple instructions on how to implement
            response procedures, and
        (c) careful supervision of activities.
    (4) Morale.
        (a) Establish a rest/refreshment area.
        (b) Provide frequent breaks.
        (c) Don't expect volunteers (and some staff) to
            continue working on the scene forever. Their
            adrenalin will wear off after 72 hours.
5. Establish security measures.
  a. Only authorized persons should be allowed in the
     building during recovery activities. They should be
     issued badges, phosphorescent vests, hard hats, etc.,
     that identify them.
  b. Secure the building when staff is not present by posting
     guards and, if necessary, enclosing the area with a fence.
6. Get clearance to enter the building. Ask the fire/safety
   personnel for permission to enter areas with especially
   valuable/vulnerable materials prior to total building clearance.
   Including fire/safety personnel on the disaster preparedness
   team will help them understand the need for such clearance.
7. Eliminate hazards such as
  a. sewage, biological agents (bacteria, etc.), chemicals, and
     other contaminants,
  b. live electrical lines,
  c. muddy, slippery floors,
  d. glass and other debris,
  e. leaning or collapsed shelves, and
  f. gas leaks.
8. Stabilize the environment by
  a. reducing the temperature as much as possible below
     70°F. Mold and mildew grow above about 70°F.
     Warming the space to dry books faster will practically
     guarantee mold growth.
  b. reducing humidity (for the same reason) by:
    (1) removing wet carpet and furnishings,
    (2) using dehumidifiers,

(3) opening windows if it is dry and cool outside,

(4) pumping out water or using industrial wet-vacuum cleaners.

Commercial services such as BMS-CAT, Cargocaire Moisture Control Services, or SOLEX, Inc., can be very helpful in providing assistance in reducing humidity. See section 9.E.2 for disaster planning and recovery organizations.

    c. increasing air circulation through the use of fans and open windows.

    d. taking frequent readings of environmental monitoring devices.

9. Carefully assess the damage by:

    a. taking extensive notes for use in planning detailed salvage strategy.

    b. taking photographs to document damage for insurance claims.

Documentation can also be used to give patrons information about damage to their areas of interest and to begin planning how or whether access can be provided to part or all of the collections (e.g., via interlibrary loan or access to neighboring libraries).

10. Retreat and develop a recovery plan.

11. Brief all assembled personnel:

    a. Give clear instructions on

      (1) lines of authority and

      (2) procedures to be employed.

    b. Provide training to all workers on how the media will be informed. Media can be very helpful in making potential suppliers aware of the problem, building public sympathy, and attracting volunteers. But dealing with the media is ticklish, and there must be a plan for handling them because they will want eyewitness accounts from everyone. This could be damaging to the recovery because of the possibility of media interfering with operations, receiving conflicting stories, and getting partial or erroneous information from those who don't know the big picture.

12. Begin packout [discussed in section 8.E.2].

8.E. Disaster Recovery: Salvage and Rehabilitation

This section addresses (1) short-term salvage of wet books and materials, i.e., packout and drying, and (2) rehabilitation, which is long-term and may take many years. In most cases where damage has been extensive, some of the collection will be unsalvageable. Time and the situation will work against complete recovery of all materials in the affected area. Consequently, decisions have to be made regarding which materials to save and which to discard. The concept of triage, i.e., the process of sorting materials during or after a disaster to determine which to salvage, the type of treatment they should receive, and which to discard, will often have to be invoked. The Inland Empire Libraries Disaster Response Network (IELDRN) and the UCLA Biomedical Library have developed sets of recommendations for establishing salvage priorities that are useful during emergency situations. [24; 9:C–41] The following section synthesizes those recommendations.

8.E.1. SALVAGE PRIORITY GUIDELINES

A salvage team must concern itself with the issues involving those materials to salvage and those to replace. These decisions must take into account the cost of the material, its value to the library, its availability if replacement is necessary, and the labor involved in acquiring and processing it. The cost of salvaging a book through freezing and freeze- or vacuum freeze-drying has been estimated at $5.00 to $10.00; replacing the standard library book costs anywhere between $20.00 and $300.00 or more. The difference depends on local labor costs and the number of items processed. These costs do not include processing replacements—searching, ordering, receiving, and so on. [9:C–41] [See section 8.G.4 for representative dollar values of library materials.]

If only a small amount of material has been affected, it is possible to review each item for salvage or discard. Usually there is not time to do this review during a packout, but once material is frozen it can be reviewed at a more leisurely pace. Therefore, it is far better to have some idea ahead of time as to which collections should be recovered first.

Many academic and public libraries give high priority for packout and salvage to records and collections containing information needed to establish or continue operations after a disaster, aid recovery operations, and assist in fulfilling the requirements of the insurance company in order to file a claim. Generally speaking, all of the materials in a library can be grouped into four or five priority categories in the event of a disaster. Some authorities use three or four categories because it is sometimes difficult to separate materials into the first and second priorities outlined in the following list. Often organizational records and rare or unique materials pose a dilemma when decisions must be made about which to save first. [See also section 5.E.1 and appendix J.]

1. First priority should be given to (1) the bibliographic records of
   the collection, e.g., the shelflist, card catalog, or some type of
   magnetic storage device (tape or disc); and (2) staff and
   personnel records necessary to continue payroll and operations.
   It is strongly recommended that both types of records be
   duplicated and stored off-site to prevent their irretrievable loss.

2. Second priority are the materials needed to support the institution's current programs, such as reference collections, reserve collections, and certain current journals. High priority is also given by many libraries (especially those having research collections) to special collections, foreign publications, rare books, restricted books, or books that would be too costly to replace and/or are not available at any price. Thought should also be given to materials that should not be frozen (such as microforms, photographs, and magnetic media) and to items that should never be air-dried (e.g., glossy materials, coated paper, and materials with water-soluble inks). These materials should be included, however, only if they cannot be replaced.
3. Third priority are materials that are replaceable: those that could eventually be acquired in print or in microform but that would involve a considerable outlay of time and funds to do so. However, if these are lost, the strength of the collection would be undermined considerably, and users would be seriously inconvenienced for a long period of time.
4. Next are materials that support the collecting and information goals of the library, can more easily and less expensively be replaced than salvaged, and, most importantly, *should* be replaced. Most of these would be in *Books in Print* or similar trade bibliographies.
5. Last are those materials that do not need to be salvaged or replaced and could be withdrawn. These could include older editions of textbooks and older treatments of subjects that have been superseded by more recent materials and are of no historical value to the collection.

When a disaster occurs, time is of the essence. Decisions must be made quickly about which materials to sacrifice and which to save. The priority list is a working guide for the salvage team. Librarians must examine the mission and goals of their own library policies and then analyze their collections in light of those policies so they will be in the optimum position to resume services at the earliest possible moment.

8.E.2. PACKOUT AND REMOVAL

Materials must be physically removed from the damage area. This operation may be complicated by a lack of electricity, which will affect the operation of elevators and reduce visibility. But wet items must be removed in order to lower the humidity in the affected spaces and to facilitate drying and the eventual decisions for disposition.

Stairways may be unsafe to use. Libraries have coped with these problems by forming human chains and having workers pass single books or boxes of books from one person to another; building ramps down stairways and/or out of windows so boxes can be slid down to workers waiting below (be sure to build a bumper at the bottom so the boxes don't tumble onto the ground); or using cranes to raise dumpsters to the affected floors.

The original shelf location of the materials and the number or code of the box they are packed in must be clearly and accurately documented so they may be found, if necessary, either during or after the salvage and rehabilitation periods. It is not necessary to record the exact location of each item, but call number groups must be recorded in a log by shelf, range, classification, record group, storage room, and box. Portable microcomputers and database management software can be used to accomplish this task quickly and accurately. [13:51–60] This record is very important for insurance and/or financial planning. An institution usually has to prove to insurance companies that it actually owns (or owned) the items for which it is requesting reimbursement. Also, almost invariably after a fire, people who have a great interest in certain parts of the collection want to know its condition and how soon it can be used. An accurate record of the location of the materials they want to use will facilitate its expeditious recovery, salvage, and rehabilitation.

Wet books are slippery. Paper-based media are very fragile when wet, and they tear easily. Books and paper often become distorted when wet. Do *not* try to straighten them, unless the plan includes freeze-drying, and then only very gently urge those that are grossly distorted back toward their original shapes. Oversized materials should be left in cabinets or transferred to bread trays or plywood boards.

Materials will often require cleaning. Cleaning should usually not be done until after books are dry, but if proper care is taken, they can be lightly rinsed to get rid of mud and sewage. This must be done very carefully, holding the item with *both* hands and gently dunking it in a series of buckets or bins filled with clean, cold, flowing water. Several buckets should be used so each piece can be dipped in successively cleaner water. Running hoses should be placed in each bucket so the water will constantly be changing. *Never* try to scrub dirt or mud off a wet book or paper. Scrubbing grinds the dirt into the fibers and seriously complicates cleaning later. It may also tear the material and make it virtually impossible to successfully salvage.

For years milk crates were thought to be the best container for packing out wet books, and they do have advantages. They are strong, the right size, easy to stack, and they let air get to the materials. But they are often difficult to obtain quickly in large quantities and sometimes leave an imprint of their pattern on the materials stored in them. Consequently, 200 pound burst test cardboard boxes of 1.0 cubic foot (12″ x 15″ x 10″) or 1.5 cubic feet (12″ x 18″ x 12″) are often recommended in place of milk crates. [13:15] The boxes are relatively inexpensive and easy to acquire in most communities, but a supply should be on hand because it may be difficult to get them quickly on short notice. Whatever containers are used should be uniform in size for stacking purposes; otherwise they may tip over. Some experts say cardboard boxes should have holes in them so the materials inside can breathe, but there is no general agreement on this point. However, boxes should be sealed loosely enough so moisture can easily escape if the packed books are vacuum-dried.

Books should be separated from each other by loosely wrapping them with waxed or freezer paper and then placing them spine down in the packing containers. Wrapping the books prevents them from sticking together and stops the dyes in the covers from bleeding into the covers of the adjacent books. It does slow the packing process, however, and if books are to be vacuum dried, less than 5 percent will stick together anyway. *Never* stack books on top of each other in the containers, unless an oversized book must be laid on top of those already in the box because it will not fit anywhere else. Cramming books into the boxes will force them out of shape, causing them to become permanently deformed when they dry.

Manuscripts or loose papers should be wrapped in packages less than two inches thick. After wrapping the sheets, turn the container on its side and stack the wrapped packages on top of each other in the box until it is full. Then turn the box bottom side down so the packages are standing erect and not lying on each other. This will prevent the sheets from compressing together and forcing debris into the paper fibers.

Boxes should be sealed with tape, labeled according to their contents (e.g., call numbers and/or building, floor, and shelf codes as appropriate) and stacked on pallets. They should never be stacked more than three or four boxes high because they tend to lean and fall over, especially if they become damp. They should be secured on the pallets with strapping or shrink-wrap and sent to a freezing facility within two or three days of the time the books became wet.

8.E.3. STABILIZATION

Wetted materials must be dried or stabilized within 48 to 72 hours, depending on the temperature and humidity of the area. Mold and mildew will begin to grow within that time if precautions are not taken. The best way to stabilize wet books and papers is by freezing them. Freezing prevents mold growth, inhibits swelling of the books while they are frozen (they will swell again when thawed, if still wet), and prevents further diffusion of dyes. Probably the biggest advantage of freezing is that it buys time for the disaster recovery team (or staff) to find the means to dry the materials without further damage occurring.

When just a few books have been wetted, they can be frozen in a home-type frost-free freezer. They should be loosely wrapped in freezer paper, as described in section 8.E.2, and placed upright in the freezer; in fact, the equipment will probably dry them if they are left in the freezing compartment for several weeks or months. Larger numbers of materials should be quick or blast frozen to at least -10°F in a commercial freezer. See section 8.E.4.b for an explanation of this procedure.

Freezing is not without its disadvantages. In a large disaster, it may be difficult to locate adequate facilities nearby and at reasonable cost. Also, federal and local health regulations must be checked. Some states, for example, do not allow wet books (even in boxes) to be placed in the same freezer with seafood, although they may allow them to be frozen with vegetables.

8.E.4. DRYING TECHNIQUES

The information in this section is based on material in the Toronto manual and Peter Waters' pamphlet on salvaging water-damaged library materials. [20; 27] Appendix I contains a synopsis of these techniques.

8.E.4.a. Air-drying

Damp, uncoated papers and books may be safely air-dried if they can be processed within 72 hours. Do not attempt to air-dry materials that are dripping wet unless the temperature range is between 70 °F and 77 °F (or lower) and the relative humidity is stabilized at 50 percent or less. These conditions must be maintained and the air kept moving all the time with an air-conditioning system or fans. If the air-conditioning system is used to move the air, care must be taken to avoid pumping the moist air back into the stacks and raising the humidity in other parts of the library, thus creating conditions elsewhere for the growth of mold. This will happen if the staff attempts to dry wetted materials in the library or in the space where they originally became wet. The moisture from the wet books will recycle into the air, raise the relative humidity of the area, and slow the drying process, possibly to the point where it becomes impossible for books to dry.

Waters says that if just the edges of the text blocks are wet, the books can be air-dried in about two weeks in temperatures of 50 °F to 65 °F and relative humidity of 25 to 35 percent. [27:21] Wet materials that are exposed to the air will continue to swell; the boards and paper will become more distorted, and the book cloth will bubble. The longer it takes them to dry, the greater the chance of mildew forming. Air-drying requires lots of space and is back-breaking work. Volunteers may disappear before the job is completed, and the staff may not have time to do the work. If the temperature, humidity, and air movement cannot be controlled, then another drying technique should be considered.

Air-drying, however, does not require much expense, except for time and labor. It can be used efficiently for fewer than 500 books, or by taking groups of books at a time out of the freezing facility and air-drying them in small batches. Air-drying is the preferred method for photographic prints.

Tables, boards, or plywood sheets raised on blocks and covered with plastic sheeting should be used for the drying work surface. Raising the work surface will reduce the amount of bending and lifting and will delay workers' fatigue. The plastic sheeting will protect the drying surface from the damp books. The sheeting should be covered with clean, unprinted newsprint that will help absorb the moisture from the books; it should be removed whenever it becomes too wet to perform that function efficiently. Slightly open the books to be dried (so they won't sag), and very carefully place them on their heads (top edge) on the table. Small pieces of Styrofoam™ or sponge rubber may be placed under the edges of the covers so the books will be slightly tilted toward their spines, helping to keep them open. Toothpicks can be placed between the covers and text to keep them separated from each other. Aluminum foil can also be placed between the covers and the text block so dyes from the cover will not bleed into the paper in the book. Books that are very wet should be placed on several sheets of absorbent paper. After they dry a little, interleave paper towels or blank newsprint, cut to the approximate size of the book, every few pages. Interleaving should not exceed one-third of the book's thickness. Both the interleaving sheets and those on which the books are sitting should be removed as soon as they become wet and replaced with dry ones. The wet sheets should be taken immediately from the drying area in order to avoid adding to the humidity of the room. As the books begin to dry, they should be reversed periodically from their heads to tails, back to the heads, and so on. [20:67]

Books that have swollen to the point at which their spines are becoming concave, when viewed from the bottom or top, but *aren't saturated with water and don't weigh more than six pounds*, may be hung to finish drying on three or more monofilament fishing lines. The lines should not be more than 1/32 inch in diameter or more than 6 feet long, and they should be about 1/2 inch apart from each other. If done improperly, books can be damaged when hung from the lines, primarily from spine adhesives running down the pages, which causes staining and the adhesion of adjacent pages. This method should be used only as a last resort. *Heavy, saturated books should not be dried this way.* [20:67]

Pamphlets, vertical files, and other light materials have been successfully dried on monofilament lines. It has been reported that spraying Lysol™ in the air around the drying items might reduce the likelihood of mold occurring. The materials in the area to be sprayed should be pretested first to determine if they contain any inks that will run. Also, if too much spray is used, it might discolor the paper. [10:102]

Stacks or groups of wet manuscript papers or sheets are extremely difficult to separate for drying because they will tear when an attempt is made to pull one from another. A three-ply piece of Mylar™ polyester sheet, cut to a size bigger than the wet sheets to be salvaged, can be used to safely separate them. The Mylar™ is laid on top of the stack of paper and gently pressed down (not so much as to squeeze the pile) or rubbed with a bone folder or soft cloth. The surface tension of the water between the polyester and the paper will cause the top sheet to cleave to the Mylar™ and separate from the other sheets without damage as the polyester and the sheet are gently peeled back. The polyester, with the paper so attached, should then be placed on a nylon sheet or plastic webbing. The polyester then can be peeled back, starting from a corner, and another sheet of nylon or webbing placed on top of the wet sheet. The wet sheet can then be air-dried. Additional Mylar™ sheets are used to repeat the procedure until all the leaves are separated. The polyester with the wet sheet still attached could also be hung from a clothesline using plastic clothespins. The sheets should be watched because as they dry, they will separate and fall from the Mylar™. As they do, they can be transferred to the table and dried as the other sheets.

After separation, single sheets should be laid out on a clean blotting paper or unprinted newsprint on the tables. As they begin to dry, increasing pressure should be applied in order to flatten them. Before they are entirely dry, they may be interleaved between pellon and blotting paper (i.e., blotting paper on the bottom, pellon, a damp sheet, pellon, another damp sheet, another sheet of pellon, and so on, with blotting paper on top). Weights, such as bricks wrapped in kraft paper, should be placed on top of the stack overnight so they will dry flat.

The only practical way to successfully dry coated papers, such as those found in many magazines and art and photographic works, is by freezing and then vacuum freeze-drying them. If they are only slightly damp, however, they may be air-dried using the technique described above and fanning the pages frequently. The end result will probably be more cockling than would be expected from freeze-drying.

One of the more difficult tasks in drying wetted materials is determining when the item is actually dry. Some suggest weighing the items before and after drying to determine the rate of water removal. This procedure is probably not practical for most situations, however. A more accurate method is the use of a moisture meter, an instrument that measures the amount of moisture in the paper (or other items) by determining the amount of impedance generated by a weak electrical current between two electrodes. The instrument is inserted into the book or laid on the paper, and the amount of moisture remaining is indicated by a reading on the dial. If the reading is seven or less, the paper is considered dry. See section 9.E.2 for companies that handle this type of equipment.

When the books are almost dry, they should be taken from their upright positions, closed, laid flat on a table, and, if misshapen, gently formed into their normal shape, e.g., squared away with a convex spine and concave fore edge (if appropriate), and held in place with light weights or a book press. England and Evans note that they should not be pressed with other drying books. They may still be interleaved, if necessary, at well-spaced intervals. [10:101]

8.E.4.b. Freezer drying

This technique requires the use of a self-defrosting blast freezer. (Note: this is *not* vacuum freeze-drying.) It is suitable for materials that are damp and/or wet around the edges. Saturated books take too long to dry using this method. Temperatures in the freezer should be -10 to -40 °F. The lower the temperature the less distortion will occur in the books. Materials should be wrapped or supported to minimize initial swelling, keep them from sticking together, and avoid dye transfer. The process is analogous to meat drying out in a home freezer. Materials should be placed in the freezer as soon as possible after being wetted in order to keep swelling and distortion to a minimum. This method is relatively inexpensive but can take from a few weeks to several months to dry the materials. Freezer drying will permit the return of books to a usable state, but will not restore them to anything near their original condition. This procedure can cause the formation of large ice crystals in the cellulose structure of the paper if the temperature is not low enough for quickly blast freezing, rupturing the cells in the paper, adhesives, and bindings, which causes loss of strength and can lead to further deterioration. Cockling of pages, shrinking of the bindings, and distortion will almost always take place. Coated papers should not be dried in this manner because they will adhere to each other. [10:99]

8.E.4.c. Dehumidification

A number of companies have developed a technique whereby entire buildings are dried out without having to remove and/or wrap or prepare the contents for the drying process. Large dehumidifiers are brought to the site and placed in the building. Dry air pumped into the facility replaces the moist air and stabilizes the temperature and relative humidity. Large numbers of damp materials can be successfully dried in this manner. Film-based media and photographic prints can be very successfully handled by this method. Names of the companies that provide this service are listed in section 9.E.2.

8.E.4.d. Vacuum thermal drying

Materials are boxed as described above and placed in a vacuum chamber. Depending on the size of the chamber, several hundred volumes can be processed at once. A near vacuum is drawn and the water molecules are pulled out of the materials. This process requires heat and is accomplished at temperatures above 32 °F. After the vacuum pulls the water out (it remains in its liquid state), warm, dry air is pumped into the chamber to complete the drying. If the materials are frozen when they are placed in the chamber, some of the water molecules will sublimate from ice to vapor, but most will first pass through the liquid state before vaporizing. Thermal vacuum drying takes about four to six weeks per load of books and costs about $3.00 per volume (1988 prices). It is suitable for nonpermanent, unbound records, but not for valuable manuscripts or bound books. Since the water leaves the materials in a liquid form, there will be cockling. Radiant heat is sometimes used inside the vacuum chamber to speed up the drying process. This may cause acids to migrate from papers having high acid content to those with a lower acid content. Therefore, early manuscripts and rare books should not be mixed with acidic or embrittled materials. Heat also affects the sizing in such materials and causes it to migrate toward the edges, staining or embrittling the paper. The same caution applies to vacuum freeze-drying since heat may also be used in that process. Vacuum thermal drying tends to increase distortion of the books and thereby increase the need for rebinding. It is not recommended for bound volumes. Coated papers will almost always become blocked. However, it is easier than air-drying for large numbers of bound materials and for those that have suffered extensive water damage. [20:66–67]

8.E.4.e. Vacuum freeze-drying

Vacuum freeze-drying is the most effective way to dry large quantities of water-damaged materials. [20:66] Frozen books and materials are placed in a vacuum chamber; a vacuum is pulled, heat introduced, and the items are dried at temperatures below 32 °F. Since they remain frozen, the water molecules leave the materials as ice crystals and sublimate directly into vapor, bypassing the liquid state. Therefore, no additional swelling, cockling, or other distortion takes place, and the volumes will dry looking about the same as before they were wetted (assuming they were frozen quickly before much swelling or distortion took place). Little or no rebinding or additional shelf space after drying is necessary; and the volumes are easier to clean because the sublimation process seems to bring dirt and mud to the surface of the paper. Vacuum freeze-drying may be suitable for leather, vellum, and coated papers, if the latter had been frozen or placed in the chamber within six hours after being wetted. Leather and vellum, however, may not survive. Vacuum freeze-drying takes about one to two weeks per load and costs about $3.00 to $7.00 per volume for large numbers of books: about $5.00 per volume on the average. It is suitable for large quantities of very wet books or records. It may cause some damage to film-based materials, leaving impurities behind as the water sublimates. Photographs should not be freeze-dried because the process will cause them to lose their surface gloss. A possible exception are photos mounted in albums that have captions of historical interest. In both vacuum freeze-drying and vacuum thermal drying, the books and papers must be rehumidified to restore them to their natural condition of about 7 to 8 percent moisture content.

8.E.5. PHOTOGRAPHIC MEDIA

Salvage techniques for photographic media are still being developed and are in a state of flux. Before attempting any of the procedures described below, consult a professional conservator who is a specialist in photographic materials. If a conservator is not available, contact the

Eastman Kodak Company Information Center in Rochester, New York, or another reputable photo processing firm [see section 9.E.2 for more information]. If possible, before a disaster happens, it would be wise to make copy negatives of all photographic prints in the collection and store them off-site. Prints made from the copy negatives could then be used for everyday use. The original photographs can then be packaged and stored more securely. [10:107]

Photographic media should be air-dried under most circumstances; however, any photographic medium will be difficult to salvage after a fire or flood. The image is held by the emulsion, which is destroyed by high temperatures, humidity, and steam. Emulsions will be softened if kept under water for long periods, and soft emulsions will stick to adjacent materials. The amount of damage wet photographic materials will sustain depends on the type of photograph, its physical condition, whether or not it was hardened during processing, the immersion time, and the water temperature. Unprocessed exposed films and wet collodion glass plate negatives are very sensitive to water damage and probably will not survive. [20:69] If attention cannot be given to the materials within two or three days (two days for color), blast-freeze them until they can be salvaged. Freezing is chancy because if photographs are frozen slowly, the formation of ice crystals may rupture the emulsion layer and leave marks on the film. Freezing, however, does retard the growth of mold and allows time for rational decision making. Priorities dictate that prints should be salvaged first (film appears to be more stable), followed by freezing of photographs (if they cannot be cleaned and air-dried immediately). Whenever water is used to help separate photographs, keep the immersion time to a minimum and the water temperature below 72°F. [10:108]

8.E.5.a. Black-and-white photographic prints

Wet black-and-white photographic prints should be cleaned by agitating them in a tray of clean, cold water for about 30 minutes. Change the water frequently. After cleaning they should be air-dried either by hanging them with plastic clothespins on a line or spreading them out on blotters. A technique used to inhibit curling during drying is to place blotters on the drying surface, place the print on the blotter, lay pellon over the print, put another blotter on the pellon, and then apply weights. The blotters should be changed as they become wet. [16]

8.E.5.b. Color prints

Color prints should be dried the same way as black-and-white prints, but not washed as long. If they cannot be salvaged within two days, freeze them until they can be given proper attention. Even then, they may be lost. [20:69]

8.E.5.c. Processed films

Never let water-damaged photographic material dry out. Processed films and glass plate negatives should be soaked in clean, cold water (65 °F or below) containing 15 ml of 37 percent formaldehyde solution per liter of water. The films should be carefully separated from their sleeves, enclosures, and each other. If they are not very dirty, rinse them for 10 to 15 minutes in the solution. Otherwise, wash them for 30 minutes in the solution by gently sponging their surfaces under water with a foam rubber brush or soft sponge. Dry at room temperature in a dust-free area. [20:69–70]

Black-and-white films, Kodachrome transparencies, and X-ray films should be dipped or rinsed in a wetting agent such as a dilute solution of Kodak PHOTO-FLO. If PHOTO-FLO is not available, use a mild detergent and then rinse. The Kodachrome transparencies should be rinsed again in running water for about five minutes, then placed in Kodak SH-1 Special Hardener solution for another five minutes. Remove the excess solution with a soft sponge. Dry at room temperature in a dust-free area. [20:70]

Ektachrome transparencies should be rinsed for about 10 to 15 seconds in Kodak E6 stabilizer. Dry at room temperature in a dust-free area. [20:70]

Color negatives should be rinsed for one minute in Kodak C41 stabilizer. Dry at room temperature in a dust-free area. [20:70]

Eastman Color Film should be handled only by a processing laboratory. Dry at room temperature in a dust-free area. [20:70]

8.E.5.d. Microfilm and motion picture film

These should be handled by a processing laboratory, if at all possible. They can be kept safely in clean, cold water for 48 hours (up to three days for black-and-white film). Black-and-white film can be preserved for up to two weeks by the addition of a 1 percent solution of Formalin to the water. If transportation to a processing laboratory is not possible, remove the film from its reels and store the film in a solution of 10 grams of magnesium sulfate and 10 ml of 37 percent formaldehyde solution per liter of water. Reprocess the film in white light by (1) feeding the film on rollers without emulsion contact, (2) starting the film in a prehardner solution followed by a solution of 10 grams sodium carbonate and 10 ml of 37 percent formaldehyde solution per liter of water, (3) running it though a spray rack if possible, and (4) taking up the dry film on cores and reassembling on reels. Always wear protective eyeglasses and gloves when handling these solutions and make sure the ventilation is adequate. [20:70]

8.E.6. MAGNETIC MEDIA

The higher the technology, the less likely the success of the salvage effort. This is especially true for magnetic media; thus, the most prudent course of action is to make backup copies of all information that is important enough to keep and store it off site.

8.E.6.a. Magnetic tape

Magnetic tapes on reels are fairly heat resistant and can withstand temperatures of 160 °F (70 °C) for up to one hour without suffering severe damage. Smoke damage poses few problems, and generally only the exposed edges have to be cleaned. Prolonged exposure to water is more serious since it causes leaching of chemicals from the tape. In any event, if a backup is available, discard the original and use the backup. [See sections 6.E.1.c.1 and 6.E.1.c.2 for related information on care of magnetic tape.]

8.E.6.b. Computer tapes

If recorded tapes have been subjected to fire and heat, do the following:

1. Separate out those reels that appear to have sustained the least amount of physical fire or heat damage as soon as possible.
2. Clean all fire debris, fly ash, and smoke residue from canisters, wraparounds, and flange surfaces. Do this before opening the canisters or wraparounds.
3. Use the slowest speed transport available to perform at least two full wind-rewind passes. Instrumentation tape recorders that run at 0.762 m/s (30 in/s) and that can accommodate 12.7 mm (0.5 inch) computer tapes are a good choice. Inspect the tapes as they are being wound. If they are badly warped or display layer-to-layer adhesion that is damaging the coating, or if they are shedding significant amounts of coating debris, the chances for data recovery are poor. Clean the transport after each tape is run.
4. Give promising tapes two full cleaning passes on a tape cleaner/winder (preferably constant tension type). Rewind the tapes onto clean or new reels and make new labels.
5. Relax these rewound and cleaned tapes for 24 to 48 hours in the normal operating environment (60 °F to 90 °F and 20 to 80 percent relative humidity).
6. Perform a read (and recopying) pass. If the tapes will not load onto the transport at this time, store them in a low humidity environment and retry at intervals.
7. Repeat these steps for the next least damaged group of tapes. [12:32]

When tapes become wet, the National Institute of Standards and Technology recommends the following:

1. Quickly separate the wet and dry tapes. Also separate the vital records from the less important. If possible, move the wet or dry tapes out of the storage area; shift whichever group consists of a smaller number of tapes. Move all tapes quickly out of standing water.

2. Check all wet tape labels and make sure they are legible. Replace or make existing labels legible, but do not paste new labels over the wet originals.

3. Begin a general drying of the storage area, including shelves, floors, canisters, safes, and vaults. Standing water may continue to inundate the tapes, particularly if the water has entered a closed tape safe or vault; dry theses areas immediately. Quickly open, check, and drain any water that may have entered the tape canisters. Tape reel hubs are often capable of trapping and holding water; check by shaking and rotating reels to empty the water. Use wet-dry vacuum cleaners to absorb all standing water wherever accessible.

4. The tape drying process should begin immediately. Do not replace wet tapes into their canisters; this allows the air-drying process to begin. Dry all accessible external wet surfaces by hand. Do not force-dry the wet tape pack with a heated airflow; this can cause high internal humidity, which can lead to binder damage and layer-to-layer adhesion. Gently separate the reel flanges with spacers such as rubber grommets to allow airflow through the tape pack-flange interface. This will reduce the probability of tape-to-flange sticking damage when the tapes are first run. It will also permit additional water runoff from the vertically standing tapes. If possible, maintain a forced, room temperature airflow through this tape-to-reel configuration.

5. The most effective drying phase begins when the individual tapes are run reel-to-reel on a device such as a tape cleaner or winder. Never attempt to run wet tape on a regular tape drive. The tape will not perform correctly in the vacuum columns, and there is a strong possibility that the wet tape will adhere to the column walls or onto the capstan, with ensuing tape tearing or other damage. Run over cleaning tissues only, not over the blades.

6. Try data recovery methods, even after a period of total water immersion (but only after all of the steps described above have been accomplished). After all accessible surfaces are hand dried, store the tapes for 48 hours in the normal operating environment (60 °F to 90 °F and 20 to 80 percent relative humidity). Then run the tapes for six or seven passes on a tape dry cleaner unit over tissue cleaners only. When the tapes are reasonably dried, perform two cleaning passes over tissues and

cleaning blades. Immediately read and copy the tapes onto new reels. This procedure has been successful for salvaging tapes that were immersed in dirty river water and others that were submerged in salt water for a period of time. [12:34–35]

8.E.6.c. Audio tapes

If no backup is available, wash the exposed edges with clean water and leave the tapes to dry without heating. After it is dried, fast wind the tape against a felt pad (without the tape contacting the heads) to remove dried dirt and soil from the oxide and base surfaces. Unless it is absolutely mandatory to salvage them, discard the original cassettes and cartridges. If they must be saved, open and clean them in clean water. After the cleaning is completed, re-record the information onto a new tape and discard the old one. Be careful to identify the tapes during the cleaning process, and do not lose or switch labels. A wax crayon can be used to temporarily identify the tapes while they are being cleaned. See sections 6.E.1.c.1 and 6.E.1.c.2 for additional information.

8.E.6.d. Computer disks (floppy diskettes)

If a backup copy is not available, store the wet computer disks upright in cool distilled water. When they are to be cleaned, remove them from their jackets and agitate them in multiple water baths; then insert them into new jackets and copy the information. Do not use your own equipment to copy the information. Several companies listed in section 9.E.2 provide data recovery services.

Floppy disks can also be cleaned and dried using common household equipment, i.e., a hand hair dryer. Disks have a cloth-like lining inside the black plastic, permanent sealed jacket. This lining absorbs moisture. Disks that are only slightly damp can be dried using a hand-held hair dryer at the "air" setting. Hold the disks so the air is directed into an opening on either side of the disk, very gently turning the disk jacket as the lining dries. Peel dripping wet disks out of their jackets and wipe them dry with clean, lint-free rags. Sometimes jackets can be popped open or trimmed on one edge with a paper cutter. Open a new (dry) disk jacket by trimming about one-sixteenth inch of the write-protect edge off of the paper cover. Remove the new diskette from the plastic cover and set it aside for later replacement. Slip the bare, old disk into the dry cover; run and copy it. [18:15]

Larry Osborne describes this salvage technique in detail: [19:10]

1. If the top or bottom of the disk itself can't be easily identified, use a non-water-soluble felt-tipped pen to mark the top side of the disk, very near the center hole.

2. Slit (or otherwise open) the plastic jacket of the inundated disk; it would be a good idea to use an unmagnetized pair of scissors

for this. A modicum of care is called for, because ANSI standards call for only about .0125 inches of clearance between the disk and the inner edge of the jacket. Slide the disk gently away from the edge you intend to cut by pushing on the appropriate side of the center hole.

3. Gently remove the disk.

4. Rinse off as much of the substance as you can under tepid running water.

5. If grease remains, wash with a mild soap and rinse well.

6. Blot and air dry (. . . forced air drying with a hair dryer on its AIR-ONLY setting may speed things up . . .).

7. Carefully slit (or otherwise open) the top of a good but expendable disk, and replace that disk with your now-clean one. Be careful to place the disk right-side-up (and, if your computer can't read the disk at all, suspect you have it upside down . . .).

8. Copy the files from the salvaged disk to a new good one. . . . Use one of the many head-cleaning products afterwards.

There is no guarantee this procedure will save data, but it usually works. If using an AT or AT clone disc with its higher densities, this procedure may not help in all cases. Be careful not to physically damage the disk when removing debris from its surface. Any scratch will irrevocably destroy data.

8.F. Fire Damage

8.F.1. SMOKE AND SOOT REMOVAL AND DEODORIZATION

In most cases books and papers damaged by fire are beyond salvage. If the only damage is by soot deposits on the outside of the book and there is no charring or other evidence of heat damage, it may be possible to remove most of the soil by mechanical cleaning. It may be best to employ a cleaning firm that specializes in soot removal, deodorization, and sterilization to ensure that the job is done correctly and thoroughly. [8:104] The cost of cleaning and deodorizing varies from $1.95 to $2.95 per book. Two companies that specialize in soot removal and deodorization are Re-Oda Chem Engineering of Chagrin Falls, Ohio, and BMS-CAT of Fort Worth, Texas [see section 9.E.1].

If contracting with a cleaning firm is not possible, chemical sponges can be used to reduce and/or eliminate soot and odors. Recommended are Chem Clene or Chem-Glide. A chemical sponge does not contain chemicals to assist in the removal of soot and dirt; the name refers to the manufacturing process of producing a sponge that is much more dense than the ordinary household cleaning aid. The sponges can be cut in half to fit the cleaner's hand better and can be washed and reused several times. They should be used on a closed book with gentle stroking motions in one direction away from the spine toward the fore edge on the head and/or tail of the text block until no more soot or debris can be removed without damaging the surface area. Use the same procedure on the fore edge, spine, and covers. If non-library staff are used, be sure the cleaners are trained and supervised to remove as much soil as possible and the cleaning materials are changed frequently.

Another way to remove soot and debris is by having a library binder remove the case and trim and rebind the text block.

Charcoal and/or baking soda can be used to deodorize fire-damaged materials. Place charcoal briquettes and/or bowls of baking soda in the area to absorb the odor. The process will be shortened if the materials to be deodorized are placed in a closed or semi-enclosed chamber. See section 2.I.5 for more information.

Ozone can remove odors but must be used with care and should not be used with books or papers that are wet or damp. Ozone is formed (in this application) by a generator that draws air (O_2) through an electrical charge and causes it to separate into two elements of oxygen (O). Since oxygen is an unstable gas, it seeks out and combines with other molecules of air (O_2), forming ozone (O_3). When the ozone comes in contact with an organic odor, the extra element of oxygen combines with the odor-producing compound, and oxidation of the odor (chemical burning) takes place. [2:12–13] A qualified cleaning firm should be able to use the equipment safely. The ability of ozone to combine with water molecules to form hydrogen peroxide (a bleach) might discolor some materials and weaken them. Ozone will break down cellulose molecules and, consequently, age paper more quickly. Ozone should not be used in occupied areas because high concentrations can result in respiratory irritation.

Lysol™ spray has also been used to effectively cover odors.

8.G. Insurance

Most of the information in this section is taken, with permission, from England and Evans' *Disaster Management for Libraries*. [10]

Responsible personnel in the library must understand the library's insurance policy, establish a method for keeping an adequate, secure inventory, obtain technical details and plans of the library, decide appropriate cost parameters for claim preparation, and work with an insurer. "In most libraries, insurance is handled by an administrative officer who may or may not be part of the library's staff." [10:59–70] These officers, often called risk managers, are knowledgeable about insurance, available for consultation, and, in most cases, involved in insuring library collections. Risk management concerns are those activities, methodologies, and strategies undertaken to protect against and prepare for losses. Risk management is often closely associated with the purchase of insurance, but goes far beyond that. For example, the risk manager searches for methods to stabilize losses through the establishment of reserve or contingency funds, self-insurance programs, or the purchase of insurance policies. Many public agencies set aside funds in order to self-insure (i.e., the agency must itself pay for recovering from a disaster) operations that need protection, perhaps up to a level of $500,000 or more. Losses above that level would be covered by insurance provided by private companies. Risk managers can be invaluable in helping obtain the correct coverage for the library's collections.

Selecting the proper insurance coverage is not a task to undertake without the help of an established broker or agent who represents a variety of carriers. It is also wise to seek the occasional advice of a second professional to review the program.

It is important to review the insurance schedule frequently, since the value of collections increases. [14:93–94]

Accidents and other incidents that may result in claims should be reported at the earliest possible time to the insurer, agent, or broker. It is prudent to write a letter as well as make a telephone call for this purpose at once, particularly in any situation in which the insurer needs to make an investigation at the library. [14:100]

8.G.1. POLICIES

8.G.1.a. Coverages

Policies are written as either "all risk" or "specified risk" (i.e., named peril). All risk policies, which cover fires, sprinkler leakage, water damage, vandalism, riots and civil commotion, and so on are normally recommended, because any loss is covered except for written exclusions (e.g., staff personal property and interlibrary loans in transit). [10:60]

In a fire, loss designates that portion entirely consumed by fire; damage designates property that is not destroyed but is injured, e.g., by immersion in water.

A common problem for libraries is that of discovering, too late, that parts of the collection were either not insured or underinsured. The following definitions are helpful in understanding coverage written in the library's policy:

CONTENTS (other than books) usually includes, without limitations, furniture, furnishings, fittings, fixtures, machinery, tools, utensils and appliances, records and books of account, and generally all materials and supplies, and all other contents of every description. "Records and books of account" extend the coverage under this definition to the inventories of a collection, e.g., a card catalog, computer database, or microfiche, however they are kept.

BOOKS includes, without limitation, all books (except records and books of account) and papers, magazines, manuscripts, periodicals and other publications, catalogs, microfilm, special and other collections and clippings, and generally all contents kept or used by the Insured in connection with their operations, other than those insured under the heading CONTENTS.

"Other collections" implies coverage of audiovisual media and/or computer software. Note: If the library has extensive collections in audiovisual media, or if large bulk loans and/or exhibits are part of the library's frequent operating procedure, coverage should be specifically extended to these areas. These items are a library's operating stock, which BOOKS is generally intended to define.

Property covered in standard insurance forms may also include items removed from the premises for processing, repair, storage or exhibition.

The policy can also be written to specifically include a "Records" clause stating that the insurer covers loss to:

books of account, drawings, card index systems, other records
. . . not exceeding the cost of the blank books, blank pages or other materials, plus the cost of labor for actually transcribing or copying; media, data storage devices, and program devices for electronic and electro-mechanical data processing or for electronically controlled equipment, which shall not exceed the cost of reproducing from duplicates or from originals. . . . No liability is assumed for cost of gathering or assembling information or data for such reproduction. [10:63]

This clause applies to card catalogs, shelflists, computer and microform catalogs, etc. The cost of reconstructing the catalog, however, is *not* covered, and it behooves the library to store a master copy off-site to avoid the considerable expense of re-creating what is often the single most expensive item in the library. Note: Policies should be extended to cover the labor and research costs of re-creation of the catalog.

Standard policies used for libraries may also be written with an extended cover to include valuable papers and records. This extension tends to echo a "Records" clause and covers:

"the cost of reproducing books of account, abstracts, drawings, card index systems or any other records, including but not limited to film, tape, disc, drum, cell, magnetic recordings, or any other storage media." [10:64]

A separate multiperil "Valuable Papers and Records" form may be used to cover the card catalog and other special items. These valuable papers are:

"written, printed, or otherwise inscribed documents and records, as books, maps, films, drawings, abstracts, deeds, mortgages, and manuscripts." [10:64]

This form provides very broad all risks coverage, but has certain disadvantages. Some risk managers modify it to cover the replacement cost for items that are *actually* replaced and also provide a single agreed upon amount of blanket insurance. [14:99]

"Another form used by libraries is the 'Fine Arts,' which also covers manuscripts and rare books and is a form primarily used for those items associated with museums or galleries." [10:64] Inland marine insurance can be purchased to cover the extraordinary replacement costs of rare books and manuscripts, special collections, fine arts, and bookmobile contents. Best strongly recommends fire detection and suppression systems for libraries that house irreplaceable books and works of art. The coverage may also require that high-value items be confined to a well-guarded and regularly patrolled area. [1:105–106] Best also states that "when fine arts are borrowed by a library for an exhibit, it is customary for that library to secure and pay for insurance to and from the premises and during the exhibition." [1:106]

Many libraries have a blanket property policy to bring together a number of locations under one coverage with a single premium. In the event of loss, blanket coverage relieves the library of concern about errors in the valuation of individual locations. It insures the books along with the furniture, fixtures, and equipment at 90 percent co-insurance [see section 8.G.4] and with an agreed amount clause by which the library annually adjusts the valuation of the collections. [14:99]

"Property of others held by the library or for which the library assumes responsibility should also involve a written agreement as to the value of the property in the event of a loss. This will avoid any misunderstanding, embarrassment, or litigation that might arise if a loss occurs without an agreement. Fine arts, rare books, and sculpture should be priced by a curator in the appropriate field in order to insure it properly. By insuring such an item on the "valued" policy form, the carrier accepts the stated value if a claim is made later for the theft or destruction of the item." [14:98]

"The Hartford library policy is a specialized coverage program written only by some insurers and requires an annual declaration of agreed upon values. These values become the basis of any claim, without regard to the actual value or the replacement value of the individual items that are destroyed. This model policy was developed as a joint project of the American Library Association, Gage-Babcock & Associates, Inc., and the Hartford Fire Insurance Company. [21:184] It has been used, with modifications, by other insurance carriers. However, it lacks the flexibility of the blanket form, which does not limit the library to a specific value for each book or category of books, nor to a total value for all books and library materials." [14:99]

8.G.1.b. Loss exposures

Some common perils may be excluded from a library's property policy and would require extended or special coverage. The following list is extracted from Morris's *The Library Disaster Preparedness Handbook*. [14:95–96]

1. Autos, trucks, and bookmobiles, whether owned, leased, or hired by the library, as well as vehicles owned by others and driven on library business.
2. Burglary, theft, and robbery.
3. Collapse of buildings or structures.
4. Earthquake.
5. Employee dishonesty.
6. Explosion (except steam boiler, see below).
7. Extra expense. This coverage will pay for the additional costs of temporarily doing business at another location following a severe fire or other disaster, or for rented facilities of any kind necessitated by such an event. See also *Service interruption* below.
8. Fine arts. Specialized property coverage is available for higher valued art works.
9. Fire and lightning.
10. Flood, backing up of sewers, and surface waters.
11. Glass breakage from other than designated perils.
12. Plate glass. Breakage of plate glass is covered under the extended coverage portion of the fire policy, except for any breakage due to vandalism.
13. Property in transit. Books and works of art loaned outside the library are subject to loss. Libraries should check with their insurance person about the need for a transportation floater.
14. Riot, riot attending a strike, and civil commotion.
15. Service interruption. Fire, flood, or other catastrophic conditions may force the closing of the library. Computers and databases may have to be replaced. Such situations may require the addition of extra expense insurance to cover rental charges for replacements until new equipment can be obtained or the damaged ones repaired. [1:105]
16. Smoke damage (from faulty heating plants).
17. Sonic boom.
18. Sprinkler leakage.
19. Steam boiler explosion. The standard property policy excludes damage to or caused by steam boilers, so they have to be endorsed on the policy with an extra premium; this entitles the insured library to inspection services for this vessel and for other pressure vessels, if insured, such as hot water heating boilers. Local or state law requires inspections of large steam boilers, and the carrier's inspection satisfies this need.

20. Vandalism and malicious mischief.
21. Water damage from defective plumbing, heating, and air-conditioning systems.
22. Weather (e.g., windstorm, cyclone, tornado, hail).

All risks policies will cover some of the above items, but may exclude things such as "inherent vice," e.g., damage to books from mold, fungus, and various infestations. [17:2–4]

8.G.2. COLLECTION INVENTORIES

The shelflist is often considered an inventory of the library's collections. But to be effective for insurance claims purposes, it must contain the exact copy count (including disposition of withdrawn volumes), descriptions, and original cost of library materials. In addition, it must be kept up-to-date by regularly checking the books, both on the shelves and in circulation. Problems in settling claims can be aggravated both by incomplete and old records and by the difficulties in showing where the collections covered by the inventories are housed. An inventory of a collection must be reasonably up-to-date and complete to be of use in an efficient claims settlement. [10:64–65]

8.G.3. PROOF OF LOSS

When making a claim, the insured must prove both that the incident occurred and that the damage was due to that incident. Police and fire department records will provide proof of the event, but producing evidence of loss of all or part of the collection might be more difficult, because these losses involve the records of the library.

Requirements for proof of loss typically ask for the following: [10:61]

1. a complete inventory of destroyed and damaged property, showing in detail quantities, costs, actual cash value and particulars of amount of loss claimed;
2. a statement of when and how loss occurred, as far as the insured knows or believes;
3. a statement that the loss did not occur through any wilful act, neglect, procurement, means, or contrivance of the insured;
4. the amount of other coverages and names of other insurers;
5. the interest of the insured and all others in the property, with liens, encumbrances, and other charges upon the property;
6. the changes in title, use, occupation, location, possession, or exposures of property since issue of the contract; and
7. a demonstration of the place where the insured property was at the time of the loss.

Further requirements can include:

1. a complete inventory of undamaged property, showing quantities, cost, actual cash value; and
2. a provision of the books of account, invoices, receipts, stock inventories, and so on.

This list indicates the need for careful planning before a catastrophe occurs because of the difficulty of securing this information after the fact.

8.G.4. LOSS ADJUSTMENT AND COLLECTION VALUATION

The following material is excerpted from *Disaster Management for Libraries: Planning and Process* by Claire England and Karen Evans. Published by the Canadian Library Association and reprinted by permission of Claire England and Karen Evans. [10:65–68]

A loss settlement is theoretically intended to be on the value of each individual item. But individual settlement is virtually impossible in a collection of any size, and a valuation of collections is frequently a difficult and semi-satisfactory procedure. Value is a matter of opinion; it is only occasionally a matter of certainty, and some method must be agreed upon in order to arrive at a settlement. All advice urges that the value be determined before, not after, a disaster. The question of establishing a valuation for the collection . . . goes back to a basic insurance principle—namely, that the insured [i.e., the librarian] has the best knowledge of cost or values and is in the best position to know how much insurance is required.

Basically, there are four ways of dealing with the problem of value and loss: 1) by surveying with estimate and determination of value, 2) by accepting cost and quantity shown in records, 3) by replacing or repairing, and 4) by sale of salvage. [22:47–48] Coverage for loss or damage of collections is optimally made by a mix of ways (one to three), and a value is agreed upon before loss happens. Using a survey can mean arriving at some estimated average value. Using records can mean settling at original cost, while replacement involves the cost of a new item, sometimes less a depreciation factor, or cost of repair or restoration.

Repair or restoration may apply with damaged stock. In this area the librarian may be more aware than the insurer about costs to the library for restoration above the amount the policy covers. Deciding to dispose of an item rather than try to restore it may make a replacement for loss a better insurance decision than attempted restoration. While the decision to replace, repair or restore is the insurer's, a good relationship between insured and insurer allows for the librarian's judgement to be a determining factor in the decision.

A definition of what the insurance means in relation to the book stock might show that:

"In the event of loss or damage to books, manuscripts, papers, magazines, periodicals and other catalogs, microfilms, special and other collections and clippings, this Company shall not be liable for more than the cost of purchasing books in replacement, provided said books are in print and available in the continental United States or Canada or the United Kingdom of Great Britain and Northern Ireland. If such material be not obtainable, this insurance shall cover only for the insured's original purchase cost, and this basis moreover shall be adopted in values, calculations with relation to, or for the purpose of the Co-insurance clause." [22:8]

This definition introduces co-insurance, a clause that provides for the sharing of loss unless the policy holder maintains insurance on property or contents up to a stipulated percentage of its value. Eighty or ninety percent is a usual situation, although the percentage may vary for the particular happening. The co-insurance benefits both insurance underwriters and the public, and a rate reduction is normally given for the inclusion of this clause. Insurance texts explain the theory and use of standard co-insurance practice. [22:8]

Replacement cost for the same or equivalent new titles is a method of coverage that works well in most libraries, such as general public libraries and undergraduate collections, where circulating stock can be replaced with reasonable ease. The replacement cost should be stipulated to include replacement and processing costs. In the insurance paragraph quoted above, replacement (without processing) and default to original cost is the coverage. Replacement means that the lost items must indeed be replaced, or else loss settlement will be achieved on some other basis, usually the original or actual cash value. Actual cash value is the current value of the insured article at the time of loss; it usually involves the price of the article less some depreciation (or possibly appreciation) since purchase. An average or other predetermined value may also be agreed upon; ideally the policy should state that the agreed value is guaranteed to be paid upon loss. Average values are estimated for a whole collection or for categories within a collection. It might be argued that some average value works well for collections that are special in some respect, perhaps with items that cannot readily be replaced from in-print sources. In practice, average value, while not ideal, is used with any collection as a workable solution to the problem of value. But it must be used cautiously. Rare books in a special collection (or imbedded in the main collection) would be valued at only the average cost of all books in the library. Therefore, separate coverage should be written for the special collection if the library is to be able to replace lost items.

The procedure for most library materials is to arrive at an average value for material in the general collection, using categories like:

> Adult fiction @ $ per vol.
>
> Adult non-fiction @ $ per vol.
> (may be further categorized)
>
> Juvenile materials @ $ per vol.
>
> Reference books @ $ per vol.
>
> Periodicals @ $ per vol.
> (may be further categorized)
>
> Periodicals (bound) @ $ per vol.
>
> Newspapers @ $ per issue/vol.
>
> Microforms @ $ per unit
>
> Pamphlets @ $ per unit (or collection)
>
> and so on [8:16–17]

The cost is normally adjusted by a factor for depreciation, but may be further adjusted for appreciation of value or foreign exchange rates. The quantity in any category multiplied by the cost produces the agreed average value. For lost items, this value applies; for damaged items, the claim is for repair costs or value less salvage costs.

A library may use its own figures over a period of recent years to arrive at cost estimates, and the procedure is elaborated depending on the accuracy of estimation desired. The library's own figures are the most accurate estimators. Alternatively, a library may use figures from the book trade. *The Bowker Annual of Library and Book Trade Information* reviews average costs for U.S. and foreign books, both hardcover and paperback, and for serials and library materials. These figures cover a range of recent years. They should be used to find a library cost that is averaged over a span of years, because the collection was itself built in this manner.

The solutions to the problems of valuation are complicated by a number of factors. Replacement may mean purchase through a used book market, where the purchase price is normally higher than for currently available items. Bound serials are a nearly impossible cost replacement case, for which microfilm may be a suitable, but not equivalent, substitute. Average costs of library items are not equal to average prices from the book trade because of the varied ways in which libraries buy their books (e.g., from wholesalers or library suppliers) and process them. Deciding on methods of evaluation and the collecting, adjusting and updating of figures is a major commitment if near accuracy is to be achieved. It is sound, although easily given, advice from risk managers that insurance programs be revised annually and that policies be brought up to value with separately insured items (rare books, art objects) or groups of valuable items (a number of unique items taken together) given additional attention. If such material is insured on an appraised basis (i.e., not on a purchase price basis) and the value is increasing, reappraisal should be done regularly because the last appraised value is the normal basis for payment.

8.G.5. UNDERSTANDING INSURANCE COVERAGE

The following instructions and guidelines will be useful in determining the current insurance coverage, needs, and continuing protection requirements of the library or archive. All of the information in this section was developed by the Inland Empire Libraries Disaster Response Network and is used with the permission of Sheryl Davis, Preservation Officer, University of California, Riverside; Chair of the Inland Empire Libraries Disaster Response Network. [25]

1. What is the replacement cost per book? _____.
   Total replacement cost should include the average price of a book and all processing costs. It should be revised every year to reflect inflation. [See section 8.G.4 for a discussion on replacement cost, and the text following this list for 1986–87 values assigned by the University of California.]
2. Find out how the library or archive is insured and determine the policy's exclusions [see 6 below]. Most institutions are self-insured. This means a certain amount of money must be held in reserve as bond for the insurance.
3. Ask what can be done to reduce the premiums. Sometimes having a written disaster plan, installation of smoke and heat detectors, sprinkler systems, fire extinguishers, water detectors, and other safety equipment can significantly reduce premiums.
4. Determine which risks are covered (water, fire, explosion, smoke, vandalism, riot, civil commotion, aircraft, vehicles, theft). Are "Acts of God" (floods, tornadoes, earthquakes, windstorms, tsunamis) covered? Most policies will not cover earthquake damage but might cover damage [indirectly] caused by a quake (i.e., a fire caused by an earthquake). The most frequent cause of damage to library materials is water. Therefore, good water damage coverage is vital, especially

for such perils as worn pipes bursting and sewers backing up.

5. Have the insurer's permission in writing to begin salvage efforts immediately, without waiting for a company representative. To do this, the library must be able to answer these questions in advance: what records does the insurer require? _____ Photographs? _____ A copy of the shelflist or catalog cards? _____ An inventory of each item or just a numerical count? _____ Does an adjuster need to view the items before they can be removed from the site, or before any restoration or discarding? _____ Remember to notify the insurance company as soon as possible when disaster strikes.

6. What is the deductible for fire? _____ Water damage? _____ Theft or vandalism? _____ Other? _____ What is the maximum amount that can be claimed per occurrence? _____

7. For rare and valuable items a special policy covering each piece individually against all risks will be necessary. A list is compiled of the books and their specific declared value. This list must be updated every year.

8. Find out what the requirements and liabilities are for workers helping with a pack-out, whether they are staff or volunteers.

The University of California estimated unit dollar values for the 1986-87 fiscal year. [26:C–72] They are useful in estimating the total replacement cost (in 1986-87 dollars) for the types of materials listed.

Bound volumes	$110.50
Current serial subscriptions	122.00
Personal manuscripts	24.50
Maps	8.50
Microfilm	86.50
Microcards, fiche, prints	8.50
Audiodiscs	86.50
Audiocassettes, reels, compact discs	83.50
Video recordings (tape, disc, etc.)	462.50
Motion pictures	599.00
Filmstrips	97.50
35 mm slides	1.04
Pamphlets	2.21

Use the formula below to compute the current replacement value of the collection if it were totally destroyed. A reminder: These are values established for the University of California in 1986–87; the current value for other libraries or archives may be more or less.

No. of Volumes x Unit Dollar Value (e.g., $110.50) = Replacement Cost.

REFERENCES

1. A. M. Best Company. "Guide to Underwriting (Libraries)." In John Morris, *The Library Disaster Preparedness Handbook*. Chicago: ALA, 1986.

2. Bishop, L. J., Jr. *Comprehensive Deodorization*. Dothan, AL: Clean Care Seminars, 1983.

3. Bohem, Hilda. *Disaster Prevention and Disaster Preparedness*. Berkeley: University of California, Task Group on the Preservation of Library Materials, 1978.

4. Buchanan, Sally. *Remarks during the Tallahassee, Florida, Disaster Preparedness Workshop*. March 3–4, 1988. Sponsored by the Florida Library Disaster Preparedness and Recovery Project. The Division of Library and Information Services, Florida Department of State, Tallahassee, FL.

5. Butler, Randall. "Earthquake! The Experience of Two California Libraries." *Conservation Administration News* 32 (January 1988): 2, 23–24.

6. California State Library. *Manual of Recommended Practice: Seismic Safety Standards for Library Shelving*. Sacramento, CA: California Library Foundation, 1990.

7. Central Sprinkler Corporation. *Flow Control-FC On-Off Automatic Sprinkler*. Central FC Product Report 5-87. Lansdale, PA: Central Sprinkler Corporation, 1987.

8. *Disasters: Prevention & Coping*. Stanford, CA: Stanford University Libraries, 1981.

9. "Emergency Procedures Manual and Collection Disaster Salvage Plan." UCLA Biomedical Library. In *Management Strategies for Disaster Preparedness*, July 8, 1988, New Orleans, Louisiana. Sponsored by the Resources & Technical Services Division, American Library Association. Chicago: American Library Association, 1988.

10. England, Claire, and Karen Evans. *Disaster Management for Libraries: Planning and Process*. Ottawa: Canadian Library Association, 1988.

11. Fox, Lisa. *Notes for the Fort Lauderdale, Florida, Disaster Preparedness Workshop*. May 19–20, 1988. Sponsored by the Florida Library Disaster Preparedness and Recovery Project. The Division of Library and Information Services, Florida Department of State, Tallahassee, FL.

12. Geller, Sidney B. *Computer Science and Technology: Care and Handling of Computer Magnetic Storage Media*. Washington, DC: Department of Commerce, National Bureau of Standards, 1983.

13. Lundquist, Eric G. *Salvage of Water Damaged Books, Documents, Micrographic and Magnetic Media*. San Francisco: Document Reprocessors, April 1986.

14. Morris, John. *The Library Disaster Preparedness Handbook*. Chicago: American Library Association, 1986.

15. Morris, John. *Managing the Library Fire Risk*. 2d ed. Berkeley, CA: Office of Risk Management and Safety, University of California, 1979.

16. Murray, Toby. *Recovery of Water-Damaged Materials. A Workshop Sponsored by the Illinois Cooperative Conservation Program*. A slide-tape program. Carbondale, IL: Illinois Cooperative Conservation Program, Morris Library, Southern Illinois University at Carbondale, July 1986. Now available from the Illinois State Library, Preservation Office, Room 288, Centennial Building, Springfield, IL 62756.

17. Myers, Gerald E. *Insurance Manual for Libraries*. Chicago: American Library Association, 1977.

18. Olson, Nancy B. "Salvaging Wet Disks." *The U*N*A*B*A*S*H*E*D Librarian* 59 (1986): 15.

19. Osborne, Larry N. "Those (In)destructible Disks; or, Another Myth Exploded." *Library Hi Tech* 27 (1989): 7–10, 28.

20. *An Ounce of Prevention: A Handbook on Disaster Contingency Planning for Archives, Libraries and Record Centres,* edited by John P. Barton and Johanna G. Wellheiser. Toronto, Canada: Toronto Area Archivists Group, 1985.

21. *Protecting the Library and Its Resources,* edited by Edward M. Johnson. Chicago: American Library Association, 1963.

22. Reed, P. B., and P. I. Thomas. *Adjustment of Property Losses.* 3d ed. New York: McGraw-Hill, 1969.

23. Reitherman, Robert. "Earthquake Vulnerabilities of Shelving." Paper given at *Earthquake Preparedness: What We Can Learn From Past Quakes.* November 9, 1989. Workshop sponsored by the Los Angeles Preservation Network (LAPNet), California Institute of Technology, Pasadena, CA.

24. "Some Guidelines for Establishing Salvage Priorities." *Inland Empire Libraries Disaster Response Network Guide.* Riverside, CA: University of California, Riverside, Libraries, March 21, 1988.

25. "Some Guidelines for Understanding Insurance Coverage." *Inland Empire Libraries Disaster Response Network Guide.* Riverside, CA: University of California, Riverside, Libraries, March 21, 1988.

26. University of California. Office of the President. Memo dated May 19, 1987. In *RTSD Preconference Binder, Management Strategies for Disaster Preparedness.* July 8, 1988, New Orleans, Louisiana. Sponsored by the Resources & Technical Services Division, American Library Association. Chicago: American Library Association, 1988.

27. Waters, Peter. *Procedures for Salvage of Water-Damaged Library Materials.* 2d ed. Washington DC: Library of Congress, 1979.

9.
PRESERVATION SERVICES, SUPPLIERS, AND EDUCATIONAL OPPORTUNITIES

This chapter contains information about selecting a conservator and lists institutions that offer conservation and preservation educational opportunities, organizations that can supply disaster planning and recovery assistance, equipment and supply companies, services for preservation microfilming, regional preservation centers, and preservation services in general.

9.A. Selecting a Conservator [7]

The American Institute for the Conservation of Historic and Artistic Works (AIC) has published a set of guidelines to help archivists, librarians, and custodians or owners of rare and valuable materials find competent professionals who will repair and/or restore bindings, books, manuscripts, photographic materials, and other cultural property. Finding and selecting a competent conservator can be a difficult and trying task. Complicating the selection of the right person is the lack of universally recognized standards for certification of book and paper conservators. Using AIC recommendations to select a conservator, however, will give some assurance that the individual or organization is trustworthy and will follow those recommended procedures and standards that do exist.

Learn as much as possible about the field of conservation.

Ask for advice and recommendations from other conservators and museum personnel when looking for a qualified conservator.

Contact several conservators so their services and qualifications can be compared.

Contact a prospective conservator's previous clients for information about the quality of his or her work, costs, and documentation of treatment applied to the artifact.

Be sure to contact the conservator's references.

Request information about the prospective conservator's background, training, and professional affiliation.

Determine if treatment costs are by the day or by the hour and if there are separate rates for preliminary examinations and evaluations. Check if these rates are separate or deductible from any subsequent contract. Determine the costs for insurance, packing, shipping, and any extras.

Don't rush into a contract precipitously just because it is convenient to do so.

Every conservator should provide his or her customer with:

1. A written preliminary examination evaluating condition, proposing treatment, describing limitations of the treatment, and providing estimates of treatment costs and duration.
2. Notification during treatment of major changes in the original proposal.
3. Written and photographic documentation of the treatment and, when appropriate, recommendations for continued care and maintenance.

The American Institute for the Conservation of Historic and Artistic Works (AIC), the International Institute for Conservation of Historic and Artistic Works (IIC), the International Council of Museums: Committee for Conservation (ICOMUS), and the International Centre for the Study of the Preservation and the Restoration of Cultural Property (ICCROM) are four organizations that can supply information about conservators. They cannot recommend individuals or businesses, but will be able to give names of institutions, such as archives, libraries, and museums, that can provide more specific information about conservation professionals. Other organizations such as the Conservation Center for Art & Historic Artifacts (CCAHA), the Northeast Document Conservation Center (NEDCC), and the Southeastern Library Network (SOLINET) can also provide similar information. CCAHA and NEDCC also treat books and paper. They are all in the list of organizations that give advice.

9.B. Library Binding Institute

The Library Binding Institute is a trade association of commercial library bookbinders, primarily in the United States, but also with members in Australia, Canada, England, Japan, and Scotland. Membership includes bookbinding equipment and supply companies and institutional binders. One of the goals of the Institute is to develop standards for library binding. No library bindery whose binding fails to meet the Institute's standards can warrant its binding to be in compliance with all the requirements of the *Library Binding Institute Standard for Library Binding.* [9]

"The Standard specifies methods and materials appropriate for the binding of books and periodicals that must withstand the rigors of library use." [9:1] Binders adhering to the Standard may warrant to a customer as follows:

"Warranty: We warrant that the binding represented by us as conforming to the *Library Binding Institute Standard for Library Binding* complies with all requirements of the *Library Binding Institute Standard for Library Binding* as amended. This statement is made pursuant to Sections 2.0 and 3.0 of the *Library Binding Institute Standard for Library Binding* issued by the Library Binding Institute, and applicable federal and state laws relative to representations by a seller to a purchaser regarding the quality of a product and its adherence to a standard." [9:1] Library Binding Institute members are listed periodically in issues of *The New Library Scene,* or a list may be requested from the Library Binding Institute. [8:16–17]

9.C. Preservation Educational Programs

Many organizations offer courses, seminars, and workshops on conservation and/or preservation. They vary in level of sophistication from the most basic, e.g., simple repairs to books and paper, to those granting degrees in conservation or preservation technology. The American Library Association publishes the *Preservation Education Directory* [11], updating it irregularly every few years. The directory lists educational opportunities at accredited library schools, associations, and other educational institutions. The American Institute for Conservation of Historic and Artistic Works includes educational information in its annual directory. [3] The Society of American Archivists also distributes information about preservation workshops. A more complete list of organizations providing various types of educational opportunities is included in the guide to preservation services in section 9.C.1.

9.C.1. CONSERVATION TRAINING IN NORTH AMERICA [12]

The institutions listed below provide the basic training needed for becoming qualified, professional book, paper, or library conservators. Contact the institution or the Library of Congress for more information.

9.C.1.a. Library and archives conservation

Columbia University
School of Library Service*
Attn: Director, Conservation Education Program
Butler Library, Room 516
New York, NY 10027-1993
212-854-4178

University of Delaware/Winterthur**
Attn: Director, Art Conservation Program
303 Old College
Newark, DE 19716
302-451-2479

9.C.1.b. Museum conservation—including paper and books

New York University
Conservation Center of the Institute of Fine Arts
14 East 78th Street
New York, NY 10021
212-772-5800

Queen's University
Attn: Director, Art Conservation Programme
Kingston, Ontario K7L 3N6, Canada
613-545-2156

9.C.1.c. Museum conservation—including paper

Buffalo State College
Attn: Director, Art Conservation Department
230 Rockwell Hall
1300 Elmwood Avenue
Buffalo, NY 14222-1095
716-878-5025

* The School of Library Service will close in 1992. The Conservation Education Program will probably find a new home elsewhere.

** To begin Fall 1993.

University of Delaware/Winterthur
Attn: Director, Art Conservation Program
303 Old College
Newark, DE 19716
302-451-2479

9.C.1.d. Advanced level museum conservation—including paper

Harvard University Art Museums
Attn: Administrative Director, Center for Conservation and
Technical Studies
32 Quincy Street
Cambridge, MA 02138
617-495-2392

9.C.2. COURSES IN BOOK REPAIR [6:9]

The following organizations offer courses designed to teach librarians and archivists the basics of book repair and binding. These organizations offer semester and weekend courses as well as workshops. See issues of *The Abbey Newsletter* [1] and *Conservation and Administration News* [5] for continuing information about educational opportunities.

Artists Book Works
1422 West Irving Park
Chicago, IL 60613
312-348-4469

Center for Book Arts
24 North Third Street
Minneapolis, MN 55401
612-338-3634

Center for Book Arts
626 Broadway
New York, NY 10012
212-460-9768

Pyramid Atlantic Workshop
6925 Willow Street NW
Washington, DC 20012
202-291-0088

Saturday's Gallery
235 South Broadway
Geneva, OH 44041
216-466-9183

The following organizations offer workshops and courses from time to time that cover a variety of binding, book repair, disaster preparedness, and preservation topics. Contact them for upcoming programs.

American Association for State and Local History (AASLH)
172 Second Avenue North
Nashville, TN 37201-1902
615-255-2971

American Association of Museums (AAM)
1225 I Street NW, Suite 200
Washington, DC 20005
202-289-1818

American Institute for Conservation of Historic and Artistic Works (AIC)
1400 16th Street NW, Suite 340
Washington, DC 20036
202-232-6636

American Library Association
Association for Library Collections and Technical Services (ALCTS)
Preservation for Library Materials Section (PLMS)
50 East Huron Street
Chicago, IL 60611
312-944-6780
800-545-2433

Association for Image and Information Management (AIIM)
(formerly National Micrographics Association—NMA)
Resource Center
1100 Wayne Avenue, Suite 1100
Silver Spring, MD 20910
301-587-8202

Canadian Bookbinders and Book Artists Guild
P.O. Box 1142, Station F
Toronto, Ontario M4Y 2T8, Canada

Canadian Conservation Institute (CCI)
1030 Innes
Ottawa, Ontario K1A 0C8, Canada
613-998-3721

Conservation Center for Art and Historic Artifacts (CCAHA)
264 South 23rd Street
Philadelphia, PA 19103
215-545-0613

Getty Conservation Institute
4503 Glencoe Avenue
Marina del Rey, CA 90292-6537
213-822-2299

Guild of Book Workers (GBW)
521 Fifth Avenue, Suite 1740
New York, NY 10175
212-757-6454 (mailing number)
914-354-7101 (direct number)

Image Permanence Institute
R.I.T. City Center
50 West Main Street
Rochester, NY 14614
716-475-5199

Library Binding Institute (LBI)
8013 Centre Park Drive
Austin, TX 78754
512-836-4141

Northeast Document Conservation Center (NEDCC)
100 Brickstone Square
Andover, MA 01810-1428
508-470-1010

Rochester Institute of Technology
College of Graphic Arts and Photography
One Lamb Memorial Drive
Rochester, NY 14623

Society of American Archivists
600 South Federal Street, Suite 504
Chicago, IL 60605
312-922-0140

Southeastern Library Information Network (SOLINET)
Preservation Program
400 Colony Square, Plaza Level
1202 Peachtree Street NE
Atlanta, GA 30361
404-892-0943
800-999-8558

9.D. Regional Conservation Centers

Most libraries and archives cannot assemble the staff, equipment, and facilities necessary to adequately address more than their simplest conservation needs. This problem is not unique to libraries; museums also find it difficult to find the sometimes considerable sums of money needed to finance such installations. Over the last two or three decades a number of conservation programs have been established by consortia or individual organizations, because it is impossible for many libraries (even in concert) to develop and continually support such activities. Several conservation facilities have staff and laboratories that now serve archives, libraries, museums, and/or the public. They provide a variety of sophisticated services supporting a wide spectrum of preservation activities including consulting, contingency planning for disasters, educational programs, repair and restoration of most formats collected by libraries, and surveys of buildings and collections. They primarily support conservation and preservation needs in their own regions of the country, but many will provide assistance anywhere they are needed. A brief summary of services is given for most of the facilities listed below.

Balboa Art Conservation Center
P.O. Box 3755
San Diego, CA 92103
619-236-9702
Services: Conservation of paintings, paper, and polychrome sculpture. Surveys and slide lectures.

Conservation Center for Art and Historic Artifacts
264 South 23rd Street
Philadelphia, PA 19103
215-545-0613
Services: Conservation of paper, photographs, and library and archive material. Surveys, workshops, and emergency assistance.

Harvard University Art Museums
Center for Conservation and Technical Studies (Fogg Art Museum)
32 Quincy Street
Cambridge, MA 02138
617-495-2392
Services: Conservation of paintings, paper, objects, and sculpture. Surveys and workshops.

Intermuseum Laboratory
Allen Art Building
Oberlin, OH 44074
216-775-7331
Services: Conservation of paintings and works on paper. Surveys, workshops, and seminars.

New York State Conservation Consultancy
c/o Lower Hudson Conference
2199 Saw Mill River Road
Elmsford, NY 10523
914-592-6726

Northeast Document Conservation Center (NEDCC)
100 Brickstone Square
Andover, MA 01810-1428
508-470-1010
Services: Conservation of library and archive material, works of art on paper, and photographs. Surveys, workshops, and disaster assistance.

Pacific Regional Conservation Center
P.O. Box 19000-A
Honolulu, HI 96819
808-847-3511
Services: Conservation of objects, paintings, and paper. Surveys and education programs.

Rocky Mountain Regional Conservation Center
University of Denver
2420 South University Boulevard
Denver, CO 80208
303-733-2712
Services: Conservation of paintings, paper, objects, and textiles. Surveys and workshops.

Textile Conservation Center
Museum of American Textile History
800 Massachusetts Avenue
North Andover, MA 01845
617-686-0191
Services: Conservation of textiles and costumes. Surveys and workshops.

Textile Conservation Workshop
Main Street
South Salem, NY 10590
914-763-5805
Services: Conservation of textiles and costumes. Surveys and workshops.

Upper Midwest Conservation Association
c/o The Minneapolis Institute of Arts
2400 3rd Avenue South
Minneapolis, MN 55404
612-870-3120
Services: Conservation of Oriental pictorial art, paintings, paper, ceramics, sculpture, and textiles. Surveys and education programs.

Williamstown Regional Art Conservation Laboratory
225 South Street
Williamstown, MA 01267
413-485-5741
Services: Conservation of paintings, paper, furniture, and decorative arts. Surveys and workshops.

9.E. Preservation Sources

There are two lists in this section. The first is of sources of conservation and preservation advice, education, equipment, services, and supplies. It contains addresses and telephone numbers for the companies or organizations mentioned throughout this book. The second list, section 9.E.2, is an alphabetical subject index providing access to the services of these sources.

9.E.1. ALPHABETICAL LIST OF SOURCES

These names are provided for information only, and their inclusion should not be considered an endorsement of any company, individual, or organization. The listing is not inclusive and the omission of any organization, person, or supplier does not imply disapproval. Most addresses and telephone numbers are correct as of July 1990. Additional information about products, services, and educational and professional opportunities can be found in issues of *The Abbey Newsletter* [1], *AIC Newsletter* [2], *Conservation Administration News* [5], and the *SAA Newsletter* [13]. Buyers' guides are also published in the *Library and Book Trade Almanac* [4] and the annual "Sourcebook" issue of *Library Journal*. [10]

Aabbitt-Jade Adhesives
1403 N. Oakley
Chicago, IL 60647
312-227-2700
800-222-2488

AB Bookman's Weekly
P.O. Box AB
Clifton, NJ 07015
201-772-0020

Abbeon Cal, Inc.
123-231A Gray Avenue
Santa Barbara, CA 93101
805-966-0810 or 963-7545

Abbey Publications
320 East Center Street
Provo, UT 84601
801-373-1598

Absorene Manufacturing Co.
1609 North 14th Street
St. Louis, MO 63106
314-231-6355

Aiko's Art Materials Import, Inc.
714 North Wabash
Chicago, IL 60611
312-943-9475

Airdex Corporation
[see SOLEX, Inc.]

Aldrich Chemical Company, Inc.
940 West St. Paul Avenue
Milwaukee, WI 53233
800-558-9160

American Association for State and Local History (AASLH)
172 Second Avenue North
Nashville, TN 37201-1902
615-255-2971

American Association of Museums (AAM)
1225 I Street NW, Suite 200
Washington, DC 20005
202-289-1818

American Film Institute
[see National Center for Film and Video Preservation]

American Freeze Dry, Inc.
411 White Horse Pike
Audubon, NJ 08106
609-546-0777

American Institute for Conservation of Historic and Artistic Works
(AIC)
1400 16th Street NW, Suite 340
Washington, DC 20036
202-232-6636

American Library Association
Association for Library Collections and Technical Services (ALCTS)
Preservation for Library Materials Section (PLMS)
50 East Huron Street
Chicago, IL 60611
312-944-6780
800-545-2433

American National Standards Institute (ANSI)
1430 Broadway
New York, NY 10018
212-354-3300

American Printing Equipment and Supply Co.
42-25 Ninth Street
Long Island City, NY 11101
718-729-5779

American Society for Testing and Materials (ASTM)
1916 Race Street
Philadelphia, PA 19103-1187
215-299-5585

AMIGOS Bibliographic Council, Inc.
11300 N. Central Expressway, Suite 321
Dallas, TX 75243
214-750-6130
800-843-8482

Andrew Mellon Foundation
Arts Program
140 West 62nd Street
New York, NY 10021
212-838-8400

Andrews/Nelson/Whitehead
31-10 48th Avenue
Long Island, NY 11101
212-937-7100

Antiquarian Booksellers Association of America
John H. Jenkins
Security Chairman
50 Rockefeller Plaza
New York, NY 10020
212-751-5450

Applied Science Laboratory
2216 Hull Street
Richmond, VA 23224
804-231-9386

Archival Aids, Ltd.
P.O. Box 5
Spondon, Derby DE2 7BP, England
0332-666400

Archivart
Division of Heller & Usdan, Inc.
7 Caesar Place
Moonachie, NJ 07074
201-804-8986

Art Handicrafts Company
3512 Flatlands Avenue
Brooklyn, NY 11234
212-252-6622

Artists Book Works
1422 West Irving Park
Chicago, IL 60613
312-348-4469

Association for Image and Information Management (AIIM)
[formerly National Micrographics Association—NMA]
Resource Center
1100 Wayne Avenue, Suite 1100
Silver Spring, MD 20910
301-587-8202

Association of College & Research Libraries (ACRL)
The Security Committee
Rare Books & Manuscripts Section
ACRL/American Library Association
50 East Huron Street
Chicago, IL 60611-2795
800-545-2433
800-545-2444 in Illinois

Association of Records Managers and Administrators International
(ARMA)
4200 Somerset, Suite 215
Prairie Village, KS 66208
913-341-3808

Association of Research Libraries (ARL)
Preservation Program Officer
1527 New Hampshire Avenue NW
Washington, DC 20036
202-232-2466

B & G Equipment Company
P.O. Box 130
Plumsteadville, NJ 18949
215-766-8811

Balboa Art Conservation Center
P.O. Box 3755
San Diego, CA 92103
619-236-9702

BAMBAM
[see Bookline Alert/Missing Books and Manuscripts (BAMBAM)]

Basic Crafts
1201 Broadway
New York, NY 10001
212-679-3516

Beckman Instruments
2500 Harbor Boulevard North
Fullerton, CA 92635
714-871-4848

Bendix Corporation
National Environment Instruments Division
P.O. Box 520, Pilgrim Station
Warwick, RI 02888

Bill Cole Enterprises, Inc.
P.O. Box 60
Randolph, MA 02368-0060
617-986-2653
800-225-8248

Blackmon-Mooring-Steamatic Catastrophe (BMS-CAT), Inc.
One Summit Avenue, Suite 202
Fort Worth, TX 76102
817-332-2770
800-433-2940 (24-hour hotline)
(regional offices in Los Angeles and Atlanta)

BMS-CAT
[see Blackmon-Mooring-Steamatic Catastrophe, Inc.]

Bookbinder's Warehouse
31 Division Street
Keyport, NJ 07735
201-264-0306

BookLab, Inc.
8403 Cross Park Drive, Suite 2E
Austin, TX 78754
512-837-0479

Bookline Alert/Missing Books and Manuscripts (BAMBAM)
Daniel and Katherine Leab
P.O. Box 1236
Washington, CT 06793
212-737-2715

Bookmakers
6001 66th Avenue, Suite 101
Riverdale, MD 20737
301-459-3384

Borrell Fire Systems, Inc.
3601 N. Nebraska Avenue
Tampa, FL 33603-5094
813-223-2727
800-282-6527
(check telephone directory for local distributors)

Bridgeport National Bindery, Inc.
104 Ramah Circle South
P.O. Box 289
Agawam, MA 01001-0289
413-789-1981

Brodart Company
500 Arch Street
Williamsport, PA 17705
717-326-2461
800-233-8467

Buffalo State College
Attn: Director, Art Conservation Department
230 Rockwell Hall
1300 Elmwood Avenue
Buffalo, NY 14222-1095
716-878-5025

Cadillac Plastics and Chemical Co.
134 Railroad Avenue Ext.
Albany, NY 12205
518-459-3377

California State Library Foundation
P.O. Box 942837
Sacramento, CA 94237-0001
916-445-4027

Calumet Photographic, Inc.
890 Supreme Drive
Bensenville, IL 60106
708-860-7447
800-CALUMET (225-8638)

Canadian Bookbinders and Book Artists Guild
P.O. Box 1142, Station F
Toronto, Ontario M4Y 2T8, Canada

Canadian Conservation Institute (CCI)
1030 Innes Road
Ottawa, Ontario K1A 0C8, Canada
613-998-3721

Cargocaire Moisture Control Services
79 Monroe Street
Amesbury, MA 01913-4740
508-388-0600

Center for Book Arts
24 North Third Street
Minneapolis, MN 55401
612-338-3634

Center for Book Arts
626 Broadway
New York, NY 10012
212-460-9768

Charrette Corporation
31 Olympia Avenue
Woburn, MA 01801
508-935-6000

Cole-Parmer Instrument Company
7425 North Oak Park Avenue
Chicago, IL 60648
312-647-7600
800-323-4340 (except Alaska)

Collectors Color Prints
Ataraxia Studio
2301 York Road
P.O. Box 343
Jamison, PA 18929
215-343-3214

Color Image Systems, Inc.
2906 Rubidoux
Riverside, CA
714-787-8310

Columbia University
School of Library Service
Attn: Director, Conservation Education Program
Butler Library, Room 516
New York, NY 10027-9973
212-854-4178

Columbia University Libraries
Preservation Department
535 W. 114th Street
Butler Library, Room 110
New York, NY 10027
212-854-5757

Comdisco, Inc.
6400 Shafer Court
Rosemont, IL 60018
708-698-3000

Commission on Preservation and Access (CPA)
1785 Massachusetts Avenue NW, Suite 313
Washington, DC 20036
202-483-7474

Conservation Analytical Laboratory (CAL)
Museum Support Center
4210 Silver Hill Road
Suitland, MD 20746
301-238-3700

Conservation Center for Art and Historic Artifacts (CCAHA)
264 South 23rd Street
Philadelphia, PA 19103
215-545-0613

Conservation Information Network (CIN)
4503 Glencoe Avenue
Marina del Rey, CA 90292
213-822-2299

Conservation Lab, SCCIM
P.O. Box 10017
Columbia, SC 29202
803-737-4921

Conservation Materials, Ltd.
340 Freeport Boulevard
Box 2884
Sparks, NV 89431
702-331-0582

Conservation Resources International, Inc.
8000-H Forbes Place
Springfield, VA 22151-2203
703-321-7730

Cunha, George Martin
4 Tanglewood Drive
Lexington, KY 40505
606-293-5703

Custom Microfilm Systems, Inc.
J. Mack Creager
3221 Kansas Avenue
Riverside, CA 92507
714-369-3456

Dalhousie Law Library
c/o Killam Library
Halifax, Nova Scotia B3H 4H9, Canada
902-494-2124

Datasonic, Inc.
255 East Second Street
Mineola, NY 11501
516-248-7330

Delmhorst Instrument Company
P.O. Box 68
Towaco, NJ 07082
201-334-2557

Dick Blick
Route 150 East
P.O. Box 1267
Galesburg, IL 61401
800-447-8192
800-322-8183 in Illinois

Dickson Company
930 South Westwood Drive
Addison, IL 60101
708-543-3747
800-323-2448

Dinh Company, Inc.
803 N.E. First Street
P.O. Box 999
Alachua, FL 32615
904-462-3463

Disaster Recovery Institute
5647 Telegraph Road
St. Louis, MO 63129
314-846-2007

Document Reprocessors of San Francisco
41 Sutter Street, Suite 1120
San Francisco, CA 94194
415-362-1290
800-4-DRYING (437-9464)

Dorlen Products
6615 West Layton Avenue
Milwaukee, WI 53220
414-282-4840
800-533-6392

Dual Office Suppliers, Inc.
[see University Copy Services, Inc.]

DuPont Electronics
Customer Service Center
P.O. Box 80019
Wilmington, DE 19880-0019
800-237-2374

Durasol Drug and Chemical Company
1 Oakland Street
Amesbury, MA 01913
508-388-2020

Eastman Kodak Company
Information Center
343 State Street
Rochester, NY 14650
800-242-2424 (or nearest office)

EDP Security, Inc.
7 Beaver Brook Road
P.O. Box 740
Littleton, MA 01460
617-890-6666

Emory University
University Libraries
Preservation Office
Atlanta, GA 30322
404-727-0306

Environmental Tectonics Corporation
County Line Industrial Park
Southhampton, PA 18966
215-355-9100
800-523-6079

Film Life, Inc.
141 Moonachie Road
Moonachie, NJ 07074
201-440-8500

Film Technology
6900 Santa Monica Boulevard
Hollywood, CA 90038
213-464-3456
(movie film only, 16mm & 35mm)

Fisher Scientific Company
711 Forbes Avenue
Pittsburgh, PA 15219
412-562-8300
800 number available in certain regions
(check telephone directory for local distributors)

FMC Corporation
Lithium Division
Highway 161
Box 795
Bessemer City, NC 28016
704-868-5506

Foundation for the Preservation of Recordings, Inc.
4317 Barrington Road
Baltimore, MD 21229
301-242-0514

Franklin Distributors Corporation
P.O. Box 320
Denville, NJ 07834
201-267-2710

Gallard-Schlesinger Industries, Inc.
584 Mineola Avenue
Carle Place, NY 11514-1731
516-333-5600
800-645-3044

Gane Brothers & Lane, Inc.
1400 Greenleaf Avenue
Elk Grove Village, IL 60007
708-593-3360

Garnet Projects
Box 30241, Station B
Calgary, Alberta T2M 4PI, Canada
403-250-5429

Gaylord Brothers, Inc.
Box 4901
Syracuse, NY 13221-4901
800-448-6160

Getty Center for the History of Art and the Humanities Library
401 Wilshire Boulevard, Suite 400
Santa Monica, CA 90401-1455
213-458-9811

Getty Conservation Institute (GCI)
4503 Glencoe Avenue
Marina del Rey, CA 90292-6537
213-822-2299

Getty Trust
[see J. Paul Getty Trust]

Graham Magnetics, Inc.
[see Pro Arc Services]

Guardsman Chemicals, Inc.
Consumer Products Division
3503 Lousma Drive SE
Grand Rapids, MI 49508
616-247-7651

Guild of Book Workers (GBW)
521 Fifth Avenue, Suite 1740
New York, NY 10175
212-757-6454 (mailing number)
914-354-7101 (direct number)

Hamilton Industries
1316 18th Street
Two Rivers, WI 54241
414-793-1121

Hammermill Papers
6400 Popular Avenue
Memphis, TN 38197-7000
901-763-7800

Harvard University Art Museums
Center for Conservation and Technical Studies (Fogg Art Museum)
32 Quincy Street
Cambridge, MA 02138
617-495-2392

Hervic Electronics, Inc.
14225 Ventura Boulevard, #204
Sherman Oaks, CA 91423

Highsmith Company, Inc.
W5527 Highway 106
P.O. Box 800
Fort Atkinson, WI 53538-0800
800-558-3899

Hollinger Corporation, Archival Division
P.O. Box 8360
Fredricksburg, VA 22404
703-898-7300
800-634-0491

Holliston Mills
Route 11 West
P.O. Box 478
Kingsport, TN 37662
800-251-0451

Humanities Research Center
Attn: Conservation Department
University of Texas at Austin
P.O. Box 7219
Austin, TX 78713
512-471-9117

Huntington Library & Art Gallery
Conservation Department, Head
1151 Oxford Road
San Marino, CA 91108
818-405-2196

I.C.I. Americas Inc.
Films Division
Wilmington, DE 19897
302-575-3000
800-MELINEX (635-4639) ext. 3123
(check telephone directory for regional offices)

Image Permanence Institute (IPI)
R.I.T. City Center
50 West Main Street
Rochester, NY 14614
716-475-5199

Image Prints, Inc.
2730 Alpha Street
Lansing, MI 48910
800-782-4502

Information Conservation, Inc. (ICI)
Preservation & Conservation Division
911 Northridge Street
Greensborough, NC 27403
919-294-1443

Institute of Museum Services (IMS)
1100 Pennsylvania Avenue NW, Room 510
Washington, DC 20506
202-786-0536

Interleaf, Inc.
212 Second Street North
Minneapolis, MN 55401
800-942-6224

Intermuseum Laboratory
Allen Art Building
Oberlin, OH 44074
216-775-7331

International Centre for the Study of the Preservation and the
Restoration of Cultural Property (ICCROM)
13 Via di San Michele
00153 Rome, Italy

International Council of Museums (ICOMUS)
Committee for Conservation
Maison de l'Unesco
1 rue Miolis
Paris XVe, France

International Institute for Conservation of Historic and
Artistic Works (IIC)
6 Buckingham Street
London WC2N 6BA, England
01-839-5975

International Organization for Standardization (ISO)
One Rue de Varenbe
Case Postale 56
CH-1121 Geneva 20, Switzerland

J. Paul Getty Trust
Grant Program
1875 Century Park East, Suite 2300
Los Angeles, CA 90067
213-277-9188

JoAnna Western Mills Co.
Industrial Products
220 Broad Street
Kingsport, TN 37660
800-251-7520
800-251-7528

Joliet Public Library
150 N. Ottawa Street
Joliet, IL 60431
815-740-2660

Jon Kennedy Cartoons
301 Donaghey Building
P.O. Box 1488
Little Rock, AR 72203
501-372-7466

José Orraca Company
32 East 68th Street, #6
New York, NY 10021
212-879-5490

Keith Monks Audio Lab (KMAL)
c/o Allied Broadcasting Equipment
P.O. Box 1487
Richmond, IN 47375
317-962-8596

Kenco Chemical Company
P.O. Box 6246
Jacksonville, FL 32236
904-359-3080

KF Industries, Inc.
2310 North American Street
Philadelphia, PA 19133
215-425-7710

Kimac Company, Ltd.
478 Long Hill Road
Guilford, CT 06437
203-453-4690

The LAST Factory
2015 Research Drive
Livermore, CA 94550
800-223-LAST (5278)
800-222-LAST in California

Library Binding Institute (LBI)
8013 Centre Park Drive
Austin, TX 78754
512-836-4141

Library Binding Service (LBS)
2134 East Grand Avenue
P.O. Box 1413
Des Moines, IA 50305
515-262-3191
800-247-5323

Library of Congress
Attn: Robert B. Carneal
Head, Laboratory Services
Motion Picture, Broadcasting, and Recorded Sound Division
Washington, DC 20540
202-707-9077

Library of Congress
Preservation Information and Education Office
LM-GO7
Washington, DC 20540
202-707-1840
202-707-5634 (conservation office)

Library of Congress
Attn: Robert E. McComb, Ph.D.
Physical Scientist Research and Testing Office
LM-G38
Washington, DC 20540
202-707-5607

Library of Congress
Attn: Peter Waters
Restoration Officer
Research and Testing Office
LM-G38
Washington, DC 20540
202-707-5608

Light Impressions Corporation
439 Monroe Avenue
P.O. Box 940
Rochester, NY 14603-3717
800-828-6216

Limited Edition Photographics
136 Doyle Street
Santa Cruz, CA 95062
408-423-6453

Littlemore Scientific Engineering
Railway Lane
Littlemore, Oxford 0X4 4PZ, England
6865-747437

Los Angeles County Museum of Art
Attn: Victoria Blyth-Hill
Paper Conservator
Conservation Center
5905 Wilshire Boulevard
Los Angeles, CA 90036
213-857-6167

Los Angeles Public Library
7400 E. Imperial Highway
P.O. Box 7011
Los Angeles, CA 90241-7011
213-940-8462

Loss Control Services
3333 Nutmeg Lane
Walnut Creek, CA 94598
415-933-3365

McDonnell Aircraft Company
Box 516
St. Louis, MO 63166
314-232-0232
(large problems only)

Magnetic Aids, Inc.
133 North 10th Street
Paterson, NJ 07522
201-790-1400

Matrix Division
Leedal, Inc.
1918 South Prairie Avenue
Chicago, IL 60616
708-842-6588

Metronics Associates, Inc.
3201 Porter Drive
Palo Alto, CA 94304
408-737-0550

MAPS, The Micrographic Preservation Service
9 South Commerce Way
Bethlehem, PA 18017
215-758-8700

Moisture Control Services
[see Cargocaire Moisture Control Services]

Museum Services International
Attn: Roger Wulff
1716 17th Street NW
Washington, DC 20009
202-462-2380

National Archives and Records Administration (NARA)
Conservation Laboratory
NNPD, Room B-1
Washington, DC 20408
202-523-5360

National Archives and Records Administration (NARA)
Motion Picture, Sound, and Video Branch
Attn: William T. Murphy
Washington, DC 20408
202-523-3063

National Archives and Records Administration (NARA)
Preservation Officer
Washington, DC 20408
202-523-5496

National Archives of Canada
395 Wellington Street
Ottawa, Ontario K1A 0N3, Canada
613-995-5138

National Association of Government Archives
and Records Administrators (NAGARA)
New York State Archives, Room 10A75
Cultural Education Center
Albany, NY 12230
518-473-8037

National Center for Film and Video Preservation
American Film Institute
2021 North Western Avenue
Los Angeles, CA 90027
213-856-7637

National Center for Film and Video Preservation
American Film Institute
The John F. Kennedy Center for the Performing Arts
P.O. Box 27999
Washington, DC 20566
202-828-4000

National Endowment for the Arts (NEA)
1100 Pennsylvania Avenue NW, Room 803
Washington, DC 20506
202-682-5400

National Endowment for the Humanities (NEH)
Office of Preservation, Room 802
1100 Pennsylvania Avenue NW
Washington, DC 20506
202-786-0570

National Fire Protection Association (NFPA)
1 Batterymarch Park
P.O. Box 9101
Quincy, MA 02269-9101
800-344-3555

National Historical Publications and Records Commission (NHPRC)
National Archives Building
Washington, DC 20408
202-523-5386

National Information Standards Organization (Z39)
P.O. Box 1056
Bethesda, MD 20817
301-975-2814

National Institute for the Conservation of Cultural Property (NIC)
3299 K Street NW, Suite 403
Washington, DC 20007
202-625-1495

National Institute of Standards and Technology (NIST)
Administration 101, Room E-106
Gaithersburg, MD 20899
301-975-2814

National Science Foundation
1800 G Street NW, Suite 520
Washington, DC 20550
202-357-9859

Natural History Museum
Attn: John Cahoon
Archivist
900 Exposition Boulevard
Los Angeles, CA 90007
213-744-3355

New Jersey Department of State
Bureau of Archives and Records Preservation
2300 Stuyvesant Avenue
Trenton, NJ 08625
609-292-6265

New York Public Library
Lauren Botwick, Personnel Representative
Human Resources Department
8 West 40th Street, 2nd Floor
New York, NY 10018
212-930-0800

New York Public Library
Preservation Division
5th Avenue & 42nd Street
New York, NY 10018
212-930-0631

New York State Conservation Consultancy
c/o Lower Hudson Conference
2199 Saw Mill River Road
Elmsford, NY 10523
914-592-6726

New York University
Conservation Center
Institute of Fine Arts
14 E. 78th Street
New York, NY 10021
212-772-5800

Newberry Library
60 West Walton Street
Chicago, IL 60610-3394
312-943-9090

NEWCO, Inc.
P.O. Box 616051
Orlando, FL 32861-6051
305-293-7700

Nitty Gritty Record Care Products
4650 Arrow Highway, #F4
Montclair, CA 91763
714-625-5525

Northeast Document Conservation Center (NEDCC)
100 Brickstone Square
Andover, MA 01810-1428
508-470-1010

Northern Archival Copy
4730 Lorinda Drive
Shoreview, MN 55126
612-483-9346

Northstar Freeze Dry Manufacturing
Highway #371 North
P.O. Box 409
Nisswa, MN 56468
218-963-2900
800-551-3223

Northwestern University
University Libraries
Conservation Office
1935 Sheridan Road
Evanston, IL 60208
708-491-7599

Océ-Business Systems, Inc.
1351 Washington Boulevard, Suite 3000
P.O. Box 30
Stamford, CT 06904-0030
203-323-2111

Online Computer Library Center (OCLC)
6565 Frantz Road
Dublin, OH 43017-0702
800-848-5878

Pacific Regional Conservation Center
P.O. Box 19000-A
Honolulu, HI 96819
808-847-3511

Paper Source
730 N. Franklin Street
Chicago, IL 60610
708-337-0798

Paper Technologies, Inc.
25801 Obrero, Suite 4
Mission Viejo, CA 92691
714-768-7497

Pest Control Services, Inc.
c/o Dr. Thomas Parker
14 East Stratford Avenue
Lansdowne, PA 10950
215-284-6249

Photofile
2000 Lewis Avenue
P.O. Box 123
Zion, IL 60099
708-872-7557

Pine Cone
Blake Building
P.O. Box 1378
Gilroy, CA 95021-1378
408-842-7597
408-842-4797

Plastic Reel Corporation of America
Brisbin Avenue
Lyndhurst, NJ 07071
201-933-5100
212-541-6464

Pohlig Brothers, Inc.
Century Division
2419 E. Franklin Street
P.O. Box 8069
Richmond, VA 23223
804-644-7824

Preservation Technologies, Inc.
Farmhill Road
Sewickley, PA 15143
412-741-4875

Princeton University Library
Attn: Conservation Librarian
Princeton, NJ 08540
609-452-3180

Print File Inc.
3903 State Street
P.O. Box 100
Schenectady, NY 12304
518-374-2334

Pro Arc Services
464 Vista Way
Milpitas, CA 95035
408-945-9411
817-281-9450

Process Materials Corporation
[see Archivart]

Pyramid Atlantic Workshop
6925 Willow Street NW
Washington, DC 20012
202-291-0088

Queen's University
Attn: Director, Art Conservation Programme
Kingston, Ontario K7L 3N6, Canada
613-545-2156

Randomex, Inc.
Data Recovery Division
1100 East Willow Street
Signal Hill, CA 90806
213-595-8301

Raychem Corporation
TraceTek Products Group
300 Constitution Drive
Menlo Park, CA 94025-1164
415-361-3333
415-361-4602
(check telephone directory for local distributors)

Re-Oda Chemical Engineering Co.
100 Industrial Parkway
P.O. Box 424
Chagrin Falls, OH 44022
216-247-4131 (call collect)

Research Libraries Group, Inc. (RLG)
1200 Villa Street
Mountain View, CA 94041-1100
415-962-9951

Ris Paper Company
9101 East Hampton Drive
Capitol Heights, MD 20743
301-336-8833

Rising Paper Company
Housatonic, MA 01236
413-274-3345

Robert Jacobson: Design
P.O. Box 8909
Moscow, ID 83843
208-882-3749

Rochester Institute of Technology
College of Graphic Arts and Photography
One Lamb Memorial Drive
Rochester, NY 14623

Rocky Mountain Regional Conservation Center
University of Denver
2420 South University Boulevard
Denver, CO 80208
303-733-2712

Rohm & Haas, Plastics Division
Independence Mall West
Philadelphia, PA 19105
215-592-3000
(check telephone directory for local distributors)

S. & S. Brush Manufacturing Co.
915 Broadway
New York, NY 10010
212-260-5959

S. D. Warren Company
225 Franklin Street
Boston, MA 02101
617-423-7300

Samuel H. Kress Foundation
174 West 80th Street
New York, NY 10021
212-861-4993

San Diego Historical Society
Attn: Larry Booth
P.O. Box 1150
San Diego, CA 92112
714-232-9544

Science Associates, Inc.
11 State Road (Route 206)
P.O. Box 230
Princeton, NJ 08540
609-924-4470
800-247-7234
800-923-0055 in California

Shield Pack, Inc.
2301 Downing Pines Road
West Monroe, LA 71291
318-387-4743

Signet
4701 Hudson Drive
Stow, OH 44224
216-688-9400

Smithsonian Institution
[see Conservation Analytical Laboratory]

Society of American Archivists
600 South Federal Street, Suite 504
Chicago, IL 60605
312-922-0140

Solar-Screen Company
53-11 105th Street
Corona, NY 11268-1718
718-592-8223
718-592-8222
800-862-6233 (get dial tone, dial 1978)

SOLEX, Inc.
2700 Post Oak Boulevard, Suite 1530
P.O. Box 460242
Houston, TX 77056
713-963-9405

Solomat Partners L. P.
Solomat Instrumentation Division
652 Glenbrook Road
Stamford, CT 06906
203-348-9700
800-932-4500

SOS International
377 Oyster Point Boulevard, Suite 19
San Francisco, CA 94080
800-223-8597

Southeastern Library Information Network (SOLINET)
Preservation Program
400 Colony Square, Plaza Level
1202 Peachtree Street NE
Atlanta, GA 30361
404-892-0943
800-999-8558

Spectronics Corporation
956 Brush Hollow Road
P.O. Box 483
Westbury, NY 11590
516-333-4840

Spiro-Wallach Co., Inc.
42-16 13th Street
P.O. Box 1110
Long Island City, NY 11101
718-392-1400

Stanford Archives of Recorded Sound
Attn: Barbara Sawka
Stanford, CA 94305
415-497-9312

Stanford University Libraries
Cecil H. Green Library
Stanford, CA 94305-6004
415-723-9108

TALAS
Technical Library Service
213 West 35th Street
New York, NY 10001-1996
212-736-7744

Taylor Made Company
P.O. Box 406
Lima, PA 19037
215-459-3099

Taylor Technologies, Inc.
31 Loveton Circle
Sparks, MD 21152
301-472-4340
800-638-4776 (orders only)

TCA-Taylor
Consumer Products Division
Sybron Corporation
95 Glen Ridge Road
Arden, NC 28704
704-684-5178

Technical Association of the Pulp and Paper Industry (TAPPI)
Technology Park/Atlanta
P.O. Box 105113
Atlanta, GA 30348-5113
404-446-1400

Terminex International, Inc.
Memphis, TN 38117
901-766-1358
901-766-1105
(ask to speak to the Technical Director)

Textile Conservation Center
Museum of American Textile History
800 Massachusetts Avenue North
Andover, MA 01845
617-686-0191

Textile Conservation Workshop
Main Street
South Salem, NY 10590
914-763-5805

Thomas Scientific
99 High Hill Road
P.O. Box 99
Swedesboro, NJ 08085-0099
609-467-2000
800-345-2100

3M
Film and Allied Products Division
3M Center
St. Paul, MN 55101
612-733-1110

Total Information Group Ltd.
4 Maylands Court, Maylands Avenue
Hemel Hempstead
Hertfordshire HP2 7DE, England
0442-217282

Transilwrap Company
2615 N. Paulina
Chicago, IL 60614
312-528-8000

TRW Fasteners Division
10544 West Lunt Avenue
Rosemont, IL 60018
708-296-7161

UNESCO
Division of the General Information Program
UNESCO, 7, Place de Fontenoy
75700 Paris, France

University Copy Services, Inc.
2413 Bond Street
University Park, IL 60466
708-534-1500

University Microfilms International (UMI)
300 North Zeeb Road
Ann Arbor, MI 48106
800-521-0600

University of California, Berkeley
General Library
Attn: Nancy Harris
Conservation Department
Berkeley, CA 94720
415-642-8843

University of California, Berkeley
Lowie Museum
Attn: Jeff Brown
Berkeley, CA 94720
415-642-3681

University of California, Berkeley
University Libraries
Attn: Lynn Jones or Barclay Ogden
Conservation Department
416 Main Library
Berkeley, CA 94720
415-642-4946

University of California, Riverside
The University Library
Attn: Sheryl J. Davis
Preservation Officer
Riverside, CA 92517
714-787-3221

University of Connecticut, Storrs
University Libraries
Preservation Office
Box U-5, Library
Storrs, CT 06268
203-486-2597

University of Delaware/Winterthur
Attn: Director, Art Conservation Program
303 Old College
Newark, DE 19716
302-451-2479

University of Michigan Libraries
Preservation Department
Ann Arbor, MI 48109-1205
313-764-9356

University of Pittsburgh Libraries
Attn: Sally Buchanan
Pittsburgh, PA 15260
412-648-7710

University of Tulsa
McFarlin Library
Attn: Toby Murray
Archivist/Preservation Officer
600 South College Avenue
Tulsa, OK 74194
918-592-6000, ext. 2864

University of Wyoming Library
P.O. Box 3334, University Station
Laramie, WY 82071
307-766-3279

University Products
517 Main Street
P.O. Box 101
Holyoke, MA 01041
800-628-1912

Upper Midwest Conservation Association
c/o The Minneapolis Institute of Arts
2400 3rd Avenue South
Minneapolis, MN 55404
612-870-3120

Vacudyne Inc.
375 E. Joe Orr Road
Chicago Heights, IL 60411
708-757-5200

Verd-A-Ray Corporation
615 Front Street
Toledo, OH 43605
419-691-5751

VL Service Lighting
200 Franklin Square
Somerset, NJ 08873
201-563-3800

V.P.I., Inc.
460 County Road, Suite 162
Cliffwood, NJ 07721
718-845-0133

Washi No Mise
R.D. #2, Baltimore Pike
Kennitt Square, PA 19438

Wei T'o Associates, Inc.
21750 Main Street, Unit 27
P.O. Drawer 40
Matteson, IL 60443
708-747-6660

William Minter Bookbinding and Conservation
3605 N. Damen Avenue
Chicago, IL 60613
708-248-0624

Williamstown Regional Art Conservation Laboratory
225 South Street
Willliamstown, MA 01267
413-485-5741

Winterthur Museum Technical Library
Winterthur, DE 19735
302-888-4630

Xerox Corporation
100 South Clinton Avenue
Xerox Square
Rochester, NY 14644
800-832-6979

Yale University Libraries
Preservation Department
120 High Street
P.O. Box 1603 A, Yale Station
New Haven, CT 06520
203-432-1713
203-432-1710

9.E.2. SUBJECT INDEX TO PRESERVATION SERVICES

The organizations and/or persons in the preceding source list provide a variety of services. Those services are listed below in alphabetical order, cross-referenced where necessary. The field is changing rapidly, and some organizations render a wide variety of support; therefore some services, equipment, and so on provided by a particular organization may not be included in this index. Refer to the alphabetical list of sources in section 9.E.1 for the full name, address, and telephone number of each supplier.

Adhesives
Aabbitt-Jade Adhesives
Archival Aids, Ltd.
Basic Crafts
Bookmakers
Conservation Materials, Ltd.
Gaylord Brothers
Light Impressions
Process Materials Corporation
TALAS

Aqueous Deacidification Titration Kits
Taylor Technologies

Art on Paper
[see **Disaster Recovery—Art on Paper**]

Art Supplies
Charrette Corporation
Dick Blick

Audio Recordings—Cleaning, etc.
Hervic Electronics
Keith Monks Audio Lab
The LAST Factory
Nitty Gritty Record Care Products
Plastic Reel Corporation of America
Shield Pack
Signet
V.P.I., Inc.

Barrow Test Kit
Applied Science Laboratory

Binder Board
Ris Paper Company

Binding—Information about Binders
Library Binding Institute

Binding Equipment
Gane Brothers & Lane
TALAS

Binding Materials
Andrews/Nelson/Whitehead
Bookmakers
Library Binding Service
TALAS

Binding Supplies
Aiko's Art Materials Import
Andrews/Nelson/Whitehead
Art Handicrafts Co.
Basic Crafts
Bookbinder's Warehouse
Gane Brothers & Lane
Hollinger Corporation
Library Binding Service
TALAS

Blotting Paper, Acid-Free
Archivart
Bookmakers
Conservation Materials, Ltd.
Light Impressions
TALAS
University Products

Board
Archivart
Conservation Resources International
TALAS
University Products

Board Shear
American Printing and Supply
TALAS

Bone Folders
Aiko's Art Materials Import
Basic Crafts
Bookmakers
Light Impressions
TALAS

Book Cloth
Bookmakers
Gane Brothers & Lane
Holliston Mills
JoAnna Western Mills Co.
TALAS

Book Measuring Devices
[see **MEASUREpHASE Book Measuring Device**]

Book Presses
American Printing and Supply Co.
TALAS

Bookends, Non-knifing
Magnetic Aids

Books and Documents—Disaster Recovery
[see **Disaster Recovery—Books and Documents**]

Box Making
BookLab

Boxes
[see also **Disaster Recovery—Boxing of Materials**]
Archival Aids, Ltd.
Conservation Resources International, Inc.
Hollinger Corporation
Pine Cone
Spiro-Wallach

Bristol Board
Archivart
TALAS
University Products

Brittle Books Service
Library Binding Service

Brushes, Glue, and Paste
Aiko's Art Materials Import
Bookmakers
Brodart
S. & S. Brush Manufacturing Company
TALAS
Washi No Mise

Buckram
Bookmakers
Holliston Mills
JoAnna Western Mills Co.
TALAS

Calcium Carbonate Powder
TALAS

CD-ROM Cleaning Supplies
The LAST Factory
Nitty Gritty Record Care Products

Cleaning
[see also **Dustcloths; Disaster Recovery—Cleaning; Erasers**]
American Freeze Dry, Inc.
Document Reprocessors of San Francisco
TALAS

Cleaning—Paper Surface
[see also **Erasers; Opaline™ Dry Cleaning Pads**]
Absorene Manufacturing Co.
Aiko's Art Materials Import
TALAS

Cold Storage
Check locally

Computers
[see **Disaster Recovery—Computer Media; Disaster Recovery—Computers; Disaster Recovery—Corrosion Control of Electronic Equipment**]

Conservation Training Programs
[see **Education—Conservation Training Programs**]

Conservation Treatments
BookLab
Conservation Center for Art and Historic Artifacts
Information Conservation
Northeast Document Conservation Center

Conservators, Book (Practicing)
Conservation Center for Art and Historic Artifacts
Information Conservation
Northeast Document Conservation Center

Conservators, Information on Location of
American Institute for Conservation
Columbia University Libraries, Preservation Department
Columbia University, School of Library Service
Conservation Analytical Lab, Smithsonian Institution
Conservation Center for Art and Historic Artifacts
Emory University Libraries, Preservation Office
Library of Congress: Preservation Information and Education Office
New York Public Library, Preservation Division
Northwestern University Libraries, Conservation Office
Research Libraries Group
Southeastern Library Network, Preservation Program
University of California, Berkeley, Libraries, Conservation Department
University of Connecticut, Storrs, Libraries, Preservation Office
University of Michigan Libraries, Preservation Department
Yale University Libraries, Preservation Department

Conservators, Paper (Practicing)
Conservation Analytical Lab, Smithsonian Institute
Conservation Center for Art and Historic Artifacts
Information Conservation
Northeast Document Conservation Center

Conservators, Photographs (Practicing)
José Orraca Company
Northeast Document Conservation Center

Corner Rounder
Highsmith
Hollinger Corporation
Light Impressions
TALAS
University Products

Cutters and Trimmers
Basic Crafts
Bookmakers
Gane Brothers & Lane
Gaylord Brothers
TALAS
University Products

Damage Appraisal
[see **Disaster Recovery—Damage Appraisal**]

Deacidification Equipment
[see also section 5.D]
Wei T'o Associates

Deacidification Information
Canadian Conservation Institute
Commission on Preservation and Access
FMC Corporation
Information Conservation, Inc.
Interleaf, Inc.
Library Binding Institute
Library of Congress: Preservation Information and Education Office
Library of Congress: Research and Testing Office
National Archives and Records Service
National Archives of Canada
Northeast Document Conservation Center
Preservation Technologies, Inc.
Southeastern Library Information Network
Wei T'o Associates

Deacidification Supplies
[see also **Aqueous Deacidification Titration Kits; Calcium Carbonate Powder**]
TALAS
Wei T'o Associates

Debris Removal
[see **Disaster Recovery—Debris Removal**]

Dehumidification, On-site
Blackmon-Mooring-Steamatic Catastrophe
Cargocaire Moisture Control
SOLEX, Inc.

Dehumidifiers
Dinh Company

Dessicants
Light Impressions
TALAS

Disaster Planning
Conservation Center for Art and Historic Artifacts
Cunha, George Martin
Library of Congress: Preservation Information and Education Office
Northeast Document Conservation Center
Southeastern Library Information Network

Disaster Recovery—Advice and Assistance
American Institute for Conservation of Historic and Artistic Works
Association of Records Managers and Administrators International
Canadian Conservation Institute
Columbia University Libraries, Preservation Department
Columbia University, School of Library Service
Conservation Center for Art and Historic Artifacts
Conservation Lab, SCCIM
Cunha, George Martin
Dalhousie Law Library
Getty Center Library
Getty Conservation Institute
Humanities Research Center
Joliet Public Library
Library of Congress: Preservation Information and Education Office
Los Angeles Public Library
National Archives and Records Service
National Archives of Canada
Natural History Museum
New Jersey Department of State, Bureau of Archives
   and Records Preservation
Newberry Library
Northeast Document Conservation Center
Northwestern University Libraries
Princeton University Library
Research Libraries Group
Rocky Mountain Regional Conservation Center
Society of American Archivists
Southeastern Library Information Network

Disaster Recovery *(cont.)*
Stanford University Library
University of California, Berkeley, Conservation Department
University of Connecticut, Storrs
University of Pittsburgh Libraries
University of Tulsa, McFarlin Library
University of Wyoming Library
Winterthur Museum Library
Yale University Libraries

Disaster Recovery—Air-drying of Materials
Cargocaire Moisture Control Services
Document Reprocessors of San Francisco
SOLEX, Inc.

Disaster Recovery—Art on Paper
The Getty Conservation Institute
Los Angeles County Museum of Art: Victoria Blyth-Hill
University of California, Berkeley: Nancy Harris

Disaster Recovery—Books and Documents
Document Reprocessors of San Francisco
Huntington Library & Art Gallery
Library of Congress: Robert E. McComb, Ph.D.
Library of Congress: Peter Waters
Natural History Museum: John Cahoon
University of California, Berkeley, University Libraries
University of California, Riverside: Sheryl J. Davis
University of Tulsa: Toby Murray

Disaster Recovery—Boxing of Materials
Blackmon-Mooring-Steamatic Catastrophe

Disaster Recovery—Cleaning of Interiors
Blackmon-Mooring-Steamatic Catastrophe

Disaster Recovery—Cleaning of Materials
American Freeze Dry, Inc.
Document Reprocessors of San Francisco

Disaster Recovery—Computer Media
Pro Arc Services
Graham Magnetics
Randomex

Disaster Recovery—Computers
Blackmon-Mooring-Steamatic Catastrophe
Comdisco
EDP Security
Pro Arc Services

Disaster Recovery—Controlled Demolition
Blackmon-Mooring-Steamatic Catastrophe

Disaster Recovery—Corrosion Control of Electronic Equipment
Blackmon-Mooring-Steamatic Catastrophe

Disaster Recovery—Damage Appraisal
Blackmon-Mooring-Steamatic Catastrophe
Cargocaire Moisture Control Services
Document Reprocessors of San Francisco
SOLEX, Inc.

Disaster Recovery—Debris Removal
Blackmon-Mooring-Steamatic Catastrophe
Cargocaire Moisture Control Services

Disaster Recovery—Dehumidification
Blackmon-Mooring-Steamatic Catastrophe
Cargocaire Moisture Control Services
SOLEX, Inc.

Disaster Recovery—Document Reproduction
Blackmon-Mooring-Steamatic Catastrophe

Disaster Recovery—Equipment Rental
(Check locally)

Disaster Recovery—Film Restoration, Advice, and Recommendations
[see also **Film—Motion Picture Restoration**]
Eastman Kodak Company
National Center for Film and Video Preservation
Northeast Document Conservation Center

Disaster Recovery—Fire Damage
Blackmon-Mooring-Steamatic Catastrophe
Loss Control Services
Re-Oda Chemical Engineering Company

Disaster Recovery—Fire Protection
Loss Control Services

Disaster Recovery—Freeze-drying
American Freeze Dry, Inc.
Blackmon-Mooring-Steamatic Catastrophe
Document Reprocessors of San Francisco

Disaster Recovery—Freezer Storage
American Freeze Dry, Inc.
Document Reprocessors of San Francisco
(also check locally)

Disaster Recovery—Fumigation
American Freeze Dry, Inc.
Blackmon-Mooring-Steamatic Catastrophe
Document Reprocessors of San Francisco
Library of Congress, Research and Testing Office:
  Robert McComb (Information)
Museum Services International
Pest Control Services
Terminex International

Disaster Recovery—Inventory of Materials
Blackmon-Mooring-Steamatic Catastrophe
Document Reprocessors of San Francisco

Disaster Recovery—Microfilm
Custom Microfilm Systems
Document Reprocessors of San Francisco
Eastman Kodak Company (Information)

Disaster Recovery—Moisture Removal
Blackmon-Mooring-Steamatic Catastrophe
Cargocaire Moisture Control Services
SOLEX, Inc.

Disaster Recovery—Mold Removal
Blackmon-Mooring-Steamatic Catastrophe

Disaster Recovery—Objects
Conservation Center For Art and Historic Artifacts
Getty Conservation Institute
University of California, Berkeley: Lowie Museum

Disaster Recovery—Photographic Materials, Film & Video
Color Image Systems
Eastman Kodak Company
Film Life
Film Technology
José Orraca Company
Library of Congress: Motion Picture, Broadcasting, and Recorded
  Sound Division: Robert B. Carneal
National Center for Film and Video Preservation
Northeast Document Conservation Center: Gary Albright
San Diego Historical Society: Larry Booth

Disaster Recovery—Rebinding
Document Reprocessors of San Francisco
(also check with Library Binding Institute binders)

Disaster Recovery—Refrigerated Trucks
(check locally)

Disaster Recovery—Removal of Airborne Contaminants
SOLEX, Inc.

Disaster Recovery—Restoration of Materials
Document Reprocessors of San Francisco
Northeast Document Conservation Center

Disaster Recovery—Services
American Freeze Dry, Inc.
Blackmon-Mooring-Steamatic Catastrophe
Cargocaire Moisture Control
Document Reprocessors of San Francisco
Loss Control Services
McDonnell Aircraft Co.
Northeast Document Conservation Center
SOLEX, Inc.
SOS International

Disaster Recovery—Smoke Odor Removal
American Freeze Dry, Inc.
Blackmon-Mooring-Steamatic Catastrophe
Document Reprocessors of San Francisco
Re-Oda Chemical Engineering Company

Disaster Recovery—Sound Recordings
National Archives and Records Service: William T. Murphy
Stanford Archives of Recorded Sound: Barbara Sawka

Disaster Recovery—Thermal Vacuum Drying
Blackmon-Mooring-Steamatic Catastrophe

Disaster Recovery—Water Damage
Blackmon-Mooring-Steamatic Catastrophe
Cargocaire Moisture Control Services

Disaster Recovery—Water Pumping
Blackmon-Mooring-Steamatic Catastrophe
Cargocaire Moisture Control Services

Disaster Recovery—Water Vacuuming
Blackmon-Mooring-Steamatic Catastrophe
Cargocaire Moisture Control Services

Document Repair Tape (Filmoplast™)
[see **Tape—Document Repair**]

Double Sided Tape (#415)
[see **Tape, Double Sided #415**]

Dry Cleaning Pads
[see **Opaline™ Dry Cleaning Pads**]

Dryer—Freeze-drying Chambers
Northstar Freeze Dry Manufacturing
Wei T'o Associates

Drying, Freeze-
[see also **Disaster Recovery—Freeze-drying**]
American Freeze Dry, Inc.
Wei T'o Associates

Drying, Vacuum
McDonnell Aircraft Co.

Drying, Vacuum Freeze-
Document Reprocessors of San Francisco

Dustcloths, One-Wipe™
Guardsman Chemicals
TALAS

Earthquake Preparedness
California State Library Foundation

Education—Conservation Training Programs
[see also **Internships** and section 9.C]
Buffalo State College, Art Conservation Department
Columbia University School of Library Service, Conservation
   Education Program
Conservation Analytical Laboratory, Smithsonian Institution
Harvard University Art Museums, Center for Conservation and
   Technical Studies
New York University, Conservation Center of the Institute of Fine Arts
Queen's University, Art Conservation Programme
University of Delaware/Winterthur, Art Conservation Program

Education—Courses in Book Repair
[see also section 9.C.2]
Artists Book Works
Center for Book Arts (MN)
Center for Book Arts (NY)
Northeast Document Conservation Center
Pyramid Atlantic Workshop
Southeastern Library Information Network

Education—General
[see also section 9.C]
American Library Association, Association for Library Collections and
Technical Services, Preservation for Library Materials Section
Guild of Book Workers
Southeastern Library Information Network

Encapsulation
Information Conservation, Inc.
Northeast Document Conservation Center

Encapsulation—Ultrasonic Welder
William Minter

Envelopes, Acid-Free
[see also **Photographic Storage Supplies; Storage Supplies**]
Conservation Resources International
Hollinger Corporation
TALAS
University Products

Environmental Monitoring Equipment
Beckman Instruments
Cole-Parmer Instrument Company
Conservation Materials, Ltd.
Conservation Resources International
Dickson Company
Environmental Tectonics Corporation
Fisher Scientific Company
Light Impressions
Metronics Associates
NEWCO
Science Associates
Solomat Partners
TALAS
TCA-Taylor
Thomas Scientific

Equipment
Abbeon Cal
Archival Aids, Ltd.
TALAS

Erasers
[see also **Magic Rub™; Opaline™ Dry Cleaning Pads**]
Charrette
TALAS

Film—Motion Picture Restoration
Film Life
Film Technology
Library of Congress: Motion Picture, Broadcasting,
   and Recorded Sound Division
National Center for Film and Video Preservation

Film Salvage Information
Eastman Kodak Company
Library of Congress: Motion Picture, Broadcasting,
   and Recorded Sound Division
National Center for Film and Video Preservation

Filmoplast™
[see **Tape—Document Repair (Filmoplast™)**]

Fire Damage Recovery
[see **Disaster Recovery—Fire Damage**]

Fire-Damaged Items, Restoration of
Re-Oda Chemical Engineering

Fire Suppression Systems (Halon)
Borrell Fire Systems

Freeze-Dry
[see **Drying, Freeze-;** see also **Disaster Recovery—Freeze-Drying**]

Fumigation
[see also **Disaster Recovery—Fumigation**]
American Freeze Dry, Inc.
B & G Equipment Company
Document Reprocessors of San Francisco

Fumigation Chamber, Vacuum
Vacudyne Inc.

Gas Detector Kits
Bendix Corporation

Glassine Paper, Neutral pH
Paper Technologies

Gloves, Cotton
Light Impressions
TALAS

Granting Agencies
The Andrew Mellon Foundation
Institute of Museum Services
J. Paul Getty Trust
National Endowment for the Arts
National Endowment for the Humanities
National Historical Publications and Records Commission
National Science Foundation
Samuel H. Kress Foundation

Heat-set Tissue
Bookmakers
TALAS
University Products

Humidity Control
Dinh Company

Hydrogen Sulfide Indicator Cards
Metronics Associates

Information
American Association of Museums
American Association for State and Local History
American Institute for Conservation of Historic and Artistic Works
American Library Association
AMIGOS Bibliographic Council
Association of Records Managers and Administrators International
Association of Research Libraries
Balboa Art Conservation Center
Canadian Conservation Institute
Commission on Preservation and Access
Conservation Analytical Laboratory, Smithsonian Institution
Conservation Center for Art and Historic Artifacts
Conservation Information Network
Harvard University Art Museums, Center for Conservation
  and Technical Studies

Information *(cont.)*
Humanities Research Center
Institute of Museum Services
Intermuseum Laboratory
International Centre for the Study of the Preservation
  and the Restoration of Cultural Property
International Institute for Conservation of Historic
  and Artistic Works
Library of Congress: Preservation Information and Education Office
National Archives and Records Service
National Endowment for the Humanities
National Institute for the Conservation of Cultural Property
New York State Conservation Consultancy
Northeast Document Conservation Center
Pacific Regional Conservation Center
Research Libraries Group
Rocky Mountain Regional Conservation Center
Society of American Archivists
Southeastern Library Information Network
Textile Conservation Center
Textile Conservation Workshop
University of California, Berkeley
University of Connecticut, Storrs
University of Delaware/Winterthur, Art Conservation Program
University of Pittsburgh Libraries
University of Tulsa
Upper Midwest Conservation Association
Williamstown Regional Art Conservation Laboratory
Yale University Libraries, Preservation Department

Insect Extermination
Pest Control Services

Insect Extermination—Freezing
Pest Control Services
Wei T'o Associates

Insecticide
[see **No-Pest Strip™ Insecticide**]

Internships
Conservation Analytical Laboratory, Smithsonian Institution
Library of Congress: Preservation Information and Education Office
The New York Public Library, Human Resources Department
Northeast Document Conservation Center

Japanese Paper
Aiko's Art Materials Import
Andrews/Nelson/Whitehead
Bookmakers
Conservation Materials, Ltd.
Light Impressions
Paper Source
TALAS
University Products
Washi No Mise

Laboratory Supplies
Fisher Scientific Company
Thomas Scientific

Leather
Bookbinder's Warehouse
TALAS

Library Supplies
Brodart Company
Gaylord Brothers
Highsmith Company

Light Damage Calculator
Canadian Conservation Institute

Magic Rub™ Erasers
TALAS

Map Cases
Hamilton Industries
University Products

Map/Folder Paper, Lignin-free
Conservation Resources International
Hollinger Corporation
TALAS
University Products

Mat Board
Andrews/Nelson/Whitehead
Conservation Materials, Ltd.
Rising Paper Company
TALAS

MEASUREpHASE Book Measuring Device
Bridgeport National Bindery

Methyl Cellulose Adhesive
[see also **Adhesives**]
Archivart
Bookmakers
Conservation Materials, Ltd.
Light Impressions
TALAS

Microphotography
[see also **Disaster Recovery—Microfilm;
Preservation Microfilming— Information**]
Image Prints
Library Binding Service
Northeast Document Conservation Center

Micro-spatulas
TALAS

Moisture Meters
[see **Water Detectors**]

Moisture Removal
[see **Disaster Recovery—Moisture Removal**]

Mold Removal
[see **Disaster Recovery—Mold Removal**]

Monitoring Equipment
[see **Environmental Monitoring Equipment**]

Motion Picture Film—Preservation
Film Technology
National Archives and Records Service, Motion Picture, Sound,
    and Video Branch
National Center for Film and Video Preservation

Motion Picture Film—Restoration
Film Life
Film Technology
National Archives and Records Service, Motion Picture, Sound,
    and Video Branch
National Center for Film and Video Preservation

Mylar™ Rolls
[see **Polyester Sheets—Rolls and Products**]

No-Pest Strip™ Insecticide
Kenco Chemical Company

One-Wipe™ Dust Cloths
TALAS
(check local grocery and hardware stores)

Opaline™ Dry Cleaning Pads
Charrette
Durasol Drug and Chemical Company
Light Impressions
TALAS

Ortho-phenyl Phenol
Aldrich Chemical Company
Fisher Scientific
TALAS

Pamphlet Binders, Non-acidic
Gaylord Brothers
Library Binding Service
University Products

Paper, Alkaline
Aiko's Art Materials Import
Andrews/Nelson/Whitehead
Conservation Resources International
Hammermill Papers
Rising Paper Company
S. D. Warren Company
TALAS

Paper Cutters
American Printing Equipment and Supply Company
Charrette
TALAS

Paper Supplies
Archivart Division
TALAS

Paper Test Kit
Applied Science Laboratory
TALAS

Paste
[see **Wheat Starch**]

Pellon
TALAS

Pest Control
[see also **Insect Extermination**]
Pest Control Services

pH Indicator Pens
Abbey Publications
Light Impressions
TALAS

pH Indicator Strips
Archivart
Conservation Materials, Ltd.
Light Impressions Corporation
TALAS

pH Testing Kits
Applied Science Laboratory
Light Impressions
TALAS

pH Testing Materials
Cole-Parmer Instrument Company
Conservation Materials, Ltd.
Light Impressions Corporation
TALAS

Phase Box Maker—Equipment
Pohlig Brothers

Phonograph Disc—Cleaning Equipment
Keith Monks Audio Lab
Nitty Gritty Record Care Products
V.P.I., Inc.

Phonograph Disc—Cleaning Supplies
The LAST Factory

Phonograph Disc—Information
Foundation for the Preservation of Recordings
Library of Congress: Motion Picture, Broadcasting,
 and Recorded Sound Division

Photocopiers—Edge Copiers
Océ-Business Systems
Total Information Ltd.
University Copy Services
Xerox Corporation

Photocopying Service—Preservation
Image Prints
Library Binding Service
Northeast Document Conservation Center
Northern Archival Copy

Photographic Materials
[see **Disaster Recovery—Photographic Materials**]

Photographic Storage Supplies
Bill Cole Enterprises
Calumet Photographic
Conservation Materials, Ltd.
Conservation Resources International
Franklin Distributors Corporation
Light Impressions
Magnetic Aids
Photofile
Printfile
University Products

Photographic Supplies
Calumet Photographic
Conservation Materials, Ltd.
Conservation Resources International
Hollinger Corporation
Light Impressions Corporation
University Products

Plastic
Conservation Resources International

Plastic Containers for AV, Inert
Bill Cole Enterprises
Plastic Reel Corporation of America

Plastics, Inert
Kimac Company

Polaroid Permanent-Color Prints
Collectors Color Prints
Limited Edition Photographics

Polyester Sheets—Rolls and Products
Archival Aids, Ltd.
Archivart
Bill Cole Enterprises
Conservation Materials, Ltd.

Polyester Sheets—Rolls and Products *(cont.)*
Conservation Resources International
DuPont Electronics
Gaylord Brothers
Hollinger Corporation
I.C.I. Americas
Light Impressions
TALAS
Taylor Made Company
3M
University Products

Polyester Web (Pellon, Reemay)
Conservation Materials, Ltd.
TALAS
University Products

Posters—Preservation
Jon Kennedy Cartoons
Robert Jacobson: Design

Preservation Microfilming
Image Prints
MAPS
Northeast Document Conservation Center

Preservation Microfilming—Information
Association for Image and Information Management
Commission on Preservation and Access
Library of Congress: Preservation Information and Education Office
MAPS
Northeast Document Conservation Center
Research Libraries Group

Preservation Photocopying
Image Prints
Library Binding Service

Pressboard
TALAS
University Products

Presses
Basic Crafts
Bookmakers
Gane Brothers & Lane
TALAS

Pressing Boards
American Printing Equipment and Supply Co.
Basic Crafts
TALAS
University Products

Protective Enclosures
Information Conservation, Inc.
Northeast Document Conservation Center

PVA Adhesive
Light Impressions
TALAS

Rebinding
[see **Disaster Recovery—Rebinding**]

Regional Conservation Centers
[see also section 9.D]
Balboa Art Conservation Center
Conservation Center for Art and Historic Artifacts
Harvard University Art Museums, Center for Conservation
    and Technical Studies
Intermuseum Laboratory
New York State Conservation Consultancy
Northeast Document Conservation Center
Pacific Regional Conservation Center
Rocky Mountain Regional Conservation Center
Textile Conservation Center
Textile Conservation Workshop
Upper Midwest Conservation Association
Williamstown Regional Art Conservation Laboratory

Restoration Treatments
Information Conservation, Inc.
Northeast Document Conservation Center

Rivet Fastening Machines
TRW Fasteners Division

Rivets
Art Handicrafts Company
TRW Fasteners Division

Scalpels, Disposable
Fisher Scientific Company

Security—Reports of Book Thefts
[see also section 3.D.3]
AB Bookman's Weekly
Association of College & Research Libraries, Rare Books
  & Manuscripts Section, Security Committee
Bookline Alert/Missing Books and Manuscripts

Silicone Release Paper
Bookmakers
TALAS
University Products

Slides—Restoration
Eastman Kodak Company
Film Life

Sling Psychrometers
[see also **Environmental Monitoring Equipment**]
Light Impressions
TALAS

Smoke Odor Removal
[see **Disaster Recovery—Smoke Odor Removal**]

Solander Boxes
Conservation Resources International, Inc.

Sound Recordings
[see **Disaster Recovery—Sound Recordings**]

Squeegees
Conservation Materials, Ltd.
Light Impressions

Stamping Press
American Printing Equipment and Supply Company

Standards
American National Standards Institute
American Society for Testing and Materials
Association for Image and Information Management
International Organization for Standardization
National Information Standards Organization
Technical Association of the Pulp and Paper Industry

Storage Enclosures—Photographs
[see **Photographic Storage Supplies**]

Storage Supplies
Conservation Materials, Ltd.
Conservation Resources International
Gaylord Brothers
Pohlig Brothers

Sulphur Dioxide Test Paper
Gallard-Schlesinger Industries

Supplies—General
Aiko's Art Materials Import
Archival Aids, Ltd.
Bookmakers
Brodart Company
Conservation Materials, Ltd.
Hollinger Corporation
Light Impressions
Pohlig Brothers
TALAS
University Products

Surveys
AMIGOS Bibliographic Council
Balboa Art Conservation Center
Conservation Center for Art and Historic Artifacts
Harvard University Art Museums, Center for Conservation
  and Technical Studies
Intermuseum Laboratory
New York State Conservation Consultancy
Northeast Document Conservation Center
Pacific Regional Conservation Center
Rocky Mountain Regional Conservation Center
Society of American Archivists
Southeastern Library Information Network
Textile Conservation Center
Textile Conservation Workshop
Upper Midwest Conservation Association
Williamstown Regional Art Conservation Laboratory

Tacking Iron
Bookmakers
Light Impressions
TALAS
University Products

Tape—Document Repair (Filmoplast™)
Conservation Materials, Ltd.
Light Impressions
TALAS
University Products

Tape, Double Sided #415
Conservations Materials, Ltd.
Conservation Resources International, Inc.
Gaylord Brothers
Hollinger Corporation
Light Impressions
TALAS
University Products

Thefts
[see **Security—Reports of Book Thefts**]

Thermal Vacuum Drying
[see **Disaster Recovery—Thermal Vacuum Drying**]

Titration Kits
[see **Aqueous Deacidification Titration Kits**]

Trimmers
[see **Cutters and Trimmers**]

Tri-Test Kit
[see **pH Testing Kits**]

Tweezers
Charrette
Conservations Materials, Ltd.
TALAS

Ultraviolet Filtering Material
Cadillac Plastics and Chemical Company
Light Impressions
Rohm & Haas, Plastics Division
Solar Screen Company
University Products

Ultraviolet Light Meter
Conservation Resources International, Inc.
Fisher Scientific Company
Littlemore Scientific Engineering
Spectronics Corporation

UV (Low) Fluorescent Tubes
Verd-A-Ray Corporation
VL Service Lighting

Vacuum Chamber
Vacudyne Inc.

Vacuum Cleaner
Garnet Projects

Vacuum Cleaner, Mini
Pine Cone

Vacuum Freeze-Drying
[see **Drying, Vacuum Freeze-**]

Vapor Phase Deacidification
[see also section 5.D]
Interleaf, Inc.

Video
Library of Congress: Motion Picture, Broadcasting,
  and Recorded Sound Division
National Center for Film and Video Preservation

Water Damage Recovery
[see **Disaster Recovery—Water Damage**]

Water Detectors
Borrell Fire Systems
Datasonic, Inc.
Delmhorst Instrument Company
Dorlen Products
KF Industries
Raychem Corporation

Wheat Starch Paste
[see also **Adhesives; Methyl Cellulose Adhesive; PVA Adhesive**]
Bookmakers
Light Impressions
TALAS

REFERENCES

1. *The Abbey Newsletter: Bookbinding and Conservation.* Provo, UT: Abbey Publications, 1977– .

2. *AIC Newsletter: The American Institute for Conservation of Historic and Artistic Works.* Washington, DC: American Institute for Conservation of Historic and Artistic Works, 1975– .

3. *The American Institute for the Conservation of Historic and Artistic Works/Foundation of the American Institute for the Conservation of Historic and Artistic Works 1989–90 Directory.* Washington, DC: American Institute for the Conservation of Historic and Artistic Works/Foundation of the American Institute for the Conservation of Historic and Artistic Works, 1989.

4. *The Bowker Annual: Library and Book Trade Almanac.* Annual. New York. Bowker, 1955– .

5. *Conservation Administration News: A Quarterly Publication of Library and Archival Preservation*. Tulsa, OK: University of Tulsa, McFarlin Library, 1979– .

6. "Courses in Book Repair," compiled by Susan G. Swartzburg. *Conservation Administration News* 39 (October 1989): 9.

7. *Guidelines for Selecting a Conservator*, edited by Shelley Sturman. 3d ed. Washington, DC: American Institute for the Conservation of Historic and Artistic Works/Foundation of the American Institute for the Conservation of Historic and Artistic Works, 1987.

8. "Library Binding Institute Members." *The New Library Scene* 9 (June 1990): 16–17.

9. *Library Binding Institute Standard for Library Binding*, edited by Paul A. Parisi and Jan Merrill-Oldham. 8th ed. Rochester, NY: Library Binding Institute, 1986.

10. *Library Journal*. New York: Bowker, 1876– .

11. *Preservation Education Directory*, compiled by Christopher D. G. Coleman for the Education Committee of the Preservation of Library Materials Section, Association for Library Collections & Technical Services, a division of the American Library Association. 6th ed. Chicago: Association for Library Collections & Technical Services, a division of the American Library Association, 1990.

12. *Preservation Reference Service Fact Sheet: Conservation Training in North America*. Preservation Information Series: Education, February 1989. Washington, DC: Library of Congress, National Preservation Program Office, February 1989.

13. *SAA Newsletter: The Society of American Archivists*. Chicago: Society of American Archivists, 1990.

APPENDIX A
Environmental Monitors

CONDITION	EQUIPMENT	DESCRIPTION	FUNCTION	LIMITS
Temperature Ambient	mercury bulb or bimetal strip	air temperature thermometer	air temperature	noncontinuous measurement, nonrecording
Temperature Surface	surface thermometer	thermometer with direct measuring probe	surface and ambient temperature	noncontinuous measurement, nonrecording, probe touches surface, not easy to use
	infrared thermometer	thermometer measuring emitted infrared radiation	surface and ambient temperature	noncontinuous measurement, nonrecording, cannot measure through glass or plastic, needs recalibration
Relative Humidity (RH)	sling or aspirating psychrometer, e.g.,Taylor, Sling, and Assman	hygrometer with wet and dry bulb thermometers, manual (sling) or with battery powered fan (aspirating)	percent RH and ambient temperature	noncontinuous measurement, nonrecording, wicks must be maintained
	crystal hygrometer, e.g., Covey Hygrometer	hygrometer using water vapor sensitive crystals, compact, and low maintenance	percent RH and ambient temperature	noncontinuous measurement, nonrecording
	paper/coil hygrometer, e.g., Compact Thermo-Hygrometer	compact hygrometer	percent RH and ambient temperature	noncontinuous measurement, nonrecording

Environmental Monitors (*continued*)

CONDITION	EQUIPMENT	DESCRIPTION	FUNCTION	LIMITS
Relative Humidity (RH) (continued)	recording thermo-hygrographs, e.g., Isuzu Electronic Thermo-Hygrograph and Observer Recording Thermo-Hygrograph	continuous, recording thermohygrographs	percent RH and ambient temperature	requires regular maintenance
	electronic sensors, e.g., Beckman (Nova Sina Mik 3000), Intelli-sense Sensors & Computer Room Alert	continuous, recording monitors, compact, portable sensors, may have alarm or shut down capability	percent RH and ambient temperature, sometimes combined with smoke and water sensors	(untested)
	computer environ-mental monitoring and control systems, e.g., Honeywell Systems	HVAC centralized monitoring, control, and alarm system, continuous, can record	percent RH, ambient temperature, air pollutants, smoke, and water	requires HVAC system
Light	Blue Wool Light Fastness Standard	textile fade test, sensitive to UV light	exhibit of light damage due primarily to UV	delayed measurement, one time use
	UV light meter, e.g., Crawford UV Monitor	light meter	UV light measure	measures UV light only, nonrecording
Air Pollution (SO_2, H_2S, NO_x, & O_3)	Air Quality Reports	report	levels of air pollution in a city or region	general measurement, delayed reporting

Source: Unknown

APPENDIX B
Environmental Monitoring Forms

TEMPERATURE/RELATIVE HUMIDITY LOG

Date	Day	Time	Temp.	RH	Location	Remarks	Staff
	Monday						
	Tuesday						
	Wednesday						
	Thursday						
	Friday						
	Saturday						
	Sunday						

Average conditions for week:

Measuring devices used:

FIGURE B.1. Temperature and relative humidity recording form. Source: Society of American Archivists. *Archives & Manuscripts: Conservation.* Chicago: SAA, 1983, p. 33.

INSTITUTION: _____ Week: _____

Instrument(s) Used: _____

Date of Last Calibration: _____

Calibration Procedure: _____

Day	Time	Room	RH%	Temp. °C	Remarks

Continuous Records Included   Yes ☐   No ☐

Comments on Records: _____

FIGURE B.2. Relative humidity and temperature report. Source: Raymond H. Lafontaine. *Recommended Environmental Monitors for Museums, Archives and Galleries.* Technical Bulletin, No. 3. Ottawa: Canadian Conservation Institute, December 1980, p. 14.

Exhibition Illumination Report

INSTITUTION:

EXHIBITION: Date:

A - Lighting Levels

Instrument(s) Used:

Location	Time	Type of Lighting (Filters)	Light Level (Units)	Recomme- nded Level	UV-Com- ponent	Remarks

B - Surface Temperature

Instrument(s) Used:

Location	Time	Object Illuminated	Type of Lighting	Distance from Light Source	Surface Temp.	Remarks

FIGURE B.3. Exhibition illumination report. Source: Raymond H. Lafontaine. *Recommended Environmental Monitors for Museums, Archives and Galleries*. Technical Bulletin, No. 3. Ottawa: Canadian Conservation Institute, December 1980, p. 15.

APPENDIX C
Outline for Estimating Cost of Mildew Removal in a Media Center

Considerations
1. Degree of contamination—light, medium, heavy
2. Location of contamination
   a. Structure—blinds, ceiling, drapes, ductwork, floor, light fixtures, shades, walls
   b. Contents—AV equipment, AV materials, books, card catalogues, shelves, vertical files
3. Scope of job—what needs to be done
   a. Kill airborne spores—above ceiling, ductwork system
   b. Wet clean nonporous surfaces—AV equipment, carpet, computer hardware, floor, shelves, walls, windows
   c. Dry clean porous surfaces—books, card catalogues, computer software, magazines, pictures
4. Procedure—how to do it
   a. Fogging antimicrobial
   b. Wet clean with ortho-phenyl phenol and/or Lysol™ disinfectant
   c. Dry clean by wiping with cloth or paper towels
   d. Application of residual antimicrobial

Pricing
1. Estimate
   a. Number of days (hours) to complete job
   b. Number of workers needed (eight hours a day)
   c. Hourly rate (including workmen's compensation, insurance, travel, etc.)
2. Establish hourly rate for each level of personnel
   a. Level 1—supervisor
   b. Level 2—crew chief on site
   c. Level 3—technician/worker

Source: Action Fire & Soot Restoration Company. Tallahassee, Florida, October 1989.

APPENDIX D
Guidelines for Inspecting Library Bound Volumes

Reprinted, with permission, from "Guidelines for Inspecting Library Bound Volumes; University of Connecticut Libraries, March 1985." In Preservation Planning Program: Resource Notebook, *compiled by Pamela W. Darling, edited by Wesley Boomgaarden. Revised ed., 587–588. Washington, DC: Association of Research Libraries, Office of Management Studies, 1987.*

1. INSPECT THE UNOPENED VOLUME

Spine Stamping: Is the spine stamped correctly (i.e, does it match the binding slip and text)? Are lines properly positioned, both vertically and horizontally? Are letters evenly impressed, crisp and easy to read?

Covering Material: Is the covering material clean (i.e., free from dust and gluey fingerprints)? Is it smoothly and completely adhered to both boards?

Joints: Are the joints or hinges (the grooves on either side of the spine) parallel to the spine, and uniformly and adequately deep, evenly pressed, or too narrow or wide?

Rounding and Backing: Is the spine of the text block properly shaped at both the head and tail? Do the boards fit correctly below the shoulders of the spine? (If the volume is very thin, or has been recased, the spine may be square or somewhat misshapen. This is acceptable only in these cases.) See Figure D.1.

Squares: Are the squares (the edges of the boards that extend beyond the text block at the head, fore edge and tail) even, and an appropriate width (1/16 inch to 3/16 inch, depending on the size of the text block)?

Trimming: Do the edges of the text block appear to have been trimmed? They should not be trimmed if the library has a no-trim policy. If trimming is allowed, has text or have parts of the illustrations been trimmed away?

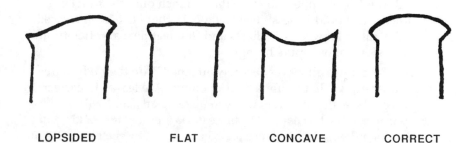

| LOPSIDED | FLAT | CONCAVE | CORRECT |

FIGURE D.1. Illustration of rounding and backing.

2. OPEN THE VOLUME TO ITS APPROXIMATE CENTER; LOOK DOWN THE HOLLOW OF THE SPINE, BETWEEN COVERING MATERIAL AND TEXT BLOCK

Spine lining: Does the spine lining extend to within 1/2 inch of the head and tail of the spine? Is it smoothly and completely adhered? If the volume is heavy or thick, has an extra paper lining been adhered over the cloth one? If the volume has been recased, was the spine well cleaned before relining? It should be free from old adhesive and paper. If the volume is adhesive bound, are there two spine linings, one stretch-firm polyester against the text block, and the second, of cloth, over the first?

3. OPEN BOTH BOARDS SO THAT THE INNER SURFACE OF EACH BOARD CAN BE INSPECTED

Endpapers: Are the endpapers smoothly and completely adhered to the boards? Are they properly positioned so that the squares of the boards appear uniformly wide? Are the edges of the endpapers straight-cut and smooth?

Turn-ins: Are the turn-ins (the margins of cloth that wrap from the front of the boards onto the inside) uniform, and approximately 5/8 inch wide? Are the edges straight-cut and smooth?

Spine Lining: Does the spine lining extend onto each board at least 1 inch? Is it uniformly wide, head to tail, on each board?

4. EXAMINE THE BINDING SLIP; LEAF THROUGH THE TEXT BLOCK

Specific Instructions: Have all instructions on the binding slip been followed, including choice of method of leaf attachment (if one has been made)?

Endsheets: Is the style of endsheet appropriate for the method of leaf attachment used? Have endsheets for recased volumes been sewn on through the fold?

Interface between endsheets and text block: Open the volume between the endsheets and the first and last pages of the text block. For text blocks that have been double-fan adhesive bound, is the endsheet tipped no more than 1/4 inch onto the first leaf? (Ideally it should be less.) For text blocks that have been recased, is the gutter between endsheets and first leaf neat and free from the residue of old spine lining?

Text Block: Are all leaves securely attached? Are their edges free from adhesive that inhibits their opening? Are leaves in correct order? Have all paper repairs been made neatly, and with appropriate materials? (If the library has a policy for making all repairs in-house, have paper tears been noted by the binder?) For volumes that have been oversewn, does sewing run into the print?

For volumes that have been adhesive bound, is there excess glue; are all leaves firmly adhered; is any text obscured?

5. A WELL BOUND VOLUME SHOULD OPEN WELL AND STAY OPEN.

For various reasons, this is sometimes not an achievable goal. The paper may be stiff, for example, or its grain may run at right angles to the spine of the volume, rather than parallel to it. A high percentage of all volumes, however, should have good openability. If this is not the case, the library and the binder should reconsider existing guidelines for selecting methods of leaf attachment.

APPENDIX E
Sample Library Binding Contract and Specifications

Compiled from Southern Illinois University's Library Binding Contract by Carolyn Clark Morrow, State of Connecticut Library Binding Contract by Jan Merrill-Oldham, and University of Virginia Department of Material Management Request for Proposal for Binding Service by Ted Kuzen.

Although this sample contract is written for a university library and contains some requirements that may be unique to the laws of Connecticut, Illinois, or Virginia, it covers all of the things any library—academic, public, school, or special—should expect of a binder. The real strength of this proposal, however, is that it incorporates the *Library Binding Institute Standard for Library Binding, 1986 Revision* in its specifications. [1] [See articles I.A.1.b and II of the sample contract.] Thus it insures that bindings will be of acceptable quality and the library will be "getting its money's worth." Individual libraries, of course, will wish to modify the terms of this sample contract to meet their own specific requirements.

The Standard itself, and more information about library binding, is available from the Library Binding Institute. The American Library Association recently published the *Guide to the Library Binding Institute Standard for Library Binding*. [2] The *Guide* clarifies the language of the Standard and helps librarians communicate more effectively with library binders.

I. GENERAL INFORMATION

A. *Discussion*

It is the Library's intent to select a Binder that will provide binding services for the *(name of the library)* to achieve these goals and objectives:

1. Goals
   a. It is expected by the Library that all materials furnished in fulfilling any binding contract shall be of the highest quality as measured by the highest standards of the trade, except where a lower grade is defined and called for in the specifications or instructions.
   b. It is also expected by the Library that the Binder must provide binding and rebinding services that meet the *Library Binding Institute Standard for Library Binding*, 1986 edition. [1]
2. Objectives
   a. To provide binding and rebinding of books, periodicals, pamphlets, reports, report sheets, newspapers, and any other materials not otherwise classified that are to be placed in permanent covers.

3. Scope (To be defined by the library, e.g., library units covered by the agreement; time period covered; library options to renew or extend the agreement, and for how long; number of serials and/or monographs expected to be bound while the contract is in force.) [2:55]

B. *Bid Prices (For example, under what circumstances, if any, can the binder change prices during the contract period; who has the authorization to change prices; "are pick-up, transportation, and delivery costs included in net binding prices?") [2:55]*

C. *Compliance with Specifications*

1. All work is to be done for the Library according to the attached specifications. These specifications apply to the binding and protective enclosure of monographs and serials, and are to be adhered to by the Binder unless instructions from the Librarian direct otherwise.

2. The Library reserves the right to specify binding styles and methods of treatment for any and all items should this decisionmaking be deemed necessary for any reason. The style (i.e., method of leaf attachment) or category (e.g., standard monograph, economy paperback) specified for each item by the Library shall not be changed by the Binder without prior consent of the Library. If an item cannot be bound in the manner specified, it shall be returned by the Binder with an explanation of the reason for its rejection.

3. The Binder shall establish the qualifications of the Binder by submitting the following evidence [see also attachment A.III]:

   a. Samples of work for examination by the *(state name of official and/or library)* including text blocks that have been double-fan adhesive bound, fitted with a new case only (original sewing structure retained), oversewn, sewn through the fold by machine and by hand, and economy paperback bound; and a selection of portfolios and boxes typical of those made by the Binder.

   b. One sample of each type of endsheet used in the bindery. These should be marked to indicate the style(s) of binding for which each is appropriate.

   c. A list of at least three (3) active accounts over $ _____ , and persons to contact for service verification.

   d. A statement of the approximate gross sales completed in the last two (2) full years of operation.

   e. Statistics regarding plant resources, including the number of:

square feet of plant space
full-time regular employees
machines for through-fold sewing
   (*state name of manufacturer*)
oversewing machines
adhesive binding machines
   (*state name of manufacturer*)

4. Prior to the contract award and at any time during the contract
   period, the Binder shall permit representatives from the Library
   or _____ to inspect the Binder during its normal
   working hours.

D. *Award of the Contract*

E. *Subcontracting*

1. All binding shall be done on the premises of the Binder unless
   written permission to do otherwise is granted by _____.
   No subcontracting will be permitted without the express
   written approval of _____.

F. *Insurance and Security*

1. The Binder shall insure, at no extra charge to the Library,
   all materials against loss of damage from any cause, from
   the time they leave the Library until they are returned.
   Each binding shipment is to be insured in the amount
   specified by the Library, but not for less than $ _____.
   The limit of liability for an item lost or destroyed shall be
   a sum that will cover the cost to the Library of reordering,
   processing, and binding the item. As proof of compliance
   with this requirement, the Binder shall furnish a certificate
   of insurance to _____.

2. In the event that an irreplaceable item is damaged or destroyed,
   the Library reserves the right to secure, at the Binder's expense,
   an independent appraisal of the damage or loss sustained. The
   Binder shall reimburse the Library in full for damage to, or fair
   market value, of the item.

G. *Communication*

1. The Binder shall be willing to accept collect telephone
   calls (or provide a toll-free number) when such calls are
   warranted because of unusual problems, changes in
   schedules, etc.

2. A representative from the Binder shall visit the Library
   periodically and be available on request. The representative
   shall be thoroughly familiar with the terms of this contract;
   and shall have in-depth knowledge of the technical aspects
   of library binding and the operations of the Binder s/he

represents, and an understanding of the relationship between library binding and the preservation of library materials.

3. The Binder shall be prepared to provide in-service training for Library staff members involved in bindery preparation activities. Training shall focus on helping the staff to better understand library binding technology and its application.

H. *Packing, Pickup, and Delivery*

1. The Library will sort all materials by category (e.g., standard monographs, standard serials) and style of binding if specified (e.g., new case only, hand sew through the fold), and pack them for shipment to the Binder. The Binder shall make regularly scheduled pickups and deliveries no less frequently than (*e.g., once every 30 calendar days*), unless a different rate of frequency is mutually agreed upon by the Library and the Binder. Materials returned to the Library shall be packed in cartons with lot number, category of contents, and specific destination legibly marked.

2. All materials shall be bound and returned within (*e.g., 30*) calendar days from the date of pickup, except when the Library and Binder agree upon a different schedule for return of specific items or shipments. Materials designated "rush" shall be bound and returned within (*a negotiated number of*) calendar days from the date of pickup. The Binder shall be allowed an upcharge per volume for "rush" work.

3. All pickups and deliveries shall be made indoors at a location specified by the Library, unless the Library agrees to an alternate arrangement. At sites other than those designated in (*section number*) of this contract, the Binder shall be allowed an upcharge per volume for those pickups that are smaller than the minimum size specified by the Binder in the proposal schedule.

4. All pickups and deliveries shall be made by the Binder's own vehicle and driver representative.

5. The Binder must be able to retrieve an individual item from any regular shipment in order to "rush" bind and "rush" return it at the Library's request. The Library will endeavor to keep this type of retrieval to a minimum, and will pay transportation costs for those items that must be returned to the Library by some means more expedient than the Binder's trucking service.

6. Shipping cartons, preprinted address labels, and binding tickets shall be provided by the Binder at no extra charge.

I. *Errors and Delays*

1. Any errors made by the Binder shall be corrected (provided corrections do not damage the text block) without additional charge to the Library, and returned within (*a negotiated number of*) days of the Binder's having received the items for correction. Any extra transportation costs resulting from such errors shall be paid for by the Binder. Errors that require the skills of a conservator to correct, or which cannot be corrected, shall be subject to Section I.F, *Insurance and Security,* of this contract.
2. The Binder shall pay a liquidated damages charge of one dollar per calendar week, or any part thereof, for each overdue item. No penalty shall apply in cases in which the Library has been notified that the return of an item will be delayed due to the need for special treatment.

J. *Uniform Binding of Serials and Sets*

1. The Binder shall be able to match the binding pattern, placement of lettering on the spine, and color of stamping foil and cloth on already-bound volumes of the Library's periodical, serial, and set titles. To ensure this, the Binder shall make and maintain, at no extra cost, rub-offs, a computerized file, or other records by which uniformity shall be achieved. This undertaking should be completed within (*a negotiated number*) days of the effective beginning date of this contract, and before the initial serials pickup is made.

K. *Computer Services*

1. The Binder shall make available, at no extra cost, computer produced services. These shall include, but not be limited to the following:
   a. A computerized system for producing preprinted tickets for serials binding. The Binder shall be able to provide, within _____ days of receipt of records supplied by the Library, a multiple part binding ticket for each volume of each serials title to be bound during the contract year. Thenceforth, the Binder must be able to produce a complete file of tickets in advance of each contract year.
   b. An alphabetized list of all titles for which binding tickets have been generated to be printed out on request. A separate alphabetized list shall be furnished for each participating Library. The list must include the following information: (1) name of Library; (2) title number; (3) binding category; (4) cloth color; (5) title, worded precisely as it will be stamped on the spine of the volume; and (6) variable information profiles in correct sequence.

{2. Optional Data Base [see also Attachment IV]

 a. The Binder shall specify and provide separate price quotes for the purchase and the maintenance of hardware and software for a Data Base: However, the Library shall have the option of purchasing the hardware and of procuring maintenance on the hardware separate from this contract if desired. The Binder shall provide complete information on telecommunications costs, showing which costs are borne by the Binder and which are borne by the Library; this shall include information on the requirements (if any) for the Library to provide dedicated telephone lines. The Binder shall also include information on supplies for the system.

 b. Equipment

 Provide a complete list of equipment that would be required to establish this Data Base.

 c. Price

 State the price of creating a Data Base for establishing binding information on periodicals, serials, and set titles.

 d. Schedule

 Provide a schedule for establishing the On-line Data Base System.

 e. Training

  1) Provide the name(s) of personnel who would train the library staff responsible for utilizing the Data Base System.

  2) Provide a resume detailing the individuals' experience.

  3) State the number of hours of training to be provided.

  4) State the price of this described training period.

 f. Supplies

 Provide a complete list of supplies and the costs that will be necessary to maintain the Data Base System.

 g. Maintenance

 Provide the price breakdown for maintaining the equipment of the Data Base System on a time and material basis and on annual fee, per item.

 h. References

 Provide names, addresses, and phone numbers of at least two (2) customers of comparable or larger size than the Library for whom the Binder has established a Data Base System.}

L. *Invoices*

 1. The Binder shall provide detailed invoices for each shipment within _____ days of delivery of the shipment to the

Library. Invoices shall reflect the price structure delineated in the bid proposal. Each type of equipment shall be listed separately, and include the number of items so treated, the charge per item, and the total charge for that treatment.

II. SPECIFICATIONS FOR MATERIALS

Unless otherwise specified, all work and materials shall conform to the *Library Binding Institute Standard for Library Binding*, 1986 revision (herein referred to as the LBI Standard). [1]

A. *Thread*

1. Thread used for oversewing shall conform to section 18.0 of the LBI Standard. Thread used for other methods of leaf attachment shall be of highest quality, and of an appropriate weight, thickness, strength, and fiber for those applications.

B. *Paper*

1. All paper used in conjunction with the Library's materials (e.g., for endpapers, stubs, pockets) shall conform to section 14.0 of the LBI Standard and shall have a pH of not less than 7.5 (cold extraction, Tappi T 509 om-88), and a minimum alkaline reserve equivalent to 2% calcium carbonate based on oven dry weight.
2. All endpapers shall conform in weight and strength to sections 14.1.2 and 14.1.3 of the LBI Standard, as shall the fabric with which they are reinforced. Grain direction shall run parallel to the binding edge.

C. *Endpaper Construction*

1. Endpapers shall be double folio, and the spine of the outermost folio reinforced with a 1-1/4 inch strip of fabric, in the following cases:
   a. For volumes to be sewn through the fold;
   b. For volumes in which the original sewing structure is intact;
   c. For single signature materials, such as music scores.
2. Endpapers shall conform to the relevant sections of the LBI Standard in the following cases:
   a. For volumes to be oversewn (see LBI Standard 6.1.3), and
   b. For volumes to be fitted with a new case only, but which have been oversewn previously and so must have endpapers whip stitched on (see LBI Standard 6.4.3).
3. Endpapers shall be single folded sheets in the following cases:
   a. For standard monographs and serials to be double-fan adhesive bound, as per LBI Standard 6.3.3., and
   b. For volumes to be economy paperback bound.

D. *Adhesives*

1. All adhesives shall conform to section 17.0 of the LBI Standard. Adhesives used for leaf attachment, back lining, case making, casing-in, and construction of boxes and portfolios shall be high grade co-polymer polyvinyl acetate emulsions with good aging characteristics. A high grade animal glue is also acceptable for some of the procedures used in case making and construction of boxes and portfolios.

E. *Back Lining Material*

1. Back lining material shall conform to section 10.0 of the LBI Standard except when volumes are economy paperback bound, in which case a stretchable back lining material that meets BL-80 specifications of the Library Binding Institute is acceptable. Standard double-fan adhesive bound volumes may also be lined with stretchable material, but must conform to section 16.2 of the LBI Standard.

F. *Board*

1. Board shall conform to section 15.0 of the LBI Standard. Board thickness shall be appropriate for the size and weight of the volume to be bound, and shall be available in thicknesses ranging from approximately .060 to .126 inches.

G. *Covering Material*

1. Covering material for bound volumes and boxes shall conform to section 16.4 of the LBI Standard unless a different type of material is requested by the Library for specific items or a specific class of items. Choice of colors for both monographs and serials will normally be specified by the Library.

H. *Inlays*

1. Inlays shall conform to section 14.3 of the LBI Standard and shall be alkaline and buffered.

I. *Stamping Foil*

1. Stamping foil shall conform to section 20.0 of the LBI Standard; color shall normally be specified by the Library.

III. SPECIFICATIONS FOR STANDARD BINDING OF MONOGRAPHS AND SERIALS

A. *Definitions*

1. *Monographs*
A monograph is defined as one piece of graphic material submitted for binding or rebinding as a single unit

without reference to another or with no demand placed on the Binder to match the unit to another. Although some items in this category may be bibliographically classed as serials or may be part of a set, the Library assumes responsibility for uniformity of cloth color and cover stamping.

2. *Serials*

A serial publication is defined as a single piece of graphic material bound separately, or a series of two or more serially numbered graphic units bound together, for which the cloth color must be selected and the cover stamped with information so as to match other publications in the same set or series. The Binder assumes responsibility for this uniformity, based on information initially supplied by the Library.

B. *Examination and Collation*

1. *All volumes*

All volumes shall be examined according to LBI Standard 5.0 to detect damaged leaves and peculiarities of paper or construction that might make first-time binding or rebinding inadvisable.

2. *Monographs*

Monographs shall be collated to ensure completeness and correct sequence of pages as per LBI Standard 5.1.

3. *Serials*

Serials shall be collated as per LBI Standard 5.2.2 to insure completeness and correct sequence of parts and pages, unless otherwise specified by the Library. If the Binder offers alternate pricing for various levels of collating services, this should be stated in the proposal and the price structure described.

a. Incomplete or imperfect volumes shall be returned unbound unless the Library has acknowledged the incompleteness in some way.

b. Covers, advertisements, and similar material shall be retained in place, unless otherwise specified by the Library on a per title basis.

4. Departures from articles B.2 and B.3 above shall be made only when the Library provides the Binder with special instructions.

5. *Special Preparation*

Whenever necessary, the Binder shall set out (with strips of alkaline paper or cloth of an appropriate weight) all double leaves, maps, and inserts in order to preserve printed matter that would otherwise be destroyed by trimming and/or sewing along the spine edge

6. *Mending*

Tears are not to be mended, as stated in LBI Standard 5.3. Torn items are to be returned unbound, including items damaged by the Binder. The Binder may repair only tears along the binding edge if necessary to bind the volume.

C. *Removing Backs*

1. Rounded and backed text blocks that must be rebound, and for which it is not possible to preserve the original sewing structure, shall have boards removed and the old rounding and backing taken out by nipping before the spine edge is trimmed or milled.

2. For text blocks that must have the spine edge trimmed or milled away in preparation for oversewing or double-fan adhesive binding, as little as possible (and not more than 1/8 inch) of the edge shall be removed, in order to preserve as much as possible of the inner margin. Trimming shall conform to LBI Standard 7.0.

3. Very bulky serial issues that are saddle stitched, and which cannot be sewn through the fold (e.g., when they must be bound together with non-saddle stitched issues), shall be prepared for adhesive binding or oversewing by slitting through the fold rather than by trimming or milling.

4. All staples must be pulled from side stitched text blocks to provide an inner margin of maximum width. No text blocks shall have staples removed by trimming or milling. Staples shall be removed from all saddle stitched issues prior to their being sewn through the fold.

5. Where margins of sewn text blocks are narrow and the text blocks are not suitable for sewing through the fold or double-fan adhesive binding, the text blocks shall be oversewn with the original folds intact. Where margins of adhesive bound text blocks are extremely narrow, the pages shall be pulled away from the original adhesive if this can be done easily (which is sometimes the case when the original adhesive is a hot melt type), and left untrimmed.

D. *Leaf Attachment*

1. The Binder shall select the leaf attachment method in accordance with the specifications listed below. The Library's preferred order of choice for leaf attachment is new case only (or recasing), sewing through the fold, double-fan adhesive binding, oversewing. The Binder shall adhere to that order of preference using the specifications listed below to determine the appropriate

method for each volume. On selected titles, the Library will state a specific leaf attachment method. When specified on the binding slip, the Binder shall follow those instructions; however, if the Binder determines that the specified leaf attachment method would be inappropriate for the volume, the Library shall be so advised in order to select a different method.

2. *New Case Only*

This method shall be used for all text blocks, either monographic or serial, that will be bound as a single unit (i.e., not with other pieces) and that are already sewn using an adequate number of stitches and sturdy thread. The sewing structure must be in good condition. Recasing shall be done according to LBI Standard 6.4. The original hard or paper cover shall be removed and the old back lining and glue lifted from the spine in a manner that does not disturb the original sewing.

3. *Sewing Through the Fold*

This method shall be used for the following materials: all serials issued in single, saddle stitched signatures; and monographs that can be bound in no other way without destroying printed matter in the inner margin, and that have special value. Sewing through the fold shall be done according to LBI Standard 6.2. Preparation of monographs for hand sewing through the fold shall not include the sewing of slots at the spine edge, nor shall monographs be cut with a saw as described in LBI Standard 6.2.1. The Library prefers that the third type of endpaper described in LBI Standard 6.2.3.1 (2 folded sheets, nested) be used whenever possible.

Extremely thick or heavy text blocks and those requiring hand sewing shall be sewn on highest quality linen or cotton tapes of suitable width, spaced no more than 2 inches apart.

4. *Double-fan Adhesive Binding*

This method shall be used for the following materials: monographs and serials that are not suitable for new casing only or sewing through the fold, are less than 2-1/2 inches thick, and are not printed on glossy, stiff, or other types of paper unsuitable for the process. Double-fan adhesive binding shall conform to LBI Standard 6.3, except that the spine is not to be notched as described in LBI Standard 6.3.1. The spine edge of the text block shall be fanned out, glued up, then fanned out in the opposite direction and reglued so that the adhesive slightly penetrates the inner margin of the volume. Any mechanized process for applying the adhesive as in LBI Standard 6.3.2 shall have the prior approval of the Library and shall be described in the proposal if applicable.

5. *Oversewing*

This method shall be used for the following materials: monographs and serials printed on sturdy, flexible paper with a margin of at least 5/8 inch, for which no other method of leaf attachment is possible. Oversewing shall conform to LBI Standard 6.1, except that the Binder is not to use the alternate endpaper described in LBI Standard 6.1.3. Items to be oversewn shall be divided into uniform sections not to exceed 0.055 inch in thickness, except those printed on flexible, pulpy paper, which may be thicker sections but not to exceed 0.065 inch. Sewing shall not be closer to the head and tail of the text block than 1/4 inch.

6. *Items Unsuitable for Binding*

Items that are unsuitable candidates for any of the above methods of leaf attachment shall be boxed in accordance with special instructions provided by the Library, or returned to the Library unbound.

7. *Stubbing*

a. When serial parts of different heights are to be bound together, the bottom of the resulting text block should be flush, not the top. Stubbing conforming to LBI Standard 14.2 shall be used whenever practical to make up for size differences. In no case shall one piece be trimmed excessively for the purpose of making it conform to a smaller piece with which it must be bound.

b. Stubbing per LBI Standard 5.4 shall be added to volumes to compensate for thick pockets on back covers, and to correct text blocks that flare out towards the fore edge.

c. At the Library's request, perforated stub sheets shall be bound in volumes to retain space for missing issues to be tipped in by the Library when they are received. Unlike stubbing, to allow space for map pockets and issue size differences, the sheets will be kept intact (except for trimming) until torn out by the perforations at the Library prior to tipping in the missing issue(s). The width of the sheets bound in will conform to the average issue width of the volume, unless otherwise specified by the Library.

E. *Application of Endpapers*

1. When text blocks are to be oversewn, application of endpapers shall conform to section 6.1.3 of the LBI Standard.

2. When text blocks are to be sewn through the fold, the double folio endpapers shall also be sewn through the fold.

3. When text blocks are to be double-fan adhesive bound, the endpapers shall be placed on either side of the text block before the gluing up process, and shall be attached during that process.

4. When text blocks with original sewing structure intact are to be fitted with a new case only, endpapers shall be attached by sewing through the folds of the endpapers and the two outermost signatures, front and back (four signatures in all), of the text block.

5. When text blocks have been oversewn previously, and so must have endpapers whip stitched on, the stitching shall be done as follows: holes shall be punched or drilled at a 45° angle, 1 inch apart, along the spine edge of the text block, front and rear. The endpapers shall be hand sewn to the block by passing the needle through the holes twice, from first hole to last and back.

6. When endpapers must be tipped onto the first page of a text block, adhesive shall be applied at the spine edge of that page in a swath at least $1/8$ inch, but no more than $1/4$ inch wide.

7. In no case shall a strip of reinforcing fabric be adhered directly to the spine edge of any page of a text block.

F. *Trimming*

1. The Library requires a "no-trim" policy for monographs, unless otherwise specified on a per title basis. When trimming is done, the heads, fore edges, and tails of text blocks shall be trimmed as slightly as possible, and under no circumstances shall printed matter be trimmed away. Volumes in which text and/or illustrations bleed to the edges of pages shall be left untrimmed. Trimming of periodical text blocks shall be done according to LBI Standard 7.0. Trimming shall not be used to remove staples from a side-stapled item; they shall be carefully pulled from the item instead. Periodicals issued in signatures that are to be oversewn or adhesive bound shall be prepared by slitting through the fold rather than by trimming or milling.

G. *Gluing Prior to Rounding and Backing*

1. Spines of all text blocks shall be glued prior to rounding and backing.

H. *Rounding and Backing*

1. All text blocks shall be rounded and backed to conform to section 9.0 of the LBI Standard, except the following: those

that will be fitted with a new case only—and that the Binder deems sufficiently rounded and backed, or too fragile to be subjected to rounding and backing without risk of damage to the text block or sewing structure; and very thin items, including saddle stitched pamphlets and music scores.

I. *Back Lining*

1. Backs shall be lined to conform to section 10.0 of the LBI Standard. Text blocks over 2-1/2 inches in thickness, or which are very heavy, shall have an extra lining of alkaline paper applied over the cloth lining for additional support. Double-fan adhesive bound volumes (standard, not economy paperback) shall be lined with a stretchable backlining material *and* a standard lining.

J. *Case Making*

1. Case construction shall conform to section 11.0 of the LBI standard.
2. Boards and inlay shall be securely adhered to the inside of the covering fabric. The inlay shall be cut to the same height as the boards and the same width as the back of the text block.
3. On all volumes 1/2 inch thick or more, a piece of cord of appropriate thickness shall be placed at each end of the inlay before the fabric is turned over the boards, in order to provide additional strength at the head and tail of the spine. (Cord must be omitted at the tail of text blocks bound flush with the bottom of the case.)
4. Hinges shall be no more than 1/4 inch wide, and covering material shall be uniformly turned in at least 5/8 inch. Cases shall be neatly made.

K. *Lettering*

1. *Type Size and Style*
   Lettering shall be done to conform to section 11.2 of the LBI Standard. All lettering shall be in 18 point type, except for volumes thinner than 1 inch, which may be lettered in 14 point type. All call numbers, however, shall be stamped in 18 point type. Characters must be available in both upper and lower cases, for use as appropriate in call numbers. Stamping foil shall conform to section 20.0 of the LBI Standard.
2. *Placement of Call Numbers*
   The order of priority for placement of call numbers on the covers of classified volumes is (a) in horizontal lines on the spine and (b) when volumes are thinner than 5/8

inch, in horizontal lines in the upper left-hand corner of the front cover, as close to the spine as possible. In no case shall the call number be stamped in vertical lines.

3. *Placement of Author/Title Information*
The order of priority for placement of author/title information on the covers of volumes is (a) in horizontal lines on the spine, and (b) when volumes are thinner than 5/8 inch, in vertical lines running down the spine.

4. *Volume, Issue, Page, and Year Designation (or other Variables)*
Volume, issue, page (if applicable), and year designation or other such variable designations are always to be stamped horizontally. Stamping shall be done consistently from one bound volume to the next. If variations in the size of bound volumes require modifications in the stamping of this information, then the Binder shall establish and adhere to patterns so that stamping is done consistently for volumes of the same size.

L. *Casing-in*

1. Casing-in shall conform to LBI Standard 12.0.
2. Volumes shall be cased-in and pressed between metal edged boards or in a hydro-press (i.e., a building-in machine). If the hydro-press is used, the heat, pressure, and dwell time shall be sufficient to set the joints, insure good adhesion, and permit the boards of the book to open easily. The adhesive used for casing-in shall be completely compatible with that used for making the case.
3. The square that projects around the head, fore edge, and tail of the text block shall be proportionate to the size and weight of the text block, as per LBI Standard 12.0.

M. *Flush Binding*

1. When the text block is extremely thick or heavy, it shall be bound flush with the bottom of the case at the request of the Library. Boards must be custom cut to eliminate the square at the tail of the volume. The Binder shall be allowed an upcharge for flush binding.

N. *Binding Slips*

1. Binding slips shall be attached to the page following the title page in a nondamaging fashion. They must be easily removable.

O. *Pockets for Supplementary Materials*

1. Pockets shall be made of alkaline paper, tear resistant fabric, or fabric and board, depending on the bulk and weight of the materials they are designed to protect as per LBI Standard 5.4.

They shall be constructed so that the materials they contain are firmly supported and are not easily damaged as they are inserted in or removed from the pocket.

P. *Inspection*

1. All bound volumes shall be carefully and critically inspected for defects in all aspects of construction and lettering, as per LBI Standard 13.0, and shall be wiped clean before packing if necessary.

IV. ECONOMY PAPERBACK BINDING

Binding procedures for economy paperback binding are the same as those for standard double-fan adhesive binding except as follows:

A. Volumes to be economy paperback bound must be paperbound originally, not thicker than 2 inches, and not more than 5 pounds in weight. Collating shall not be required.

B. A Grade C covering material shall be used, the color to be chosen by the Binder. The Library reserves the right to specify color to match volumes in a set. At the discretion of the Library, the complete original cover shall be removed from the text block and laminated with clear polyester film. This sheet shall be used for the board covering, as in regular case making, except that no cord is added at the top and bottom of the inlay for spine reinforcement.

C. Double-fan adhesive binding, as specified in LBI Standard 6.3, is the only acceptable method of leaf attachment, except when otherwise specified by the Library. Cleat sewing is never acceptable. After the spine of the text block is milled and adhesive applied using the double-fan method, it shall be lined with stretchable cloth, according to procedures used for standard adhesive binding. While a second lining is applied to books bound in the standard style, it need not be for economy paperback bound volumes.

D. Volumes shall be rounded, backed and cased-in in accordance with procedures used for standard double-fan adhesive bound volumes.

E. Call numbers shall be printed horizontally on either the spine or the upper left hand corner of the front cover. Brief author and brief title information shall be printed in vertical lines running down the spine of Grade C covers. No title, author's name, or call number shall be printed on spine of laminated covers.

F. All paperback bindings shall be carefully inspected as to workmanship and to verify that the volume opens properly.

V. PORTFOLIOS, BOXES, AND MISCELLANEOUS BINDING TREATMENTS

A. *Portfolios*

Portfolios shall be constructed of materials that conform to the materials specifications of this contract. Boards shall be of a weight suitable for the size and weight of the contents they are meant to protect. The grain shall run in the direction of the longest dimension of the portfolio. Ties shall be a high quality dye fast cotton twill or nylon tape, or unbleached linen tape. A portfolio shall have three or four flaps, each flap completely covering its contents so that there is no overlap line in contact with the contents. A portfolio shall not be more than 1/8 inch larger all around than its contents, and must be able to accommodate irregularly shaped materials. The lining shall be of alkaline paper, or the board must be free of lignin and have a pH of higher than 7.5 with an alkaline reserve of no less than 2% calcium or magnesium carbonate (based on oven dry weight).

B. *Double Tray Book Boxes*

Double-tray book boxes shall be constructed of materials that conform to the materials specifications of this contract. Boards shall be of a weight suitable for the size and weight of the contents they are meant to protect. Boxes shall be made plain, or shall have a drop-back construction; shall provide firm support for their contents; and shall be made so that the contents can be easily removed and replaced in a nondamaging fashion.

C. *Phase Boxes*

Phase boxes shall be constructed of strong, flexible, alkaline buffered board that will crease without splitting. The Library shall designate choice of gray/white barrier board (approximately 55 point), or lignin-free board of approximately the same thickness.

Box configuration shall be two custom cut strips of board, crossed and adhered to form a floor and four flaps that wrap around a book and support it firmly. The flap to be folded over the book first shall cover its entire front board, and shall be stamped "Fold This Flap First." The box shall be held closed by very strong waxed linen cord ties and rivets. Rivets shall be attached to the fore edge (not to the front or rear face), so that the box does not damage materials that will be shelved beside it. Using black foil, brief author/title information and call number shall be stamped on the spine of the box.

D. *Miscellaneous Binding Treatment*

Styles of binding other than those specified in this contract may occasionally be requested by the Library. Specifications for services not described in this contract (e.g., budget binding), and rates charged for those services shall be included by the Binder in the bid proposal. Any special treatments (or extra labor for standard treatments) for which an hourly rate is to be charged shall not be carried out by the Binder without the express permission of the Library.

E. *Improvements and Innovations in Methods and Materials*

Any improvements in traditional methods and/or materials used by the Binder shall be acceptable to the Library within the terms of this contract under the following conditions: the methods and/or materials must undergo extensive, documented testing that measures their strength, durability, and functional qualities (e.g., openability of the bound volume); and tests must clearly indicate that the innovation(s) will lead to better protection and greater longevity of the text block. Adoption of any technical innovation must be approved in writing by the Library.

ATTACHMENT A.   DESIRABLE SPECIFICATIONS FOR MATERIALS AND SERVICES

I. DETECTION STRIPS

Detection strips for the *(name of the system)* detection system shall be inserted into the spine of each volume during the case-making operation for the materials from the Library.

II. BINDING TICKETS

A. The Binder shall describe the methods for handling binding tickets both for a manual operation and for a computerized operation.

B. The copy of the binding ticket that is returned with the volume shall be attached to the page following the title page in a nondamaging fashion. It must be easily removable.

III. UNIFORM BINDING OF SERIALS AND SETS

The Binder shall demonstrate in the Proposal the ability to match the binding pattern, placement of lettering on the spine, and the color of stamping foil and cloth on already-bound volumes of the Library's periodical, serial, and set titles.

{IV. DATA BASE SERVICES (ALTERNATE PROPOSAL)
[see also section I.K.2]

A. The Library requests as part of the proposal information on the On-line Data Base services offered by the Binder (if any).

B. The Binder wishing to include this Alternate Proposal shall respond to the following desired specifications:

1. The Binder shall provide at its expense, including the cost of setting up, an automated system for storage and manipulation of all the Library's current periodical titles, and of any other active titles, for binding purposes.
2. The system shall allow the Library to prepare items for binding by calling up a specific binding record, adding variable information, and designating a shipment date. The system shall function without a need for patterns or preparation of tickets by the Library. However, each bound item shall be returned to the Library with a ticket documenting the exact binding instructions as indicated by the Library for that item.
3. The system shall allow recall of a specific title by its call number or by its title.
4. In order to benefit from on-screen editing capabilities, the system shall provide the capability for preparing binding tickets to be printed at the Library for monographic titles.
5. The proposal shall indicate whether the system can maintain a Data Base file of monograph titles and call numbers for materials that are in preparation, at the Binder, or in process of inspection.
6. The system shall allow the Library to manipulate the Data Base for the purpose of adding new titles and making corrections.
7. The Data Base shall be capable of maintaining, at minimum, a history of the previous six (6) volumes bound for a specific title, including shipment dates.
8. There shall be a permanent note area for each specific title. This note area shall print on the binding ticket if the Library so chooses. It shall be able to accommodate at least 160 characters.
9. The system shall allow for the printing of lists of titles prepared for binding on a daily, weekly, or shipment basis. The Library shall be able to sort the titles for these lists by location, by call number, or by title.
10. The Binder shall be responsible for creating the Data Base within *(number of weeks)* of the awarding of this contract from the Library's binding records and for providing adequate training for Library personnel.
11. The system shall be capable of handling separate Data Bases for each of the Library departments included in this contract.
12. The equipment needs would be as follows (note, however, that each *(department or branch, etc.)* will evaluate the Alternate Proposal independently and may or may not elect to procure the on-line services):

Library, department or branch, etc.: (delineation of equipment for each library, department, or branch, etc.)}

ATTACHMENT B. MANDATORY CONTRACTUAL PROVISIONS

   I. Goods and services
  II. Nondiscrimination
 III. Conflict of interests
 IV. Assignment and/or subcontracting
  V. Amendments to the contract
 VI. Notices to either party
VII. Tax exemption for the Library

ATTACHMENT C. PREFERRED CONTRACTUAL PROVISIONS

    I. Payment terms
   II. Payment of invoices
  III. Acceptance of shipments
  IV. Inspection by Library personnel of binding shipments
   V. Start-up costs (by the Binder for the Library's file, etc.)
  VI. Consent for advertising
 VII. The Library's authorized representatives
      (persons who legally speak for the Library)
VIII. Waivers
  IX. Governing law
   X. Compliance with laws
  XI. Indemnification
 XII. Contractual claims
XIII. Assignment subcontracting

REFERENCES

1. *Library Binding Institute Standard for Library Binding,* edited by Paul A. Parisi and Jan Merrill-Oldham. 8th ed. Rochester, NY: Library Binding Institute, 1986.

2. Merrill-Oldham, Jan, and Paul Parisi. *Guide to the Library Binding Institute Standard for Library Binding.* Chicago: American Library Association, 1990.

APPENDIX F
Plastic Film Identification Tests

A. *Physical characteristics, burning, heating, and odor tests*

TYPE OF FILM	PHYSICAL CHARACTERISTICS	BURNING TEST (Watch both flame and film)	HEATING TEST (Check odor and acid-alkalinity)
Cellulose			
Acetate	Poor extensibility	Melts and drips, burns slowly when removed from flame, beads at burnt edge	Mixture of acetic odor and burning paper
Nitrate	Similar to cellulose	Burns rapidly with an intense, white flame	Odor of camphor
Triacetate	Fairly easy to tear, easier than polyester to stretch		
Polyester			
(Mylar™ or Melinex™)	Clear, very tough nontearable, poor extensibility	Ignites, but extinguishes on removal from flame, bending back without dripping, leaves an ash residue	Faintly sweet

Plastic Film Identification Tests (*continued*)

TYPE OF FILM	PHYSICAL CHARACTERISTICS	BURNING TEST (Watch both flame and film)	HEATING TEST (Check odor and acid-alkalinity)
Polyvinyl chloride (PVC)			
Flexible	Softness is that of rubber; extensibility proportionate to plasticizer used	Burns with yellowish sooty flame; melts freely to form pearl-like drops	Sharp, acrid odor; fumes turn Congo paper blue
Rigid	Hard, greasy feel; white fracturing will show up in creasing line	Self-extinguishing	Sharp, acrid odor; fumes turn Congo paper blue

Source: Taken from a pamphlet issued by the Taylor Made Company, Lima, PA, 1985.

Note: Melinex is a trademark of ICI; Mylar is a trademark of DuPont.

B. *Hot copper wire test for PVC*

Strip the insulation off a two-foot section of #8 or #10 *copper* wire leaving a good length for a handle because the wire gets hot. Burn off any residual plastic coat on the wire with a butane torch. This will show a green flame because most wires are covered with PVC. When the flame turns orange, touch the red hot copper to the unknown film sample. Then place the wire back in the flame. If a green flame appears, the sample is PVC, PVDC, or a PVDC-coated film. If no green flame appears, the sample is another material and other tests (above) will show the film type. Make sure the wire is burned "clean" before testing another sample.

Source: Taylor Made Company, Lima, PA, 1985.

APPENDIX G
Collection Condition Survey Form

I. IDENTIFICATION AND SHELVING INFORMATION
A. Fill in while locating book:
   Team _____
   Date _____
   Random No. _____

B. As book is pulled:
   Shelved (check only if applicable)
   ___ dusty   ___ on fore-edge
   ___ flat   ___ on spine
   ___ leaning

C. Information from spine label or title page:
   Location _____
   Call No. _____

D. Title page or verso :
   Date of publication _____
   Country of publication ___

   Circulating _____

II. EXTERNAL COVER OR CASE (Outside of the item)
A. Cover material
   (Check all that are applicable)

B. Cover condition
   (Check only if applicable)

Cover:
___ boards
___ buckram
___ cloth
___ leather
___ paper
___ plastic
___ vellum
___ none
___ other:

Added casing:
___ envelope
___ acid-free
___ Hollinger box
___ orig. portfolio
___ other box
___ pamphlet binder
___ acid-free
___ slip case

Cover, general:
___ insect damage
___ light damage
___ mold or mildew
___ red rot
___ repaired
___ scratched
___ stained
___ warped or mis-
       shapen

Front & back covers:
___ detached
___ loose
___ missing
___ torn

Spine cover:
___ damaged
___ detached
___ missing

___ Dust jacket on
___ Rebound

Extraneous materials:
___ adh. tape
___ cloth tape
___ rubber band

Primary protection functional? ____

III. INTERNAL PAGES & BINDING (Textblock & leaf attachment)
A. Attributes and characteristics:
   (Check all that are applicable)

B. Physical condition:
   (Check only if applicable)

Paper:
___ book/matte
___ glossy
___ newsprint
___ photo-dup

Leaf attachment:
___ fold-sewn
___ glued
___ loose-leaf
___ oversewn/cleat
       sewn
___ stabbed
___ stapled
___ other:
___ unknown

End leaves:
___ detached
___ loose
___ missing
___ sp. broken
___ other:

Extraneous materials:
___ adh. tape
___ clips
___ paper additions
___ paper slips

Pages:
___ foxed
___ marked
___ stained
___ stuck
___ torn
___ yellowing

Acidic (Check with pH pen):
___ green
___ yellow
___ Test not done

___ Fold outs
___ Plates
___ Tissue guards

___ Edges uncut
___ Gutter margin
       less than 5/8"

Suppl. material:
___ microform
___ paper
___ phono/disc
___ slides
___ other:

___ Insect damage
___ Insect presence
___ Mold or mildew

Brittle test: ___ folds
_____ Test not done

Explanation of the Collection Condition Survey Form

This information is based upon the Smithsonian Institution Libraries' Condition of the Collection. [1:Attachment 3]

Part I. Identification and Shelving Information

The survey is accomplished more efficiently if two persons are assigned to each team.

A. While one individual locates the book or item to be examined, the second fills in the team and date information on the form. [See section 7.C.2 for book selection and random number procedures.]

B. As the book is being pulled from the shelf, its shelving condition is noted:

Dusty. Visible or touchable dust, grit, etc., on tops of books or on shelf surfaces. Do *not* blow or rub it off. This condition should be corrected by the use of a vacuum cleaner [see section 3.B.2].

Flat. The book is lying flat on its back, either on folio shelving or on top of other, upright books on a regular shelf.

Leaning. If the book is leaning at a significant angle (20 percent or more off the vertical), note it on the form. After the survey form is completed, reshelve the book correctly.

On fore edge. The book is standing on the front edges of the cover. This should also be corrected by shelving the book upright.

On spine. The book is standing on its spine.

C. Location and call number information is taken from the spine label or title page:

Location. The abbreviation or acronym of the library, which may be located at the beginning or end of the call number. The inclusion of such information helps locate books precisely in collections that are distributed among reference or circulating, by type of user, or in branches, etc.

Call number. This should be recorded completely, as written on the spine and/or title page.

D. Information from the title page or its verso:

Date of publication. The year of publication or reprint from the title page or verso. Record the latest if more than one is listed. If no date is available, the shelflist should be checked. Lack of information should be noted in the comments area [use the back of the form].

Country of publication. Take from the title page or verso. See the list of country abbreviations in Table G.1 for a sample list. If a city is given, but the country unknown, use an atlas, gazetteer, or the shelflist to supply the information.

TABLE G.1. Abbreviations for frequently used countries of publication.

ABBREVIATION	COUNTRY	ABBREVIATION	COUNTRY
ARGE	Argentina	ISRL	Israel
AUSL	Australia	ITAL	Italy
AUST	Austria	JAPN	Japan
BELG	Belgium	LUXG	Luxembourg
BOLV	Bolivia	MEXI	Mexico
BRZL	Brazil	NETH	Netherlands
BULG	Bulgaria	NICA	Nicaragua
CANA	Canada	NIRE	N. Ireland
CHIL	Chile	NORW	Norway
CHNA	China (People's Republic)	NWZL	New Zealand
CLMB	Colombia	PAKI	Pakistan
CSTR	Costa Rica	PANA	Panama
CUBA	Cuba	PERU	Peru
CZEC	Czechoslovakia	PHIL	Philippines
DENM	Denmark	PORT	Portugal
DOMR	Dominican Republic	PRGY	Paraguay
ECUA	Ecuador	SAFR	South Africa
ENGL	England	SCOT	Scotland
FINL	Finland	SPAN	Spain
FRAN	France	SWDN	Sweden
GERM	Germany	SWTZ	Switzerland
GREC	Greece	TAIW	China (Nationalist)
GUAT	Guatemala	TAIW	Taiwan
HOND	Honduras	USAM	United States
HUNG	Hungary	USSR	Russia
IREL	Ireland	VNZL	Venezuela

Source: Gay Walker, et al. "The Yale Survey: A Large Scale Study of Book Deterioration in the Yale University Library." *College & Research Libraries* 46 (March 1985): 131.

Does the book circulate? Some surveys include this information to find if there is a relationship between the condition of the book and its use inside or outside of the library. In the Yale survey, however, circulation information was inconclusive in regard to the condition of the book. [12:121]

Part II. External Cover or Case (the primary protection, the outer protective covers)

A. Covering material

Cover definitions:

Boards. Thick cardboard, whether plain or covered with paper.

Buckram. A coarse woven fabric coated to form a thick, hard exterior surface (over boards); the standard material used by commercial library binders.

Cloth. A woven fabric of any kind (over boards).

Leather. Tanned or tawed animal skin of any kind, usually brown or reddish-brown (often over boards).

Paper. Limp paper covers with no boards; i.e., paperback books.

Plastic. A smooth, impermeable, synthetic material (often over boards).

Vellum. Extremely smooth calf leather, usually creamy white (often over boards).

None. Unbound materials such as pamphlets without attached covers of any kind.

Dust jacket. Detached paper cover enfolding the regular cover.

Rebound. The book has a new (as opposed to the original) cover, usually with new endsheets; usually a strong binding with buckram over boards and reinforced internal hinges.

Additional casing (additional external protection):

Envelope. Paper envelope of any kind. Mark "acid-free" only if it is so identified (pH number printed on the envelope) or it is new and white.

Hollinger box. A gray, folding cardboard box, usually quite large, with overlapping fore edge sides.

Original portfolio. Any kind of container, holding loose sheets or signatures, that was part of the original publication. Materials and condition should be noted in the comments.

Other box. Any kind of box not listed above.

Pamphlet binder. Thick cardboard, usually brown, gray, or speckled, with a cloth or tape spine holding slim paperback materials. The method of interior attachment should be noted in the comments. Only binders with marbleized gray-green boards and green or tan cloth spines are acid-free.

Slip case. Box (usually cardboard) encasing a bound book and open on one end to show the book's spine, which was part of the original publication.

B. Cover condition

General condition:

Insect damage. Small holes, tunnels, etc. through the cover; bite marks and/or ragged, nibbled edges.

Light damage. Faded cover, often on the spine.

Mold/mildew. Fuzzy or speckling stain or growth, usually gray/green/brown, often with a musty smell. Books with active mold or mildew should be pulled off the shelf and isolated immediately.

Red rot. Dry, crumbling leather that usually leaves a dusty red or brown smear.

Repaired. Self explanatory.

Scratched. Lines, marks, etc., breaking the surface of the cover material.

Stained. Discoloration (from water, grease, blood, whatever), whether a solid blotch or merely a residual outline.

Warped/misshapen. No longer flat with squared (right-angle) corners; bent, bowed.

Extraneous materials:

Adhesive tape. Any kind of tape that sticks to a surface; used to repair tears.

Cloth tape. Books in poor repair are often held together with a cloth tape wrapped and tied around them.

Rubber band(s). May be used to hold the book together.

Front and back covers:

Detached. Present but no longer actually attached. Pull the book for attention.

Loose. Still attached but only loosely (e.g., the sewing is coming undone and the signatures can be pulled away slightly from the spine; the cover hinges are cracking/tearing so that the front or back cover wobbles away from the rest).

Missing. Not present with the book on the shelf.

Torn. Whether a partial tear or a complete tear resulting in the loss or separation of part of the page or cover.

Spine cover:

Damaged. The spine is torn in any way (check the headcap especially).

Detached. Present but no longer actually attached. Pull the book for attention.

Missing. Not present with the book on the shelf.

Primary protection functional. The primary protection is the hard cover or paper binding on a book or pamphlet, or the box or wrapper in which the item is housed. Boxes and other protective enclosures that are worn, damaged, or that for any reason do not provide sound support are considered nonfunctional. To determine whether a binding is nonfunctional, inspect both the inner and outer hinges and look for the conditions listed below. If these conditions exist, the binding is usually considered nonfunctional:

If an *inner* hinge is torn more than 25 percent, the primary protection is nonfunctional.

If the *outer* hinge is torn, but the boards still give firm support, manipulate the text block. It is nonfunctional if it can be easily moved so that it protrudes from the binding.

If a board is broken or mutilated to the point at which it no longer protects the text block, or the endpapers are pulling away from the boards along the inner hinge, it is nonfunctional.

If a paper binding will not keep the book upright, it is nonfunctional. The binding is supposed to support and protect the text block; if it is not performing that function, it is nonfunctional. On the other hand, it may *look* as though it is nonfunctional and still be doing its job. For example, the spine covering may be torn or missing, but the boards are still providing secure support; thus it is functional.

Part III. Internal Pages and Binding (text block and leaf attachment)

A. Attributes and characteristics

Paper:

Book/matte. Regular book paper, slightly rough with no sheen.

Glossy. Extremely smooth, shiny paper.

Newsprint. Thin, porous paper like that used in newspapers.

Photo-dup. Standard paper, smooth, used in photocopying.

Foldouts: Any bound-in paper materials that fold out.

Plates: Pages containing illustrations, maps, etc., that may be interspersed in the text block or may form an entire volume of their own, but that contain no text themselves, aside from captions.

Tissue guards: Very thin sheets of tissue paper placed between an illustration and the facing page of text.

Edges uncut: Pages still connected from being folded into signatures, usually along the top edge.

Gutter margin: The inner margin of a page between the text and the binding. A margin of about 5/8 inch is necessary for rebinding without loss of text.

Leaf attachment (the primary method of attachment between the inside and outside of the book) [see section 4.C]:

Fold-sewn. The text block is sewn together through the central folds of the signatures. The threads run vertically in the center of the folds.

Glued. The text block is formed by gluing the inner edges of the paper to a spine strip. This can look something like sewing, but no threads are visible. The backs of the gatherings or signatures are cut off or sewn in intervals.

Loose-leaf. Self-explanatory.

Oversewn/cleat sewn. The text block is sewn together from front to back through the inner edges of pages. The thread goes horizontally through holes in the gutter margin. The book opens only to the sewing thread, visible at about 1/4-inch intervals. In cleat sewn books the adhesive looks like rubber bands, visible at intervals of about 3/4 inch in the gutter.

Stabbed. These usually show three to six holes. The thread is at a right angle to the plane of the book or pamphlet.

Stapled. The pages are attached to each other by staples, either through the central signature folds (like fold-sewing) or from front to back through the inner edges of the pages.

Other. Leaves or pages are held between the covers by means of rings, metal or plastic spirals, plastic comb bindings, or plastic pegs.

Unknown. The leaf attachment cannot be determined without damaging the book.

Supplementary materials:

Microforms. Thin plastic cards or translucent sheets, designed to be used on an enlarging viewer.

Paper. Self-explanatory.

Phono/disc. Any kind of recorded material, usually a thin, flexible plastic circle.

Slides. Small transparencies held between frames.

Other. Maps, diagrams, etc., may be included, either in a pocket or loose within the book.

B. Physical condition [see section 4.B for an explanation of book structure]:

End leaves (blank pages at the beginning and end of a book):

Detached. Present but no longer actually attached. Take the book off the shelf for further attention.

Loose. Still attached but only loosely (e.g., the sewing is coming undone and the signatures can be pulled away slightly from the spine; the cover hinges are cracking/tearing so that the front or back cover wobbles away from the rest).

Missing. Not present with the book on the shelf.

Spine broken. Self-explanatory.

Pages:

Foxed. Brownish speckling on paper.

Marked. Pen or pencil marks in the text (e.g., annotations, underlines, etc.). Note extensive annotations in comments.

Stained. Discoloration (from water, grease, blood, whatever), whether a solid blotch or merely a residual outline.

Stuck. Pages stuck together within the text block. Pages should *not* be separated by hand.

Torn. Whether a partial tear or a complete tear resulting in the loss or separation of part of the page or cover.

Yellowing. Internal discoloration of paper where it's turning yellow or brown.

Insect damage. Small holes, tunnels, etc., through the text block; bite marks and/or ragged, nibbled edges.

Insect presence. Visible insect bodies or body parts in the book or on the shelf.

Mold/mildew. Fuzzy or speckling stain or growth, usually gray/green/brown, often with a musty smell. Books with active mold or mildew should be pulled off the shelf and isolated immediately. See section 2.I for a more detailed account of mold and mildew.

Extraneous materials:

Adhesive tape. Any kind of tape that sticks to a surface or is used to repair tears.

Clips.* Metal or plastic paper clips, whether attached to pages or loose inside.

Paper additions. Informative material (book jackets, newspaper or magazine articles, etc.) loose inside the book. If the material is bound or tipped in with the text, it should be considered part of the text and not extraneous or supplementary material.

Paper slips.* Any kind of extraneous paper, usually inserted as a bookmark.

Acidic test: Check with a pH pen (a felt-tipped pen filled with chlorophenol red used for testing the acidity of paper) by making a short line with the acid pen in an inconspicuous place near the inner margin of the middle of the page near the middle of the book. Avoid doing this on plates. If the book consists entirely of plates, choose an inconspicuous spot on the *back* of the page. The line will become one of three colors:

purple signifies that the paper is acid-free; green indicates some acidity in the paper; and yellow shows high acidity. If the line turns green or yellow, check off the appropriate place on the form; if it turns purple, leave it blank. Do *not* do this to pre-1800 materials. See section 1.D.1 for an explanation of pH testing.

Brittle test: Bend the upper corner of a page in the middle of the book, backward and forward up to four folds. Once backward plus once forward equals one fold. Write down how many times it would bend before breaking off. If it breaks off before one complete fold, write down "1," if it breaks off before two complete folds, write down "2," etc. If it does not break off by four complete folds, leave the line blank. Do *not* do this to pre-1800 materials or to any illustration.

*Materials marked with an asterisk should be removed *gently* from the book after noting them on the survey form.

REFERENCES

1. Smithsonian Institution Libraries. *Condition of the Collections.* Smithsonian Institution Libraries Preservation Planning Program: Report of the Task Force on the Physical Condition of the Collections. Typescript. Washington, DC: Smithsonian Institution, February 13, 1986.

2. Walker, Gay, Jane Greenfield, John Fox, and Jeffrey S. Siminoff. "The Yale Survey: A Large Scale Study of Book Deterioration in the Yale University Library." *College & Research Libraries* 46 (March 1985): 111–132.

APPENDIX H
Program Code for Random Book Number Generator

```
Program randbk;
{Created by James L. Divilbiss on March 10, 1983, and
used with his permission. Revised and compiled under
Turbo Pascal 3.01 for John N. DePew, School of Library
and Information Studies, Florida State University,
Tallahassee, FL, by David R. Miner on December 15, 1989.}
{This is an interactive program that will take the
specifications of a library and generate a set of random
locations. It is intended to be fairly general and useable
by persons with no special programming skills.}

TYPE
str50 = string[12];

VAR
   samples    : integer;  {number of samples to be generated}
   copies     : integer;  {number of 'duplicate' sets}
   areas      : integer;  {number of areas to be sampled}
   ranges     : integer;  {number of ranges in a room}
   sections   : integer;  {number of sections in a range}
   shelves    : integer;  {number of shelves per section}
   books      : integer;  {number of books/shelf (approx maximum)}
   cop        : integer;  {index for number of copies}
   n          : integer;  {index for samples}
   randarr    : array[1..4975] of str50;
   temp1      : str50;     {temporary variable for
                            conversion and sorting}
   i          : integer;  {counter for loops}
   fileout    : text;     {for selection of printer or
screen output}

PROCEDURE Sort; FORWARD;

Procedure generate; {creates random numbers}
Var
   book       : integer;
   shelf      : integer;
   section    : integer;
   range      : integer;
begin
    for n := 1 to samples do
      begin
         range := succ(random(ranges));
         str(range,temp1);
         if length(temp1) = 1 then temp1 := '0' + temp1;
randarr[n] := temp1 + chr(32);
         section := succ(random(sections));
```

```
            str(section,temp1);
            if length(temp1) = 1 then temp1 := '0' + temp1;
            randarr[n] := randarr[n] + temp1 + chr(32);
            shelf := succ(random(shelves));
            str(shelf,temp1);
            if length(temp1) = 1 then temp1 := '0' + temp1;
            randarr[n] := randarr[n] + temp1 + chr(32);
            book := succ(random(books));
            str(book,temp1);
            if length(temp1) = 1 then temp1 := '0' + temp1;
            if length(temp1) = 2 then temp1 := '0' + temp1;
            randarr[n] := randarr[n] + temp1;
        end;
end;

PROCEDURE Check;
Var
  m,n        : integer;
  temp2      : str50;
Begin
  n := samples;
  for m := 1 to samples -1 do
    begin
      if randarr[m] = randarr[m+1] then
        begin
            temp2 := randarr[m+1];
            randarr[m+1] := randarr[n];
            randarr[n] := '';
            n := n-1;
          end;
      end;
   if n < > samples then
      begin
        sort;
        m := samples;
        samples := samples - n;
        generate;
        samples := m;
        sort;
        check;
      end;
end;

PROCEDURE sort;   { this is a standard shell sort  }
var
  jump, m, n  : integer;
  temp        : integer;
  alldone     : boolean;
begin
  jump := samples;
  while jump > 1 do
    begin
      jump := jump div 2;
```

```
      repeat
        alldone := true;
        for m := 1 to samples - jump do
          begin
            n := m + jump;
            if randarr[m] > randarr[n] then
              begin
                temp1 := randarr[m];
                randarr[m] := randarr[n];
                randarr[n] := temp1;
                alldone := false
              end
          end
      until alldone
    end
end;

Procedure Output;
Var
   ch : char;
Begin
    Write('Do you want output to the Printer or to the
Screen (P/S)? ');
    readln(ch);
    if ch in ['P','p']
       then begin
            assign(fileout, 'lst:');
            end;
    if ch in ['S','s']
       then begin
            assign(fileout, 'con:');
            end;
    rewrite(fileout);
    writeln;
End;

Procedure input;
Var
   ch : char;
Begin
  randomize;
  writeln ('Subject to a maximum of 4975 samples');
  write   ('How many samples are to be generated?  ');
  read    (samples);
  writeln;
  write   ('                         How many copies?  ');
  read    (copies);
  writeln;
  write   ('   How many areas are to be sampled?  ');
  read    (areas);
  writeln;
  write   ('                         How many ranges?  ');
  read    (ranges);
```

```
     writeln;
     write    ('                    How many sections?  ');
     read     (sections);
     writeln;
     write    ('                    How many shelves?  ');
     read     (shelves);
     writeln;
     write    ('                    Books per shelf?  ');
     read     (books);
     writeln;
     writeln;
write ('           Do you want to change anything? ');
read(ch);
if ch in ['Y','y'] then input;
writeln;
writeln;
end;

Begin {main}
input;
output;
for cop := 1 to copies do
  begin
     writeln (fileout,'Copy:   ',cop:3);
     for i := 1 to areas do
        begin
           writeln (fileout,'Area:   ',i:3);
           writeln;
           writeln (fileout,'R  S   S   B ');
           writeln (fileout,'A  E   H   O ');
           writeln (fileout,'N  C   E   O ');
           writeln (fileout,'G  T   L   K ');
           writeln (fileout,'E      F   ');
           writeln (fileout);
           generate;
           sort;
           check;
           for n := 1 to samples do
              writeln (fileout,randarr[n]);
           for n := 1 to 5 do writeln(fileout);
        end;
  end
end.
```

APPENDIX I
Drying Techniques for Water-Damaged Books and Records

TECHNIQUE	PROCEDURE	SPEED	DIRECT COST	STAFF & LABOR	AVAILABILITY	RESULTS
Air-drying	Items dried by circulating air in a low-temperature, low humidity space	days or weeks	negligible	high	very good	—swelling —cockling —blocking —inks run —mold threat
Dehumidification	Large, commercial dehumidifiers installed to dry buildings, furnishings, and collections *in situ*	varies		low	good	—limited cockling, if used only on damp items
Freezer drying	Items placed in self-defrosting freezer (under -10°F) are frozen, then ice is slowly sublimated	weeks or months	negligible if done at home)	moderate	very good	—swelling —blocking
Vacuum Thermal drying	Items placed in chamber; vacuum drawn; heat introduced to melt and/or "boil out" water	4–6 weeks per load	$3–5 per volume	low	good	Potential —swelling —cockling —ink runs —blocking —damage to film media
Vacuum Freeze-drying	Frozen items placed in chamber; vacuum drawn; small amount of heat introduced (below 32°F); ice crystals drawn out by sublimation	1–2 weeks per load	$5–7 per volume	low	good	—leather and vellum may warp —photos may lose gloss

Source: SOLINET Preservation Program. Atlanta, GA: Southeastern Library Network, Inc., February 1989.

APPENDIX J
Intrinsic Value

The National Archives and Records Service published a staff information paper in 1982 that defines intrinsic value in relation to archival material. [1:2–3] It is a very useful guide to establishing the value of records, and it can be used in conjunction with the other guides in section 5.E.1. A portion of it is reprinted here.

Qualities and Characteristics of Records with Intrinsic Value

All record materials having intrinsic value possess one or more of the following specific qualities or characteristics. These qualities or characteristics relate to the physical nature of the records, their prospective uses, and the information they contain.

1. Physical form that may be the subject for study if the record provides meaningful documentation or significant examples of the form.

Documents may be preserved in their original form as evidence of technological development. For example, a series of early press copies, glass-plate negatives, or wax-cylinder sound recordings may be retained. All records having a particular physical form would not be considered to have intrinsic value because of this characteristic; however, a selection broad enough to provide evidence of technological development would be considered to have some value.

2. Aesthetic or artistic quality

Records having aesthetic or artistic quality may include photographs; pencil, ink, or watercolor sketches; maps; architectural drawings; frakturs; and engraved and/or printed forms, such as bounty-land warrants.

3. Unique or curious physical features

Physical features that are unique or curious might include quality and texture of paper, color, wax seals, imprints and watermarks, inks, and unusual bindings. All records having a particular physical feature would not be considered to have intrinsic value because of this feature; however, an exemplary selection of each type would be considered to have such value.

4. Age that provides a quality of uniqueness

Age is a relative rather than an absolute quality. Generally, records of earlier date are of more significance than records of later date. This can be because of a historical change in the functions and activities of the creator of the records, the scarcity of earlier records, a change in record-keeping practices, or a combination of these. Age can be a factor even with comparatively recent records. The earliest records concerning, for example, the development of the radio industry or of nuclear power could have intrinsic value because of age.

5. Value for use in exhibits

Records used frequently for exhibits normally have several qualities and characteristics that give them intrinsic value. Records with exhibit value impressively convey the immediacy of an event, depict a significant issue, or impart a sense of the person who is the subject or originator of the record. In these cases, the impact of the original document cannot be equaled by a copy.

6. Questionable authenticity, date, author, or other characteristic that is significant and ascertainable by physical examination.

Some records are of doubtful authenticity or have informational content that is open to question. Although it is impossible to foresee which documents will be questioned in the future, certain types of documents are well known to have the potential for controversy and, if the original records are extant, handwriting and signatures can be examined, paper age can be ascertained, and other physical tests can be performed. In some cases the controversy can be resolved by recourse to the original item (such as by an examination of the handwriting, the age of the paper, or the original negative of the photostatic print), while in other cases the item will not be conclusive but will provide the researcher with the best evidence from which to draw conclusions (original photographs of UFO's, for example).

7. General and substantial public interest because of direct association with famous or historically significant people, places, things, issues, or events.

This criterion is not only the most difficult to apply, but also the most important in terms of the volume of records to which it could be applied. It could be used to justify preserving in original form almost all permanently valuable records because of their historical importance. On the other hand, if limited to records of unusual significance, it would be used to justify disposal of almost all original records. Archival judgment is the crucial factor in determining whether there is general and substantial public interest, whether the association is direct, and whether the subject is famous or historically significant. Generally, those series with a high concentration of such information should be preserved.

8. Significance as documentation of the establishment or continuing legal basis of an agency or institution.

Agencies or institutions are founded and acquire or lose functions and responsibilities through the actions of the executive, legislative, and judicial branches of the Government. Records documenting these actions may be found concentrated in series or scattered in various series. They have in common the characteristic of documenting the shifts in function of the agency or institution at the highest level.

9. Significance as documentation of the formulation of policy at the highest executive levels when the policy has significance and broad effect throughout or beyond the agency or institution.

Numerous records reflect policy decisions; however, most policy decisions have a relatively limited impact and reflect a relatively small area of authority. The characteristics that give policy records intrinsic value are the origin of the records at the highest executive levels, breadth of effect, and importance of subject matter.

See section 5.E.1 for a more detailed discussion of selection of materials for preservation, replacement, withdrawal, or no action at all.

REFERENCE

1. National Archives and Records Service. *Intrinsic Value in Archival Material.* National Archives and Records Service Staff Information Paper No. 21. Washington, DC: National Archives and Records Service, General Services Administration, 1982.

GLOSSARY

This glossary contains terms used in the text that need definition or qualification. The context in which they are used can be seen by finding their location in the index and then turning to that page in the handbook. Terms in **boldface** in the definitions are defined elsewhere in the glossary.

albumen emulsion A coated light-sensitive layer in photographs made from egg whites.

alum Potassium aluminum sulphate (alum) is added with **size** made of **rosin** to wood pulp to impart a harder and more water resistant surface to the finished sheet. Alum helps the fibers to retain the rosin and also aids in dispersing the paper fibers in the vat. Alum is acidic when dissolved in water and is a primary source of acid in paper. [16:87] Fortunately, many paper mills are now switching to alkaline sizing processes.

basis weight The basis weight indicates the actual weight of a ream (500 sheets) of paper measuring 38 inches by 25 inches. The more dense and thick each sheet of paper in the ream, the heavier the ream. The standard, or basic, size ream varies with different grades of paper. [18:19]

bone folder A flat piece of bone or plastic, six to nine inches long, about one inch wide and 1/8 inch thick, with rounded corners and edges; used to rub along the fold of a sheet of paper to bend it squarely into position.

bristol A lightweight, thin paperboard with a smooth surface; used for lining the spine of a book cover or case and for book pocket or small portfolio construction. [13:213]

buckram A strong, coarse woven cotton (sometimes linen) cloth that has been dyed and filled with starch under heat and pressure. Buckrams are frequently coated with **pyroxylin** or acrylic and used for commercial library binding. [13:213]

buffer "An alkaline reserve in paper, usually a calcium carbonate filler which maintains the pH in the neutral or alkaline range by reacting with acidic gases from the environment or from the deterioration of the paper itself." [11:20]

calender A series of horizontal cast iron rollers (similar in appearance to the rollers in old domestic washing machines equipped with clothes wringers) with hardened, chilled surfaces resting one on another in a vertical bank at the dry end of the papermaking machine. The newly made, dried paper **web** is passed between the calender rolls to increase the smoothness and gloss of its surface. [18:44]

cambric "A fine, closely woven white linen fabric, used in library bindings for hinges, spine linings, extensions, etc." [18:45]

cellulose "The basic **filler** in paper. It is a complex polymeric carbohydrate $(C_6H_{10}O_5)_n$, having the same percentage composition as starch, i.e., 44.4 percent carbon, 6.2 percent hydrogen, and 49.4 percent oxygen." [18:49] It is the chief component of the cell walls of plants, wood, etc. These fibers have the unique property of adhering together to form a mat, i.e., paper, from a water suspension.

cellulose nitrate A material produced by the action of nitric acid on **cellulose;** used extensively as a film base until 1951. It was the first of the modern plastics that replaced cellulose acetate as a disc or cylinder recording medium. Because it is highly unstable, subject to oxidation and denitration, and is extremely flammable, cellulose nitrate has been largely replaced by cellulose acetate and cellulose triacetate.

coated A coating of clay, calcium carbonate, or other pigment or mixture of pigments applied to the surface of paper to provide a smoother base for printing.

cockle The wrinkling or puckering caused when paper (or any sheet) dries unevenly.

collodion emulsion "A coated, light-sensitive layer in which the medium is a solution of **cellulose nitrate (pyroxylin)** in alcohol and ether." [15:29]

conservation "The treatment of library or archival materials, works of art, or museum objects to stabilize them chemically or strengthen them physically, sustaining their survival as long as possible in their original form." [6:14] See also **preservation.**

couch "(1) The operation of transferring or laying sheets of hand-made paper from the mold to the **felts** for pressing. (2) To press the newly made sheets of paper on the felts. (3) To press a sheet on the wire of a cylinder papermaking machine and transfer it onto the felt for pressing and drying. (4) To press water from a sheet on a couch roll of a fourdrinier machine, or extract water by means of a suction couch preparatory to transferring it to a felt." [18:67]

cross direction The direction across (right angles to) the direction a machine-made paper travels through a papermaking machine. The cross direction of paper usually has less strength and folding endurance than the **machine direction.** [18:69]

deacidification (neutralization) The removal of acid (or alkali) from a material, such as paper, that causes its pH to approach 7 (neutrality).

degauss To neutralize the magnetic field of a material (such as electrical equipment or magnetic tape) by means of electric coils that create a magnetic field cancelling that of the material.

desiccant A nonvolatile chemical that absorbs moisture from the surrounding atmosphere. Silica gel is the desiccant typically employed to keep documents, photographs, and other materials dry while in exhibit cases in humid surroundings.

diazo Materials (coated films or papers) containing sensitized layers composed of diazonium salts that react with couplers to form azo dye images.

esparto "A coarse grass grown chiefly in Southern Spain and Northern Africa, containing short fibers that are usually extracted by alkaline pulping processes. Esparto pulp is most often used in the production of book papers. Esparto is also known as alfa, esparto grass and Spanish grass." [5:165]

felt "A continuous belt on a̅ papermaking machine, generally made of wool, but also as a combination of wool, cotton, asbestos, and synthetic fibers. Felts perform the function of mechanical conveyors or transmission belts, provide a cushion between the press rolls, and serve as a medium for the removal of water from the wet **web**." [18:99]

filler A material, typically clay or calcium carbonate, added to the furnish of paper mainly to increase the smoothness of the paper surface and make it a better printing surface. [11:20]

flashing Pieces of sheet metal or the like used to cover and protect where a roof comes in contact with a wall or chimney.

formalin A solution of formaldehyde in water, 37 to 50 percent by volume.

foxing Small, usually brownish spots appearing on paper; variously attributed to action of fungi on trace metal (iron) in paper under humid conditions. [16:88] Many questions about the actual source and development of foxing stains still remain to be answered.

fungistat An agent or preparation inhibiting the growth of a fungus.

glassine A dense, glazed, semi-transparent paper often used to make envelopes and sleeves for storing photographic negatives. It is usually acidic. [16:88]

goyu Japanese handmade paper, white in color and made from 90 percent **kozo**. It is acid-free, has chain lines, and is used for printing, for printmaking, and for hinges in the mounting of paper objects.

guard "A strip of cloth or paper pasted around or into a **section** of a book so as to reinforce the paper and prevent the sewing thread from tearing through." [18:124]

gum arabic A water soluble gum used in the bichromated colloid photographic process to form a relief image.

headband An ornamental piece of colored silk or cloth attached to and projecting slightly above the head of the book at the spine. Originally, the headband consisted of a thong core, similar to the bands on which the book was sewn, around which the ends of the threads were twisted and then laced into the boards of the book. In edition binding they are almost always manufactured separately and then attached, while in library binding they have mostly been replaced by a length of cord around which the covering material is rolled at both head and tail. [18:129]

hemicelluloses Cellulose having a degree of polymerization (DP) of 150 or less (i.e., smaller molecules with fewer "building blocks"). A collective term for beta and gamma cellulose, cellulose that is soluble in hot alkali. The contribution of hemicelluloses to development of initial strength in paper is well recognized. It is related to fibrillation and bonding. But hemicellulose-rich pulps have a strong tendency to discolor during thermal aging. [11:20]

HEPA High efficiency particulate air filter.

Japanese paper A very thin, strong paper made in Japan from long-fibered stock, such as **kozo,** the paper mulberry. It may be used for mending, for the overall lining of paper as reinforcement, for reinforcing the folds of **sections,** or for mending hinges. Known for its properties of flexibility, strength, and permanence. Papers used in conservation and bookbinding include **goyu, kitakata, kizukishi,** misu, mulberry, **okawara, sekishu, sekishu kozogami mare, sekishu kozogami turu,** and **udagami.** [13:216]

jordan A pulp refiner consisting of a conical plug rotating in a matching conical shell. The outside of the plug and the inside of the shell are fitted with cutting bars, which macerate fibrous material in a water suspension that is passed between them.

Kalvar See **vesicular film.**

kaolin "A whitish earthy material composed primarily of the clay mineral kaolinite, a form of aluminum silicate. In refined form, kaolin is used in papermaking as a filler, coating component and opacifying agent." [5:238]

kettle stitch The stitches closest to the head and tail of each **signature** of a text block; used to secure each **section** or signature together. Kettle stitches lock the sewing thread after each complete pass of the thread along the spine of the text block and link each signature to the one sewn on previously. [9:15] The term may be a corruption of "catch-up stitch," or "kettle stitch" (the stitch that forms a little chain). [18:146] See also **lock stitch.**

kitakata An acid-free paper handmade in Japan from mitsumata and sulfite pulp. Buff in color and silky to the touch. Used for the mending of older books and documents. See also **Japanese paper.**

kizukishi Japanese handmade paper, buff in color and silky to the touch, made from 100 percent **kozo,** and acid-free. Used for mending and bookbinding since its fibers are compact and can be torn into a strong web. See also **Japanese paper.**

kozo One of the three principal plants that yield fiber for the production of **Japanese paper.** (Others are mitsumata and gampi.) The name is loosely applied to several plants of the mulberry family, which have fibers suitable for papermaking. In general, the long kozo fibers make it the strongest and most dimensionally stable of Japanese papers, and its absorbent surface makes it useful for printing and printmaking. [10:116]

Krylon™ No. 1301 A crystal-clear acrylic coating for strengthening worn and decayed leather. Sometimes used for consolidating the surface of powdery suede bindings because the water in the potassium lactate solution may darken and spot the suede. Leather bindings that are so powdery that the covering material cannot be restored by oiling alone can be sprayed with Krylon. Also recommended for spraying bookplates to prevent acid transfer to the flyleaf. [8:24, 53] The spray propellant does not contain fluorocarbons or vinyl chloride.

Krytox™ An industrial lubricant made of fluorocarbons by Dupont. Used in conjunction with other compounds to clean metallic media such as magnetic tapes.

lignin A three-dimensional amorphous **polymer** with a variable structure so complex that a definitive formula for it has never been written. It makes up 17 to 32 percent of wood; it surrounds the **cellulose** fibers and provides the stiffness that enables trees to stand upright. It is chemically stable in wood, but it becomes unstable when the wood is broken down to make paper. It is removed in pulping with the use of hot chemicals, followed by bleaching. Fully bleached pulp contains practically no lignin. [11:20]

lock stitch "Any method of sewing with thread whereby the stitching at each operation is 'locked' and cannot unravel if cut on either side of the completed stitch. Lock stitches are the type made by household sewing machines, although the machines used by library binders are often larger. Stitches are formed by a primary thread that runs along the top surface of the text block being sewn, and a bobbin thread that runs along the bottom surface and locks with the thread at regular intervals." [9:15] See also **kettle stitch.**

machine direction "The direction in which paper travels through a paper making machine. Most of the fibers lie in this direction; therefore paper folds more easily along the machine direction (or 'with the grain'), and a sheet of paper when wetted expands mainly across this direction, with a corresponding shrinkage of the paper on drying. The paper is stronger in the machine direction." [7:487] See also **cross direction.**

mold-made paper A deckle-edged paper resembling that made by hand, but produced on a machine. It is made on a cylinder or cylindrical mold revolving in a vat of pulp. [5:275]

monomer   A simple molecule that can combine with identical or different molecules of low molecular weight to form a **polymer.**

neat's-foot oil   A pale yellow, fatty oil produced by boiling the feet and shin bones of hoofed animals. "Cold-tested" neat's-foot oil has been held at the freezing point for a period of time and then filtered. Neat's-foot oil is used in the preparation of some leather dressings, and in the fat-liquoring of leather. [18:175]

nitrate film   Photographic film with a film base composed principally of **cellulose nitrate.** [14:193]

okawara   A **Japanese paper** handmade from 100 percent **kozo.** Strong, soft, and supple, with laid lines. Good for **conservation** purposes.

overcasting   A method of hand binding in which one **section** is sewn to another by passing the thread through the back edge and diagonally out through the back. [1:161]

Pellon™   A variety of polyester, nonwoven, long-fiber fabrics. Will not stick to most adhesives. Used for interleaving between newly mended or repaired materials so they will not stick together while adhesive or paste is drying. Used as a barrier between heat-set tissue and the tacking iron.

plasticizer   (1) A material, such as glycerin (glycerol), sorbitol, triethylene glycol, etc., incorporated into an adhesive during manufacture to increase its flexibility, workability, or distensibility. (2) A material added to the stock in the manufacture of a paper such as **glassine,** or used in the papermaking mixtures to impart softness and flexibility. [18:199]

points per pound   A ratio derived by dividing the **basis weight** of a sheet of paper in pounds by its thickness in mils. It is used to describe the density of paper or board. The term is most frequently applied to the bursting strength. [18:201]

polyethylene   A chemically inert, stable, highly flexible, transparent, or translucent thermoplastic material. It has a low melting point and, when made with no surface coatings or additives, is suitable for enclosures for photographs. [17:155] It is also used in preservation as a protective liner or sleeve for discs and tapes. It furnishes a smooth fungi-resistant surface and is also a moisture barrier for both the disc or tape and the external packaging (jacket or box). [2:299]

polymer   A naturally occurring or synthetic substance consisting of giant molecules derived either by the addition of many smaller similar molecules (e.g., **polyethylene**) or by the compaction of many smaller molecules with the condensation of water, alcohol, or the like (e.g., nylon).

preservation   The activities associated with maintaining library and archival materials for use, either in their original physical form or in some other format. Preservation is considered a broader term than **conservation.** [3:20; 4:24]

princeton file   A free-standing, boxlike container open at the top, back, and the lower half of the front. It is used to hold pamphlets, periodical issues, single sheets, etc., usually for storage on the book shelves.

pyroxylin   A compound consisting of lower-nitrated **cellulose nitrate,** usually containing less than 12.5 percent nitrogen. It is used in the manufacture of pyroxylin coated and impregnated book cloths. [18:209] See also **collodion emulsion.**

realia   Three-dimensional objects such as museum materials, dioramas, models, and samples. [7:650]

red rot   "Deterioration of leather in the form of red powdering, found particularly in East India leathers prepared with tanning of the catechol group." [12:36] See also **Krylon™.**

reprography   A generic term for copying or reproduction, etc., including the reproduction of printed, typed, or handwritten material by processes other than printing or photography.

risk manager   The person in an organization who is responsible for protecting it from predictable losses. Through insurance and/or other strategies designed to recover from any losses sustained, the risk manager implements measures to control and reduce the possibility of loss.

rosin size   A solution or dispersion obtained by treating rosin with a suitable alkali. When properly converted in the papermaking process, usually by the addition of **alum,** the **size** precipitates and imparts water (ink) resistance to paper. [18:221] Rosin is the residue obtained after distilling off the volatile matter (turpentine) from the gum of the Southern pine (chiefly from long-leaf and slash species). [5:351]

section   The unit of paper that is printed and folded into sets of 4, 8, 16, 32, 64, or 128 printed pages, and which, together with other like units, plates, and inserts, makes up a complete book. A section is usually folded from one sheet of paper, but it may consist of one and one-half or two sheets, or even one sheet and an additional leaf or leaves. The outside folds (bolt) are trimmed, leaving the center, or inside, fold intact. Consecutive sections are sewn through-the-fold to form the text block. Each section of a book bears a different signature identification. *Signature* originally referred to a letter or numeral placed at the bottom of the first page of each printed sheet of paper to assist in collating the book. Modern books are collated by a diagonal solid line across the spine. [13:219] Today, however, little if any distinction is made between *section* and *signature,* and the terms are sometimes used synonymously with *quire* and *gathering.*

sekishu   Japanese handmade paper, white or natural in color and made from 80 percent **kozo.** It is acid-free and is used for printing and **conservation.** See also **sekishu kozogami mare** and **sekishu kozogami turu.**

sekishu kozogami mare   Japanese handmade paper, off-white in color and made from 100 percent **kozo.** Very similar to **sekishu kozogami**

turu except it has doubled chain lines. It is acid-free and is used for mending.

sekishu kozogami turu Japanese handmade paper, off-white in color and made from 100 percent **kozo**. It is acid-free and is used for all types of mending.

signature See **section**.

silicone release paper A thin, white, translucent paper coated with silicone resin on one or both sides to render the surface slippery and resistant to sticking. It will withstand the application of heat without sticking to or otherwise damaging the work. Used with heat-set tissue.

size An additive that makes fiber surfaces hydrophobic and keeps paper from acting like blotting paper when written or printed upon. Early papermakers dipped their handmade sheets into vats of gelatin to size them, but the productive capacity of the papermaking machine called for an internal size that could be added directly to the slurry. For 150 years, **rosin** was the only practical internal size available, and it had to be used with **alum** in order to coat the paper fibers. Today a growing variety of sizing compounds and systems makes it possible to size paper at any pH from 4 to 10. [11:21]

smyth sewing A method of sewing through the center folds of **sections**. Named for the inventor of the first practical through-the-fold book sewing machine. [13:219]

Solander box Invented by Dr. Daniel Charles Solander, a botanist, while at the British Museum (1773–1782). The Solander box, which is made of wood, is generally of a drop-back construction. When properly fabricated, the Solander box is almost dust and water proof. [18:243]

square The part of a book's cover or case that extends beyond the edges of the text block to protect the pages.

strengthening (of paper) "Restoring the mechanical stability of brittle paper through chemical means." [19:5]

stub (1) The portion of the original leaf that remains in the volume after most of it has been cut out. Can be used as a support for tipping-in a replacement leaf. (2) A narrow section or strip bound into a book for the purpose of attaching plates, maps, etc.

tentelometer A gauge for measuring the tension of magnetic tape as it is wound on a reel or hub.

terylene (1) A generic name for a synthetic thread that has the advantages of nylon thread, but does not have the undesirable high degree of elasticity. Because of its lower elasticity, it does not present the problem of thread retraction after cutting. (2) Terylene is also used in sheet form in the repair of documents and the leaves of books. [18:262]

udagami A Japanese paper made of 100 percent **kozo**. Very lightweight, with narrow laid lines. While looking very delicate and fragile, it is strong and opaque. Useful for mending art objects on paper.

μm   Micrometer (10⁻⁶ meter); also referred to as a micron.
μw   Microwatt (10⁻⁶ watt).

Van der Waals' forces   Weak, nonspecific forces between molecules.

vellum   (1) Originally, a translucent or opaque material produced from calfskin. Today, however, vellum is generally defined as a material made from calfskin, sheepskin, or virtually any other skin obtained from a relatively small animal, e.g., antelope. Some authorities do not distinguish between vellum and parchment, although traditionally the former was made from an unsplit calfskin, and consequently had a grain pattern on one side (unless removed by scraping), while the latter was produced from the flesh split of a sheepskin, and consequently had no grain pattern. [18:277] (2) A strong, high-grade natural or cream-colored paper made to resemble vellum. (3) A term applied to a finish rather than a grade. Social and personal stationery are often called vellums. [5:435]

vesicular film   A duplicating film, usually sign-reversing, which uses heat alone to develop latent images after exposure to ultraviolet light. The light-sensitive component of the film is suspended in a plastic layer. On exposure, the component creates optical vesicles (bubbles) in the layer. These imperfections form the latent image. The latent image becomes visible and permanent by heating the plastic layer and then allowing it to cool. [14:196] It is not generally considered to be of archival quality. At one time the film was referred to as Kalvar, after the company that originally produced it. [1:239]

web   The sheet of paper coming from the papermaking machine in its full width or from a roll of paper in any converting operation. [18:281]

REFERENCES

1. *ALA Glossary of Library and Information Science.* Edited by Heartsill Young. Chicago: American Library Association, 1983.

2. Association for Recorded Sound Collections, Associated Audio Archives Committee. *Audio Preservation: A Planning Study: Final Performance Report.* 2 vols. Prepared by the Associated Audio Archives Committee for the National Endowment for the Humanities. Silver Spring, MD: The Associated Audio Archives Committee, Association for Recorded Sound Collections, 1988– .

3. Darling, Pamela W. "To the Editor." *Conservation Administration News* 22 (July 1985): 3, 20.

4. DeCandido, Robert. "Out of the Question." *Conservation Administration News* 38 (July 1989): 24.

5. *Dictionary of Paper: A Compendium of Terms Commonly Used in the U.S. Pulp, Paper and Allied Industries.* 4th ed. New York: American Paper Institute, Inc., 1980.

6. "Glossary of Selected Preservation Terms." *ALCTS Newsletter* 1:2 (1990): 14–15. Association for Library Collections and Technical Services, American Library Association.

7. *Harrod's Librarians' Glossary of Terms Used in Librarianship, Documentation and the Book Crafts: A Reference Book.* 6th ed. Compiled by Ray Prytherch. Aldershot, Hants, England: Gower Publishing Company, Ltd., 1987.

8. Horton, Carolyn. *Cleaning and Preserving Bindings and Related Materials.* 2nd ed., revised. LTP Publication No. 16. Conservation of Library Materials, Pamphlet 1. Chicago: American Library Association, 1969.

9. *Library Binding Institute Standard for Library Binding.* Edited by Paul A. Parisi and Jan Merrill-Oldham. 8th ed. Rochester, NY: Library Binding Institute, 1986.

10. Luebbers, Leslie Laird, "Glossary." *Paper—Art & Technology.* Edited by Paulette Long. San Francisco: World Print Council, 1979.

11. McGrady, Ellen. "A Glossary for the March Issue." *The Alkaline Paper Advocate* 3 (May 1990): 19–21.

12. Middleton, Bernard C. *The Restoration of Leather Bindings.* Rev. ed. LTP Publication No. 20. Chicago: American Library Association, 1984.

13. Morrow, Carolyn Clark, and Carole Dyal. *Conservation Treatment Procedures: A Manual of Step-by-Step Procedures for the Maintenance and Repair of Library Materials.* 2nd ed. Littleton, CO: Libraries Unlimited, Inc., 1986.

14. *Preservation Microfilming: A Guide for Librarians and Archivists.* Edited by Nancy E. Gwinn for the Association of Research Libraries. Chicago: American Library Association, 1987.

15. Rempel, Siegfried. *The Care of Black and White Photographic Collections: Identification of Processes.* Technical Bulletin No. 6. Ottawa: Canadian Conservation Institute, 1979.

16. Ritzenthaler, Mary Lynn. *Archives & Manuscripts: Conservation: A Manual on Physical Care and Management.* Chicago: Society of American Archivists, 1983.

17. Ritzenthaler, Mary Lynn, Gerald J. Munoff, and Margery S. Long. *Archives & Manuscripts: Administration of Photographic Collections.* SAA Basic Manual Series. Chicago: Society of American Archivists, 1984.

18. Roberts, Matt T. and Don Etherington. *Bookbinding and the Conservation of Books: A Dictionary of Descriptive Terminology.* Washington, DC: Library of Congress, 1982.

19. Turko, Karen. *Mass Deacidification Systems: Planning and Managerial Decision Making.* Washington, DC: Association of Research Libraries, 1990, 4–5.

INDEX